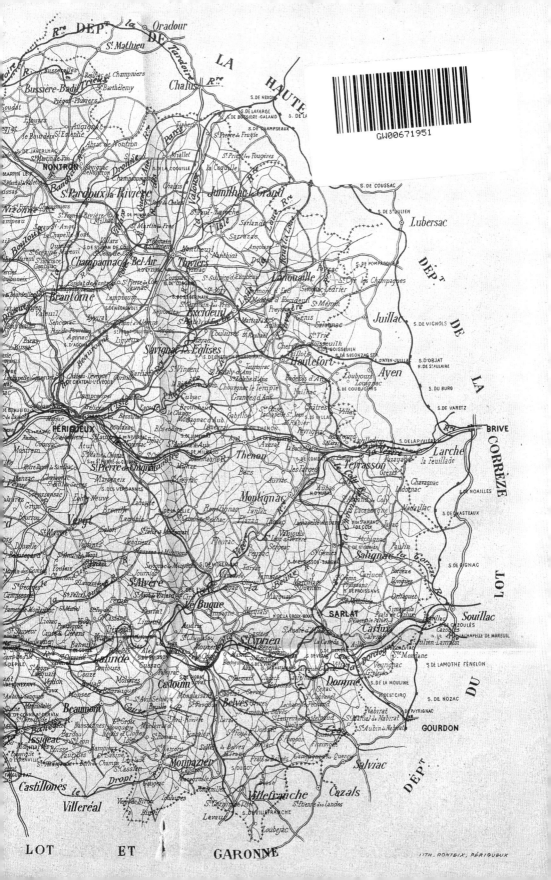

DEFYING
VICHY

'Pacey and engaging, this study explores the drama and complexity of the German occupation and resistance, highlighting moral ambiguities, deceit, betrayal and violence. A fascinating contribution to the field.'

Robert Gildea, author of *Fighters in the Shadows*

'Robert Pike has not only produced a meticulously researched and valuable contribution to the history of the German occupation, but a reminder of how courageously and selflessly many ordinary French men and women behaved.'

Caroline Moorehead, author of *Village of Secrets*

'This vivid and evocative account of the Resistance in Dordogne details the exploits of some remarkable personalities and makes us acutely aware of their courage and the dangers they faced. Robert Pike is to be applauded for bringing these stories to a wider readership.'

Hanna Diamond, author of *Fleeing Hitler*

'Robert Pike skilfully shows how ordinary people responded to the German occupation: some heroically, others less so. Above all, this story is rooted in the towns, villages and wooded hillsides of the Dordogne, which Pike knows so well, and which come alive in this moving account of the darkest and brightest period in French history.'

Matthew Cobb, author of *The Resistance*

'Pulsating with action and detailed stories.'

Rod Kedward, author of *In Search of the Maquis*

DEFYING VICHY

BLOOD, FEAR AND FRENCH RESISTANCE

ROBERT PIKE

To my wife Kate, my boys Joseph and Elliot, and my late mother Mary, whose love of history inspired me.

First published 2018

The History Press
The Mill, Brimscombe Port
Stroud, Gloucestershire, GL5 2QG
www.thehistorypress.co.uk

© Robert Pike, 2018

The right of Robert Pike to be identified as the Author
of this work has been asserted in accordance with the
Copyright, Designs and Patents Act 1988.

British Library Cataloguing in Publication Data.
A catalogue record for this book is available from the British Library.

ISBN 978 0 7509 8552 9

Typesetting and origination by The History Press
Printed and bound in Great Britain by TJ International Ltd

CONTENTS

'There was something within me that viscerally refused enslavement. I am against dictators, whoever they may be. As for Nazism, at the time I didn't know what it was. But I refused to no longer be a free man.'

Louis de la Bardonnie

'Rather servitude than war.'

Léon Emery

INTRODUCTION

'Resistance, in its multiple forms, has become the fundamental reaction of the French … It is everywhere, fierce and effective … It is in the factories and in the fields, in the offices and schools, in the streets and in the houses, in hearts and in thoughts.'

General Charles de Gaulle, 3 November 1943.

Inspirational leader though he was, General de Gaulle was far from the mark in 1943 with his assertion that the idea of resistance had permeated through the thoughts and actions of all French people. He knew this full well. De Gaulle's great achievement while guiding the Free French movement from London and later Algiers was to provide leadership for a vast array of different groups with a broadly common goal. In time he helped to rekindle French pride and inspired the spirit of its people to emerge triumphant. He managed to work side by side and toe to toe with the United States and the United Kingdom, whose leaders did not much like him. The French collective psyche throughout the 1930s, still rebuilding after the devastation of the First World War, was one of self-questioning and low self-esteem. The Front Populaire, a left-wing and partially communist alliance that claimed power in 1936, had offered brief hope to the masses but ultimately ended in financial crisis. The right wing placed the blame for the swift defeat of the once great French army in May 1940 squarely at the feet of the Front Populaire, led by Léon Blum, a politician of Jewish descent. Anti-Semitism was common in the country's political classes, as was a fear of communism, but defeat also meant an opportunity to establish an authoritarian and nationalist government forged on the ideals of France's monarchical past. Those deemed anti-French, which included militant communists and Jews, would be chased out of influential positions and, in some cases, underground.

Few people in France had heard of de Gaulle in June 1940, when he made his famous call to carry on the fight over the airwaves of the BBC, and the number that heard the speech – which was firmly aimed at the military – was also small. Many more knew of and trusted Marshal Philippe Pétain, who carried an almost mythical aura having earned himself the title of 'victor of Verdun'. Some politicians behind his coming to power had assumed and hoped that, at 84 years of age, he would be a malleable figurehead for France. His influence, however, was profound in the creation of the new state through a process commonly and officially called a National Revolution, though Pétain himself abhorred this term, which he associated with communism; he preferred the notion of a renewal.

In his 1977 book, *Quarante millions de Pétainistes*, French popular historian Henri Amouroux claimed that those who openly applauded de Gaulle on the Champs Elysée in 1944 were the same as those who had applauded Pétain in the summer of 1940. His book was an indication of the mood that followed the release of Marcel Ophuls' 1969 film *Le Chagrin et la pitié (The Sorrow and the Pity)*, in which a revisionist view of occupation and resistance emerged. Up until then France had shied away from its guilt in the period known as the 'Dark Years' of occupation. Such works questioned whether France should consider its own role in the years of oppression of its own people, as well as its guilt in supplying Germany with a cupboard of men and materials to empty for the wider war effort. The Vichy government created police forces to subdue its own people who protested, and it offered up Jews for deportation before even being asked to do so, going so far as to include children in deportations to reach targets negotiated with its Nazi 'partners'. The default position of the French population, both Amouroux and Ophuls argued, was compliance and therefore collaboration. Only a small number protested or refused – minuscule in the early days.

Following the war only 250,000 'membership cards' were given out by the veterans' administration to those who had actively fought in the Resistance, which was anything but a mass movement. During its early days right up to the liberation it attracted hostility and initially only muted support by some, while the events of the *épuration* (summary punishment for those thought to have collaborated) further undermined its reputation. On signature of the armistice with Nazi Germany, few career soldiers were behind de Gaulle and most scorned his efforts. General Philippe Guillain de Bénouville wrote later that 'those who dedicated themselves to the active Resistance from the start know how few we were in those early days just as those at the end'.

What follows is a story of resistance, inauspicious to begin with against an ever-greater force. It is the tale of how the notion of refusal took root in the minds of French people, driving them to respond through action, whether in a clandestine and fighting sense, or in a more restrained but equally dangerous manner, in full sight of the authorities. Looking at the department of the Dordogne – an area where Resistance flourished – the events here demonstrate the resilience of a people under inordinate amounts of pressure as the military powers of Nazi Germany combined with the politicians of Vichy to turn the public against the very notion of Resistance. The resulting story demonstrates the best of humanity, and the worst. The people of South-west France were fearful, were force-fed propaganda and were uncertain of their own fates should they commit to either side. By 1944, when reprisals were reported daily, battles and ambushes raged in the countryside, and acquaintances were summarily executed, the default position was to lock the door and retreat. In the Dordogne, as was the case elsewhere in the southern zone, a large number refused to give in and instead, some way or another, chose to defy Vichy.

MAPS

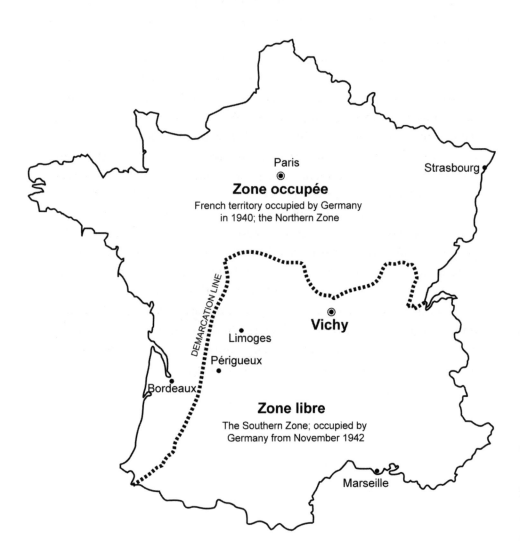

Paris

Strasbourg

Zone occupée

French territory occupied by Germany
in 1940; the Northern Zone

DEMARCATION LINE

Vichy

Limoges

Périgueux

Bordeaux

Zone libre

The Southern Zone; occupied by
Germany from November 1942

Marseille

Occupied France, 1940–44.

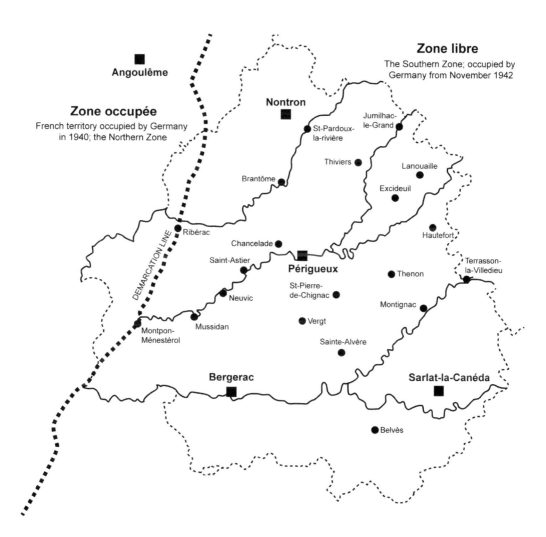

Zone libre
The Southern Zone; occupied by
Germany from November 1942

Angoulême

Zone occupée
French territory occupied by Germany
in 1940; the Northern Zone

Nontron

St-Pardoux-
la-rivière

Jumilhac-
le-Grand

Thiviers

Lanouaille

Brantôme

Excideuil

DEMARCATION LINE

Ribérac

Chancelade

Hautefort

Saint-Astier

Périgueux

Thenon

Terrasson-
la-Villedieu

Neuvic

St-Pierre-
de-Chignac

Montignac

Montpon-
Ménestérol

Mussidan

Vergt

Sainte-Alvère

Bergerac

Sarlat-la-Canéda

Belvès

The Dordogne, showing the demarcation line that seperated the northern and southern zones.

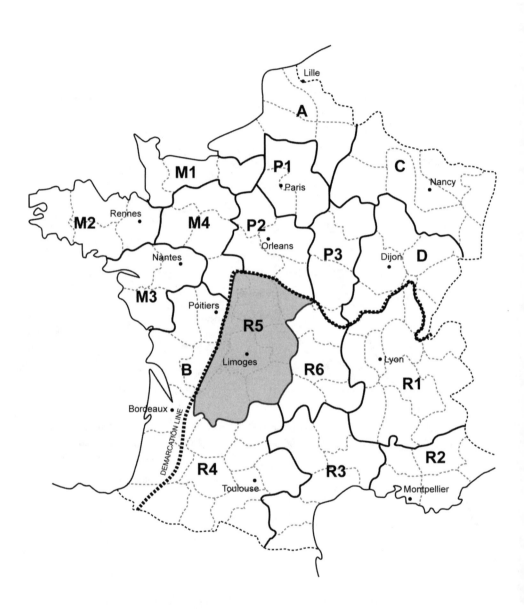

The military regions of the Resistance in spring 1944.

1

PEACE AND WAR

The Byzantine cathedral of Périgueux is unmistakeable. Approach from the south and it appears to hover over the sharply descending hill on which the old town is constructed, at the foot of which runs the River Isle. The shapes of the basilica are eastern and sharp edged, out of place against the medieval architecture. It is a patchwork city, old and new, modern and ancient, traditional and forward thinking. The administrative capital of the department of the Dordogne, it can be bustling but is more often than not quiet and unspectacular, with few tourists to clog its streets. The contrast could not be more striking as the pedestrian emerges from the car parks and open spaces of the Place Francheville and Boulevard Montagne through a virtual doorway into the close walls of the winding streets of the old town. It is easy to pass by when travelling south, the motorways and orbital roads allowing the tourist to steer clear and head for the better-known Bergerac or Sarlat further south. But those who go find it charming, its roman remains and pretty boutiques along the meandering rue Limogeanne enough to occupy the single-day visitor.

Formerly the ancient county of Périgord until after the revolution of 1789, the people still often refer to themselves as Périgourdin. The same is true for their gastronomy, history and heritage. The countryside is home to farms full of ducks and geese, many of which are destined for the dinner table served as fatty confit, or lean *magret*, often with creamy mushroom sauces. Most restaurants still offer the Périgourdin menu of salads featuring walnuts, warm goat's cheese and *gésiers*, followed by poultry of which nothing is wasted. Wine is white and sweet; prunes and apricots are abundant and the local *eau de vie pruneaux* best taken in moderation. To taste the local truffles, 'black diamonds' which were for centuries snuffled out by pigs in the woodlands, best to do so in an omelette.

Its green luscious countryside has played host to those seeking a slower pace of life for hundreds of years. Visitors have always wandered amongst the impressive châteaux that stud the countryside, paddled along the rivers Isle or Dordogne, or lazed amongst the many farm buildings built amongst the fertile farmland. Life is still lived at a slow pace, and its people glow with the healthy bronze of a long, warm summer. Situated between Bordeaux to the west and Limoges to the east, it is a wide area often only passed through by those who holiday elsewhere. Once home to the four tribes, or Petrocore from which the Périgord derived its name, it is located between the Loire Valley and the Pyrenées. The Petrocores resisted the Romans, leaving behind ruins such as the enormous tower and arena on the south side of the River Isle, in the part of the city formerly known as Vesone. Bastide towns like Sarlat and Montpazier are reminders of the violent Middle Ages.

The Dordogne river is some 30km south, bisecting Bergerac, the region's second town. This is a farming region, vast, leafy and filled with slow-moving rivers and gentle slopes. It has been inhabited by tribes since prehistoric times, as testified by the famous cave paintings of Lascaux and Rouffignac, and the troglodyte dwellings of La Roque Saint-Christophe and Les Eyzies. The river that runs through Périgueux is the Isle. The department's major towns and villages are found along its rivers, but its people have never relied upon them other than as tourist attractions. This is a farming region, and its people rely on the land, and its animals. It is also a place where the rural world and the towns intermingle and co-depend. The people of the countryside, over the past millennium, have been identified as the *paysans* (peasants). They and the landowners have co-existed happily since the days of the revolution. Around the villages are towns where small factories sprang up, mirroring the more industrial towns of Brive and Limoges further east. Some of the *paysans* became *ouvrieurs* (factory workers), while others who worked on the railways became *les cheminots*. In the towns themselves, additional layers such as the professional classes thrived.

According to a census held in 1936 the region was home to 386,900 inhabitants. The sparsity of population when compared to the 918,383 hectares of ground was testament to the open spaces of this idyllic corner of

France. Even as heavy industry developed across the country and elsewhere in Europe, life remained slow in pace and agriculture was by far the biggest industry. For the people of the Dordogne the polyculture of wheat, rye and maize complemented the potatoes, fruit trees and vegetables. Vast vineyards adorned the hilly land around Bergerac while the rearing of cattle and poultry enriched the local economy throughout the rest of the department into something approaching idyllic but precariously balanced self-sufficiency.

A huge number of agricultural businesses nestled between the rivers and wooded areas that divided the region into four 'Périgords'. The centre of the region, the '*grenier de blé*', or grain store of the Périgord, deserved its name: le Périgord blanc. In the north of the region le Périgord vert is a vast area packed with woodland taking in the beautiful towns of Brantôme and Nontron. Le Périgord pourpre of the south-west is home to the large wine-producing areas that surround Bergerac. The south-east of the region, or le Périgord noir, houses the ancient Bastille towns of Sarlat and Domme. Well-populated valleys with steep escarpments were surrounded by forests, scattered throughout the region, vast and empty.

Of those inhabitants recorded in 1936, very few lived in large towns. The largest of these towns was Périgueux, with Bergerac next in line. Those were the only urban centres with populations of more than 20,000. Other slightly larger towns such as the medieval Sarlat, Ribérac, Nontron and Mussidan were at that time still rather small by comparison.

The population of the late 1930s was not cosmopolitan, although the area did host many retreats for more wealthy Parisians. The year 1939 saw some changes due to an exodus from Spain of Republicans chased out by Franco's new regime, and from Eastern Europe as Nazism engulfed the continent, but these numbers were relatively small. The overall demographic of the Périgord was typical of the rural provinces: primarily French, white and Catholic. In the fields there was a significant influence of militant socialism, but generally the region was rather conservative. The gentry, a significant proportion of which were in the wine-producing west, were patriotic and Conservative. Some believed in the ideas of fascism and wished for a strong and stable France that could hold its place at the negotiation tables of the world.

Whatever their social status, those living in the southern half of France in late 1938 and 1939 could be forgiven for feeling insulated from events elsewhere in Europe. The local population had been spared the horror of trench warfare that engulfed much of the north-east only twenty years previously, so for many of the *paysans* (peasant farmers) the prospect of another war was distant, almost imperceptible. In Bergerac, brothers Léon and Robert Bondier, professional photographers, recorded scenes from the *foire-exposition* of June 1939. Amongst the parades were men dressed as Nazi dignitaries, parodied in no uncertain terms. The most flagrant of these was a comical 'Hitler' piloting a tiny plane, encouraged by a laughing crowd.

★★★

Away from the calm of the rural south-west, France was a country in political and economic turmoil. Its people, politically aware and engaged, were fed up with a political system whose instability and vulnerability to outside influences had led to economic and social failures that profoundly affected most layers of society.

The Third Republic was creaking, bending under the weight of the inter-war years that had taken their toll on France's standing in European and world theatres. German militarisation had already galloped ahead of France.

In 1936 the Front Populaire, a combination of the far and middle left, came to power. Led by Léon Blum, the party promised reform and some respite from the economic downturn that had plagued France since the great depression of 1929. It swept to power on the promise of a shorter working week, paid holidays and new rights for workers through trade unions. Staunchly anti-fascist, it distanced itself from the success of Hitler and the Nazis, but took pains to persuade the French that it was not run from Moscow. This pushed it into a strange middle ground that pleased neither the far-left communists, numerous in the factories and mines of northern France, nor the right wing, on which the future collaborationist government would be founded.

Ever since the creation of the Parti Communiste Français (PCF) at the congress of Tours in 1920, just three years after the Bolshevik revolution in Russia, communism played an increasing role in French politics. Often involved in just as much conflict with the socialist parties as with the bourgeoisie, the sworn enemies of its Russian cousin, the party played its part in the democratic life of the Third Republic without threatening a revolution. Socialist leader Léon Blum had distanced himself from Marxism, however, defining himself as a leader of the moderate left. He was more concerned with the threat on the other side of the Rhine, concentrating on opposing an ongoing appeasement of Hitler, rather than on the irritant of a Communist Party that preferred to emphasise its non-affiliation to Moscow. Every government of the Third Republic had, in fact, been concerned with curbing the excesses of the far right – in particular Action Française – and the first year of the Front Populaire was the height of leftist influence in the interwar years. The traditionally right-wing Third Republic had a history of hatred towards the communists, as well as other foreign influences, particularly the Jews. When the coalition government became partially infused with communists with the 1936 election victory, led by the Jewish Blum, the divisions that already existed within the system were only reinforced.

The period of the Front Populaire's incumbency began with a general strike between the months of May and June 1936, which did little to endear the movement to the bourgeoisie. Then came a period of relative success over twelve months as the social reforms promised by Blum were introduced. Shorter working weeks and paid holidays were popular, but the ground had not been properly laid for such major changes.

The Lichtenbergs were a Jewish Polish family who moved to Paris from Siedlce near Warsaw in 1928 because of growing anti-Semitism in Poland. While at primary school in the Marais area of the French capital, Léon lived with his grandmother, a practising Jew, and became accustomed to Jewish practices. His parents, however, gave little thought to their being Jewish, his mother being far less of a believer than his father. With his grandmother Léon spoke Yiddish, and rarely Polish, while with his parents he spoke Polish and French.

In 1936 the family began to once again feel uncomfortable as anti-Semitic sentiment swelled, combined with the rise of Hitler and his German National Socialists, so they relocated to the Périgord. Hitler's thoughts on Aryanisation and anti-Semitism were becoming well known, albeit linked to civil persecution rather than anything more severe. Nevertheless, the threats to livelihoods weighed heavily on the minds of many in the Jewish Parisian communities.

Still only 11 years of age in 1936, Léon Lichtenberg had begun to understand the nature of politics and was aware of the advent of the Front Populaire, taken in by the progressive atmosphere and material benefits enjoyed by those of his class. His family were left-leaning – repulsed by right-wing ideology – and Léon revelled in the 'festival atmosphere' that left him with 'very warm memories' of the short period: 'People were happy, there was … an atmosphere of brotherhood, not this tension of previous years.' The paid holidays were spent as a family, cycling on tandems. 'It was a kind of liberation. There was change in the air … The atmosphere, it was one of humanism.'[1]

The Front Populaire's brief time in power left Léon politicised, and convinced of his socialist inclinations. However, as the party's power began to crumble, Jewish sections of society began to feel the force of blame for France's political strife. Despite not being subject to direct discrimination by the French people they knew, the Lichtenbergs were concerned by the language of the press and politicians' speeches. This *violence verbale* was enough to persuade the family to relocate to the Dordogne, a 'forgotten corner of France' where Léon's uncle had set up business. They arrived in Périgueux in 1936 and Léon continued his schooling there, due to sit his *baccalauréat philo* in 1942.

The Dordogne was a department anchored in leftist tradition. Between 1919 and 1940 two thirds of all *députés* elected to Parliament in the department belonged to left-wing parties. This tradition stretched back into the nineteenth century and would be strengthened during the two world wars. in 1936 the first two communist *députés* in its history were elected in Paul Loubradou of Bergerac and Gustave Saussot of Nontron. Only one out of the six *députés* elected that year did not belong to the Front Populaire. The Dordogne and the neighbouring Lot-et-Garonne were examples of the influence of rural communism.[2] This combined with the large increase in population – first in 1938 with the arrival of swathes of Spanish Republicans, and later with the arrival of evacuees from Alsace-Lorraine, of whom nearly 50,000 stayed until the end of the war – resulted in a substantial rural left-wing element. This set the stage for a leftist-influenced Resistance earlier rather than later.

By June 1937 a downward economic spiral set in. Higher wages were neutralised by the rise in prices due to inflation. Due to the higher costs of running factories in which working conditions had been skewed to benefit the workforce, owners scaled back production and businessmen took their funds abroad for investment in healthier markets. This turn in the economy and a Senate controlled by conservatives forced Blum to take many backward steps, stopping his social reforms and devaluing the franc. A further complication for the Front Populaire had been events on the other side of the Pyrénées in Spain. General Franco's revolution had gathered momentum and many on the left were keen for France to reinforce the left-wing republican democrats against the far right-wing Franco. Blum had resisted this, not for ideological reasons but because he was worried that such a war would spill over the borders into France.

The politicians of the Front Populaire no longer presented the united front that was needed in times of potential war. A chasm appeared between pacifist socialists and communists not willing to look beyond the protection of workers from the march of imperialism. As Blum fell the Radicals – who, despite the name, were far less radically socialist than the communists – took over power on 10 April 1938.

By the autumn of 1938 the Front Populaire dissolved itself, a victim of its lack of preparedness for the continued ill effects of the global downturn after the great depression. It also failed because of a right wing that was so entrenched in the political system, that it bid to undermine everything the Front Populaire tried to achieve. It had been too much, too soon, and too left wing for a conservative country like France. By the end of April, Blum had been replaced by the Radical Édouard Daladier as président du Conseil, who remained in post from April 1938 to March 1940. During this time he steadied the ship by repealing much of the social reform of the Front Populaire and distancing himself from it. He got some big businesses to reinvest in France and presented a strong diplomatic force abroad. Backed by his Finance Minister, Paul Reynaud, he oversaw a good recovery of the economy, but he knew that the Republic of France was in trouble. He went to Munich in 1938 knowing that France would be playing second fiddle to Britain, and took a back seat to Georges Bonnet, a French politician and leading figure in the Radical Party, not involving himself in Chamberlain-style triumphalism on his return. Nevertheless, he was well received in the chamber after his visit and was perceived to have done what all of France wanted: avoid a war

After Munich Daladier began to realign himself, courting the Soviet Union once he was sure that any links to the Front Populaire were firmly cut, but making it clear that he in no way intended to promote Bolshevism, only peace. When Hitler occupied Prague, he stepped up rearmament and stood on the side of Britain over the Polish corridor, changing France's policy of appeasement to one of diplomatic resistance. This in itself was a result of a swing in public opinion – from determination to avoid war, to regret at having avoided international responsibilities.

Nevertheless, France was restricted to a defensive strategy; the aim of the leaders was to engage in a defensive war, making France's borders impenetrable and hitting Germany with economic blockades. A series of concrete armament installations, fortifications and obstacles, the Maginot Line was built on the French side of her borders with Switzerland, Germany and Luxembourg, with construction beginning well before the Second World War, in 1928. The concrete structures were served by a complicated system of underground tunnels and railway lines, meaning those manning it could go for weeks without seeing sunlight. Its primary role was to avoid a repeat of the types of losses that had been endured in the First World War. These losses, both human and material, had been disastrous for France, where so much of the fighting had taken place.

Neither Marshal Pétain nor Pierre Laval, traditionally the villains of the story of Vichy collaboration, expressed an attitude towards Germany that was out of kilter with the right-wing French politicians of 1939. For them, it was far better to deal with Germany, led by a strong, charismatic leader like Hitler, than to be infiltrated by the internal enemy, or the 'anti-France'. These dangers to the *patrie française* were the internal Communist Party, the Jewish establishment that had infiltrated France's economic infrastructure and the influx of immigrants from the east – even more Jews that presented a danger to Catholic idealism.

The far right of French politics, in which the ideologies of leagues such as Action Française and Croix de Feu played a central part, were more concerned by the enemies within than the enemies without. Hatred of the Germans had been intense throughout the 1920s due to the catastrophic physical and emotional results of the First World War, and the far right had openly criticised the governments of that decade for not making Germany pay heavily enough. However, by the mid 1930s admiration had grown for Germany's resilience and this, together with a huge distaste for the success of the Front Populaire, meant that the personality and success of Adolf Hitler held some allure for those with fascist leanings. They also saw the success of nationalist movements by Franco in Spain and Salazar in Portugal, while Mussolini had created ties with Hitler that were benefiting Italy.

The majority of French people in the mid 1930s were not concerned about Germany's remilitarisation; rather, the overriding concern – of the people and most French politicians – was the avoidance of war. Nobody wanted bloodshed such as had been witnessed twenty years earlier, and foreign and defence policy was hugely influenced by a finely balanced pacifism. The governments of the Front Populaire were the first to employ a hurried programme of remilitarisation due to events over the Rhine, but in fact remilitarisation had begun even earlier, in 1934. Blum, however, increased spending significantly, upping the ante by putting concerted effort into building tanks after Germany's *Anschluss* with Austria in 1938.

French defence policy in the 1930s was in turmoil. The left wing, including the communists, was eager to put the brakes on Hitler's progress. Having to tread carefully, Blum's left wanted a policy of a strengthened national defence. The right, on the other hand, were urging negotiation and co-operation with Hitler's Germany. For them a peaceful co-existence with a strong Germany as a bulwark against Soviet communism and internal left-wing forces was far preferable to Blum and his Front Populaire. A slogan emerged, 'Rather Hitler than Blum' – an invitation to peace, rather than one to invade.

In a thinly veiled reference to Jews and communists, Pierre-Étienne Flandin, former French conservative prime minister and leader of the Democratic Republican Alliance (ARD), wrote that 'occult forces' were 'dragging the country to war', while right-wing publications supported the Munich agreement by openly articulating a refusal to go to war for the 'Judeo-Bolshevik' refugees, who were themselves seeking revenge on Germany. Blum called for the Munich delegation to make a firm stand against Hitler. He was caught between 'relief and shame' at the appeasement – it was the Communist Party who vehemently opposed the accord.

These opposing ideas on France's foreign policy were little more than a conflict of ideology until things came to a head in 1939, as the overall policy of a defensive approach was challenged very little if at all. With the Maginot Line in place, it was considered inconceivable that German troops would be able to penetrate the Ardennes, so that area was lightly defended – the River Meuse, it was believed, would be impossible to traverse, and much of the terrain would be impassable anyway. France had not wanted to offend its neutral neighbour Belgium, so the Maginot Line stopped at the beginning of the Belgian border. Stretching south from the

English Channel to the Ardennes, the Seventh, First and Ninth Armies dug into what would become known as the Daladier Line – a series of lighter defences. France had developed its strategy based on a public belief that war must be avoided at all costs, and so no military planning could be seen to threaten an outbreak of conflict; even Pétain advocated the defensive nature of France's policy. The creation of the Maginot Line was a visual embodiment of this: concrete structures took the place of iron machines, and the well-photographed underground passageways and book-adorned living quarters bathed in artificial lighting spoke of a determination to dig in. When comparisons were made with the horrors of First World War trenches, it was claimed 'defence was now about concrete rather than human flesh'. Additionally, despite Belgium's declaration of neutrality in 1936, those in office believed – based on gentlemen's agreements and personal 'links' – that Belgium would allow French soldiers on her land to take up advanced fighting positions, and that they would benefit from any intelligence provided by the Belgians. France's view of the army was outdated and focused, even relied, on such nostalgic concepts.

To compound these misapprehensions, both the French army and population at large regarded the French armed forces as highly effective, well equipped and highly skilled. The French military leadership insisted that conscription continued to be the best way to procure an effective and fresh fighting force, and the professional soldier was only required to lead vast reserves of men, called upon when needed. There was no recognition that Germany had moved on and continued to do so while France concentrated on her internal enemies in an unstable political climate that kept tearing itself apart.

Paul Reynaud, Finance Minister in Édouard Daladier's post-Blum government and in 1940 président du Conseil, was one of the very few politicians to recognise that France's army was in need of modernisation. He read and was heavily influenced by a little-known book published in 1934, *Vers l'armée de métier* (*Towards a Professional Army*), written by an unknown lieutenant colonel called Charles de Gaulle. Reynaud put in front of Parliament its ideas, such as moving the machinery of war forward to reflect the technology of the modern age, and making up the armed forces with professional soldiers rather than conscripted civilians. These soldiers would be retained and upskilled, leading to fewer losses and more efficient fighting, and they would be complemented by the use of up-to-date machinery that would require fewer fighters. Reynaud's suggestions were defeated by a comfortable majority, and de Gaulle's foresight was lost.

At the end of August 1939, Germany and the Soviet Union were at loggerheads over Poland. It seemed possible that the world was about to be at war again unless Hitler backed down. It was also conceivable that the two opposing ideologies of fascist Germany and the communist Soviet Union would blow each other apart. Instead, during the second half of August 1939 news broke that Nazi Germany had signed a commercial accord with the Soviet Union. On 23 August Europe gasped when a pact of non-aggression was signed between the two countries, and suddenly the USSR, seen since the Munich Agreement of 1938 as the absolute foe of Nazi Germany, became a mighty enemy to France and Britain. Daladier declared that the unknown terms of the vague treaty increased greatly 'the chances of an attack against France's allies, or against France herself'. As well as precluding a unilateral attack against each other, the accord also ensured that the world knew that, should Britain or France uphold the promise to support Poland should Germany invade, the USSR would not side with them. When Molotov and Ribbentrop announced this Nazi–Soviet Pact of non-aggression, Stalin opened the door to Poland for Hitler, and war was inevitable.

So began the systematic destruction of the PCF, now considered a dangerous satellite organisation of Moscow within French borders that could and would collaborate with an ever-strengthening and ever more belligerent Nazi Germany. The last few years of the Third Republic bore witness to a methodical crushing of the communists that would lay the foundations for the harsher realities of the Vichy police state.

Communist party members and militants had been caught off guard by Stalin's negotiations with Hitler, and many felt aggrieved at the betrayal. Gustave Saussot, a former mechanic and now *député* for Nontron in the Dordogne, responded by announcing, 'This pact concerns us all directly. By signing this treaty with Nazi Germany, Stalin has stuck a knife into the backs of England and France.' Other communist leaders preached the idea of trusting in the judgement of Stalin, and avoiding appearing traitorous to Moscow, but Saussot was of the persuasion of the French Communist Party, which had adopted the ideals of Marxism but for whom patriotism as a Frenchman came first.

Even as a meeting took place on 25 August of the parliamentary Communist Party, the premises of the printer of the communist newspaper *Humanité* was raided by police. The following day Saussot, along with his colleague from and representing Bergerac, Paul Loubradou, sent his resignation letter to Jacques Duclos, secretary of the parliamentary Communist Party. In his letter, Saussot spoke of his admiration of the Soviet Union's defence of republican Spain, Czechoslovakia and China, but criticised Moscow's passivity towards Hitler's threat of taking Danzig. According to Saussot, if a defensive position had been adopted there, Hitler would have been pushed back and it was for this reason he no longer wished to work with the Communist Party.

A few days later Loubradou explained his own resignation. He believed that the only guarantee of peace would have been if an Anglo-Franco-Soviet pact – something that would have, in the case of war, meant the 'crushing of racism' – had been made. Instead, claimed Loubradou, the new pact only served to encourage aggression, and he made a statement that sounded like an ominous death knell but would prove remarkably prescient: 'It took Hitler five years of effort and savagery to crush communism – and freedom – in Germany, in Austria … in Czechoslovakia; it will only have taken five days for Stalin to crush it in France.'

Whereas the social idealism of the communists had always been unpopular with the French ruling classes and support for Marxism reached little further than the industrial north, these policies were not what ultimately sharpened the Third Republic's knives towards the Communist Party. Rather it was the Nazi–Soviet pact that caused utter outrage. Despite public declarations by many militants that they took their orders from Paris rather than Moscow, communism became, for several years, public enemy number one.

On 26 September 1939 a government decree was made ordering the dissolution of all communist organisations, including affiliates. Daladier announced on 18 November that 'just as foreigners, French individuals dangerous for national defence and public security could be interned by préfets.'

The Soviet invasion of Finland in November exacerbated matters for the remnants of the Communist Party, now underground. Images of the Finnish suffering on a snowy battlefront led the likes of right-wing writer Charles Maurras to declare that the Soviet Union should be broken in Finland as elsewhere. By January 1940 the right-wing Catholic *député* for

the Gironde, Philippe Henriot, was ready to claim that 'whoever is a follower of Stalin is a follower of Hitler'. The embattled communists were
subject to a full-scale purge.

While not yet a police state, the dogged pursuit of those judged '*dangereux
pour la défense nationale ou la sécurité publique*' preoccupied many officials
during the last days of the Third Republic. The resulting *centres de séjour
surveillé pour indésirables* were created out of what became an important
government policy that pre-dated the Daladier government, but on which
it could build. The first of the centres was in Rieucros near Mende in the
Lozère, and from 21 January 1939 tens of thousands of foreigners were
interned there. Initially inmates were predominantly Spanish, but when
war broke out Daladier's government stepped up surveillance of political groups considered 'subversive', and allowed for the internment of any
individual, foreign or otherwise, who was considered a threat to national
defence or public safety. Once the Vichy state became established they were
joined by Austrians, Poles, German Jews and further French communists.

★★★

With war on the horizon, action had been taken since June 1937 to evacuate those parts of Alsace-Lorraine in north-east France that fell within
a contested zone. In all, 485,000 inhabitants from 417 communes within
the Moselle, Haut-Rhin and Bas-Rhin would be required to travel south.
Much of the population of the Bas-Rhin, including Strasbourg, would
relocate towards the Dordogne, and parts of the Haute-Vienne and
Clermont-Ferrand. The peoples of the Haut-Rhin would set off in the
direction of the Landes, Lot-et-Garonne and Gers. No amount of planning
could have made the operation run smoothly. Trains were prepared, but
comfort was at a premium: many of the locomotives pulled agricultural or
commercial transport wagons with little in the way of sanitation or access
to food and water. The travellers had been told to bring supplies for 'several
days' of transit but for many the journey was much longer.

In the first week of September 1939, Anne Vergez, aged 17, along with
her family, was one such traveller. She was sitting near the doorway of a carriage designed for cattle: 'I said to my mother, "Look I've got tanned legs!"
She said to me: "Wait till you are washed, you'll see if you are tanned!" In
fact, I was just dirty! Nobody was able to wash for twelve days.'[3] For others

the journey was stop–start, with half-day pauses while the overcrowded rail network creaked under the weight of a simultaneous population migration and military mobilisation.

In less than a week seventy-eight trains transporting 87,300 people from the Strasbourg area were headed towards Périgueux. On 5 September, the Mayor of Périgueux asked for the city's population to take in Alsatian families, estimating 3,000 new arrivals per day. The numbers would be higher, on certain days peaking at 10,000 people. The Croix Rouge set up teams in the Gare de Périgueux that provided much-needed food and comfort, as well as information about stations for ongoing transit – for many their journey was unfinished. Cars with loudspeakers circulated the streets confirming when the first trains had arrived. In all, Périgueux took in 11,375 Strasbourgeois, in doing so doubling its population and becoming Alsace-Lorraine's first city. On 18 September 1939, the prefect of the Dordogne sent a letter to a colleague in Limoges saying, 'We have arrived at a degree of saturation that is worrying me a lot'[4]

The refugees were sometimes treated suspiciously, particularly as the Strasbourgeois dialect sounded German. In some instances, the newcomers were referred to as '*les Boches*', while in schools children were often called 'ya-yas' because of the sound groups of youngsters seemed to make together. The Périgourdins had their own patois as well, and their clipped regional accent was hard to understand for those unfamiliar with it. Country life required some getting used to for those from much more urban settings such as Strasbourg, where the quality of life was higher; indeed, some Alsatians noted that by going to the Périgord it felt like they were regressing by 150 years. In this environment, some hosts were put out by the request to provide for their 'guests', but most accepted it despite having little to spare.

The Belgian family of Marie-Josèphe Pauwelÿn came to the Dordogne in 1937 in search of a farm to rent, becoming French citizens and first settling in Normandy before seeking to diversify elsewhere. Marie-Josèphe was 4 years old when she arrived in Sencenac-Puy-de-Fourches near Brantôme, and the family soon grew with the arrival of a sister – the fourth child – in late September 1939. However, when her father was mobilised in summer 1939, life became harder: that autumn her mother was unable to pull up the beetroot and 6-year-old Marie-Josèphe had to help so it would not spoil. Even when her father was sent back that December, his absence meant it would be a difficult time ahead for the farm. Marie-Josèphe recalled him crying each night because he had returned far too late in the year to successfully sow wheat.

An already difficult period was made far more difficult by the arrival of the Alsatians and Strasbourgeois:

> I remember that my sister was in her cot and my mother had put a big table in between the cows. She cooked potatoes and gave milk to all these people that had arrived from Agonac. They slept in the corner on the hay. A few days later some got up and left but a few remained.[5]

Those refugees who were found a space in a family home, though restricted for space, learned that their lot was a fortunate one. For many, their initial accommodation was in a school. Others were set up in man-made sheds or even caves that were little more than hovels, without heating, electricity or water. To ease the problems, it was decided that 165 barracks would be built around the larger towns – huge sheds to shelter up to 100 people each.

Space was not the only commodity at a premium: funds were also sparse, meaning that most welfare tasks had to take place in the larger towns, usually Périgueux. Other important administrative functions were relocated around the immediate area. The Hôpital civil de Strasbourg was transferred to Clairvivre in Périgueux, but, despite large spaces and a convenient location, preparations for the ill and the workers were nowhere near complete. Meanwhile, a huge task was undertaken so that the new hospital for the refugees, with its 120 beds, could be opened.

Mobilisation

At 4.15 a.m. on 1 September 1939 a general mobilisation of the French military was decreed for Saturday 2 September at midnight. TSF radio sets were rare so, as in 1914, bells rang out to alert the population, and to announce the mobilisation of all army reservists. A muted sadness reigned. Some felt as though the war graves completed just twenty-one years previously were still warm. Jean Marotin, who had travelled to Mussidan to visit his son Robert, a railway worker, when the invasion of Poland had taken place, recorded his thoughts in a private diary: 'From now on, after the departure of each train leading the men of Mussidan away, fathers, mothers, wives, children file away along the street, overcome, in tears, handkerchief on the eyes or on the mouth. It is like coming back from the cemetery after the funeral.'[6]

Reservists were surprised at the lack of readiness they encountered. Alphonse Dureisseix was just 20 years old when he was allocated to the 196th Régiment d'Artillerie in Bordeaux:

> Nobody was ready for war like in 1914. When we left Bordeaux, we went to Bassens to collect lorries and pieces of artillery. There were tractors and lorries that were brand new. I asked my captain why we were taking old lorries and not the new ones. He said that we would have them when the time came. Some reservists had neither guns nor uniform.[7]

Throughout the country the feeling was one of resignation.[8] 4.5 million men were drafted in France and her colonies, and there was very little refusal to sign up even if there was a distinct lack of enthusiasm for war: no one wanted a repeat of the 1914–18 conflict. Nevertheless, recalled veterans of the First World War passed on much-needed positivity created by the 1918 victory.

Writer Roland Dorgelès, while visiting the front line in October 1939, commented in the publication *Gringoire* that 'war was not *drôle* [funny], but it was certainly *une drôle de guerre* [a funny war]'. The following nine months would be defined by this term: very little happening, few signs of German aggression and French soldiers battling with little other than boredom. The British called it a 'phoney war'.

France had wanted, and had planned, its resources for a long-term, defensive battle, hoping to force Germany to retreat and rethink. But the blitz of the victorious German effort quickly extinguished this hope. France's fall not only came quickly, but her allies seemed to have deserted her. Britain's retreat via Dunkirk would prove vital in the course of the war, but at the time it was perceived by some French as a cowardly abandonment. A lack of assistance from Holland and neutral Belgium meant that France was under-informed as to the state of the defences of those countries. Despite some examples of feeble resistance such as the second-class troops along the Meuse, there had also been some stern and heroic defence, such as in Lille. There was no absolute collapse in morale, just poor tactics and jumbled leadership as Hitler and his generals remained nervous of a counter-attack that never came. In being defeated thus, France lost a whole army to prisoner-of-war camps within Germany.

Still the defeat was a shock. Just nine months earlier France considered itself to have one of the strongest armies in the world, but it had collapsed in a period of six weeks, having come up against 136 well-equipped, effective and thoroughly modern divisions. The lack of modernisation and forward-thinking among the military leadership meant that the French forces were routed by extraordinary German gains between 10 May 1940 and 17 June 1940. The French army was well resourced, and its tanks were among the best – but the French method of using them statically was outdated in comparison to Germany's blindingly quick forward manoeuvres. The men on the ground, the leaders and the public were shocked by the losses they had endured in so short a space of time.

★★★

On 17 June 1940 two schoolboys looked disbelievingly at the newspaper headlines that shouted from the kiosks along the leafy boulevard Montaigne in Périgueux. The French army was defeated, France's Prime Minister – now Paul Reynaud – had resigned and Marshal Philippe Pétain, a general during the last war, had offered himself as a gift to the French people. An armistice with the enemy loomed. The boys, both 15, were shocked – not so much by defeat but by the manner in which France had given up.

The two boys were both French, and 'Périgourdins'. One, Léon Lichtenberg was originally from Poland and the other was his best friend, Raphael Finkler, who, like his friend, was brought to Périgueux in the mid 1930s. His parents were Romanian and had fled to France when they felt threatened by rising anti-Semitism in their own country, but they also sought a better life. They moved to Paris where Raphael was born, but stayed for only a matter of months. Having family in Périgueux, they headed there for an easier existence. Life in the open spaces and fresher air, and in the semi-rural surroundings of the region's capital, suited them far better than what they had known in Paris.

The Finkler family fled the economic and social difficulties of Paris just like the Lichtenbergs, who were equally concerned by the uncomfortable anti-Semitism swelling in France. In the Périgord, however, where Jews were few and far between, danger seemed some way off. The two families became firm friends.

Neither of the boys fully understood the international politics that had led to war nor had insight into the level of significance their cultural and religious background would have in the years to come – raised in France and a product of the secular republican school system, religion meant very little to either of them. Indeed, if asked, Raphael would define himself as atheist, and even his parents respected certain traditional dates and festivals primarily only to catch up with family and friends.

Both Raphael's and Léon's parents had taught the boys to know that racism and fascism were unwelcome scourges on the world, so on that June day, they knew enough to decide that something had to be done. The boys had followed events abroad more closely than most, and recognised the 1938 Munich agreement as the failure that it was. However, they regarded themselves not as Jewish but as concerned onlookers with socialist leanings. They believed that war would be avoided, then watched as 'Poland was crushed, and nobody made a move. We had a general staff of imbeciles and politicians who were capitulators.'[9] They worried about the reaction of the population, both locally and nationally – it was muted, and worryingly almost satisfied: a blind deference to Pétain, the *victor de Verdun*. The cessation of fighting seemed for most to be a blessed relief. Raphael and Léon saw it differently. They knew something had to be done, but had no idea what. The majority of the population had no such thoughts and were content to see normality resume. But as sparse and isolated as they were, like-minded individuals refused to accept France's lot.

Defeat and the Birth of Vichy France

During June 1940 the roads leading south became packed with refugees fleeing northern France, Belgium and Holland. Many columns of terrified men, women and children, estimated to number between 6 and 10 million individuals, travelled slowly in carts, on bikes, in vehicles or on foot. The roads were blocked, the sound of engines was, in places, deafening and in towns the hot air mixed with engine fumes. Further south, vehicles were abandoned having run out of fuel. As far south as Angoulême these slow-moving columns of people, scared for their future plight, were caught up in attacks on the retreating army, costing hundreds of civilians their lives.

The French government was also on the move, adding to the feeling of fear, chased from Paris by the advancing German army. Beleaguered politicians were headed south-west: a long land train making its way slowly over the damaged roads to Bordeaux, after a short stay at Tours. In the Périgourdin town of Mussidan drivers of packed trains refused to leave the station. There was no bread left to buy and the water was each day being cut off for several hours. Windows were left open with radios on so that passers-by could hear the news, and inhabitants gave of what little they had: some townspeople made cauldrons of soup, while others allowed refugees to sleep in their homes or outbuildings.

The last president of the Third Republic, Albert Lebrun, called on Marshal Philippe Pétain to replace Reynaud at the head of the government. Reynaud was torn, not wanting to give up but out of options as his military persuaded him that innocents were dying with every passing day. Germanophile and career politician Pierre Laval worked behind the scenes to manoeuvre Pétain into place, and Reynaud was persuaded that Pétain would act as a figurehead, nothing more. Pétain accepted Reynaud's job, which he occupied for just under a month before assuming Lebrun's own role. Lebrun met with Pétain envisaging a plan to continue the military resistance against the Germans from the North African colonies, but instead Pétain produced a list of ministers favourable to capitulation, from which he formed his government.

Having secured his place as the new prime minister, Marshal Pétain called for arms to be laid down by the French army. He made a speech on 17 June 1940 at 12.30 p.m., declaring, 'With a heavy heart I say … that it is necessary to try and stop the fighting [*C'est le coeur serré que je vous dis aujourd'hui qu'il faut tenter de cesser le combat*].' During the speech he cleverly offered himself as a 'gift' to the French people. He was yet to even request armistice terms, but even so many Périgourdins breathed a sigh of relief when he appeared at the head of the government. After all, here was a trusted pair of hands to safeguard the country as he appeared to save it from the brink of defeat.

On the ground, military units were ordered to retreat, with divisions headed into southern regions not knowing whether they would be returning to the fight. During the retreat, Payzac, in the north-west of the Dordogne, played host to an armoured division. Its local population helped to accommodate personnel, including General Charles Delestraint, later the first leader of the AS. The following month, at the camp of Caylus in the Tarn-et-Garonne, Delestraint spoke to his soldiers before they were demobilised:

> France is caving into a terrible disaster. It is up to us now, it is especially up to you, the young, to see that France does not die … If we keep faith in the destiny of the country, if we behave as Frenchmen and not as beaten dogs or slaves, if we know how to want it, France will one day be reborn from its current ordeal.

In Réthondes on 22 June, in the same railway carriage where German defeat had been sealed in 1918, the armistice was signed between Hitler and Pétain. For Pétain, the main aim was to ensure France was not subjugated by its occupiers.★ He began with partnership with the Germans in mind but intended to negotiate with Hitler in the months to come. Determined that France should rekindle her own identity and re-establish herself on the world stage, Pétain was an ambitious 84-year-old. His view, however, of what collaboration with Germany might look like differed from Hitler's, as events of the next fours years would demonstrate.

After a short stay in Clermont-Ferrand, it became clear that the nearby spa town of Vichy offered more and better hotel facilities for the new seat of government, so it was chosen for the new state. Pétain arrived on 2 July, and Parliament met eight days later, with what remained of the *députés* and *senateurs*, at the Grand Casino de Vichy. Also present was Pierre Laval, who used all his skills to persuade opponents to accept the proposition to hand over full powers to Pétain, and to end the Republic. Eighty voted against the motion, twenty abstained and 569, whether through belief, fear or opportunism, voted in favour.

★ Some of those who joined Resistance after the war refer to the defeatist general of 1917 – the man who had wanted to abandon Verdun. He was the man of all the rebellious anti-republican movements, a man wishing to impose authoritarianism on the country to whom he was a traitor. This was not the popular opinion of 1940, however.

Laval's desire for France to lock arms with its, in his eyes, stronger neighbour was foolhardy. He saw France as key to Germany's future, but, although the armistice was not particularly harsh on the French, Hitler had very different ideas. Politically the armistice was only meant to be a short-term deal to be replaced, it was assumed, by a peace settlement progressively more beneficial to France. But, even so, it didn't take long for the French economy to feel the pinch of the agreement. Trade and exports became expensive as monies had to go through a German-imposed clearing system, not to mention that the French had to pay for the upkeep of the German army: an estimated 20 million Reichsmark a day.

France's defeat had hurt the political classes as well. Vichy propaganda painted the Third Republic as too concerned with leftist social policy to prepare for a war, and Édouard Daladier, Léon Blum, Paul Reynaud and General Gamelin (head of the French army) were locked up as a result. In his later speeches Pétain blamed the parliamentarians and the temperament of the French people themselves for the defeat – making no mention of the poor decision-making and incoherent command of military leaders.

As a government minister under Reynaud and an army general during the Battle of France, and unhappy with the state of affairs, de Gaulle found himself unwelcome in his own country for fear of arrest. On 17 June he flew to London with his entourage and worked to establish a French army from there, based largely around Frenchmen who were already in England following the evacuation of Dunkirk. The next day he responded to Pétain's calls to put down arms by encouraging the military in France and overseas to do the opposite. His famous speech, broadcast by the BBC, drew on sentiments of France as eternal and encouraged a continuation of the struggle that Pétain had given up. For the French people this *appel* summarised all that de Gaulle – someone they didn't know at all – would become to them: a beacon of hope, a man of action and a rallying point for refusers.

For Charles Sarlandie, of Les Monts, near Saint-Mesmin, the new regime had led to chaos. After his unit, Groupe Aérien d'Observation (GAR 1/52) de Limoges, had been disbanded, he returned to Sarrazac, where he took up a teaching job. He commented, 'Back in France we came into a total upheaval. It was a monstrous shambles. Everything was disorganised: services, supplies. The army, well there was no longer one. It was decimated and scattered around. The armistice treaty had practically feudalised France to Germany …'[10]

He also proclaimed the new regime a pseudo-government, and an illegal entity. For de Gaulle '*la France libre*', or as he preferred to call it, '*la France*', was the only legitimate authority, though he stopped short at claiming it to be a constitutional governance. Several months later, he proclaimed:

There no longer exists a government that is properly French. Effectively the body situated in Vichy and which claims to carry that name is unconstitutional and submissive to the invader. In this state of servitude, this organisation is only, and can only be, an instrument used by France's enemies, against the honour and the interests of the country.[11]

As German columns began their journey north into the occupied zone they passed many hundreds of malnourished, unshaven demobilised soldiers heading in the other direction. No longer having to look out for German bombers above, these were the men who had escaped death or captivity and were headed either home or to their barracks. Lieutenant Georges Friedmann, a philosopher who later had a part to play in the creation of the first Resistance networks in the southern zone, commented on what he had seen in mid June in Niort, a few days after Pétain had made his famous speech:

A whole country seems suddenly to have given itself up. Everything has collapsed, imploded ... Today, among many French people, I do not detect any sense of pain at the misfortunes of their country: during the days of this perfectly pure summer in these villages, towns, and camp stations of Limousin, Périgord, and Guyenne, among so many civilians and soldiers ... I have only observed a sort of complacent relief (sometimes even exalted relief), a kind of base atavistic satisfaction at the knowledge that 'for us it's over' ... without caring about anything else.[12]

As part of the armistice agreement France was divided into four zones for strategic, political and economic reasons; the two largest were separated roughly by the Loire and reached from the Swiss to the Spanish border. The occupied zone covered the western coastline and extended into northern France. Here troops would be stationed, and the country would be fully militarised by the Germans. The 'unoccupied zone' covered much of the south of the country, including the Mediterranean coast. All would be governed by the new Vichy government, though in practice Pétain's grip was not as tight on the occupied zone. The demarcation line was no loose border but a heavily armed frontier that the Germans opened or closed depending on their needs. Crossing points were installed in various towns, villages and *bourgs* around the west and north-west of the Dordogne, passing directly through the towns of Ribérac and Montpon. Women were often allowed to pass unquestioned by armed soldiers, but the same was rarely true for men. Wherever a crossing point was established, so too was a German sentinel with anything up to 100 German troops. Schools and private homes were used as their accommodation, and the munici-pal administration requisitioned goods for them. The occupied north and western coast became a playground for Germans benefiting from the prof-itable exchange rate, while the unoccupied zone became something of a concession to the French and an excellent target for German economic pressures – a cupboard for the thousand-year Reich to empty.

The French were, under the terms of the armistice, entitled to an army of 100,000 men, mainly for internal peacekeeping. Only a small amount of armaments, machinery and transport was allowed. As defeat loomed General Gabriel Cochet, commander of the air force of the Second Army and a *vichysto-résistant*,★ put into place a secret initiative called Camouflage de Matériel (CDM). In July 1940 Colonel Emile Mollard was named responsible for the official Matériel section, and took over the organisation of it, progressing the CDM into a movement. All around the country teams were charged with securing armaments and munitions. Caterpillar track vehicles were distributed by the CDM under the auspices of being tractors for use in forestry, while arms were sent to private properties, caves were used to hide munitions and forests were used to store vehicles. At its height Mollard's CDM comprised some 3,000 agents.

Due to its lack of metalworks – meaning less surveillance – and a large number of suitable workplaces such as caves, quarries and other shelters set into hilly countryside, the Dordogne became a favoured destination

---

★ This is a term forged in the 1990s to define those who resisted by fighting against the German occupation whilst remaining followers of Pétain and the politics of the *Révolution nationale*; alternatively they might have broken with that, but their seperation was never formalised, allowing them to remain active within the corridors of power or within the army. e.g. Generals Cochet and Giraud.

for storage of equipment: 65,000 individual arms, 100,000 collective arms and 1,000 tonnes of various munitions were hidden in the Dordogne. The Renault tank engineer Jean-Jacques Ramon, under the pseudonym Joseph Restany, worked hard at establishing a network of workshops where adaptations could be made and creations could be constructed. In one of these workshops a prototype of the automatic machine gun was produced and tested in the grounds surrounding the Château de la Carrière in Marquay.

Protest

When Charles Tillon, a former metalworker and war veteran, and a leader of the now clandestine PCF, heard Pétain's call to lay down arms, he responded by publishing a widely distributed tract. In it he proclaimed that the 'French people do not want slavery, misery, fascism. No more than they wanted the war of the capitalists.' He called for the 'immediate arrest of the traitors' and implored the people 'of the factories, of the fields, of the shops and offices, shopkeepers, artisans and intellectuals, soldiers, sailors, pilots still under arms' to 'join in action'. Tillon's call was not representative of the official Communist Party line, chained to an uncomfortable middle ground since the Soviet Union's 1939 accords with Germany that had resulted in the party being driven underground in the first place during the final days of the Third Republic. For Tillon and other like-minded communists, the party line of an end to combat in order to fall into line with Moscow came a distant second to refusing the armistice and carrying on the fight.[13]

Edmond Michelet, already a well-known figure in his home town of Brive as a Christian Democrat, was visible on the streets of the town providing social and material assistance to the thousands fleeing south during the exodus that followed the May defeat. Over time Michelet set up several bodies that allowed him numerous trips to Vichy, where he established a group of contacts while continuing to do good work for families in need. On 17 June, with the help of members of his various associations, including a number of communist members who had refused to accept the Germano-Soviet pact, he distributed a tract that included phrases from Charles Péguy's *L'Argent Suite*, which helped Michelet express his refusal. Michelet managed to convince some of those who had been involved with the refugee crisis to help those who opposed Nazism. It was from one of those close friends from Brive, L'Abbé Jean Alvitre, that on 20 June 1940 Michelet learned about General de Gaulle's call made from London two days earlier. He studied the works of de Gaulle, some of which he already owned and thereafter dreamed of going to London himself, going so far as to pack his suitcase on three occasions. Each time, however, he was dissuaded by the thought of the seven children he would have to leave behind.

Small acts of sabotage began as early as 21 June 1940, when a group of boys in the Charente interfered with several aircraft that had been seized by the occupier in Angoulême. In Bordeaux, midway through August, a young man named Joël Libouban crossed the esplanade des Quiconces and slashed ten enormous German propaganda signs, stamping and daubing graffiti on a further dozen. On 8 September, German officers attending a performance of Bizet's *Carmen* were annoyed at spontaneous bouts of applause from the audience when the British were mentioned, and similar happened in cinemas throughout the country at the mention of Allied troops on newsreels.

As early as 17 June 1940 in Chartres, capital of the Eure-et-Loir, southwest of Paris, the departmental prefect was arrested by the Nazis. Faced with having to sign a protocol that unjustly laid the blame for ill-treatment and violence towards civilians on Senegalese infantrymen rather than the guilty Germans, he refused. Rather than confronting further questioning and torture, he cut his own throat, seriously injuring himself. After being relieved of his post by the Vichy authorities he escaped to the unoccupied zone, from where he managed to travel to London and de Gaulle. The prefect was Jean Moulin – a name that in later years would become synonymous with the spirit of resistance. He was sent back to France by de Gaulle on a number of occasions over the next three years and became instrumental in bringing the many factions together into an effective resistance network that was able to co-exist and eventually work together. In famous images of him, he can be seen wearing a scarf around his neck, covering the scars of his attempted suicide.

The Confrerie Notre-Dame

Le Pleix is a village on a large bend of the Dordogne River, overlooked by green hills of forest and farmland. On one of these hills, set back from the main roads by a rough mud track, stood an isolated farmhouse, Le Gabastou. It was here that seven men would regularly gather and meet. Later it would become an important outpost for Maquis activity and a safe haven for fighters to meet following dangerous missions. The farm was owned by Paul Armbruster, a practising Catholic and a former journalist for the right-wing nationalist newspaper *Action Française*. The publication and accompanying movement preached the ideas of Charles Maurras, including a rejection of the republican legacy of the revolution and accepting Catholicism as the national religion. It was also anti-Semitic, having opposed the influence of left-wing liberal interventions in the controversial trying of the Jewish captain Alfred Dreyfus. Armbruster came from a milieu that was staunchly pro-Pétain in its ideology, but his sense of patriotism and religious beliefs made him one of the country's first active members of the Resistance.

Armbruster already knew Louis de la Bardonnie, a winegrower and the owner of Château Laroque in nearby Saint-Antoine-de-Breuilh. A typical gentleman farmer, de la Bardonnie was a man of fine tastes, familiar with the grind of hard labour. His hands were hard and rough, and his head bald with a tuft of drab blonde hair and on his face was a cropped moustache. Thirty-eight years old and already a father of eight (a further child would be born in 1942), he attempted to sign up for armed service in 1939 only to be told that his pension would be too expensive if he was killed. He was well known for his kindness and cordiality and cared little about what others thought of him or his actions. Speaking in 1972 and reflecting on his personal interests at the time, de la Bardonnie said: 'I had nothing to do with politics, because anyone in politics gets himself dirty. I wanted to stay clean. I was a man of the Right, a man of order, and for this reason I opposed the Front Populaire because it was revolutionary.'[14]

De la Bardonnie had stumbled upon de Gaulle's *appel du 18 juin* by accident at six o'clock in the evening and later claimed that the short broadcast gave him a new reason to hope – and to resist. He called together a small group of friends and acquaintances, including a priest, l'Abbé Louis Charles de Dartein, and friends of both Armbruster and de la Bardonnie.

Early activities included turning around signposts on the other side of the demarcation line, just 8km away. The group recognised that whatever they did, they would need good, trusted links with the Allied forces, especially England, given de Gaulle's placement there.

The group developed a four-point plan, which they intended to carry out according to their own modest means. Firstly, safe crossing points across the demarcation line with contacts on either side needed to be established. Secondly, they undertook to sabotage, as much as possible and with maximum prudency on their part, anything that might prove useful to the occupiers, such as lines of communication. Thirdly, they sought to establish observation points, especially around Bordeaux and the Gironde where information could be garnered on German naval movements. The final point of action would be information gathering of every ilk: names of French and Italian military units (Italy had been awarded a part of south-east France) and their movements; emblems or symbols seen on vehicles, matriculation numbers on submarines and vessels coming in and out of the ports at Bordeaux; and names and functions of enemy officers from the grade of commandant up on ships or of units. This information would then be transmitted to England, thereby helping the war effort.

Communication with London was through an existing channel. Paul Armbruster would physically transport bundles of information to Switzerland by travelling via his established business route, using his known identity to meet with a contact from the British embassy in Berne. Four packages were transported in this way during the months of July, August and September 1940, initially by Armbruster, later accompanied by de la Bardonnie, but on each occasion nothing happened as a result. British intelligence was not open to acting on information from an unknown, untrusted and unproven source that it had not laid down itself. On the fourth visit the two men were told in no uncertain terms by the Swiss police that future visits of the like would not be tolerated.

A different approach was needed to procure orders and funds: L'Abbé de Dartein, was 71 years old and less likely to be stopped. Finally, the group's information was shared directly with the intelligence services, and information doubted for being 'too exact' in the past was this time accounted for. André Dewavrin, widely known as Colonel Passy, of the French intelligence services decided that an envoy would be sent to meet the group and establish what role could be played by a London intelligence-sharing network.

The man chosen to travel to establish the sought-after links and provide stewardship for de la Bardonnie's group was Gilbert Renault, known as Rémy. Originally from Brittany, Renault abandoned a career as a partially successful film director and joined his brother on a boat from Lorient in June 1940 for London, leaving his family behind. Keen for the opportunity to return to France, this fervent Jesuit-educated man of strong Christian principles and belief in a royalist future for France was sent by Passy to Périgord to meet with Paul Armbruster, his initial mission being to establish an escape route through the Pyrenées. He arrived in Bergerac in early November and travelled to Le Gabastou by bicycle from Sainte-Foy-la-Grande. He received a warm welcome and asked Armbruster if he would like to work with him. The answer was a resounding '*Bien sûr*'.

Renault had to get into the nearby occupied zone as soon as possible so Armbruster took him to Saint-Antoine-de Breuilh to see de la Bardonnie. Dining on a fine meal that included a foie gras perfumed with La Roque *1e cru classé* from de la Bardonnie's own vineyards, it was agreed that Rémy would be taken across the demarcation line the following evening, using the network's contacts on either side and de la Bardonnie's *permis frontalier*. Rémy would need to take his shoes off, roll up his trousers and cross through a stream that marked the border.

In time Rémy's personality and drive led to the creation of the Confrerie Notre-Dame (CND), an intelligence-gathering network linked firmly to the Bureau Central de Renseignements et d'Action (BCRA), de Gaulle's London-based intelligence service. Having managed to collect information from Bordeaux and pass into Spain via contacts provided by de la Bardonnie's group, Rémy returned to London to vouch for the veracity and efficacy of the embryonic network, later returning at the beginning of December to begin in earnest. De la Bardonnie claimed in 1977 that, at that time, the network was in possession of thirty-two well-placed and valuable individuals in La Rochelle, Bordeaux, Pau, Toulouse, Angoulème, Lyon and, importantly, Vichy itself. The group could also claim safe crossing points across the demarcation line in the Dordogne and the Jura, a solid link with Switzerland and many secure letterboxes that could be used to exchange information and enable contacts to communicate. A radio transmitter was installed at de la Bardonnie's château in February 1941, along with an agent to operate it. This radio was the only clandestine set in France for several weeks before two more were installed in Thouars and Saumur in April 1941. It remained at Château Laroque for six months.

One of the CND's members from nearby Périgueux was Laure Gatet, the incredibly gifted daughter of a local educationalist. A biochemist, Gatet had immersed herself in the study of vines used in wine-making, and after the war her thesis would be commended by the Office International de la Vigne. Deeply moved by the fall of France in June 1940, Gatet began to preach the ideals of the resistance that autumn. She found her way into the CND in January 1941 and acted as a liaison agent, with a rank of *sous-lieutenant*. Having gained an *Ausweiss* (ID card),[15] she was able to move relatively freely to carry messages to and from the Spanish border, as well as pass through the demarcation line on a weekly basis on the Périgueux–Bordeaux train. She passed messages onto agents for transmission on to London and each week she left a package at a letterbox in Sainte-Foy-la-Grande for de la Bardonnie, who would transmit the information to London. Each week she would undergo a strip search at Montpon, but nothing was ever found – she carried the information in a box of cleaning powder.

An unlikely haven for resistance had also appeared at the Château des Milandes, 10 miles south of Sarlat in the south-east of the region, on the banks of the Dordogne. Since de Gaulle's *appel* of 18 June 1940, famous singer and scantily clad dancer Josephine Baker had taken up residence at her rented home along with Jacques Abtey, her lover. Baker was a black American star born in St Louis who had found her place in the music shows of Paris; in 1939, as Nazi Germany struck its deals with the Soviet Union and invaded Poland, Abtey asked her to be an 'honourable correspondent' to the Deuxième Bureau (France's intelligence service). He wanted her to provide information gleaned from the many parties and concerts she attended with well-connected people around France and beyond its borders. This work continued until the pair moved to the Dordogne, where not only was Château des Milandes installed with a powerful radio, but weapons were hidden in the cellar and a point of contact was established for members of the Forces Françaises Libres (FFL) who were en route to North Africa. The singer did all she could to use her contacts to provide information about troop movements in the area. Having already declared herself 'ready to give my life for France' and having, along with Maurice Chevalier, entertained the bored troops on the Maginot Line in

1939, she continued her work even after she was denounced and had to flee the Dordogne. She travelled to North Africa via Portugal and, with Abtey playing the role of her private secretary, continued to provide important intelligence, playing a full role in the Resistance in North Africa. She not only carried messages in invisible ink on sheet music, but sometimes scrawled information she had found on her arm, convinced that she would never be suspected. To be on the safe side, she occasionally carried messages in her underwear.

As dispersed as they were, French people were showing signs of refusal, protest and resistance. France was occupied, but in the unoccupied zone the government of Vichy was about to embark on a campaign of renewal, a 'National Revolution'.

2

NATIONAL RENEWAL

Following the full cessation of hostilities on 25 June 1940, the newspaper *L'Avenir* reported that the 'region lived through none of the horrors of war except for the sight of the exodus of the evacuated populations'. The *Journal de Bergerac* noted, 'Happily, the enemy is not coming, and only the supply of milk and vegetables to our town suffers.' Families wanted for food, warmth and safety. They also wanted the 1.8 million men back from the prisoner-of-war camps established in Germany and eastern France. This had left a hole in the workforce, and in the hearts and minds of the population.★

Local administration was, from July 1940, restructured and personnel replaced. Departmental *préfets* (prefects) were reminded that they were expected to replace mayors of municipalities with whichever member of the *conseil municipal* they saw fit. On 14 January 1941, the *préfet* of the Dordogne, Maurice Labarthe, received a telegram from Pierre Pucheu, *secretaire d'État à l'intérieur* (Secretary of State for the Interior), that all municipalities opposed to the *Révolution nationale* must be toppled immediately. This strengthening of Vichy power at a local administrative level was further extended in September 1941 when René Rivière replaced Maurice Labarthe as the new *préfet* of the Dordogne.

Restrictions began almost immediately and much of the region's raw materials were directed towards the Reich. An order from the prefect

---

★ Pétain had promised to prioritise the return of this potential workforce as a point of French policy, for which he was lauded. In the Dordogne alone, 13,750 men were missed almost as much by their abandoned employers as they were by their young wives.

outlawed the production and sale of bread less than 2.5kg in weight, so as to avoid wastage through staleness. The sale of flour was prohibited, as was the production and sale of patisserie. A diet of three days without meat was ordered, as was the careful use of tripe and offal. Prudence and moderation were strongly recommended in using spices or comestibles. 'The prefect calls for discipline by the people of the department, in yielding to the measures described which have as an aim, if scrupulously respected, the avoidance of harsher restrictions in the near future.'[1]

Pétain's new state was born as a 'National Revolution', though Pétain disliked the term, since it reminded him of communist anarchism. He preferred 'renewal' as his primary aim was to rediscover the 'eternal' France soiled by so-called excesses, 'decadence' and moral deterioration. The new state was to be post-monarchist and authoritarian – not quite fascist, but with Pétain as a God-like figure, returning to the people their forgotten traditionalist morality. Inward-looking and intensely anti-British (the eternal enemy responsible for so many of the ills that had beset the French), Pétain played the public on the idea of finding and removing those responsible for the defeat of June 1940.[2] Painting himself as a 'providential saviour', his programme was drawn around several loose guidelines: a loyal application of the armistice through a policy of collaboration in order to lead France into a preferential position after German victory; a transformation of the country under the National Revolution; and finally a systematic call to national unity which included the designation of internal enemies and the repression of all those who did not agree.[3] Through a disciplined following of the leader, reactionary values could be cultivated and the exclusion of 'undesirables' such as Jews and Freemasons (*Francs-maçons*), deemed guilty for the decadence of the previous regime, could be achieved.

The propaganda machine ensured that the Vichy government was recognised as the legal heart of government. Many felt a sense of relief, if not elation. Those with families were comfortable in the knowledge that the Vichy government was committed to pumping money into an education system that would throw off the shackles of secularism and embrace the Catholic ideals of prayer and worship. An insistence on clean living and family ideals was welcome. Family and purity were central to the Vichy ideals in a revolutionised France. Pétain ensured that the republican motto of '*Liberté, égalité, fraternité*' was replaced by '*Travail, famille, patrie*'. In agricultural areas such as the Dordogne Pétain succeeded in highlighting the ideals of family, patriotism and hard work in alignment with the cult of personality so vital in the establishment of an anti-democratic regime. His image appeared everywhere: in public places and in classrooms, where pupils were to sing the new anthem, '*Maréchal, nous voilà*' in place of the 'Marseillaise'. The role of the young person in the new *état français* was emphasised and celebrated. As well as being messianic, redemption focused and paternalistic, ideology behind the 'National Revolution' emphasised the need to train and manage the country's youth.

An army-influenced youth organisation, Les Chantiers de la Jeunesse, was set up in 1940 in order to avoid draft-age unemployed youths becoming restless. Located near big towns and cities, the camps were based in forests, and the following year it became compulsory, akin to national service. Young men were obligated to attend camps involving lectures and activities to promote healthy minds and bodies. Well-equipped and -provisioned, they became easy targets for Maquis raids in the years to come, and around 20 per cent of their members quit to join the Maquis. Girls could voluntarily attend camps too, but their activities were based largely around craftwork and skills for home-makers. Traditional values were emphasised, as was a return 'to the earth' and the removal of the anti-France, starting with the Jews, the communists and the *Francs-maçons*. During a speech on 25 June 1940, Pétain declared that 'our defeat arose from our slackening', and his followers were struck by his message of redemption from hard work.

Initiatives began to 'rebrand' France and remove her republican past. The numerous public areas called Place de la République were renamed in honour of the new leader. Teachers were instructed to extol the virtues of the new state, and were warned that a lack of action in promoting the new ideas would be deemed an act of protest against the state. While these new policies were very difficult to enforce, teachers felt exposed in front of their charges, who could so easily report back to their families. The new *état français* placed huge importance on the Catholic Church, on France's army, on her public figures and her elite. From the summer of 1940 it began its policy of exclusion against the Jews, communists and Freemasons. The regime did all it could to remove those who resisted the national revolution. Work began to root out those who did not fit the profile of a 'Vichy Frenchman', initially using humiliation and mockery, later through material persecution and imprisonment. Romany gypsies were shut up like livestock and communists were hunted with increased regularity.

Detention camps were not new to France: even under the Third Republic camps had been set up, such as those at Le Vernet and Gurs. Originally built to house dissident Spanish Republicans, they had also been used to house illegal aliens of all nationalities and, from 1939, camps such as those at Château du Sablou had been used to detain militant communists. Conditions were not good and gradually got worse. With labour widely available, the government voted in a law enabling the detention of foreign men between the ages of 18 and 45 as long as there was an excess of labour in the economy.

In all, 15,154 naturalisation papers issued since citizenship had been simplified were returned and of these 6,307 were Jews. Charles Maurras applied the pejorative term *métèques* to his own ideas of 'anti-France': Protestants, Masons and Jews. This theory worked well for readers of *Action Française* and government leaders, except that Protestants were too influential and ingrained to remove, so their place in the triumvirate of enemies was taken by communists. Pressure was exerted on those associated with the Third Republic. Secret societies were outlawed in mid-August and public officials were made to swear that they were no longer members. Freemasons' behind-closed-door meetings of politicians and business-men in towns throughout France were, for Vichy, 'a kind of clandestine shadow government'.[4] The Masons' lodges of Bergerac, Périgueux and Sarlat were shut down and property was auctioned off. Masonic symbols were removed from buildings and ironwork. In Périgueux the rue des Francs-maçons became the rue de la Bienfaisance. With a long-term rivalry between the lodges and the Catholic Church that went back several hundred years, French Masons were generally anti-religion, which meant they were also anti-monarchy, and anti-right wing. Good Catholics, and thus good Frenchmen, were prohibited from joining. The attack on the Masons was not due to any pressure from the Germans and probably did little other than to dissuade many middling Frenchmen to back the regime.

The Communists

Though only 14 years old when power passed to Pétain, Lucien Cournil was already politically aware. His father, a glass-maker in the Brardville glass factory in Saint-Lazare, just a few miles west of Terrasson, was an *ancien combattant* who had been at Verdun, and who had been an anti-Pétainiste ever since. The area around Terrasson was something of an industrial corner of the department. As well as the glassworks at Brardville there was another in Terrasson itself and the Progil chemical works in Le Lardin. Pétain's career as France's representative in Spain, where 'he had participated in fascist movements', meant that for Lucien, 'our family was not part of the eighty percent of Frenchmen who were for this false victor of Verdun.'[5]

Lucien was the middle of three brothers. His younger brother had died of meningitis several years earlier, while his older brother Jean became one of the first in the region to join the Maquis. Near the Cournil family in Le Lardin lived the family Ranoux. The Cournil boys were close friends of the three Ranoux brothers, Guy, Paul and Roger, whose mother had died when the children were young. Their father, Alexandre Ranoux, was a railway worker (*cheminot*) and a war veteran, mobilised from 1911 to 1918. His experiences over seven years had taught him to be anti-military, a pacifist. He was, however, intensely politically minded and a keen union member; while many Communist Party meetings and conversations happened in the many cafés along the riverside of Terrasson, a great number of such debates also took place in the Ranoux household. The families spent many evenings in each other's homes, where Alexandre regaled them with tales of the war, and they chatted about life, work and politics. Having experienced the Front Populaire, the fathers of both families had felt robbed when the benefits were snatched away from them and power was handed to the anti-republican Pétain. But both, like workers throughout the region, had developed a political consciousness and their sons all joined the Jeunesses Communistes ready to make sure their voices were heard.

Indeed, after engaging early on with Jeunesses Communistes, Lucien met with other young communists in a small building behind the large glass factory in Brardville and, despite this activity being clandestine, one of his roles, assigned to him through contacts in Paris, was to bring other like-minded individuals on board. This meant making them politically aware and informing them of the ills from which France was currently suffering.

Equally in Terrasson were a number of members of Croix de Feu, a league of former combatants – far-right nationalists led by

Colonel François de la Rocque. The militants of the left, driven by the union Confédération Générale du Travail Unitaire (CGTU), protested throughout 1934 and 1935, never more so than during a visit to La Roque when a counter-demonstration by the right wing led to heated exchanges in the town. Amongst the Croix de Feu faithful that day were a number of future Vichy officials including Adolphe Denoix, who would play a large role in years to come as departmental chief of the Milice.

★★★

The Communist Party had been banned in the autumn of 1939 when its official allegiance was pro-German–Soviet. Communism was seen to represent the worst of the Front Populaire of the late 1930s and was linked with the Jews of Eastern Europe. Many known militants had already been arrested and the advent of Vichy led to further tracking of those with Marxist links. In the Dordogne, the Camp du Château du Sablou was put to use throughout most of 1940. This eighteenth-century construction, located near Fanlac, was requisitioned by the local prefect to house militant communists and 'immigrants from enemy states'; they were interned due to their *activité antinationale*. The relative isolation of the property, surrounded by 130 hectares of grounds and hidden by the surrounding forest, was perfect for penning in its inmates without provoking too much curiosity.

Between 17 January and 30 December 1940, 300–400 political prisoners were interned in the camp *'par mesure administrative'*, meaning that there was no need for them to be charged with anything. The inmates arrived in waves from all of France. Transported by train, they arrived at the tiny station at Montignac, from where they would either walk or be transported by truck to Sablou. When on foot, they crossed the village watched by a local population sympathetic to their plight, until a network of clandestine support developed around Montignac. The baker Jean Gatinel lifted his beret as the bedraggled unfortunates passed by his shop – an indicator of local sentiment. While most of those arrested and brought to the camp were communists, and militants, there were also trade unionists and others thought a threat to national security. Amongst the professions of those brought to Sablou were teachers, railway workers, miners (primarily from the region of Pas-de-Calais) and postal workers. Many had already been exiled from their homes. Paul Kleinart was a refugee from the Alsace region who had been working at the explosives factory in Bergerac and living in nearby Mouleydier. In late September 1940 he wrote to his local prefect complaining that he had still not been repatriated to Alsace and he was finding it increasingly difficult to survive on the 10 francs per day allowance given as aid to refugees. Acting on local police reports that Kleinart was displaying an agitated attitude 'dangerous for public order', he was arrested on the pretext of planning a local strike.

Some internees were veterans of the First World War and infirm. A small number were released as responsible for families of eight children or more, while others were considered too old or too ill to be held. For those who did arrive at the camp at its inauguration in January 1940, there was no respite from the particularly harsh winter as few facilities had been prepared for its role as a penitentiary. The idea was to reduce the inmates materially to the level of animals, and this was achieved in an environment that would also provide a brutal psychological challenge.

Basic hygiene was not available, and neither was running water: there was only one water source, in nearby woodland, and inmates were sent under armed guard to collect what they needed for cooking. Food preparation took place in a mobile kitchen, and ingredients were turned into rough hash *ratta* or soup of little calorific value. Inmates were provided with no plates, bowls or utensils, and less than half arrived at the camp with any, so they were forced to collect food by hand from large bowls or scavenge for old tins and sharpened twigs. Initially there were no bed frames, tables or chairs. A few appeared throughout the year, but at first inmates had to make do with hay and bales of straw. The lack of basic hygiene led to a proliferation of vermin, lice and fleas and an increasing problem of dysentery.

Aware of the dreadful conditions within the camp during its early life, a handful of local communists took it upon themselves to improve the lot of the inmates. As well as providing accommodation and protection for visiting families that had arrived from throughout France, they also began to collect goods that might help the everyday life of those in the camp. Cutlery, plates, blankets and medication were all provided to prisoners, while a doctor gave free consultations and care to those who became ill.

On the inside of the camp some of the most militant men in France had been gathered, and many of those held later joined the communist resistance groups. On 29 December 1940, 231 prisoners were transferred to a new camp at Saint-Paul-d'Eyjeaux in the Haute-Vienne via the stations at Condat-le-Lardin and Limoges. Three disappeared en route. Some inmates were later sent to the penal colonies of Algeria, while others escaped and joined the Resistance. Some were shot, and some were sent to concentration camps in Germany. But contacts had been assured in and around the camp, as had a sense of sympathy for those who suffered.

The Jews

In the late 1930s Jewish families in the Dordogne and its surrounding departments were few and far between, but as war loomed Jewish organisations prospected the area and saw ample reasons to expect that Jewish communities might thrive there. Work was done prior to the exodus by organisations such as Oeuvre de Sécours aux Enfants (OSE) and Eclaireurs Israélites de France to set up homes and potential shelters to welcome Jewish children in the months and years to come. In the years preceding the evacuation others had found new homes or asylum in southern France as a result of persecution elsewhere. The region became something of a *terre de refuge*, its rural nature ideal for those who wished to disappear from view. The Jewish population did its upmost to assimilate into its new communities. While, some did their best to melt into obscurity, most carried on with a normal life now that danger and discomfort seemed to have dissipated: they attended school, and parents set up businesses, often in the field of commerce and retail.

When the evacuation of Alsace and Lorraine was carried out, a significant number of Jewish families arrived: some 10,000 registered Jews left Strasbourg officially, while many more crossed the demarcation line in an attempt to escape from the threat of the Reich and the occupied zone. Soon after the military defeat of June 1940, Alsace and the Moselle were annexed, and its population was encouraged to return, the Germans having arrived to a rather empty Strasbourg. Jewish families stayed behind, not being permitted to go back.

The Dordogne and Haute-Vienne became home to a significant Jewish population.* Children made up a significant proportion of the number of Jews headed south, often sent to family friends or extended family members, or simply to shelters for safekeeping. Also heading south were business owners from larger towns in the occupied zone who wished to set up a new life in a climate that allowed them to thrive. On first arriving Jewish families were at the behest of the local prefectures for social assistance, particularly in the allocation of housing, and the larger towns suited some whose skills would benefit the larger community. The administrators did their best to push the newcomers into rural settings, particularly if they were unskilled, as these villages had no prior experience of Jews. The idea was to avoid rejection of the newcomers even when pressure would be exerted on supplies and housing.

Rachel Tenenbaum was 13 when she arrived in Saint-Pierre-de-Chignac with other Alsatian refugees and was at first given shelter in the magnificent Château de Lardimalie along with many others, but only the Jewish contingent stayed behind. They were taken into the village and found refuge; Rachel was never shown anything other than kindness: 'I can't complain. We had food. We had milk, we had potatoes, we had vegetables and we had meat. We had everything that we needed. If we hadn't have had the Germans behind us ...' Importantly for Rachel, the local population accepted them as part of their community, but she knew things could have been very different: 'We were accepted everywhere. In farms ... we made friends ... If they hadn't been like that, I would not be here.'[6]

Yvette Molho was in her late teens during her stay in Siorac-en-Périgord, together with her sister. There she felt safe leading an almost privileged existence as they lacked for nothing: everyone could buy flour and bread without food tickets, and they could get meat because of black-market

---

* A census carried out in March 1942 in order to establish the civil state, family situation, profession and property of Jews in the unoccupied zone gives an indication. 6,065 were recorded for the Dordogne, of which 3,800 were French and 2,265 were of foreign nationality such as German, Hungarian, Polish, Yugoslav and Russian. The departments of Corrèze, Creuse, Indre-et-Loire, Loir-et-Cher and Cher all had significantly fewer. These numbers have to be considered as in part inaccurate. As well as the many Jews who decided to avoid drawing attention to themselves, there were also huge shifts in numbers through the area, particularly in the Dordogne, which was used as a passageway for the south.

supplies. Siorac was a village that benefited from a tight-lipped attitude of self-sufficiency. Later in the war Yvette learned that the local carpenter was a Resistance chief and the priest hid arms for the Maquis. It was a peaceful life, but the threat of the authorities, both Vichy and German, was never far away. Despite some perfect summer days when the refugee girls performed ballet or theatre pieces for the locals, reality hit in 1943 when Yvette's father was arrested and deported.

Despite the welcoming attitude of the locals, mispreconceptions still existed. Yvette was surprised one summer's day, after putting on a swimming costume, when one of her new friends commented that her feet were just the same as their own: in one of many Vichy posters, Jews were depicted as having Devil's feet.

When Sonya Zysman arrived in Périgueux she managed to find herself lodgings in a block of flats. Living there was an 'adorable' older woman, a widow called Madame Gadou, who Sonya described as a woman of great taste who lived for clothes and fashion. One evening Gadou returned from the shops looking dishevelled and upset, claiming that they were 'going to be submerged, invaded ... *they* are going to take everything, destroy everything.' Madame Gadou had been told that 'the Jews are going to arrive and take over.'[7] And when Sonya revealed that she was Jewish, the old woman revealed that she had never knowingly seen, let alone met, a Jew in her life.

According to Vichy, France was seeing a 'wave of anti-Semitism' but it was likely to have been propagating fears for anyone uninvolved with finance or politics. Animosities existed certainly, but during the summer of 1940 to the summer 1941, in the Dordogne this was aimed at strangers to the region, not at Jews for being Jewish, and this ill-feeling was created by problems with housing, the local *patois* and sometimes a pressure on food stocks.[8] Some, such as Edmond Michelet in Brive, supported the Jews, claiming persecution to be unchristian, especially when measures removing Jews from employment and positions of influence took effect in 1941.

Vichy anti-Semitism was different in nature to that of post-1942 Germany. Its politicians wished to limit anti-Semitism to job discrimination and expulsion or forced emigration of foreign Jews; it was not based on any wish to exterminate the 'race'. Despite this, anti-Semitic measures began under the Vichy government before any pressure was exerted from Germany. The Nazis were happy to use France as a destination for their own deported Jews – in spite of French objections – and had little care for what was going on in the country, or any particular plans to purify it of Jews. However, in France, law that had prohibited blatant anti-Semitism in the press, passed in April 1939, was repealed on 27 August 1940. On 3 October 1940 Jews were excluded from positions of authority in the military, the judiciary and the civil service, and they were also no longer allowed onto elected bodies. Further laws followed at pace, allowing prefects to intern or rehome foreign Jews and repealing French citizenship from indigenous Jews in Algeria. Vichy xenophobia was more 'cultural and national than racial',[9] and the lack of assimilation of foreign Jews related more to anti-Jewish cultural sentiments than racism. French conservative xenophobia was primarily aimed at those that lacked cultural conformity that was acquirable over time.

The 2 June 1941 Statute of Jews defined the '*notion de juif*', taking the lead of the German *ordonnances* and topping it. Vichy's definition of who or what constituted a Jew was based on race rather than religion, and this is where the net reached wider than some had anticipated. To be considered a Jew a person needed to have three Jewish grandparents, or two Jewish grandparents if married to a Jew. Contemporary cinematic propaganda focused on the genetic make-up of Jews as mongrels of Asian, African and Middle Eastern descent rather than concentrating on their religious practices or history of economic or political malpractice. Many were forced to illustrate by some means that they were, in fact, completely 'French'. This requirement created tensions throughout the southern zone: could one be Jewish and French? At first war veterans in particular were given some relief from persecution. It was widely believed that Pétain would, as a former soldier and a man of honour, protect Jewish veterans from any persecution at all. Initially this happened, but ultimately it would prove not to be the case. Those who considered themselves to have assimilated into Catholic France, having abandoned Jewish religious practices, defined themselves as '*Israélites*' rather than 'Jewish' – a label that carried pejorative overtones. These people sometimes over-compensated by displaying hostility to more recent immigrants.

The creation of the Commissariat Général aux Questions Juives (CGQJ) on 29 March 1941, led by Xavier Vallat, began in earnest a policy of state anti-Semitisim. May 1941 saw the first round-up in Paris, with 3,710 people sent to camps in Loiret, Pithiviers and Beaune-la-Rolande. A second Statut de Juifs followed in June, ordering by law a census of all Jews living on

French territory, including the unoccupied zone. The removal of Jews from businesses and areas of life that could influence the public was extended and the measures were applied to the unoccupied zone. On 22 July 1941 the Loi de Spoliation was passed, beginning the process of economic Aryanisation: businesses and goods belonging to Jews were passed into state control through liquidation of goods and the running of businesses by non-Jewish administrators.

By mid-1941 a member of the CGQJ considered the number of Jews living within the Limoges region, including the Dordogne, to be '*phénomenal*'. Initially the Limoges officials responded to the Jewish question in the area with vigour, mainly due to the personalities entrusted with carrying out the task. André Dupont was the first regional director of the CGQJ before moving to Vichy, while Joseph Antignac took control of the regional base of the Police aux Questions Juives (PQJ), whose anti-Jewish operation was considered by Vichy to be something of a model. Antignac thrived in two areas: applying pressure to prefects to implement initiatives quickly and efficiently, even when public opinion began to stock up against anti-Jewish measures; and carrying out the economic Aryanisation of Jewish property extremely well. Indeed, his performance was such that he would later be called to Vichy and appointed national director of the Section d'Enquête (SEC), a department that profiled and tracked Jews.

It was becoming increasingly apparent that, where possible, Jews in the unoccupied zone needed to fade into the background. Where censuses had been taken, it was often only practical to hide children. In the Périgord, where Jewish families had, until the war, been few and far between, individuals were needed to protect these families. It also required the involvement of small networks capable of finding hiding places quickly. Seven-year-old Marcel Wieder and his older brother Roland arrived at the station in Périgueux in late September 1940 with their parents, having fled persecution in occupied Strasbourg. The family spent a short time with relatives in nearby Chancelade before their father Bernard, a barber, took over the lease of a salon in rue Limogeanne, in the heart of medieval Périgueux. The boys were sent to the Collège du Centre, where they remained for a short time before their mother was called in by the principal, who explained that he had been asked to provide the Vichy government with a list of all Jewish children registered at the school. This, he said, he did not wish to do, so instead he asked

Madame Wieder to remove the boys from the school. It was approaching the final months of 1941.

Marcel's father had made the acquaintance of Hélène Dupuy, who took on the task of procuring a safe identity for the boys. It did not take her long to get hold of false identity documents and she took them to the Catholic school, l'école Saint-Jean. The *directeur,* Alexandre Berbonde, took the boys in and they were registered under the surname Dupuy. Marcel and Roland found themselves in a Catholic institution, taught by priests, and, as far as they knew, nobody, including their teachers, was aware that they were Jewish. Only after the war did Marcel discover that Berbonde, a 35-year-old father of five whose wife Marcelle worked as his assistant, was in full confidence of their situation. Their teachers were not – at least not all. Staying hidden could be complicated, though, and the boys were warned by their father that they must never shower with the other boys, as the circumcision would give them away and place them in grave danger. Marcel and Roland managed to succeed – almost two full school years – in not being detected.

Prior to joining the school, the brothers had never seen the inside of a church before. They learned to pray and adjusted to the Catholic *soumission* – they even became choirboys. However, at the end of the 1943 school year Berbonde called Hélène Dupuy in to say that the situation had become too dangerous. Thankfully, the boys were found new placements in La Chapelle-Fauché.

The Wieder/Dupuy brothers were not the only Jewish children that the Berbonde couple had aided. Beginning in 1941, around twenty Jewish children were helped in the same way, hidden and protected right in the heart of the school. With the help of the chaplain, L'Abbé Marcel Sabouret, they were mixed in amongst the other children, hiding in plain sight of the Vichy sympathisers in the town. Despite the various round-ups that occurred between 1941 and 1944, as well as the inspections by SS officers, staff at the school succeeded in hiding the children, all of whom had been provided with false names. Not one was arrested or deported. This included a young mother whom Alexandre Berbonde employed in the school refectory, and whose 7-year-old son he also took into the school.

Early Protest

On the first day of 1941 the people of Vichy France were given an opportunity to demonstrate their opposition to the new government, being assured of safety in numbers. Prompted by Radio Londres, the people were asked to show their discontent by staying at home for one hour. Tracts appeared in the streets with details. One such, handwritten and decorated with the symbol of France Libre said, 'General de Gaulle asks, in order to count his friends, that as a Good Frenchman you remain at home today the 1st January 1941 from 14h to 15h. *Vive Pétain! Vive de Gaulle.*'[10]

That '*Vive Pétain!*' was included alongside the name of de Gaulle is surprising, but demonstrates the regard in which Pétain was held: the man in whose hands France could be entrusted. At this stage the German occupiers were the force to be opposed and Pétain was viewed as chief negotiator for the rights of the French people. A police report to the prefect reported:

> The demonstration encouraged by British radio today between 14h and 15h was clearly visible today in town, on the streets and in the central district.
>
> Very few people were in the streets between 14h and 15h, whilst from this time onwards movement in the streets regained its normal holiday feel.

Early urban resistance began as early as 1940 in the form of civil disobedience. The drawing of a 'V' shape on a wall and the ripping down of posters were perhaps the most common means of demonstrating, but this developed into the distribution of tracts and slogans, and refusal to follow Vichy directives such as displaying Pétain's portrait at all times in classrooms. The courage of those involved cannot be overestimated.

Acts of protest took many forms. When, in early 1942, a large number of metal statues were demanded by the Vichy authorities for their value as metal, towns throughout France lost a depressing proportion of their cultural heritage to the foundry. This was the case in the Dordogne too, but some action was taken by the likes of a Monsieur Delpy, an architect who hid the statue of the Périgourdin general Daumesnil under bundles of sticks in a chapel, and even the communist resistance group Francs-Tireurs et Partisans, who hid a statue of the famous author Eugène le Roy in Montignac.

Meanwhile, politician Jean Borotra, known as the 'Bounding Basque' and one of the 'Four Musketeers' who dominated world tennis in the 1930s, came to Périgueux, and the local schools received an order to send their students onto place Montaigne for a welcoming reception. Between 5,000 and 6,000 young people gathered in rows chanting '*Vive Pétain, Vive Pétain*' while Raphael Finkler, Léon Lichtenberg and several others shouted, '*Vive de Gaulle!*' Both boys were eager to resist in some way and they knew that shouting the odd insult or ripping classroom posters of Pétain would only go so far. But it was a start.

The first groups and networks of groups emerged from the summer of 1940, the result of the work of individual men and women who refused to accept the surrender of their country. Some worked towards the twin goals of smuggling escaped prisoners or passing on information, often using *passeurs*★ either to cross the demarcation line or at least gain news of loved ones. This would develop into helping British airmen cross into the unoccupied zone, head south towards Spain and ultimately find a route back to Britain. Other networks were committed to propaganda and the politics of Resistance. Eventually certain groups looked to create designated teams committed to 'action', be it sabotage or violent attacks. None of this was easy given that early groups paid for their existence and activities themselves. In Paris the Musée de l'Homme group gathered regularly and used a printing press deep in the bowels of the museum to spread their ideas.

The group was led by a young ethnologist named Boris Vildé along with several colleagues, and it was Vildé's personality and energy that helped the network link up with other groups, including the Français Libres de France of Agnès Humbert and Jean Cassou as well as further embryonic networks of lawyers and military colonels. As Vildé's group grew in size it shifted its focus. As well as providing information of military value to allies, the group began concentrating on the production and distribution of propaganda in the form of tracts and newspapers. It also continued to help prisoners escape towards Spain and then Portugal – the only realistic escape route for onward transit to England.

★ People willing to get others across borders such as the demarcation line or into Spain or Switzerland, usually because they knew the area well and knew routes where they could cross undetected. Some did it for money, some did it as their contribution, some as part of a growing network. it was highly dangerous and many were arrested.

Crossing of the heavily guarded demarcation line was followed by a tense journey towards the south, normally by train. A number of transit stops were established in safer sections of countryside where, with the help of a *passeur* and accompanied by at least one agent, escapees could creep over rivers or through wooded areas in order to pass undetected. The demarcation line cut through the western edge of the Dordogne, passing through Montpon. The first railway stop after the line when heading towards Lyon from the occupied zone was in Beaupoyet. It was here that the hotel restaurant Jeanne d'Arc, and its owner Noëla Malard, played a valuable role hosting groups travelling south.

Ideally located close to the demarcation line and opposite the station, the hotel didn't raise suspicion with its comings and goings, given its nature of business.[11] Members of the network such as René Sénéchal and quite possibly Boris Vildé himself stayed there, as did many individuals in groups who had clandestinely crossed into the unoccupied zone. During the winter of 1940 and spring 1941, the hotel became a transit point for those heading towards the Pyrenées who had been led across the demarcation line on foot. It was during these few months that Sénéchal, known in Paris as '*le gosse*', became well known to the Malard family. Aged just 18, he was an apprentice accountant from Béthune in the Pas-de-Calais. He was keen to join General de Gaulle in London and so Sylvette Leleu, whose own network had been amongst the first to join forces with the Musée de l'Homme group, contacted Vildé to request transit for him. Vildé trusted Sénéchal but the request to travel to England was not accepted; instead Sénéchal was used by the network to guide groups of twenty or so travellers to Spain, and was asked to perform other roles as well.

Several times a month Noëla Malard and her son would open the doors of the hotel in the middle of the night, usually having been warned by groans from the family dog. Sénéchal became well known to Noëla, and he trusted the hotel and its owners implicitly. He often led his group of weary travellers into the ballroom, where mattresses allowed them to get several hours of sleep. Sometimes the guests were of a military background, and sometimes French, British, Dutch or Polish agents. The Malard family brought them hot soup, and the travellers would depart the following day.

During one visit to the Hôtel Beaupoyet, sometime in late February or early March 1941, the young Sénéchal asked Noëla Malard to look after two suitcases, saying that he would return to collect them in a fortnight.

The cases were stored in the attic, but Sénéchal never did return. After a year Noëla decided to open the cases, in the presence of her son Raymond: 'Inside we found plans for the air field in Strasbourg, maps of the Atlantic wall and other documents. We put them back in the attic, knowing fully well that we could have got ourselves killed.'[12]

It is likely that these documents included those gained by a network agent named René-Yves Creston, who used Breton contacts sympathetic to the cause to steal documents that would be vital to the Allied plans to attack the Saint-Nazaire coastal installations and submarine base. These documents passed through the hands of Jean Cassou and Agnès Humbert before being given to Sénéchal for transportation to Toulouse. Betrayed, Sénéchal was arrested at the Gare Austerlitz in Paris on 18 March 1941. He was carrying documents containing military information and plenty of incriminating names and addresses – the mistake of an early, untrained network finding its way in the bleak world of espionage. The network tumbled and *le gosse*, along with Vildé and eight other members, were sentenced to death on 17 February 1942. Three of those sentenced, including Sénéchal's first contact, Sylvette Leleu, had their sentences commuted to deportation to Germany, from where they would later return. The others were executed by firing squad on 22 February 1942 in the fortress of Mont-Valérien. Just before crumpling under the cutting bullets they sang the 'Marseillaise'.

Informers

A Service d'Information et d'Études Départmentale was established in each prefecture of the unoccupied zone, which offered career opportunists great chances to demonstrate their fidelity to Pétain through surveillance and information gathering. Born and raised in 1893 near Thenon in the east of the Dordogne, Paul Lapuyarde fought in the First World War and was invalided due to sight problems. After divorcing his second wife, he began a series of desk jobs until just after the armistice he met Raoul Blasselle, a military commander in Périgueux. Just like 30,000 others in the Périgord, Lapuyarde became a member of the Légion Française des Combattants, a Vichy organisation composed of veterans and a fusion of several existing such organisations. The Légion, led by departmental leaders such as Henri Rials in the Dordogne, was not exclusively for veterans. Women and young volunteers to the cause of the national revolution also counted amongst its membership. It was described by Pétain as '*les yeux et des oreilles du Maréchal*' (the eyes and ears of the Marshal) and was extremely officious. Lapuyarde found the official organisation too soft and slow moving, and he took on a more independent approach.

Already anti-communist, Lapuyarde was dismayed by the accords between Germany and the Soviet Union. He made the task of tracking communists his own and made sure that the police forces based in Périgueux knew about him so that he could become involved in the tracking of militants. He also spent as much time as he could in and around the office of the local branch of the Parti Populaire Français (PPF) – a political party formed in 1936 by a collection of disillusioned communists who had shifted radically to nationalism. It was headed by Jacques Doriot and was staunchly anti-Semitic and anti-Marxist and much of its backing came from supporters of other nationalistic groups, such as Action Française, Croix de Feu and Jeunesses Patriotes. In urban areas its paramilitary wing, the Service d'Ordre Légionnaire (SOL), created and headed by Joseph Darnand, attracted the ultra-committed members of the PPF and carried out physical violence towards communists and other 'enemies of France'.

In October 1940 the leader of the Service d'Information et d'Études, Étienne Dauriac, sent a confidential report to Georges A. Groussard, *inspecteur general des services de la sureté nationale* (military counter-espionage), denouncing a number of officials in the public eye. Reports such as these denounced Jews and Freemasons, while the prefect of the Dordogne, Marcel Jacquier, was critiqued with a single sentence: '*à changer département*', meaning that he had not, according to the service, fully embraced the Vichy way and should be relocated. On 30 October, Jacquier was replaced by Maurice Labarthe, who was more inclined to act as desired by Vichy. In a follow-up report Lapuyarde commented that the population was relieved by this change. In reality it meant there was more chance of personal advancement for himself and others like him.

Maurice Loupias, a later chief of the AS in the Dordogne-Sud and assistant prefect of Bergerac, described surveillance by Vichy agents:

These people could betray a French person while claiming to be good patriots themselves who were serving the nation. That was the baseness of Laval, in dividing the country in such away, under the cover and authority of marshal Pétain. Consequently, they took responsibility for all the collaborations, all the denunciations of patriots and of the hunting down of the maquis.

Roger Denoix, later a *maquisard* with Groupe Franc Roland, recalled an evening in May 1941 when he visited Le Fleix with his family. There he came across Monsieur Camille Chandou, a family friend and mayor of the town, who was involved in a card game. Denoix swapped pleasantries with him, before the two men got onto the subject of the release of French prisoners of war. Chandou pronounced his assuredness that Pétain would ensure a favourable solution. When Denoix disagreed, expressing his distaste for the Pétain government, particularly Laval, and suggesting that the presence of Pétain offered no guarantee, Chandou exclaimed, 'You are not going to talk to me about de Gaulle!' The two men had a heated exchange of ideas and Denoix predicted that de Gaulle, being the first to resist, would liberate the country along with the allied powers.

The following day witnesses encouraged Chandou to speak to the state prosecutor in Bergerac, who then ordered an investigation. One of the witnesses had sent a letter to Admiral Darlan, the vice president of the État Français, outlining his concerns over what he had overheard. Denoix was a local government employee and therefore his views on state policy and the Gaullist movement were, by nature, 'causing trouble and discord in the rural population', and that witness considered it his duty to let Darlan know.[13] The president of the Légion for Le Fleix, who had already encouraged Chandou to denounce Denoix, took the information to the leader of the departmental head in Périgueux, who passed it to the local gendarmerie and subsequently to assistant prefect of Bergerac, with the advice that such opponents of the government must not be allowed to gain ground:

That was how the chiefs of the *Légion française des combattants* who were under the orders of the Vichy government, denounced Frenchmen and women suspected of being Gaullists … Happily for me it happened in 1941 and the *miliciens*, later created by the *Service d'ordre de la légion* (SOL) did not yet exist. If it had happened a year later I would not have escaped arrest and deportation.[14]

★★★

On 16 November 1941 Louis de la Bardonnie was in one of the barns at Château Laroque, his large home on a hill overlooking Saint-Antoine-de-Breuilh. He was repairing a motor-pump when he looked up to see several French police officers gathering around him. The police told him that they knew he had a radio transmitter post – an assertion that he vehemently denied. They told him that they also knew of a certain '*capitaine Renault*' who came to visit him often. They referred to Renault as a '*chef des renseignements gaulliste*' and, together with that individual, de la Bardonnie was known to be setting up a new branch of their network in Pau. De la Bardonnie shook his head and told them that they were welcome to search his property. Around seven o'clock that evening de la Bardonnie bade farewell to his wife and eight children, and was taken by car to Périgueux to undergo a thorough interrogation. The interview lasted fifty-six hours over the course of eight days. De la Bardonnie engaged in 'pointless and endless verbosity' over the course of the interview and no evidence was found at his house.

Nevertheless, de la Bardonnie was detained, but the Périgueux prison of Béleyme was full so he was transferred instead to Saint-Georges, an old school requisitioned as training space for the new auxiliary police force, the Groupe Mobile de Réserve (GMR). On 31 December, he was transferred to a camp at Mauzac, on the edge of the Dordogne River in the eastern valley midway between Bergerac and Sarlat.

The château's radio antennae and transmitter set had been transferred to the occupied zone just weeks before a neighbour betrayed de la Bardonnie. Had it still been there when the police came, the course of events for him, his family and the Resistance in the unoccupied zone may well have run differently.

3

NETWORKS AND SECRET ARMIES

In 1941 it was still very rare for Resistance groups to be linked to outside networks and agencies. The actions of Louis de la Bardonnie and those like him were far removed from the populace. What was needed during the early years was guidance and organisation from without, along with expertise, equipment and money. De Gaulle and the Free French were based in London, where Churchill's British government was doing what it could to support the general's cause, despite an insistence on the part of Roosevelt that de Gaulle could not claim sovereignty. The proximity of London meant that the intelligence community could train agents to travel to France and organise existing Resistance networks, all the while developing means of two communications between the Allies and France through radio links.

The Special Operations Executive (SOE) was the British network set up to organise and help Resistance groups throughout Europe. Maurice Buckmaster, who was head of the French F section, insisted that through-out the years of conflict with the Germans: 'Our role at Special Operations Headquarters was not that of spy-masters but of active and belligerent planners of operations to be carried out in advance of the allied landing.'[1]

Agents, male and female, often recruited due to French lineage and trained in Britain, were sent to France to create a fighting force ready for D-Day, and to hurt the Germans in the process. SOE was looking to develop networks of agents that could train fighters. The provision of intelligence was the job of others, which sometimes confused matters with their French colleagues in London: de Gaulle's own intelligence agency, the BCRA, described by SOE agent Peter Churchill as 'De Gaulle's rival show, run from Duke Street and known as "Our friends across the road"'. According to Churchill, the BCRA 'was apparently not working in close co-operation with SOE, although the RAF served them both'.[2]

The parachute drops began in 1940, and that October a container was dropped onto Mignots, near Saint-André-de-Double, in western Dordogne – its cargo secret. When local gendarmes found the container the following morning there was no sign of either its contents or an agent. In 1941 the drops were stepped up, and one of the most important roles for local contacts was to identify potential landing areas that could be considered safe. In the early hours of 15 February 1941 two men were dropped from an RAF plane near Le Bugue: Maurice Duclos, a French agent known as Saint-Jacques, and a British radio operator, John Mulleman. One of the missions assigned to Duclos was the development of information networks, which he had already begun to set up previously while in France.

As the embryonic Resistance networks were yet to organise welcoming committees, the two men fell into dark countryside, and into the middle of a pine forest. Mulleman landed without incident but Duclos was not so lucky. His parachute only opened 50m or so from the ground then ripped on contact with a tree, causing him to fall 8m to the ground. He was knocked out and suffered a fractured fibula. Separated, Mulleman used contacts to carry out his mission, eventually installing a radio emitter in Normandy. Duclos, however, spent several hours searching for his colleague despite the pain, having managed to make a splint and hide his parachute.

The calls of Duclos in trying to find Mulleman alerted a farmer, whom Duclos persuaded to drive to Le Bugue. Duclos hid the documents he was carrying, and the farmer called a local doctor. The doctor treated Duclos but then instructed the farmer to call the authorities. When two gendarmes arrived Duclos told them that his name was Saint-Jacques, that he had arrived from England and that he would only talk in front of the military authorities. Duclos was lucky to be interviewed by officers who were happy to swallow his unlikely stories and let him go, even offering to transport him and asking for information updates once over the demarcation line. Duclos made his way to the home of Louis de la Bardonnie in Saint-Antoine-de-Breuilh, and after a three-week stay he managed to get to Pau, where he found Gilbert Renault of the BCRA.

SOE on the Ground

Georges Bégué was born in Périgueux and, in his late 20s, married an English girl named Rosemary while studying at the University of Hull. Having joined up to the French army in 1938 as a signaller, he was evacuated from Dunkirk in a state of total physical exhaustion, eventually rejoining his daughter and wife in Hull.

Determined to do something positive when he learned of the armistice, Bégué opted to join the British services with a view to helping create a situation in France wherein a landing could be facilitated later in the war. Undergoing long and at times frustrating training, his place in the scheme of things was underlined when he asked questions such as what the aim of the mission would be, who he would be working with and under what kind of conditions. He was told, 'You are radio, you will pass on the messages; don't worry about anything else. Set yourself up, camouflage yourself, have contact with no one but couriers and *letterboxes*.' He was given the alternative identity, George Nobel.

On the night of 5 May 1941 Bégué left for France, landing in Indre, north of the Dordogne. He knew it a little, and as well as being close to the demarcation line it was possible to pick up and receive radio signals from Bordeaux, Toulouse, Lyon and Marseille. On landing at 1.30 a.m. on 6 May, he became the first SOE F Section agent to be parachuted into France. He carried false papers under a second alias of Georges Mercier, food tickets and 12,480 francs. He landed some way from his intended position and, having buried his parachute, headed towards Valencay and his contact, Max Hymans, known to him as Frederic. While travelling the 30km on foot, carrying his heavy radio set at his side and not wishing to be noticed, he dined on chocolate and a can of beer. Unable to find Hymans that first night, he got some sleep in a cheap hotel then succeeded in locating his contact the following morning.

Hymans advised Bégué and gave him food tickets before Bégué moved on to Châteauroux, where he found accommodation that allowed him to lie low as a Parisian refugee. The room, in a run-down hotel, was perfect as it permitted him to face north in order in to receive a good signal. He installed an antenna in the bathroom, and on the morning of 9 May, after spending just four minutes making adjustments, he made contact with London through a coded message. He was the first to do so from France, and in that message he let London know not only that Hymans was on board to act as a point of contact, but also that he himself had found a safe house and a letterbox. As a result, more agents were sent over the following days, including Pierre de Vomécourt, who, along with his two brothers and the indispensable Bégué, set up the first SOE network in France, SOE AUTOGIRO.

Soon the sheer mass of work and messages for transmission made it very difficult to achieve what was needed using the limited channels, which were being constantly jammed. The difficulty was compounded because Bégué needed to spend as little time as possible transmitting in order to avoid detection. He proposed using BBC transmissions that contained coded lines of poetry to announce if and when missions were taking place. These lines evolved into the celebrated system of '*messages personnels*', and the technique was adopted throughout Europe for the rest of the war, especially in the lead-up to D-Day.

Towards the end of May two former French parliamentarians already implicated in early resistance made contact. One of them, Bégué's initial contact Max Hymans, sent a message to the other, Pierre Bloch, who was spending most of his time in Villamblard with occasional visits to Vichy. When Bloch arrived, he was introduced to Cardiff-born half-British SOE agent Jacques Vaillant de Guélis, whose parents were involved in coal exports in Brittany. De Guélis was in France on a month-long mission, having parachuted in blind, hurting his leg on landing and losing his co-agent, Gilbert Turck, codename Christophe, who had drifted too far away. Being bilingual and English-educated, de Guélis had been taken on by F Section as a briefing officer and became one of the few English-educated agents who could report back to the general staff on life under German occupation and the population's reaction to it. As a member of the general staff he, in principle, should not have been allowed to go to France but an exception was made – one of only two during the war. (The other was Peter Churchill.)

Bloch, de Guélis and Bégué took a walk around Châteauroux despite de Guélis' injury, discussing matters pertaining to the future of the Resistance, but while Bloch wanted to find out all about the kind of man de Gaulle was, de Guélis was interested only in knowing whether Bloch had readily available sites suitable for parachute drops. One of the places that Bégué and Hymans were looking at for future drops was the Périgord.

In Villamblard Pierre Bloch brought together a committee that included Doctor Édouard Dupuy, the mayor of Villamblard, and a blacksmith and mechanic named Albert Rigoulet, 'Le Frisé'. The men were told that within a week they should hear the message '*Gabriel vous envoie ses amities*', and after several short delays due to heavy fog in England, the message '*Gabriel va bien*' was finally received from the BBC on 10 October 1941, signalling that a drop was imminent. Rigoulet, knowing the countryside well having served in the French air force, had found a suitable site, near the hamlet of Lagudal, just a few kilometres from Villamblard. Coordinates had already been transmitted to London. The drop was to be made that night, assuming no counter orders were made, and a long nervous day of waiting lay ahead. Rigoulet was working on the harvest in his father's vineyard when he saw Doctor Dupuy's car pull up. The two men arrived at Rigoulet's home to collect what they needed; as well as a pickaxe, shovel, small saw and rope, Rigoulet packed biscuits, sweet Monbazillac white wine, chocolate, ham and bread into a backpack.

On board the plane was Jean le Harivel, a 23-year-old wireless operator and trained saboteur 'with a long face, and hair that had begun to thin out'. He spoke 'excellent French, although marked by a strong accent'.[3] Born in France to a British father, he was saddened by the humiliation that France had endured – it was inconceivable that Paris could be occupied: 'We were patriotic, we really believed in this fight against Nazism, and the fact that France had been invaded hurt terribly.'[4] Le Harivel made the jump with three colleagues, all agents of SOE's F Section, and all four were instructors in the skills of sabotage. They were Marc Jumeau, in charge of the mission (code named Corsican), Jack Hayes and Daniel Turberville. Further 'chutes would carry containers of explosive materials for sabotage missions in occupied France, and radio sets – this was a new and untested type of mission.

However, the circling plane had unfortunately drawn too much attention, and Turberville, together with the equipment 'chutes, was dropped 10km away from the drop site. Without the vital radios or other pieces of equipment, the success of the mission was already hampered. Two of the men sheltered at the nearby Rigoulet farm and a third was hidden at Doctor Dupuy's residence. Pierre Bloch told the men that it would be suicidal to go to Bergerac to meet their contact given that the authorities would have been alerted by the presence of the plane. They therefore hid in a barn for several days before finally going to Bergerac and then separately on to Marseille, against a backdrop of heightened security. They were carrying documents, revolvers and 2 million francs to pass to an emerging Resistance group in Marseille that was struggling to run without supplies.

Traps

In the early hours of the morning of 11 October 1941, just as Pierre Bloch was leading three of the four parachutists of mission Corsican to safety, gendarmes from the station at Guet who had been alerted to the circling plane were sent out to look around the area. They found two large parachutes – one hanging from a tree and one near a road. Each had attached to it a large metal cylinder, described as a 'contraption' of some sort. On closer inspection the metal cylinders, 1.8m in length and with a diameter of 40cm, contained three barrels holding detonators and explosive sabotage materials. The total weight of each was around 120kg. At around 11 a.m. two gendarmes of the Villamblard brigade were alerted to the presence of a stranger carrying a small suitcase and a briefcase in nearby Issac. The gendarmes caught up with him and arrested him. Speaking perfect French with an excellent accent, he gave his name as Jacques Dormoy and said his address was 26 rue des Capucins, Périgueux. This information was checked with the Commissariat de Police, who reported that not only did they have no record of Dormoy, but the rue des Capucins did not exist.

Under interrogation, Daniel Turberville revealed that he was an agent of the intelligence service and had been parachuted in the previous night. He revealed his real name and his nationality as English.* He admitted to living in London but refused to give any further details of his mission.[5] On being led through the streets of Villamblard, flanked by two gendarmes, Turberville was spotted by Pierre Bloch.[6] What Bloch didn't know was that the authorities had found details of a contact that he, along with the other members of the Corsican mission, were to proceed to: the villa in Marseille.

Turberville was taken to the *maison d'arrets* in Périgueux and put on a train to Lyon on 9 December 1941. Two gendarmes from the Périgueux

---

* In fact his parents were English but he was born in Tournan-en-Brie. He returned there in 1935 to marry Renée Chavannes.

brigade were allocated to carry out the transfer. Turberville was handcuffed on leaving the *maison d'arrets* in Périgueux but, once the train pulled out of Limoges, he was uncuffed. The gendarmes awoke at 6.30 a.m. to find that their prisoner had vanished.

★★★

Hayes, Jumeau and le Harivel managed to reach their destination safely, passing document checks and even searches before arriving in the sprawling southern city of Marseille. However, the Vichy authorities had pieced together details of the operation and set an elaborate trap at the Villa des Bois safehouse, which led to multiple arrests, including the three newcomers.

The roll call of those arrested in and around the Villa des Bois was impressive. As well as Marc Jumeau, Jack Hayes and Jean le Harivel of the Corsican mission, Georges Bégué and SOE agent Raymond Roche were incarcerated, as were Pierre Bloch and his wife Gaby who had travelled to Marseille to distribute money they had taken delivery of. They were all caught in the same trap and charged with treason. Earlier that month other agents sent by SOE to assist the new network had been trapped as well. Lieutenant Michael Trotobas was arrested in Châteauroux during an identity check while on his way to Marseille; Georges Langelaan, a former *New York Times* journalist, was picked up at a restaurant in Châteauxroux while waiting to meet Bégué; and Francis Garel (real name Bouguennec), a local recruit, was picked up in Antibes as a result of an indiscretion by Langelaan, who had been carrying the address of Philippe Liewer, a Jewish ex-liaison officer who had enthusiastically taken up Langelaan's offer of employment as a courier.

Mistakes had been plentiful, but SOE learned its lessons well. In 1941 agents were imprisoned by Vichy police instead of the Gestapo, which would have been the case in later years; Gestapo interrogation would have included torture and probably death by firing squad. SOE in France had been reduced to one female agent on the ground in Lyon, supported by the US embassy. She was called Virginia Hall. Those arrested were transferred to the Béleyme prison for serious offenders in Périgueux, before transfer to the Mauzac camp near Bergerac.

Forging Links

By the winter of 1941 protest and collective defiance on a small scale began to morph into something more organised. A refusal to accept collaboration, focusing less on Pétain's 'betrayal' and more on the occupying forces, served as a conduit between islands of discontent. Throughout 1941 and 1942 three larger movements emerged in the unoccupied zone that had the potential to provide a structured and cohesive movement, if only the potential could be recognised and managed. Initially these groups were intent on producing propaganda. As structures emerged, suitable candidates could be recruited to a wide variety of roles. Certain types were actively sought out, such as those who were known locally as resourceful and imaginative. Whereas in the very early days local leaders, printers and journalists were particularly desirable, over time the range of required skills and occupations broadened. Potential recruits working in town halls with access to official stamps and stationery, local clergy, teachers and garage mechanics were vital, as were café and restaurant owners, and any civilian with papers that allowed them to travel freely, especially if a vehicle was available. Crossing dangerous mountain paths into Spain was a key part of Resistance activity from the very early days, so mountain guides were sought, as were reliable *passeurs* on the demarcation line.

While *résistants* could be 'man, woman, adult, youth; Catholic, Protestant, Jew, non-believer; a French person or foreigner',[7] those who participated needed to demonstrate a capacity for secrecy, maintaining a normal life, separating their day job from Resistance activity, resilience and capacity to endure periods of fatigue and pressure. Furthermore, those who resisted needed to accept that they were breaking the law of the land, and stick to their belief that what they were doing was morally correct. The mix of people, skills and social classes made for an almost unheard-of variety, and the diversity of the various organisations was celebrated in the decades to come.

Maurice Loupias described the early period of 1941 to 1942 as '*à tatons dans le noir*' ('fumbling along in the dark'), and his own involvement in the Resistance came from discussions with friends and chance meetings amongst the 'malaise' of society. He grouped around ten friends, and together they pondered how and when they could act. Then one day the Resistance found him:

In my neighbourhood there was a brave man, Monsieur Rettien, a carpenter, who had put together a local resistance group. One day he came to find me and said: 'This is where I am. I know a little bit about how you feel, I know that I can count on you. I have no military skills at all. You are a captain in the reserves. Do you want to be my second in command?' You can imagine the joy with which I leapt at the offer. I brought my ten men, and we found ourselves being part of a movement of Resistance.[8]

Loupias took on the name Bergeret, after having toyed with the names Liber and le Large. He settled on Bergeret because it identified him with Bergerac, his sector. He also liked the 'literary memories and the shadow of Anatole France which leant a charm to the name'.[9]

The networks that formed during May 1941 were not political in nature, but through existing contacts tended to recruit from certain political spheres. One of these, Libération, recruited mainly socialists and established its own section chiefs, while the Christian Democratic Combat was popular amongst left-wing Catholics and established itself by naming sector leaders and a chain of command below. In the northern sector of the Dordogne, Charles Serre, eventually known as Yvette, was a solicitor who lived just outside Champagnac-de-Belair. He benefited from being able to hold many meetings behind closed doors because of his occupation, as well as from having a first-class agent immediately on hand – his wife, Charlotte. Combat, which emerged in November 1941, was itself a fusion of two groups from the unoccupied zone that shared broadly similar goals: Mouvement de Libération Nationale (MLN) and Liberté.

MLN was the work of Henri Frenay, the son of a career officer, who entered the École Militaire de Saint-Cyr in 1924 as a 19-year-old. While serving in Vichy he began recruiting fellow officers to the cause before resigning in January 1941.

At Grenoble in November 1941, Frenay met with François Menthon, who was also devoted to the importance of propaganda. His own developing group was called Liberté and published a Christian Democrat periodical of the same name out of Marseille. Not only did Liberté share the ideals of a denunciation of Nazism and defeatism, but it had also developed from the summer of 1941 some '*groupes francs*', primarily made up of workers, students and Spanish Republicans who had fled Franco's regime. These cells undertook the first properly organised attacks and sabotage missions.

The new group, the Mouvement de Libération Française, became widely known as Combat. Helped in no small part by money supplied by the now London-based Jean Moulin, in 1942 it became the largest Resistance group in the unoccupied zone. It was also highly structured around two operations: action and propaganda. Recrutement-organisation-propagande (ROP) worked at distributing the tens of thousands of copies of the new newspaper, *Combat*, edited first by Georges Bidault and later by Claude Bourdet. The 'action' arm included the *groupes francs*, which often used small explosives on homes of well-known collaborators, and aided the gathering and passing on of information. It also began the vital work of infiltrating police stations, post offices, town halls and Vichy offices, while further sections focused on finance, sabotaging railways and obtaining false papers. By the end of 1942 Combat could count several thousand members scattered in and around the major cities and large towns of the unoccupied zone.

Frenay, keen to create a secret army, divided the unoccupied zone into six groups, of which the fifth centred around Limoges. This area became known as 'R5' and included Haute-Vienne, Corrèze, Creuse, Dordogne, Indre, as well as the unoccupied sections of Charente, Cher, Loir and Loir-et-Cher. Despite living in Brive rather than Limoges, Edmond Michelet was given responsibility for the region, and 'backed by his faith and his patriotism, disappointed but not discouraged by the episcopal prudences, totally supported by his family'[10] he pressed ahead, surrounding himself with figures he knew and trusted from the Christian Democratic circles of Brive. One of these men, the young officer Raymond Faro or 'Fromonteil', who later became regional leader of the AS, met with Michelet in Périgueux in June 1942. They gathered in the room of L'Abbé Jean Sigala, professor of philosophy in the Collège Saint Joseph. Attendees included a teacher named André Boissière (Berthou) and Gabriel de Choiseul-Praslin. Combat had reached the area through the work of Charles Serre, but in this meeting Boissière was given overall responsibility for the area and roles were distributed such as press, propaganda, secret army and information.

The second major group differed from Combat in that its structure was slightly less concrete, but it shared a double-winged approach of propaganda and information (more political in nature than that of Combat) and paramilitary action. Initiated by Emmanuel d'Astier de la Vigerie, an aristocratic former naval intelligence officer who, 'sickened by the atmosphere of abject submission'[11] surrounding the armistice, began his search for others of the same mind in Port-Vendres. By November 1940, d'Astier de la Vigerie's plans were slowly taking shape and he founded La Derniere Colonne in Clermont-Ferrand with Jean Cavaillès, a university philosopher, Georges Zérapha and a married couple by the names of Raymond and Lucie Aubrac. Despite his aristocratic family, d'Astier de la Vigerie's target groups for membership were left wing, including syndicalists and communists.

The politics of the group, renamed Libération in July 1941 at Clermont-Ferrand when the group began a newspaper of the same name, became more and more left wing over time. The paramilitary arm of Libération, headed up overall by Raymond Aubrac, was no rival to the armed wing of Combat, and *Libération*'s reach, being more radical in its politics, was also more limited. In 1942 its 35,000 copies printed, though significant, demonstrated this. D'Astier de La Vigerie's vision for his paramilitary arms was one of quietly inspiring and training a popular uprising, but the main focus of the group was the newspaper that helped to bring in and retain membership.

As Libération became more and more socialist, it thrived in the Dordogne, where engineer Jean Worms, assigned to work in the gunpowder factories, led after joining in November 1942. Worms had already demonstrated a desire to lead, having run campaigns to serve in both the Assemblée Nationale and the Sénat prior to the war. He was known clandestinely as 'Germinal'.

The third group, composed initially of a former member of Action Française, Georges Valois, an ex-communist named Elie Peju and Antoine Avinin of Jeune République, started as France-Liberté in Lyon in November 1940, before launching its own clandestine publication, *Le Franc-Tireur*, in December 1941, at which time the group was renamed in line with the paper. Under the stewardship of Jean-Pierre Lévy, a Jewish refugee from Strasbourg, the paper drew on the talents of local Lyon-based journalists; the movement also created some of its own *groupes francs*, drawing itself into the world of sabotage and attacks on people and property on a minor scale.

In the early days arms were makeshift and had to be sought out. Dynamite was supplied by local engineers who happened to be sympathetic to the cause, as was the case with Monsieur Cruvellier, whose business was in

Ribérac. Food and other supplies were contributed, as were any and all types of weapons, be they hunting rifles or souvenirs of the Great War.

Refusers and resisters recognised the need to recruit and walked a fine line between approaching potential denouncers and those who had simply succumbed to fatalism and may still be pliable. It was vital that these people were helped to understand what fate might hold for them. By early 1942, propaganda in the form of tracts and newspapers had already proved extremely powerful. Edmond Michelet's Péguy-inspired tracts had, since first appearing in June 1940, verbalised Michelet's desire to 'prevent people from believing that all was lost, that we are beaten because we are guilty and that all remains is for us to lie flat on our stomachs before the enemy'.[12] Michelet was well known for his amiability and lack of bigotry or religious sectarianism.

Michelet's words featured in Menthon's *Liberté*, and then *Combat*, which, once Menthon and Frenay's movements had combined, amounted to several pages that appeared either once or twice a month. The papers were circulated mainly by hand to safe associates, accompanied by advice for them to do the same. This way they enjoyed a significant readership with somewhere in the region of 100,000 copies of each issue printed.[13] The appetite for papers such as *Libération* and *Le Franc-Tireur* alongside *Combat* led to distribution becoming an increasingly dangerous activity, but one which was carried out by mainly young *résistants* keen to contribute. In urban areas copies were pushed under doors or left in letterboxes; in some towns, they were even left in police stations.

The difficulty of procuring ink, paper and distribution channels made national titles difficult and dangerous to produce. At a local level these difficulties were as acute, if not more so, but small determined teams continued to overcome them in order to produce titles using outdated equipment or by hand. Printing equipment was used as available, but with difficulty: a dedicated press was installed in a cave in Montignac but had to be quickly relocated for fear of being betrayed. Local papers, such as *La Dordogne en Guerre*, *La Voix de Jacquou* or the Limoges-based *La Marseillaise du Centre*, carried messages in bold such as 'Never throw away the "Marseillaise", hand it to a friend who will thus know the truth.'[14] Successful though they were, tracts were even more widely lapped up since they were produced quickly and irregularly to report on key events without delay: Allied success could stimulate refusal, just as could word of German reprisals.

The provision of information to the Allies was a highly significant goal of early Resistance networks. In the occupied zone, Alliance was created by Commander Georges Loustaunau-Lacau, first called La Croisade, then Navarre, until Alliance was permanently adopted. It was known to the Germans as Noah's Ark as each agent took the name of an animal. One of these agents was known as Hérisson (hedgehog) because of the animal's immunity to snakes' venom and its tendency to destroy harmful species.[15] Her real name was Marie-Madeleine Bridou (later Fourcade) – a 30-year-old mother of two who lived in Paris and created a network that was particularly effective through its use of civil servants. Almost a quarter of its members were women – a higher percentage than many other groups. Bridou served as Loustaunau-Lacau's deputy up until the latter's arrest in 1941 and led the group with great distinction thereafter.

In Corrèze, a core had begun to form of men who were hard and uncompromising, and who wished to become affiliated to a network. Led by Jean Vinzant, known as 'Le Danois', they took on the names of types of dogs, and became known as the '*chiens de garde*'. The location was useful, as, due to its lack of proximity to large towns and its topography, the Corrèze was a good place to go into hiding.

★★★

North-west of Sarlat, in October 1940, Édouard Kauffmann had been developing his farm, purchased in 1930 but which he had only recently moved into full-time, when his views on the armistice army, created to uphold law and order, became incompatible with his continued service. A 'gentleman farmer', he had taught himself basic farming methodologies and, to the outsider, would appear to be happily following the 'return to the earth' mantra of the new regime. Once fully installed in his 8-hectare property, which he improved with help from his 14-year-old son Jean-Claude at the weekends, he owned 2,000 hens that were excellent layers. This together with his two dairy cows, two pigs, rabbits and a donkey kept him busy, though he received help from a local young farmhand.[16]

Kauffmann was, according to his countryfolk neighbours, so zealous about his farming activities that it would raise a smile among them. In his mid 40s with a wide, high forehead and a light moustache, he was fascinated by the slow work of the crops and the harvests, and this endeared him to those who knew him. He was considered an excellent neighbour, friendly and a good conversationalist, but never hid his lack of enthusiasm for the new regime and, being originally from Alsace-Lorraine, for their German partners. He was a subscriber to Action Française, was no fan of the politicians of the Third Republic and was almost attacked while in uniform by a group of protesters in the streets of Paris during the years of the Front Populaire, so he fitted the profile of a Pétainist extremely well. Despite this, at the end of the 1940 conflict he concealed tonnes of petrol-filled barrels in a ravine so the Germans could not procure it. Sadly, the fuel was easily recovered: Kauffmann was admonished and decided he could no longer serve the new regime.

Kauffmann was, despite his love of small-hold farming, a military man: he had joined up in 1913 at the age of just 18, became a major at 34 and later a wing commander, gaining nine citations and the *croix de guerre*. From 1923 to 1933 he had been based in Morocco, and it was here that he caught the eye of a captain serving under him, Léon Faye. After the arrest of Loustaunau-Lacau in May 1941 (Faye had himself been detained for two months), Marie-Madelaine Bridou (later Fourcade) was appointed the one and only female leader of a Resistance network, and Faye worked as her second in command in Alliance. On being asked to think of trustworthy officers he knew well, Kauffmann sprang to Faye's mind.

The Alliance network was unique in that the territory had been divided up into sectors and each of these included a patrol to gather information that might be useful to England. Movement of troops or material, changes at bases or any other information was first transmitted by letter at an extremely slow pace until radio contact was made with London. It was in this field that Kauffmann (Criquet or Manitou) came into his element. In the Sarlat region, where he had no problem in recruiting a good number of willing volunteers, he became known for his excellent leadership. Before long he was the regional boss and then responsible for the whole of the south of France. Travelling from base to base dressed in his washed-out grey greatcoat, he spent his days overseeing the vital and increasingly dangerous work of the network. Information needed to be gained, checked and transmitted, while requests that arrived from London also had to be dealt with. The teams looked for movements in railway stations and in ports throughout France, but as the numbers grew so did the danger of being caught out.

The small numbers willing to resist in the unoccupied zone some-times worked for other groups such as Libération-sud, Ceux de la France, Le Franc-Tireur or Musée de l'Homme. Conversely, some operated alone, unaware that nearby there existed a group working towards a similar goal. It was by no means unknown for double agents to operate within this dis-organisation, leading to denunciations that could bring down burgeoning groups. Still, however, the overriding shared sentiment of those involved was that something had be done.

The problem was that without guidance and skilled organisers isolated actions had only a limited effect. The boarding pupil who tore down post-ers of the Marshal in the high school in Périgueux seemingly acted alone, the police report recommending that only internal sanctions be taken, due to his age. Meanwhile other young people spent long days in garages near Château-l'Éveque, Le Bugue and Bordas folding newspaper sheets, putting them into envelopes, licking and sticking stamps, and copying addresses out of telephone directories. Some spent evenings sliding copies under doors, targeting certain known people such as the local vice president of the Légion – a lawyer based in Salignac, who received many copies of the same publication.[17]

Under the leadership of school teacher André Boissière, Combat contin-ued to grow in the Périgord, while Michelet entrusted further development of the network within the area to another friend. Dr Louis Christiaens in turn began a recruitment drive and found Dr Victor Nessmann, a demo-bilised medic who had no wish to return to the militarised Alsace – the perfect recruit to look after Sarlat. From here Nessmann lost little time in gathering a group of professional men, including the principal of the Collège La Boétie, Raymond Terrenq, whose school subsequently served from time to time as a headquarters for the new network. In nearby Carlux another medical doctor, Bezazel Auerbach, who by the new Vichy laws had lost the right to practise, committed most of his time to recruitment. In October 1942 Auerbach, who became known as 'Bernard', participated in a parachute drop before becoming a local SOE agent in the Hilaire network.

Also in south-east Dordogne, in Groléjac, the woodcutting and charcoal business belonging to Lucien Dubois thrived. Its owner, always with his ear to the ground, had become interested in matters related to local opposition and had expressed his view to friends: 'come on … the Resistance … It can't not exist.' Before long an opportunity presented itself. A local cereal miller was hiding a police captain – an agent of the new Libération-nord movement. Dubois met him and agreed to establish the network around the Bastide town of Domme. Taking the name 'Céou', he also agreed to become the representative of Le Franc-Tireur, which had begun to spread into the region from Lyon.

These groups could do little more than distribute propaganda unless they were supplied with explosive materials, armaments and ammunition. However, they were able to participate in the reception of these materials. Dubois, whose name changed from 'Céou' to 'Victor', got in contact with British SOE agents including Henri Paul Lechêne, one of three brothers who had been parachuted into France and whose wife would later join him. Dubois was one of twenty-five local agents who had, during May 1941, taken delivery of radio equipment destined for the Alliance network. The drop was made near Domme and those involved recovered the equipment and ensured its correct onward distribution. Dubois also helped receive material delivered clandestinely under the CDM programme into Brive.

Public Opinion

A report written for BCRA, France Libre's intelligence network, on 19 January 1942 described in great detail the situation in the unoccupied zone at the beginning of the year:

> The people have gone back to their normal activity and very few are considering resisting either the Germans or the government. Proportion of collaborators is quite strong. The majority are counting on the English, and lately on the Russians, to chase the Germans from France.

The Légion was described as:

> [an] obligatory thing for shopkeepers or businessmen who want to have to have some chance to succeed or even to eke out a living … The *Légion* is strong by number, and that is all, because of those that make it up, the number of those that are sincere is very small. The *Légion* is rather like a flock of sheep.

As far as politics were concerned, 'The Communists, of which the exact strength is unknown (just that it is quite considerable) seem since the outbreak of the Germano-Russian war to have gained ground.' But commitment to the ideals of the National Revolution seemed sound:

> The *Camps de Jeunesse* and the *Compagnons de France* have known success amongst the young because, in a sense, these organisations fulfil their thirst for idealism and action … [In the military] young officers, in general, are fairly Pétainist … A propaganda campaign has been waged amongst them in order to kindle their hatred against England … The older officers, especially those that took part in the last war, are more favourable towards us.

The BCRA report summed up the apathy of the French towards the possibility of resisting in some way:

> The people appear to be in search for a balance that the Vichy government has not allowed them to find. Nevertheless, people seem loath to carry out any action whatsoever for fear of losing the beautiful peace to which they aspire. On the other hand, some have the impression of resisting by listening to the BBC and contenting themselves by ranting very modestly against the Germans or against the government.

There were clear indications, however, that the country was no longer as convinced by Pétain's leadership: 'Pétain's star seems to be tarnished a little because of the restrictions which are becoming more and more hard.'

As to the potential for future organisations in the area:

> experience shows us that it is impossible to continue to work as we have done up to now. In the current climate the mass population cannot be counted on for any action whatsoever. Even those who claim to be ready give up at the first difficulty. A well organised propaganda campaign is absolutely necessary in order to give to the population a strongly instilled spirit, an ideal that it does not currently possess.

Propaganda was one area in which the BCRA felt it needed to exert further control:

we must possess a link with propaganda which, in principle, should come from London but which, for reasons of convenience as much as good sense, most originate in France … What we need to look for is a selection of people who will never let go and who will hang on in there until the end. From there the mass, being in itself quite pliable, will model itself on this elite … we must confine ourselves to searching for those from a background which, the moment arrived, will drive the masses, whose courage will have been awoken by propaganda.[18]

The report paints a picture of Vichy France at the beginning of 1942 that is realistic and appropriately downbeat. De Gaulle set up the BCRA as his own intelligence bureau to collect, examine and feed back on military intelligence. It was headed up by André Dewavrin (Colonel Passy), whose vision for any type of Resistance in France was based around military action. This included providing military personnel the means to escape to Spain and beyond, but not identifying internal groups of civilians or demobilised soldiers or encouraging their organisation into fighting groups.

Information came to the BCRA via the likes of Rémy's Confrérie Notre-Dame. But Rémy's personality and laissez-faire attitude to security made him more of a problem as time progressed. Information travelled through as few hands as possible and was examined in London, where the BCRA held a variety of addresses around Kensington.

Nevertheless, 'Resistance' was still to come together into a cohesive identity amongst the leaders of the Free French. In 1942 de Gaulle considered himself to be fighting a parallel war, with his small number of exiled fighters in England and access to a small army in North Africa. His vision was of the eternal French army that would combine with existing military within and liberate herself when the time came. For others linked to the BCRA, Resistance was a political and social matter to prepare the ground for future liberation.

Pierre Brossolette was an early *résistant* with a brilliant mind, who first engaged in 1940 through the Musée de l'Homme group and later set up a bookshop on the rue de Pompe in Paris. The shop became an important meeting place for Resistance leaders. He was a socialist and journalist who had good contacts with leaders of the embryonic information and resistance networks, including Rémy. Brossolette was able to articulate the thoughts, feelings and goals of the various leaders that gathered at the bookshop, which were sometimes wildly different to the goals of de Gaulle and the London-based Free French movement.

In April 1942 Brossolette travelled to London, where he drafted a report that touched upon the nature of dangerous collaboration in France at that time and backed up what the January report had recounted:

> In the Occupied zone the situation is clear: 95% of people are against collaboration with Germany. This 95% are almost unanimous in despising Vichy, because Vichy preaches and practises a policy of collaboration. In the Unoccupied zone things are made less simple by the government's actions, its press, its Legion and a general ignorance about the German occupation. One part of public opinion is behind the Marshal and accepts everything he does, even collaboration.[19]

It was clear, therefore, that in order for the whole country to follow the example of the occupied zone, it would not be enough for agents on the ground to organise networks. The population was behind Pétain, and London, whether through de Gaulle's Free French movement or the minuscule number of SOE agents parachuted in, had its work cut out to make an impact.

If a momentum change was to occur in regions such as the Périgord or the Limousin, then it was likely to begin with the working class. Of course, food was the first shortage that everyday folk noticed. The newspaper *L'Avenir de la Dordogne* regularly carried information as to the rations for each month. In September 1942, 180g of meat was allowed per week, along with 150g of oil, 200g of butter and a monthly allowance of 1kg of sugar was made. Other foods were rationed per three months, for example potatoes, which, by November 1942, were limited to 12kg per person for the following three months. Forging of ration vouchers was viewed harshly and a *Périgourdine* found to have falsified her allowance was sentenced to eight days in prison in late November. By early December the prefecture had outlawed the production of *fromage blanc*.[20]

As food became scarcer, the Dordogne population, 'forced each day to have to think a bit more about its own subsistence, seemed hopelessly devoted to a kind of morose depression'.[21] The Périgord region, like others in Vichy France, had few large cities but even here the pursuit of food vouchers, combined with long queues at the shops and the disappearance of such everyday luxuries as coffee and tobacco, became an almost universal preoccupation. In the countryside growers' worries were compounded by incessant controls, inspections and requisitions of crops and products, usually destined for Germany.

Persecution

As 1941 and 1942 passed, the public became more and more informed about the difficulties the Jews faced. A small number of representatives of the Catholic Church began began speaking out against their persecution, and in some cases convent doors opened for those who sought refuge, while talk of round-ups led to some public sympathy. The passage of time had also eased the feelings of blame apportioned to the 'Jewish' Third Republic, especially as the true nature of Vichy collaborationism began to emerge. General attitudes that were already in the process of softening evolved further as the Jewish exiles became neighbours and friends: in the Dordogne a non-Jewish benefactor gave 80,000 francs to the Entraide Sociale Israélite de Périgueux at the end of 1941 and people began to help Jewish neighbours whose livelihoods had been liquidated. Vichy, on the other hand, did its best to propagandise the problem of the Resistance as a Jewish phenomenon totally under the influence of Moscow. As cynical and political as this might have been, Jews had been placed in rural communities which is where early Resistance networks sprung up. That many of the early Maquis groups were led by Jews is no accident.

On 20 January 1942 a conference took place in the idyllic lakeside suburb of Wannsee. There, fifteen high-ranking Nazi dignitaries including Reinhard Heydrich and Adolf Eichmann put the wheels in motion for the 'Final Solution to the Jewish problem'. Hitler's plan to exterminate 11 million European Jews was going to put a lot of strain on German resources, and France would have to be more helpful than they had been, having resisted holding any more arrested Jews in camps in the southern zone. The creation of the CGQJ and the subsequent appointment by Darlan of anti-Semite Xavier Vallat, despite the latter's nationalism and anti-German sentiments, made dealing with the Jewish issue a shared problem. In charge of Jewish affairs since the late summer of 1940 was SS-Hauptsturmführer Theodor Dannecker, a 29-year-old fanatical anti-Semite. After the Vichy government had agreed on 4 July 1942 to the deportation of foreign Jews from both zones, mainly on the insistence of Chief of Police René Bousquet, Dannecker insisted on conducting a tour of the country, much to Bousquet's annoyance as it would undermine Vichy sovereignty of the unoccupied zone. Dannecker was disappointed by the number of internees in the camps that he visited. Hoping to see in excess of 40,000 Jews interned, he was surprised to find that many camps held fewer internees than they had in 1940, when they had held political refugees mainly from Spain. In the Gurs camp near Pau, for example where he hoped to see at least 20,000 Jews, only 2,599 were interned.

When Dannecker visited Périgueux he was told by the prefect Popineau 'that a rapid solution of the Jewish question by means of deportation was eminently desirable for his region', although he wanted to excuse a few 'decent Jews'.[22] Dannecker was impressed with the motivation of the prefects around the southern zone and felt that 'middle ranking French officials and departments are interested in the early solution of the Jewish question and are only waiting for the orders to come down.'[23]

Laval set goals that were in excess of the numbers requested by the German authorities, and round-ups of foreign Jews throughout the country began in earnest in the summer of 1942. Between 16 and 18 July, 12,884 Jews were arrested in Paris and taken to the Vel' d'Hiv' cycle stadium prior to deportation. This was the culmination of a terrible few months that had already seen Jews in the occupied zone being forced to wear a yellow Star of David on their clothes at all times and banned from visiting public places such as cafés, theatres, swimming pools and parks. The Jews of the south were spared having to wear the Star of David, but their documents had to be marked with the word '*Juif*'.

Public opinion was twitching, unsure which way to go and who to believe. In the countryside, there were complaints and denunciations. Some newcomers were unsuited and incapable of laborious work due to an innate 'idleness', while other were unsettled at the ability of some Jews to slot into already despised occupations, where they thrived at the expense of others, for example the market of livestock.[24] In the towns, members of the Légion and other collaborationist groups worked hard at propagandising problems on which the arrival of the Jews could be blamed. The rising prices and rarity of foods, housing issues and questions of employment could all be attached to the Judaic scapegoat. Centrally Vichy continued to play on these issues to prepare the ground for the round-ups that would follow, and for which they had to be prepared for a backlash – although the snitches and bigots were talking about the problems caused by the Jews, and children were name-calling in school, the gendarmeries and town halls were not having to deal with any such problems.

Rumours had begun to spread about the destination of the Jews that had been deported from the occupied zone. Resistance networks did what they could to spread the word that the Jews were not merely being relocated. There was talk of camps in the east. There was talk of death.

The Relève

At a time when the French people required strong leadership, behind the dictatorial Pétain was a Vichy government made up of politicians who were determined to position themselves to profit fully from the structure into which they were installed. In doing so France's bargaining power was being drained away as Vichy's leaders were dragged into servility that profited only the Germans. Rare were those who chose to speak up, or indeed do anything, despite the draining public moral. According to André Roulland, later a leader in the AS, 'confidence having disappeared, everyone gave up on seeing through [the Vichy government], resigning themselves to not thinking too much about it.'[25]

However, on 22 June 1942, Pierre Laval made a speech that, for many, ended any lingering hopes that the politicians of Vichy were playing an elaborate game of double bluff with the German High Command:

> I wish to re-establish with both Germany and Italy normal and trusting relations … In order to construct that Europe, Germany is in the process of engaging in huge battles. In doing so it must, with others, allow enormous sacrifices and it cannot spare the blood of its youth: in order to throw that [youth] into battle [Germany] is going to look for it in the factories and in the fields.

The following phrase was to trigger the next phase of resistance in France:

> I wish for a German victory, because, without it, Bolshevism would tomorrow install itself everywhere.

Doubts over Pétain's rocky relationship with Laval had been eliminated just days before when, in a speech to leaders of the Légion in Vichy, Pétain had declared: 'There are no more clouds between us ... we are now marching on hand in hand.'

Laval's speech that suggested France would supplement Germany's manpower created a wave of discontent. All French police forces were passed from the War Ministry to the Interior Ministry, which meant that, through René Bousquet who like Laval was hugely pro-German, the police apparatus was now in the hands of Laval. France was taking on a role that appeared more and more subservient to her German master. There was no partnership, equal or otherwise. As the German requisition of resources had demonstrated for some time, France was little more than a cupboard that Germany would happily empty. By September 1942 the Gestapo was allowed to operate freely within the unoccupied zone.

Laval's speech was accompanied by the announcement of a scheme that he had high hopes for. Under pressure from Reich Minister of Labour Fritz Sauckel for France to provide labour for the Reich within Germany, Laval had thrashed out a deal that he sold to the French people as La Relève. Under the scheme, for every three skilled workers who agreed to take up a well-paid position in Germany, one prisoner of war would return. France had, after all, begun to feel the second effect of occupation: the absence of 1.5 million prisoners of war held in German camps. Laval subscribed to the idea that rural areas were feeling the absence more than towns, and he knew that, as well as placing a moral pressure on French non-military families to contribute in a patriotic way, Vichy could claim moral currency when suffering heroes returned home.

The Relève was not an overwhelming success. At first there was a sheer lack of numbers of workers willing to sign up. A frustrated Sauckel – a wiry and rigid negotiator who had driven a hard bargain by demanding the three to one ratio – repeated his demands to Laval over summer 1942 and only allowed the first wave of prisoners to return on 11 August. Soon afterwards Sauckel announced that, within occupied Europe, men and women between the ages of 20 and 65 would be eligible for mobilisation to labour duty in Germany. Laval again negotiated, overestimating France's importance to Germany. His partial success in limiting the new conscription to men aged 18–50 and single women aged 21–35, made eligible at the discretion of Vichy, may have suggested he had a little more control of the situation, but it was an empty gesture to the French people. Prefect reports drawn from hundreds of thousands of opened letters intercepted by the Vichy postal services told the real tale. Pétain's speech and the subsequent imposition of the Relève were unpopular. Despite a modicum of support for the financial benefits of the scheme amongst the poorest rural communities, Laval's last vestige of respect had been mortally damaged. Pétain's support wavered.

Pétain, as part of the *Révolution nationale*, had encouraged a *retour à la terre* ('return to the earth'), and now he was encouraging those whose livelihoods depended on a small patch of ground to abandon it. The reports also indicated a mistrust of the scheme – an anxiety that workers would go but soldiers would not return. While the name La Relève pointed to 'return', the 3:1 ratio in reality indicated removal. Vocabulary was damaging too: whereas Laval had hoped that the end of 1942 would be about return, relief or compensation, it would instead be associated with departure, conscription and deportation. Vichy was 'becoming identified with Germany as a predatory force, responsible for absences'.[26]

The Relève was a failure despite the initial target set by Sauckel for 250,000 men being more or less met. These men were mainly from the industrialised and overpopulated northern towns, and the quality of workers was more variable than had been envisaged, as was the health of the prisoners returned. Vichy tried to photograph the returning soldiers positively, but little good was said about the scheme anywhere. The Resistance leapt on the opportunity to engage in intense pamphleteering on the issue. The BBC conducted a campaign against the scheme, painting it as a treasonous slave trade with chief slave master Laval making personal gain. It became an emotive issue that, together with the scenes of mass deportation of Jewish men, women and children during summer 1942, pushed resistance further up the agenda in the unoccupied zone. But Laval was not yet finished.

Unification

From April 1942 the leaders of the three main resistance movements of the unoccupied zone met every week or so to thrash out the difficult task of bringing the groups closer together. This Comité de Coordination de Zone Sud, with headquarters in Lyon, was chaired by Jean Moulin, who had been sent to France on behalf of General de Gaulle. Even Moulin was surprised at the difficulty in setting up a unified organisation from three existing movements that were working towards broadly the same goals, namely the liberation of France and the implementation of de Gaulle in the first instance.

Moulin, at this point known as 'Rex', came onto the scene not wanting a 'premature fusion'. In agreement with de Gaulle and the BCRA, he aimed to bring broadly similar activities into line with each other, looking past the views of the individual movements and 'behind the exaggerations … of some of their leaders'.[27] In order to do this Moulin directed the leaders to thoroughly review and tighten up their internal structures and security arrangements before advancing further.

Moulin's task was thankless, and the same questions were gone over time and time again, often from a starting point of zero. According to Colonel Passy, for many months Moulin presided over meetings full of 'sterile and noisy discussions from which nothing emerged because, each time if by some means a decision was being approached, the representative of one of the movements would, in order to win some time, hide behind the obligation that he had to consult with his *Comité directeur*'.[28] Furthermore each movement was reluctant to reveal information relating to its membership, its naming conventions and its stores of arms.

The Mouvements Unis de la Résistance (MUR) was finally created in January 1943 as a direct result of the fusion of Henri Frenay's Combat, Libération-sud, led by Emmanuel d'Astier de la Vigerie, and Le Franc-Tireur, whose leader was Jean-Pierre Lévy. Throughout the process problems arose on a number of personal political levels. There was some suspicion on the part of Henri Frenay towards Emmanuel d'Astier de la Vigerie who, in Frenay's eyes, was more left wing than was comfortable. Frenay appeared, on the other hand, a little too right wing for the tastes of d'Astier de la Vigerie. Despite the sparsity of the groups and the difficulties in bringing them together, it was vital, according to Jean Moulin's biographer sister Laure, to 'join them into a larger structure or, at the least, to act in unison at certain times in order to obtain a greater efficacy'.[29] For the members of the groups, below the leadership, the etiquette of the individual movement they had joined was less important than the fact that they were fighting against Vichy and the Germans while following the banner of General de Gaulle. While the groups certainly had their own individual characteristics, these mattered more to the leaders than to the members, who would be unlikely to abandon a group 'in order to better agree with a parallel group'. Such a move 'would seem to them an enormous sacrifice'.[30]

The leaders did their best to hang onto their autonomy but, in time, Moulin made progress. A new structure developed that brought into line strategies that had already been successful for Combat. The Armée Secrète (AS) entered into service from September 1942, as a fusion of the armed groups that had already been envisaged and planned by the movements, although now the AS would be a single organisation divided up according to location and purpose. Some smaller cells – *groupes francs* – were to be established in order to carry out immediate missions, such as the elimination of informers or sabotage, while other *bataillons* would maintain the wait-and-see approach. Other vital strategies were shaped, such as the infiltration of public administration, known as Noyautage des Administrations Publiques (NAP) which aimed to infiltrate public services – everything from prefectures, town halls and post offices to social services offices and police stations. The questions of housing and safe houses, printing and distribution of propaganda, and information networks also received due attention. Furthermore, communication with London and selection of landing sites for Lysander flights and parachute drops had to be unified. Liaison between the groups themselves and with other sections that had their own resistance presence, such as the railways and post offices, required tight security measures. In time discussions would start on the exact nature of the new, armed Maquis that had been reported scattered around the countryside, and how all could work in together.

Once it was confirmed, during September 1942, that the new AS would take on an overtly military role, local leaders of Combat, Le Franc-Tireur and Libération began to recruit those with proven military experience. Movements that had been engaged primarily in supply of information, propaganda and smuggling of people began the process of creating a new structure that could be effective in training men and preparing effective fighting units for when the time came to take up arms.

Raymond Berggren, known as 'Bordeaux 48', was the first to lead the new AS* in the Dordogne. Given the dispersed nature of the groups, mostly amounting to little more than fifty men, the Dordogne was simply too vast to control centrally and effectively. As a result, the department was divided into three sections, with three distinct leaders. The northern sector of the region – Dordogne-nord – biting into Haute-Vienne, the Corrèze and the Charente, was hilly and full of valleys, such as those of the Isle, the Auvézère the Dronne, the Loue and the Bandiat, and the countryside was cut up by woodland, hedgerows and brambles. The roads leading to Limoges from Périgueux via Thiviers, and to Angoulême through Brantôme, were perfect for ambushes. Major railway lines also ran through the area, one beginning in Périgueux (itself a major link with Bordeaux through Mussidan) working eastwards through Thiviers to Limoges, and another from Brive northwards to Angoulême, serving Thiviers, Hautefort and Nontron. This sector was run by Charles Serre (Yvette), who had already made major inroads in developing links with the likes of Edmond Michelet in Brive, where Resistance as a concept was more advanced.

Another key man in the Dordogne-nord, Raymond Boucharel, had been a 33-year-old army captain when he was taken prisoner in the Vosges on 27 June 1940. Just three months later he escaped and found his way back to Ribérac, where he re-entered his former profession of primary school teacher. Having received notification from Vichy that he had 'resigned from his role', he decided to sink into obscurity, first working in forestry where he helped to sabotage logs that were being sent to Germany for making gun handles. In February 1942 Boucharel was contacted by Didier Reynaud, departmental chief of Libération and its newly formed AS, and was given responsibility for the north of the department. In November 1942, as the groups began to merge, he was again contacted, this time by an Alsatian who represented Combat in Périgueux. Through a young woman that he knew only as Claude, Boucharel began to bring the groups together while establishing strong links with the network outside of the department.[31]

---

* He was, however, arrested at the end of May 1943. Roger Barnalier (Régine) of the Combat network took over.

The Dordogne centre area, which included Périgueux and was led by Périgueux school teacher André Boissière (Berthou), was undoubtedly the most complicated to organise and the least structured. Despite its organisational difficulties, it was here that the Dordogne witnessed its first explosive attack at the hands of the Resistance. On the evening of 3 October 1942, a kiosk in the place de Bugue, Périgueux, belonging to the Légion Française des Combattants, was blown apart by a small bomb. Nobody was hurt but the Vichy-inspired organisation, whose aim was to propagate support for the national revolution, learned in no uncertain terms that it was now a target. Similar attacks were carried out simultaneously at various locations in the unoccupied zone, but it is unclear whether the attack was carried out by members of Le Franc-Tireur or Combat. However, it can be attributed to the new AS of the Dordogne.

Maurice Loupias (Bergeret) was given Dordogne-sud: a section that included Bergerac, and a significant number of men – potential recruits from the armistice army still stationed there. Here the already existing France Combattante group was integrated, meaning that Loupias had at his disposal a potentially hugely effective fighting force.

Round-ups

EXTREMELY URGENT – Circular 12882 – Following my telegram 12464 of the 18 August confirming measures of arrest and rounding up of foreign Israelites indicated by dispatch 5 August and additional telegrams must take place 26 August – stop – It will be for you to fix the start time of these operations at the moment that it would seem to you most opportune – stop – letting you know however that it would be preferred that it takes place early morning preferably around 4 or 5 o'clock – 1210/24/8

Twenty-three miles west of Périgueux, in the small picturesque and historic market town of Saint-Astier, the dawn mist was already giving way to the hot summer sun. At six o'clock in the morning of 26 August 1942, 22-year-old Ernest Homberger woke to the sound of banging at his door. He opened it to find French police agents from the gendarmerie of

Saint-Astier, who demanded that he pack a suitcase and follow them. This he did and, in the bright morning sunshine, he was loaded onto the back of a waiting truck, open at the rear with hard parallel benches facing each other. He was not the first on board, but nobody was talking so he found himself a space. The truck rumbled through village after village around Saint-Astier, picking up more and more people as it went. After what seemed like an eternity the truck stopped at a small *collège* in Périgueux, deserted for the holidays. The vehicle's occupants were assembled, and names were ticked off lists. Those that had been collected talked amongst themselves. Throughout the day there had been plenty of opportunities to escape but nobody had thought of doing so.

The following morning Ernest and the others were boarded onto the truck once again and set off northwards in the direction of Limoges along the windy Périgourdin roads. An hour or two later they arrived at a camp not far from Saint-Pardoux-la-Rivière. They were disembarked and told which one of two barracks they were to report to. The camp was small, with between 200 and 300 internees, and Ernest noticed the barbed wire that surrounded it. The guards were French *miliciens*. Still nobody told the internees what they were there for, but this was not the first time Jews had been rounded up in this fashion. Ernest was not to know that on this day, 26 August, the southern zone's largest round-up so far was to take place – and had been planned since 5 August, when the prefecture had received secret orders to make tight arrangements. The raid of 26 August was a major push by the southern zones to meet Laval's targets for Jew deportations. The ultimate destination for the Jews arrested that day was Eastern Europe, and concentration camps.

Once at the camp the new inmates were given pre-printed forms to complete and sign. By signing the *formulaires*, the signees agreed that any fortune or belongings would legally be left to the French State in the event of exclusion from the country. Any doubts that the inmates might have had were thus dispelled: they were about to be deported. They expected to be sent to some sort of work camp to benefit the Reich, but beyond that they had no idea what fate awaited them. So far as Ernest and new friend Eric Bodenheimer were concerned, this uncertainty meant they should at least try to escape.

The morning after their arrival at the camp, while taking in some air in the yard, Ernest and Eric were pulled aside by a police inspector. He introduced himself as Strebler, saying that he was Strasbourgeois and, as a member of the Police Judiciaire, was one of those responsible for running the camp. Unexpectedly, Strebler said he couldn't understand why such young people were not at least trying to escape. Ernest replied that the thought had occurred to him, but he did not see how. An exasperated Strebler, looked at the two men and pointed to the ceiling of the barracks, said nothing, turned and left.[32] Ernest and Eric decided that they needed to find a *milicien* who might help them escape, but their attempts at communication with the guards met with no success. If they were to escape they would have to do so on their own. Ernest thought back to how Strebler had pointed to the ceiling and, when a quiet moment allowed, he investigated the structure of the barracks: the interior ceiling was false, nailed onto beams that crossed the structure, out of sight. The men climbed up and managed to squeeze through a gap into the space between the ceilings, where they could remain safely concealed.

That afternoon they found Strebler and told him that they might have found a way to escape. They asked if they could be sure that he would never betray them, and were reassured that they must do everything they could to escape. Departure from the camp was announced to take place at 5 p.m. that evening, and the two men followed the instructions given, bringing their suitcases to the edge of the camp to be loaded onto a truck. Then they climbed into the ceiling and hid. When the signal was sounded for the *rassemblement* they could hear the rest of the prisoners being embarked, but after half an hour silence fell. However, they knew it would be unsafe to do anything until they were sure that all guardians had left and the camp was quiet. They waited until around 11 p.m. then climbed back down into their hut. The camp was entirely dark and, it seemed, deserted. They climbed over the barbed wire, adrenaline masking the pain of their ripped skin. Once outside they saw a row of motorcycles that belonged to the *miliciens*, who no doubt were away accompanying the prisoners. They didn't know at the time, but the convoy had left for Drancy.

Ernest and Eric walked through the night, first southwards, skirting Brantôme, then, when they reached Chancelade, south-west towards Saint-Astier. The pair had an address for the mayor of a small village just outside Saint-Astier, and, when they knocked on his door in the glum dawn light, were told to go inside. Here they were given food and a bed to get some sleep. They spent the day and a further night there, until their feet had recovered. They were safe for the time being. Of those interned at Saint-Pardoux-la-Rivière on 28 August, Ernest Homberger and Eric Bodenheimer were the only ones who survived. None returned from the transit camp of Drancy, or from the concentration camps of Eastern Europe.

In the run-up to this, on 4 July 1942, the Vichy government had agreed to the deportation of foreign Jews from both zones, while Police Chief Bousquet offered up Jews from the so-called unoccupied zone. Furthermore, Laval had given his consent that, in the near future, French Jews would also be deported. A circular signed by Henri Cado, Bousquet's deputy, was sent to all regional prefects instructing them to prepare to send foreign Jews who had entered France since 1 January 1936 to the occupied zone. This included Jews from Germany, Austria, Poland, Czechoslovakia, Estonia, Lithuania, former inhabitants of Danzig and the Saar region, Soviet citizens and Russian refugees, with exceptions permitted in the case of unaccompanied children under the age of 18, war veterans and pregnant women. The round-ups were to be conducted under the personal charge of the prefects and without the participation of occupied forces. A directive from Bousquet on 22 August ordered the prefects to 'crush all resistance you encounter' and deal with 'passivity' or 'indiscretions' from their staff firmly to rid their areas of foreign Jews. Many of these Jews were already in camps or labour groups, and lists were already in place following the census from the previous December. Follow-up operations were carried out, with *miliciens* visiting schools and convents looking for further Jews to arrest. When ration cards needed renewal at the end of the month, more Jews fell into the net.

Ernest Homberger and Eric Bodenheimer were not the only Jewish lives saved by Aloyse Strebler, whose wife Melanie helped him by running dangerous but extremely important liaison tasks for him. The Streblers had come to Périgueux during the evacuation of 1939. Aloyse, who was born in 1895 in Uberach, was vehemently opposed to the racial policies of Vichy and had taken the difficult decision to use his position to try to warn those endangered by them. Regularly he passed on information to Jewish acquaintances about possible dangers: he had been in touch with 12-year-old Simon Lang about the upcoming round-ups, urging him to spread word of the dangers. However, the round-up of the 26th had been well planned and secrecy maintained to such an extent that he was unable to let Simon and the rest of the family know in time. Simon, his 8- and 14-year-old sisters and their parents were arrested and sent to Saint-Pardoux-la Rivière – a *camp de triage*, or sorting camp – while Simon's older brother Armand was sent to Nexon. All were in line to be transported to Drancy.

Seeing the family's name on the lists, Strebler intervened on their behalf, arguing for the family's release since two of the children had French citizenship. He rushed to Nexon and managed to free Armand before bringing the family back together and putting them in contact with several families that he knew could be counted on to help them survive. Having done all he could in a short period of round-ups, the Streblers were denounced, but Aloyse managed to limit the damage to a transfer to Annecy. There, the Streblers, who remained childless themselves, continued to work hard protecting endangered Jewish families.

Escape from Mauzac

Pierre Bloch, Georges Bégué and the rest of the pilots who had been arrested at the Villa des Bois in Marseille the previous October were transferred from the Béleyme prison in Périgueux to the Mauzac camp in the Dordogne valley, 18 miles east of Bergerac. There they were put into a single barrack – a short-sighted decision that allowed the men to plan escape. Most were frustrated at their capture and eager to return to their jobs. They had already established contact with the outside because Gaby Bloch, Pierre's wife who had also been arrested in Marseille, was released to look after her three young children. Plans had to be made to get the five 'English' officers – Marc Jumeau, Jean le Harivel, Jack Hayes, Georges Langelaan and Michael Trotobas – and the six French officers – Bloch and Bégué, Francis Garel, Philippe Liewer, Robert Lyon and Raymond Roche – out. If the men could get out of prison and find their way to Lyon, then they could use an SOE escape route that was already in operation to get to England. Georges Bégué, knowing the area well having been born in Périgueux and being an extraordinarily resourceful agent as well as a more than competent engineer, led the escape.

On Bégué's instructions Gaby Bloch contacted Virginia Hall of the SOE Lyon network, who put Lazare Rachaline (Lucien) – a close friend of the Bloch family – to work. In the barracks the men made it appear that they had no wish to escape by decorating their hut, holding bridge tournaments and putting on a solemn face around other inmates, all the while developing a daily routine that reflected a resignation to sitting out the war. When a route of escape over the Pyrenées was established, Trotobas began a programme of physical training. Afternoons were spent playing pétanque in the yard, which allowed the men to study the wire fencing. Bégué also organised the men into small working cells in order to avoid the suspicion large groups attracted.

Gaby Bloch worked with Albert Rigoulet (Le Frisé) and Rachaline to devise a plan, and weeks later she began to turn the wheels. First, she needed to establish contact with a guard or guards on the inside of the prison, so each week during her weekly visits to see her husband she stayed overnight at a hotel restaurant where the guards went to chat and play cards. There she started by chatting to them, first winning them over by discussing nothing in particular. Eventually she got to know a guard named Anton Sévilla, an Andoulousian who was happy to assist in return for a place on the journey to London.[33] Another of the officers, Frenchman Philippe Liewer, knew a local lawyer named Brissonière who regularly visited him and kept him up to date with administration changes and information, and supplied tools. In the meantime, during her visits Gaby Bloch brought her husband pots of conserve and cigarettes to share with the men, inside which she put several small files, other small tools, nails and pieces of metal. With these Georges Bégué set about making a key that would open the door of their cell, which he did by stuffing bread into the locking mechanism to create an imprint. During the evenings the men sang songs to cover up the noises of Bégué working hard at filing metal. Using items that Bloch and Brissonière supplied, Bégué was able to construct a small wooden frame – *chevaux de frise* – which would hold up barbed wire while the men could climb under it. Once the men were carried clear of the prison to safety they would need to be accommodated somewhere safe while searches took place – the guard, Sévilla, agreed to help support them with this too.

The date of the escape was set for the night of 15 July 1942 once it had been established that Sévilla would be on duty that evening in the guard post nearest the men's barracks. An elderly woman with children walked past the camp at four o'clock in the afternoon – the signal that the plan was on.[34] One of the Frenchmen, a 60-year-old who did not wish to take part in the operation because of fear of reprisals on his family, threatened to inform on the operation as he was worried he would be linked to the attempt and his family would suffer anyway. As such, Bégué organised for a heavy dose of sleeping draft to be administered to him in the early evening.

As night fell the men waited nervously for the signal – Sévilla lighting his cigarette – which was to take place after midnight and before three o'clock. The signal eventually came a few minutes before the cut-off time and Bégué led the way, attaching a false door to the barracks so that the real one could be kept open and rolling carpet over the ground to avoid disturbance. All the men wore gloves to protect their hands and socks over their boots to avoid noise. It is probable that most of the camp inmates knew of the operation, and a guard interrupted the men at least once – luckily he was in the confidence of Sévilla and carried a message from him to tell them to be quieter.

Bégué pulled out the wooden posts and undid the wire enough for the men to get through. Once through himself he pulled on a string for the next man to come. The men were through in twelve minutes, and one by one they made their way to a nearby van, where Albert Rigoulet, having been informed of the operation by Mauzac resident Madame Vincent, was waiting to drive them away. Bégué reattached the wire to the posts, which he replanted, and the men were clear. They were driven 20 miles into the forest of Liorac, where they walked the final 10 miles to an abandoned farm and barn at Église-neuve-d'Issac. They spent a fortnight at that farm, sleeping during the day so as not to be spotted and doing their best to retain fitness during the night. Rigoulet, his wife or Sévilla brought them food daily, and new identity documents were procured with the help of SOE in London. After their two-week wait, in pairs they set off to Lyon, eventually all heading to Pérpignan, the Spanish border and eventually London, ready to retake their part in the war.

4

THE RISE OF THE MAQUIS

On 8 November 1942 Allied troops landed in North Africa, partly as a result of a request by Stalin to open a second front and direct German military strength away from the Soviet Union. France's position in Hitler's European view changed as the Allies were able to take up positions in the area from where the southern coast of the country could potentially be attacked. As a result German troops rolled across the demarcation line on 11 November 1942 in what was the first major sea change in the history of the French Resistance.

The occupation of the southern zone was a crushing blow for the people of the Dordogne. In the local paper, *Périgueux-Strasbourg Chronique Locale*, new orders were given to the population as dictated by the prefecture in conjunction with the military authorities. A curfew was brought in of 10 p.m., except for those with urgent business such as doctors and midwives. Those breaking the curfew would be brought in to the gendarmerie. All cafés and bars were to close by 9 p.m., and theatres, cinemas and music halls had to remain closed until further notice. Telephone communications were suspended, except for official business relating to supplies, medicine and national defence. Personal communications picked up on these lines would instantly be cut off.

However, once Germany had occupied the southern zone, the possibility for a militarised arm of the Resistance really took off. The armistice army was disbanded just a month later and for the second time in two years several thousand military personnel in the Dordogne were dismissed from duty. Though limited in numbers and equipment, many of those military men wanted to resist but many did not know quite how to go about it.

Of course, some effort had been put into the preservation of materiel, hidden as part of the CDM programme. In the town hall of Périgueux the prefect René Rivière had grown used to visits from leaders of the burgeoning Resistance – especially from those charged with ensuring that the armaments and munitions were well maintained and hidden. In his witness statement, Rivière described these meetings with Captain Pradet and his deputy, who had been sent to the city to ensure that the materiel was dealt with and protected with a view to ensuring swift distribution of functioning equipment once the time came. It was also important that those property and business owners on whose property the equipment was being stored were reassured that their interests were being kept in mind. Any concerns raised in the open could quickly lead to denunciations that could result in the CDM programme falling like a house of cards. Within the prefecture of the Dordogne, Mollard had found an ally in Madame Henriette Lutembacher and, through her, action had been taken to move arms, munitions and other equipment from the barracks of the 35th Régiment d'Artillerie in Périgueux to various caches in the countryside.

On the morning after the demarcation line was crossed and the first German troops began to roll into the southern zone, a dishevelled and anxious Captain Pradet came to the prefect's office. It was not lost on Pradet that those charged with the storage of equipment feared for their lives should the munitions be found. Equally Pradet knew that his superiors in Vichy did not intend for the plans to come to an end. He begged the prefect for new identity cards, food cards, realistic mission orders and authorities to enable them to be able to circulate in vehicles. Only the prefect could supply this vital documentation, but even he was dependent on a number of complicit functionaries in whom he could place his absolute trust. In Monsieur Puyjanmet, amongst others, he had an administrator who he knew was well versed in producing such documentation. Pradet brought names of those that needed new identities and Rivière's team produced the necessary identity cards, together with randomised serial numbers – a detail remembered by the most experienced and trustworthy of his team and without which discovery might be all too easy. The prefect himself ensured that new handwritten orders for tasks that required travel were issued to those that needed to move around the countryside, including such details as registration numbers of vehicles. Without all of this the materiel preserved under the CDM would have disappeared all too easily.

For those non-military personnel who had gambled on being part of the CDM networks, their entire raison d'être was challenged. How could they continue to resist? Not only were the Germans armed with information about all their operations since 1940 but, following the sinking of the French fleet at Toulon on 27 November 1942, the Vichy authorities themselves ordered armaments to be handed over. Despite the best efforts and dedication of the CDM teams, most aspects of the operation were given up by traitors, several of whom had been involved in locating suitable sites for crates to be buried. Precautions had been taken, however, and materiel in sealed containers had been dispersed around the region, while paperwork had been continually disposed of. Joseph Restamy, whose company had not only produced a prototype machine gun but was in the process of mass-producing the model in its many constituent parts, decided quickly that his enterprise had to come to an end. The parts were crated up, moved out and buried, and the company personnel also dispersed. Restamy himself went into hiding. Then someone talked, and the Germans discovered the company and all of its ramifications. Within the space of two months most CDM depots had been emptied and weaponry caches dug up, the vast majority of materiel gathered up by the German army. Only a small number of lighter weapons found their way into the hands of any paramilitary units.

The Military

Whereas Resistance networks and small groups that had developed up to that point had primarily been civilian in nature, now a significant number of military men were also looking to plan a move against the occupiers. Few career soldiers were, however, behind General de Gaulle and many scorned his efforts. The French army still had a presence in North Africa under General Henri Giraud, and for the upper echelons of the army, Giraud represented the better hope for France than two-star General de Gaulle who, having fled to Britain, was branded a traitor. De Gaulle's stock had fallen since Vichy had set out its Anglophobic agenda due to the events at Mers-el-Kébir in July 1940 when Churchill authorised the sinking of French ships whose commanders would not step down or scuttle their fleet. Churchill feared the French fleet falling into the hands of the Germans, which might have all but ended the war. A massive loss of French life resulted. Giraud, on the other hand, was tried and trusted and, like many soldiers, faithful to Pétain. At the beginning of the war Giraud had been a member of the Superior War Council and held very different views to de Gaulle over the best use of armoured divisions. Active in the Ardennes during the 1940 war, he was captured by the Germans and taken to a POW camp from where he made a remarkable escape. With the aid of an SOE agent, Giraud found his way back to Vichy France where he tried to persuade Pétain that collaboration was doomed to failure.

Prior to the dissolution of the armistice army, the 35th Régiment d'Artillerie Divisionnaire was stationed in the Daumesnil quarter of Périgueux, and Bergerac played home to the 26th Régiment d'Infanterie. Before escaping France and fleeing to Algeria, Giraud believed that the Allied forces would entrust the role of commander-in-chief of the Allied forces landing in Africa and Provence to him. So, on 3 November 1942, he passed command of civil and military forces of metropolitan France to General Aubert Frère – a highly rated army general. However, events turned out differently for Giraud, with no landings in Provence, the demarcation line crossed by the Germans and the southern zone subsequently occupied. But Giraud, officially commander-in-chief in Algiers, confirmed to Frère that he wanted him to be chief of the Resistance within France itself. Frère sent trusted military men he knew had already been involved with the CDM programme into the southern zone where they were told to visit former garrisons, organise those of a similar disposition and delegate responsibility.

Colonel Henri Zeller and Lieutenant Colonel Pfister arrived in Périgueux at the end of 1942 and established contact with Colonel Marchand ('le Manchot'), who was chosen to lead a new organisation in the region. Marchand's deputies ran battalions in nearby Brantôme and in Bergerac itself. Through the local leader of Combat – then an information gathering and communication network called Mouvement de Libération Française – the new group led by 'le Manchot' soon counted sixteen officers, seventy-five non-commissioned officers and around 200 combatants. The Organisation de Résistance de l'Armée (ORA) was formed at the end of January 1943 and a core existed in the Dordogne, as throughout the southern zone. Apolitical, its leaders wished to avenge the fall of France, but its loyalties lay with Pétain.

In the Dordogne region, ORA was grouped into four sectors: Dordogne-nord, Périgord-nord, Périgeux ville et sud and Bergerac-Dordogne-sud. Its militaristic experience was used to the maximum. Lieutenants Ménard and Cossot of the 26th Régiment d'Infanterie, for example, were deployed along with many others to the *service de la garde des voies et communications* – an area in which they were already experienced. This ability to call on men of experience at any time provided ample opportunities to train new recruits. Though grown from the armistice army, ORA didn't take on large numbers outside of Périgueux and Bergerac, where AS Maquis groups formed later in 1943 from the armed wings of Combat, Libération-sud and Le Franc-Tireur thrived. But, in the long run, the Dordogne ORA groups and those very Gaullist AS groups often merged or at least worked in unison with each other. Characteristically the ORA hierarchy wished to keep a distance from the 'interior resistance' because of their view that Pétain was a prisoner of the Germans, and they recognised the legitimacy of Vichy over de Gaulle's Free French movement.

Technical knowledge of armed combat was vital to the Resistance, and it was in this area that ORA led the field. They were able to train their combatants effectively in weaponry parachuted into France from London. As the 'Giraudist' arm of the militaristic Resistance, the ORA of 1943 had no links with de Gaulle's French London-based intelligence service, Colonel Passy's BCRA, but had instead developed links with Buckmaster's SOE. As a result of its efforts in the CDM, it was the best armed of any of the early groups but the number of civilians joining its ranks never swelled, unlike the AS and Franc-Tireurs et Partisans (FTP) Maquis groups of the countryside. Those Maquis formed from the Gaullist AS were also often led by military men but were joined by a great many civilians, especially when young men were demanded for work in Germany under the Service de Travail Obligatoire (STO) from February 1943 onwards. Both organisations were ready to train new members, but neither were looking for an open fight with the Germans. Weapons training was key to their immediate functions, as was preparation of sabotage teams.

Prior to the entry of the Wehrmacht into the southern zone few German soldiers of any type were seen. But by mid November 1942 they were in most towns and, by the beginning of 1943, the sight of Germans in urban areas was part of daily life. Military vehicles drove along the main roads, soldiers sat in cafés and officers travelled around towns in luxury French and Belgian cars. Wehrmacht soldiers on garrison duty in the Périgord were largely well disciplined, despite many being no older than 17 or 18, and were drawn from Upper Silesia. They were instructed by officers to avoid interaction with the public, and when they did they were courteous. These troops posed few problems for those engaged in Resistance activity.

The same could not be said for the Gestapo. Périgueux was chosen as an *Aussenstelle* (regional base) and even though the first arrivals, housed in a first-floor town-centre office suite, comprised only two administrative bodies and an interpreter, they were given a direct telephone link to the commanders of the Wehrmacht staying in the nearby Hôtel de Commerce. The primary role of the agents was to locate and record the whereabouts of Jews – particularly those who had arrived from Alsace-Lorraine – as well as carry out checks on all those involved in local administration. This included the local French police forces. The interpreter was called Werner Gersbach and referred to himself as Willy Birkenfeld. More commonly known as 'Willy', he spoke four languages, including impressive unac-cented French, and had been a pianist on a cruise ship before the war. He became well known in Périgueux as he frequented bars and restaurants, spending vast sums of money. Initially considered one of 'the least worst' of the Germans to come to the region, his stock would fall amongst the population as the occupation went on. He was one of the last Germans to leave Périgueux.

The FTP

While Libération-sud represented the socialist side of the Resistance, the PCF, underground since 1939 due to the Germano-Soviet accord, had to bide its time. Those undeterred by having to be anti-Vichy and pro-Ger-many, but who dreamed of the past days of the Front Populaire, had been left in an uncomfortable position. Some took matters into their own hands. In Limoges, schoolteacher Georges Guingouin had no intention of waiting. For him and other militant communists the liberation and independence of France was an issue that far outweighed political consideration. Born in 1913, Guingouin proclaimed himself ready for an anti-Nazi struggle in 1940. He wrote and distributed tracts denouncing both Vichy and Hitler while making clear his communist idealism. When threatened with arrest he took to the countryside, becoming one of, if not the first, *maquisard*. In woodland near Eymoutiers in the Limousin countryside, he dug a shelter and there he typed his tracts, only emerging at night to meet friendly contacts. Those of a communist leaning who wished to express dissatisfaction but not break with the party line justified their stance by claiming that the freedom of France was a patriotic necessity and had nothing to do with the imperialist war being waged by the Allies.

The official PCF remained underground, with many of its leaders either pursued by Vichy authorities or already interned or deported. Nevertheless, in May 1941 the underground party created the Front National (FN), which was theoretically pluralist to bring together patriots from a broad spectrum of backgrounds, including Christian Democrats such as Georges Bidault, conservatives, ecclesiasticals, radicals, progressives and conservatives. In reality, however, the party was run by communists who occupied the main positions. Satellite groups such as the Fronts des Écrivains, des Médicins, des Avocats, des Commerçants and the Forces Unies de la Jeunesse Patriotique and l'Union des Femmes Françaises emerged, similarly driven by the PCF.

Paradoxically the PCF's prayers were answered by the Nazi invasion of the Soviet Union on 22 June 1941. The creation of a second front put further strain on the German war effort that later led to the need to bleed the Reich, including France, for further supplies and resources. More importantly, as far as the French population was concerned, many communists who up to that point had been torn between the Soviet Union's ties to Hitler and their own bruised patriotism now permitted themselves to declare themselves anti-Germany and anti-Vichy, leaving behind the imperialist war claims.

Hostility towards the Third Reich was assured as the international communist community confirmed its change in strategy. Up until that day criticism of the Vichy regime by the underground Communist Party had centred on points such as prisoner-of-war release and food supplies, but it now abruptly transformed into an ideological battle. In August 1941 a meeting was held in Périgueux, attended by Georges Guingouin and Clovis Chirin, a militant communist and future Maquis leader who travelled from Clermont-Ferrand. Communist committees formed from the Front National were planned, and these were the prcursor to the FTP. As a result, small military groups sponsored by the Communist Party began to form in the Dordogne around Bergerac and Mussidan. Before too long communist tracts began to appear, the wording of which worried those already involved in Gaullist Resistance. The last lines of several of them read: 'Long live the USSR, Land of the Workers – Allies of England – Allies of America – Long live Stalin, brilliant continuator of Lenin, friend of all Humanity.'

In February 1942 the underground PCF formed the FTP, tasked with taking the armed struggle to the occupier. Charles Tillon headed the new initiative, alongside Marcel Prenant who would ensure military training for members. The first group was formed near Paris in March 1942 from the Main d'Oeuvre Immigré, which, combined with communist combatants, became known as the FTP-MOI (Main d'Oeuvre Immigré). Paris and Toulouse both witnessed campaigns of violence waged by these battalions, which consisted of Slavs, Armenians, Jews, Romanians, Italians and Spaniards fighting alongside French and Germans opposed to Nazism. The early efforts of the FTP-MOI were met with satisfaction in London from the side of the British SOE, while de Gaulle's BCRA were far from happy at events. For de Gaulle not only did the action oppose his own views on warfare, but he believed that it would undoubtedly lead to wasted lives and potentially all manner of leaked information.

In a history of the FTP of the Périgord written in 1945,[1] Roger Bellanger paints in highly emotive language some of the events and motivations behind the creation of the first Maquis of the Dordogne. Written so soon after the events, Bellanger captures an interesting contemporary view of inspirations to those Périgourdin communists who decided to take up arms. He cites their inspiration as being particularly drawn from the 1st French Brigade's defiance at the bridge of Bir-Hakeim during the Battle of Gazala in May and June 1942, during which General Koenig repelled Rommel's advance. More poignantly he refers to Châteaubriand where, the previous October, twenty-seven suspected communists had been shot by a German firing squad. The group included 17-year-old activist Guy Moquet, a young man whose name became an inspiration to the Resistance. The executions followed a number of early attacks by French communists on the occupiers over a matter of days, including the derailment of a train near Rouen carried out with the aid of engine drivers and other *cheminots*, and the attempted assassination of two German officers in Nantes. One commanding officer, Karl Holtz, died of his injuries. The following day another German officer was killed in Bordeaux in similar circumstances, leading to the German demand for Vichy Minister for the Interior Pierre Pucheu to select candidates for execution. Pucheu selected communists over 'Good Frenchmen' such as veterans of the First World War.

During the summer of 1942 a request by the Allies to conduct a policy of propaganda and restrained direct 'action' was followed, alongside the creation of an ever-increasing network of *légaux* – men and women who belonged to the Resistance while continuing a normal non-clandestine existence. Then came 'Stalingrad', an event which was, according to Bellanger, a 'torch of sacrifice for which is owed to the Russian people and their valiant Red Army the esteem and gratitude of all combatants of freedom'. Those communists, whether party members or just sympathisers, who had maintained their confidence in their clandestine national leadership were particularly relieved. Early defeats for the Red Army turned into victories as winter set in, while the invasion of the Wehrmacht in November 1942 rendered the southern zone nothing more than an occupied country; this provided further recruits, as did the persecution of Jews, many of whom had come to France from Eastern Europe.

The strategy of the FTP was based on a Soviet perspective of warfare. From June 1941 it was one of 'direct action which must weaken the German army from the rear and contain the maximum possible of enemy forces'.[2] However, the lack of success and overall effectiveness of sabotages carried out by the earliest detachments at the end of 1942 and the beginning of 1943 led to the Comité Militaire Interrégional (CMR) of the FTP to call for a delay to further action, putting in place measures to mitigate the military inexperience and weakness of the recruits' overall training.

Just before the crossing of the demarcation line by the Germans, a Périgueux builder named André Jouhand accepted the immense responsibility of the underground leadership of the Communist Party for the region. He, along with several militants, set the ball rolling by distributing propaganda in the region's capital. Soon, it became clear that he would need to flee the city. In the meantime, direction was taken from the Limousin region, which bordered the north-east of the Dordogne and where a former mayor called Georges Lasalle ('Félix') was directing matters. In autumn 1942 Lasalle, in his 40s and whose 'outward debonair aspects hid a rare steadfastness',[3] came to the north of the department where conditions were, it seemed, ripe for FTP militancy. He was accompanied by Jean-Dolet Blanchou, the son of a well-respected and trusted family from La Coquille, a village north of Thiviers, on the Dordogne–Limousin border. They met at nearby La Sarlandie with a number of militants, thus developing a number of 'core' Resistance groups whose primary aim was propaganda. Despite the evident fear of those involved, areas around Jumilhac, Lanouaille and Excideuil had their own groups, usually of around three people. The implementation of these groups of *légaux* allowed for the later appearance of armed formations, providing a support structure that the Maquis could draw on.

The combination of the Allied landing in North Africa in November 1942 – a notable victory that enabled the French to return to combat alongside the Allies albeit in a minor way – the crossing of the demarcation line, the scuttling of the proud French fleet in Toulon and early 1943 news from Stalingrad that the Nazi invasion had been repelled at the city set the stage. In January 1943 Resistance by those who signed up for armed activity passed from the defensive to the offensive.[4] Groups respected neither ideological nor geographical boundaries. Just as early groups didn't attract or turn away *résistants* because of their political leanings or social or militaristic backgrounds, borders between *parois*, *communes* or *departments* counted for nothing. Very little about the way early groups came into existence was neat. Those of the north-east and the centre of the department had much to do with the more industrialised Corrèze, as well as Limousin. The early armed groups of the north-west had very clear links with the Charente while in the south the valley of the Dordogne was a geographical unit in itself that extended into the Lot in the east and the Gironde in the west.

STO (Service de Travail Obligatoire)

As it became clear that the Relève of 1942 had at least partially failed, an additional layer was added to Sauckel's quest for workers. The Service de Travail Obligatoire (STO) law of 16 February 1943 was a milestone as it created a necessity for a section of society to be sorted into categories of workers, a proportion being 'deported' to Germany. Sauckel demanded an additional 250,000 workers to those already deported in mid March. The law, which was refined and amended over the following months, began with the obligation of young men born between 1920 and 1922 to be registered at the local town hall and classified. Certain occupations were exempt, including agricultural workers and miners. Students could have their call-ups deferred until September while women saw no change to what had been put in place the previous year. These rules remained in place for all, regardless of the new STO rules. Categories were drawn up depending on workers: those men not extempt would fall into one of the two categories that enforced employment in German-owned industries within France or in Germany itself.

The new rules created distress and anger, but Vichy did listen to some of the complaints made. Some men would be entering something akin to another period of conscription having just finished their military service or having spent eight months in the Chantiers de la Jeunesse. As a result, changes were made with some categories of exemption taken away in order to balance the numbers. The changes didn't take place for two months, by which time Sauckel had requested a further 220,000 workers, which was accepted by Laval in April 1943 and was to be fulfilled by the end of June that year. The target market was largely the same, with the addition of men born in the last quarter of 1919 who had not been mobilised in 1939. Whereas the Relève had drifted rather aimlessly, the STO was precise and purposeful. Laval oversaw its implementation and ensured that prefectures and town halls were put under considerable pressure to deliver their quotas. Local administrations were pushed to breaking point by a process made difficult by both its short deadlines and public reaction. STO pushed small towns and communes hard by reducing the number of men available for work at home, while prefectures struggled to locate the numbers requested to send to the STO. Both waves, conducted in the months leading up to Sauckel's deadlines, proved difficult to refuse and escape for those targeted. Most tried to do neither. Some, however, did just that.

Referred to by Vichy authorities as *défaillants* or *insoumis*, and later as *réfractaires*, some men took to hiding. The need to melt into clandestinity was not altogether new. During the previous two years networks and centres of willing helpers had developed, and good systems of hiding had been forged for persecuted Jews as well as for early *résistants*. If found, these young men could be held in centres close to railway centres then dispatched straight to

Germany, lending the STO a straight comparison with 'de facto deportation'.[5] *Réfractaires* itself is a strong term, but for Catholics it has positive connotations with priests' resistance to the Civil Constitution of the clergy during the 1789 revolution. The valley of the Dordogne, leading into the Haute-Corrèze, had a long history of refuge, having done so for the priests as well as for Huguenots, and men escaping conscription to the armies of Napoleon.

René Sabourdy ('Tarzan'), who had gained military knowledge during his brief time with the armistice army, and Roger Faure, a baby-faced 20-year-old who used the *nom de guerre* Jim, took their places at the head of the new groups in the early summer of 1943. Both men had been in hiding after being caught up by the exigencies of Laval's new agreement with General Sauckel, known as the Service de Travail Obligatoire.

While the STO had a significant effect on the growth and make-up of Maquis groups, in regions such as the Dordogne its initial impact was tempered by the nature of the region. Agricultural workers were initially exempt from both the Relève and the STO, and then in February 1944 certain railway workers also became exempt. It followed that many young men of the farming *paysan* communities were untroubled directly at first. Around 5,500 men from the Dordogne travelled to Germany because they did not wish to become outlaws.

Fines of between 200,000 and 100,000 francs, and prison sentences of three to five months became attributable for those who didn't respect the new institution. However, those who hid, becoming *réfractaires*, were not unanimous in deciding to enter the Resistance, at least not immediately. For some, hiding out was enough. The ranks swelled much later, when Allied advances ensured that German defeat was no longer a pipe dream, and some who joined did so for the wrong reasons and did not stay on.

Despite all of these nuanced calibrations, the STO did provide a boost to numbers of recruits to the Resistance as men left villages and towns and fled to the countryside. For those who fled, Maquis groups, if they could be located, often provided the psychological and physical outlet for their frustrations, as well as a framework within which to survive.

Whether *réfractaires* joined Maquis groups or not, for Vichy they were a problem. Firstly, they were potential troublemakers. Those who evaded the STO were law-breakers by default, while those who joined the Maquis were considered by many as criminals. For the Reich they were not political opponents, but rather opponents of the civil order, which was meant to be the responsibility of the French. Vichy authorities were keen, however, to appear diplomatic and did try to draw a line between those who had made a rash decision to flee the STO and those who had become *bandits* and *terroristes* by joining the Maquis. An amnesty was offered in the latter half of 1943 for those who wished to change their mind to hand themselves in and avoid deportation. It was a huge failure.

Vichy now faced a problem. The STO had boosted Maquis numbers throughout the southern zone and the problem had to be dealt with on both a civic and political level. The idea of an insurrection was unpalatable and could even lead to civil conflict. However, the Reich had insisted on an armistice that had granted 'Vichy power on paper without actual power, a grand title and grand responsibilities but not the means to carry them out'.[6] Waiting outside cinemas and swooping into village centres in an attempt to find *réfractaires* would achieve minimal results. As gendarmes were local police, the Vichy authorities found that the rounding up of people for arrest and deportation was not being done well because of familial and friend links and local grievances. From early 1943 onwards *maquisards* would have to be hunted down and the prefects needed new tools. Denunciations would have to be dealt with seriously, and tracking would need to be carried out with brutality if required.

The Milice

On 5 January 1943 Marshal Pétain made a speech celebrating the efforts of the fighters of the Service d'Ordre Légionnaire (SOL) in North Africa. Joseph Darnand's creation was then, with the blessing and signature of Pierre Laval, turned into the Milice Française. Darnand was a right-winger of limited political ability and intelligence who had previously been involved in the terrorist group La Cagoule against the Front Populaire. This new organisation, born from the most extreme edges of the Légion was nominally the responsibility of Laval, but Darnand took up residence in Vichy and led it with vigour. Hitler had already told Laval in December 1942 that he was keen to see the creation of an internal French police force that would assist the Germans with the preservation of law and order. Darnand ensured that his troops not only looked the part in their black uniforms, but also recruited the most ruthless servants to be found. Drawing from the existing SOL, and even from known criminal networks, the aims of the Milice were set out clearly from the start. The eradication of the '*lèpre juive*' (Jewish leprosy) and communism were high on that list, as was the hunting and arrest of members of the Resistance.

The Milice that emerged as a result of the law of 30 December 1942 was a paramilitary organisation that insisted its members be 'volunteers, morally ready and physically able, not only to support the new State by their actions, but also to participate in maintaining order'. On 28 February 1943, throughout France the departmental SOL met for the official trans-formation into the Milice. The former SOL members, led by their chief, Tomasi, lay a wreath at the Monument aux Morts then marched to the municipal theatre, where speeches were given by Tomasi and the new pre-fect, Jean Popineau. The new *miliciens* were reminded of their role 'at a time when our army no longer exists and where a new organisation must rally against communism'.

Popineau arrived as prefect in the dying weeks of 1942 and presented a complex picture to those who worked under him. Approachable and softly spoken, he did little in the early weeks to try to root out Resistance within the administrative organisations over which he now held sway. He was also very supportive of the new Milice. It may be that he was keeping his options open and, being a man of intelligence, knew the importance of avoiding burning bridges. He followed instructions from Vichy with abso-lute fidelity, and did not flinch in their application. He was not, however, by any means pro-Germany. In this way he represented a large proportion of the Périgourdin population at that time. He had absolute faith in Pétain who, for him, represented *la verité française*.[7]

The Milice was not the only force that the Vichy authorities could call upon to maintain law and order. The Groupe Mobile de Réserve (GMR) was a civilian force, attached to the Service Régional de la Sécurité Publique and commanded by the *intendant de police*. It was created to restore some of the power lost to Vichy by the reduction of its army to 100,000 men, then to nothing after the southern zone was occupied. The *garde mobile* was attached to the army and had been reduced to practically noth-ing, so although it had been relied upon for interior law-and-order tasks, numbers had become insufficient. The GMR was, however, put under the overall control of René Bouquet so was not subject to the terms of the armistice. Unlike local gendarmeries staffed by police usually from the local area, members of the GMR were placed anywhere in the country, allowing them a certain additional independence of action.

Into the Maquis

In 1943, having served an apprenticeship as an engineer, Roger Ranoux was working for a flour mill as a lorry driver, delivering flour to the hundreds of *boulangeries* in the area. As he was in employment that counted as vital for the provision of food, he was exempt from a call-up to work in Germany under the STO programme. However, he had made a pact with his brothers that, should one of them be called up, they would all enter a Maquis. Both his brothers qualified in February 1943 so, spurred on by news of Soviet victory in Stalingrad and with full agreement from their father, Guy and Roger set out for the Corrèze, older brother Paul having already left. They took with them the address of a contact in Grand-Chastang, and by the summer the group Lucien Sampaix had been founded. Roger, extremely tall but approachable and clear in thought, was a natural leader and became second in command of the new group almost immediately. He took on the *nom de guerre* 'Hercule'. His brother Guy, much shorter than him to an almost comical degree, was named 'Mickey'.

During his time in the twenty-four-strong group FTP Lucien Sampaix,[*] Roger Ranoux learned a lot about running a successful Maquis from his immediate superior, a chief sergeant from the army. The Maquis troops were to behave impeccably, particularly towards the population on whom they would rely absolutely for shelter, supplies, information and secrecy. Their missions involved sabotage and suppression of agents to the enemy. Following a failed mission in July 1943, Roger was forced to tighten security, and the group moved a number of times, suffering attacks from the GMR wherever they went. The group would from that point be much more mobile, and change camps regularly. Then, in autumn 1943, some members of Lucien Sampaix came across a patrol of gendarmes and a firefight broke out in which several

---

[*] Named after a militant of the Communist Party and a journalist for the newspaper *L'Humanité* who was shot on 15 September 1941.

policemen were killed. The gendarmerie requested a meeting with the Resistance and Ranoux attended, open and diplomatic. The delegates decided that French police and French *résistants* should not fire on each other, and a deal was struck. In future the gendarmes of the Corrèze would turn a blind eye to the Resistance and the two would co-exist.

★★★

Lucien Cournil saw his older brother, Jean, join the first Maquis in the Terassonais in early 1943. This was an AS group, led by Docteur Pierre Daunois, that was named after a local communist politician Maurice Dujarric. This odd mix – a Gaullist group named after a well-known local communist – was illustrative of the unusual nature of the beginnings of the Resistance in and around Terrasson. In that small part of the Périgord the various factions of what would later become a unified Resistance, operated side by side without difficulty.[8] This was not the case elsewhere in France, in the southern zone or even in the Dordogne, where political and strategical differences created divisions between the various factions. Here in the Terassonais, just a few kilometres from the border with the Corrèze, and 20km from Brive, Resistance developed in an unusual fashion.

It began on 20 June 1942, during a meeting held in the barracks of the Terrasson fire service. Jean Rouby, captain of the fire service, was employed primarily as a plumber who travelled outside the confines of the Dordogne and into the Corrèze, servicing facilities and stations for the railway. On several occasions Rouby had seen what was happening in Brive where Resistance was evolving, and on that June evening he called a meeting to propose that such action be replicated in the eastern Dordogne. This was not the first time such opposition had been considered in Terrasson. When Edmond Michelet had produced his Péguy-inspired pamphlets in Brive in June 1940, it had only taken a matter of weeks for word and copies to spread into Terrasson, and nearby Montignac and Excideuil. There had been murmurings of 'should we, shouldn't we?', but Rouby was the first to put something in place by calling the meeting – a meeting that was, importantly, for everyone. Factions had yet to form, and attending were people who would become members of the AS as well as those who would become FTP. But the common goal and starting point was shared amongst a community that refused to be torn apart by antagonisms.

Lucien took a different path to his brother, who had taken to clandestine life as a *maquisard*. An apprentice barber in 1941, Lucien supplemented his income by delivering newspapers, *La France* and *La Petite Gironde*, around Le Lardin. He was approached by a friend already engaged in the Combat movement. It mattered not that Lucien was known to have communist views – the only views that were important were those shared by people willing to oppose the Vichy regime. Lucien agreed to take on a further task: along with the papers he was due to deliver each day, he agreed to take copies of *Combat*, the most successful clandestine paper in the area, supplied to him by contacts of Lacombe. Choosing his audience very carefully, Lucien slid a copy of *Combat* inside the newspapers of those he felt would be open to the rejection of Vichy's collaboration. Given that he was well known for making the deliveries, this opened him up to enormous potential difficulties. Happily, all went well for him on that front.

Along with his role in Combat, Lucien also became the local representative of the Forces Unies de la Jeunesse Patriotique (FUJP). As the FTP grew in the region it, like all Maquis groups, needed a network of *légaux* – men and women who supported the group while continuing to occupy their day jobs. Lucien became a vital link, copying and dispersing messages that came to him from Paris to *maquisards* throughout that sector. The FTP grew in the region and the first group, named Jacquou le Croquant, appeared soon after. Lucien used a female liaison agent to travel to and from the Maquis camps scattered around Thenon, Excideuil and Montignac.

Lessons for *Maquisards*

Roger Faure and René Sabourdy had been hiding as *réfractaires* for several months already. In their case, sufficient young *réfractaires* were arriving, ready to be formed into fighting military units. Most of the FTP 'soldiers' brought under the command of 'Tarzan' and 'Jim' in the Forêt de Vieillecour in June 1943 were *réfractaires*. Camps were set up close to each other, with only a few hundred metres of separation between them, and holes were dug into the ground, creating a semi-permanent encampment camouflaged with branches and other natural resources. When, on 10 August, several hundred GMR attacked the betrayed camp, the earliest Maquis of the Dordogne learned several harsh lessons. The groups had, over the previous few weeks, undertaken several attacks on wheat threshers because of the number of them being sent to Germany. Of course, the *paysans* were being attacked and denunciations would follow. Secondly, the groups had begun their operations before being adequately armed and trained. The groups in the Forêt de Vieillecour had received no weaponry or munitions, and had only a few old rifles between them, which proved wholly inadequate and led to most of the men being arrested. Lastly, the camp was too dug in. As Spanish Republican fighters arrived in the Maquis, they brought with them the know-how of guerrilla warfare, of which one of the most important rules was to be mobile, and not to stay in any one place for too long.

Similar lessons had been learned further west in the Haute-Corrèze just two months previously by the AS. Having established one of the first Maquis at the same time as that in the Forêt de Vieillecour, an armed camp was set up by the AS of Neuvic, Ussel, Tulle and Lapleu. It was known as the Camp de Chambon and incorporated the ideals of the AS. It was sufficiently armed, well provisioned, isolated and served as the ideal *école de cadres*, where *réfractaires* could be trained by military men. It worked well until it was surprised at dawn on 15 June by several hundred GMR. Shots wounded two *maquisards* while two others were arrested. Lessons learned included the necessity to rethink what a Maquis camp should consist of: isolation was not sufficient; security had to be tighter; and camps had to be much more mobile, located in areas that were less wild but where information could be passed along chains quickly and effectively.

The events of the Forêt de Vieillecour led to the arrest of René Sabourdy and nine of his men, who were taken to the camp of Saint-Paul-d'Eyjeaux ready for deportation. Sabourdy escaped and re-entered the Maquis several months later. Roger Faure's group had managed to escape in time and the men set off for the Sorges, where they could pass on their experiences to a new Maquis, Gabrielli, which was gathering strength. Further groups grew up in the north-east of the department, in Firbeix and Sarlande, where a former officer of the Spanish Republicans, José Gonzalvo, began with a dozen or so young men. Before long the area north of Thiviers was crowded with Maquis.

It was not just the FTP that were active in the area. René Tallet was 21 years old when he was decommissioned from the army at the beginning of 1941, returning home to Queyroi de Sarlande. There he helped run his family's company that dealt in farm machinery; on returning, his hopes of becoming a pilot in the army dashed, he discovered that his brother Emile was of a similar mind: furious about the fall of France. The Tallet brothers were not alone in their determination to do something, and when René spoke to his friend René Ségui, a garage owner in Sarlande with whom he loved to work on vehicles, they decided to gather men they knew around them. At the beginning of 1942 they began their own Resistance network, Jove, co-created and led by Marie Bartette, the daughter of an officer who had begun by distributing tracts in Arcachon. They were joined by, amongst others, Bissou, a lumberjack of immense strength who later became René Tallet's bodyguard.

The men's involvement with the Jove network resulted from contact with Colonel Giovanni, who lived in nearby Saint-Yrieux-La-Perche and had installed a hub of information, complete with a radio contact to London on all known Resistance activity in the south of France. Ségui had taken the lead and the *nom de guerre* 'Violette'. Soon, as more and more Germans circulated around the area, Colonel Giovanni was forced into hiding. Ségui followed him, taking refuge in woodland and provided with food each day by his parents.

In early 1943 René Tallet also visited Ségui, who told him that he wanted him to take on the name 'Violette', probably in a bid to retain contacts made while the latter was forced to stay out of sight. At a similar time Tallet made contact with a group of *résistants* in Thiviers that had emerged as a vital crossroads for both Resistance networks and German troop movements. Located between Limoges and Périgueux, with good roads towards Tulle and Brive to the east and the Gironde to the west, later that year the Milice would set up a headquarters at a hotel in the town, so busy was the area with Maquis activity. At Thiviers contact was made with Charles Serre (Yvette) who, as well as having developed Combat, was hard at work as head of the AS for the northern sector of the Dordogne. Serre's immediate deputy, Rodolphe Cézard, would soon become another of the leader of the Resistance in the Périgord, when he took charge of Brigade Rac.

The Tallet brothers, benefiting from the cover of the family business which helped keep Vichy police forces off their scent, helped many young men find their way into the Resistance, or into hiding in nearby farms. At Queyroi, a solid group of men gathered around René Tallet in particular, whose leadership qualities were exceptional. Before long the Groupe

Violette was a disciplined and committed Maquis, only lacking in resources. They were armed with old rifles, several revolvers and limited stocks of gun cartridges. Still yet to learn the lessons of guerrilla warfare and camp mobility, the men dug trenches in woodland, creating semi-underground shelters, and built makeshift huts. Further contacts were made, including with the Maquis de Payzac, led by Raoul Audrerie, who had founded a Maquis group at Chatreix near to the gorges of the River Auvézère. Audrerie had been a member of the special forces when, on 29 May 1940, a German bullet entered his right lung. He was first taken prisoner and transported to Germany and then released in early 1941 due to ill health. He returned to Payzac where the injury limited him physically. The bullet was never extracted and Audrerie often said that it acted as a barometer, telling him of any change in the weather.

Early in 1943 Audrerie was contacted by seven men who asked if he could help them avoid being sent to Germany.[9] Despite his injury, Audrerie had determined to fight until the very end, so with Raymond Pivert and several others, including the Mayor of Savignac Fernand Devaud, a meeting was held to discuss whether the area around Payzac-Savignac could maintain, feed and shelter an armed unit. The men decided that it had to happen. Fernand Devaud became the elder statesman and chief, as well as the civilian face of the group, becoming known as the 'Papy'. Audrerie agreed to take on the military training.

In a speech made forty years later, Raymond Pivert gave what, in his eyes, was the recipe for a good young *maquisard*, and a description of what he should expect of a life in the Maquis. Firstly, the man should be 20 years old or younger, and a fervent patriot. He should also be reckless, as an awareness of the strength of the enemy ahead required an obliviousness to danger. Pivert added that the ideal *maquisard* would have courage: all Franc-Tireurs were illegal fighters, and all international codes made it clear that such combatants could be shot if taken prisoner. After tearing himself away from his parents, his home, his work, his farm, the *maquisard* should be ready to uproot to cramped living quarters. He would expect to climb through rough thickets, collecting old barbed wire to use in the construction of fences around the camp. He would have to dig out a shelter, cover it with branches, then earth and finally sprinkle grass seed so as to camouflage it from planes overhead. Once sheltered, he should search for arms, involving trudging around the countryside and visiting the homes of combatants of the First World War, begging for or stealing any old pistols or rifles buried under rubbish at the back of sheds or stuffed next to the fireplace. The best *maquisards* would take the weapons back to camp and make them operational.

Life in the early camps was described as simple, almost sleepy, with little to be seen before midday other than the sentry guards as most activities took place at night. Mealtimes might consist of a *ragout de pommes de terres* (potato stew) prepared by a local farmer, with meat being extremely rare. However, the early days of the Camp de Payzac, as described by Pivert – serene and poetic, and far removed from the horror of deportation under STO – could not last. As more *réfractaires* arrived, it became almost impossible to shelter them sufficiently. During the summer and autumn of 1943, as Raoul Audrerie took the name 'Crapaud', the Maquis de Payzac grew to nearly 200 men. The camp could not be maintained by villagers and farmers where it was: it had become too dangerous. A new location was needed where at least some of the men could gather, and Audrerie could train them. An *école de cadres* could be set up, and men from Bataillon Violette could benefit too. They found was a deserted mill known as Pont Lasveyras, deep in a hardly accessible valley on the edge of a fast-moving river.

The Légaux and the Maquis

Claudette Négrier was 12 years old when the war broke out and 16 when she committed her first act of protest. Born in Vergt, her parents owned and ran a town-centre café called Rendez-vous des Chasseurs. Her father was an *aumonier*, skilled with servicing guns and hunting equipment, which he also sold. His shop also sold bicycles and fishing equipment. Claudette was an only child but grew up surrounded by others in the café, where she learned much about life. Her aunt and cousin, both of whom had husbands who were prisoners of war, moved in with them. Her family did not discuss politics so much as the importance of freedom and human rights. Her primary school teachers in the *école communale de Vergt* instilled in her solid republican principles and the importance of tolerance, while her grandfather told her about the Great War and the dangers of fascism. Growing up, the advent of the Front Populaire was positive for her family, not for its material benefits but for the hope it gave those she knew and loved.[10] The community of Vergt had always been home to a wide variety of people and the mix of Alsatian refugees and Spanish Republicans that came to the café and her life taught her all she needed to know about fascism, Hitler and the strain that France was under. The café had a large room that Claudette's mother sometimes used as a canteen for the refugees from Alsace-Lorraine and on market days it was also used as a cinema.

Claudette was sent to live with her grandmother in the Saint-Jean area of Périgueux in 1940, at the age of 13, in order to attend *les cours complémentaires* there, but she returned to Périgueux every other weekend to see her parents, using the *tacot* – a small train that ran from Périgueux to Vergt. When France fell to the Germans, the atmosphere in Périgueux changed noticeably, while in Vergt many locals became aware of a Maquis forming nearby. At school Claudette did all she could to protest – something at the very centre of her nature. She sewed as many metal buttons as she could find onto her coat when the Germans were requisitioning spare metal. She sang 'Vous n'aurez pas l'Alsace et la Lorraine' while passing a sentry guard on her way to and from physical education lessons, warranting a visit to the school from the Gestapo, and she refused to raise the flag at the end of the school day. However, it was for refusing to sing '*Maréchal, nous voilà*' that she was excluded from school for a short time, her grandmother being complicit in keeping that information from her parents.

In the summer of 1943, as Groupe Mireille was forming in the Durestal woods, near Cendrieux, drawing in *réfractaires* from the area around Vergt, the Rendez-vous des Chasseurs café became a meeting point for a number of local *résistants*, who Claudette came to know. Her father fixed weapons for Marc Goldman ('Mirelle') and stored some armaments and ammunition. Elsewhere in the village the local *pharmacien* André Boubaud and his wife Alice were not only directing young men to the Maquis, but were also providing shelter to Jean-Paul Seret-Mangold, who was acting as a liaison agent between the nearby Maquis and his father in Périgueux, an AS leader.

Alfred Hauswirth, called Freddy by all who knew him, arrived in Périgueux with his compatriots from Strasbourg in 1939. He was 15 years old and alone, one of the many *enfants de l'Assistance publique* and, as such, was given a home in Parrot, a Périgueux quarter where a *centre d'hébergement* was set up for refugee children under the direction of Monsieur Gagnerie, inspector for the Assistance Publique de Périgueux. The centre was run by

Alice Garrigou, who became known to the youngsters under her care as Maman Alice. As a full-time resident of the centre, Freddy became close to Alice – they were almost family.

Freddy attended the *école professionel* in Périgueux from 1939 and it was there he met Jean-Paul Seret-Mangold, son of Charles Mangold and another Alsatian refugee. Extremely able, he studied away having been awarded a scholarship in Chambery between 1942 and 1943, and on his return to Périgueux he was interested to hear from his friends from the north, including Jean-Paul, of the Resistance in the Périgord. Goldman had been arrested but a new group that had been formed in January 1943 by Antoine Diener (Ancel) had taken its place in the forest of Durestal. Importantly for both Jean-Paul and Freddy, Diener and his brother-in-law Gustave Houver were creating a Maquis that would, when the moment came, liberate their homeland, Alsace-Lorraine. Jean-Paul took Freddy to see Alice Boubaud at the *pharmacie*, and she directed him to the Ancel group.

After having spent six months at *chantier de jeunesse* (youth camp) 30 in 1942 in Saint-Pé-de-Bigorre, André Danède returned to the family home in Cornille, on the route from Périgueux to Limoges. His mother worked in a nearby château, and André took up work in the forestry alongside a number of Spanish immigrants. In 1943 he was called up to the STO but, not wishing to go to Germany, he asked for a *carte de travail* (work permit) at the Cornille town hall but was refused. Using several contacts, he got in touch with Monsieur Châteauraynaud from nearby Sorges who, André knew, was part of the Resistance, as a *légal*. He managed to get the card which exempted André from STO as a necessary worker. It also meant that he had permission to travel around the region which made him an asset to any potential Resistance groups.

It did not take long for him to be approached by Jean Damis, a local from Les Piles. Damis led him to a nearby wood, and to a clearing, where he was introduced to six more people. There, in June 1943, they began one of the very earliest Maquis groups. Their armaments were rudimentary and had been taken from a number of sources, including requisitioning the materiel that the armistice army had hidden away. The first *réfractaire* had arrived from the north in April 1943: Roger Bellanger, who had learned of the house through his contacts. He was followed soon after by two more *réfractaires*, including Gaston Naboulet.

Danède joined the Resistance as a member of a network of *légaux* that covered a wide area. He was given a radio receptor for parachute messages which he hid in the drawer of a table near where his mother routinely did the washing up. Gaston Naboulet (L'ancêtre) became the head of the small network of seven – someone Danède admired greatly, calling him 'valiant, competent and brave, a real man of the time'. Naboulet's contacts included Valentine Bussière, with whom he worked closely. Born in Beausoleil, Valentine lived on her parents' farm, and from here the whole family would contribute to the Resistance efforts. Valentine was 19 years old at the fall of France and her older brother escaped a German POW camp after eighteen months' imprisonment, leading the determined young lady to become an important link between the FTP and the civilian world.

The Bussière farm was located near a sizeable local quarry and the family had noticed night-time toings and froings of lorries, at odds with the regular work hours of the quarry owners. At various times of day the family visited the quarry to examine what had been left there: muskets, revolvers and ammunition. In discussion with contacts who were similarly keen to help build a resistance movement, the Bussière family began removing as much of the weaponry and ammunition a possible to their farm, ensuring they were not spotted while doing so. Recuperation of the equipment was not straightforward given that most of it was dismantled and stored in separate containers; however, what was recovered was vital when the time came.

One day the operation had to stop. On a trip to the quarry one of the Bussière girls noticed Germans, who had arrived in an assortment of vehicles, and a local man whom they recognised. He was wearing dark glasses and had clearly advised the Gestapo of the existence of the stock. This worried the Bussières as they had no idea that its existence was known by anyone but them and the members of the armistice army that had left it there.

The Buissières were betrayed by unknown locals who had spotted the groups of young men coming and going. As such, it was decided that the men should disperse, and so the future *maquisards* headed to the woodland of Ligueux, 15km north-east of Périgueux. Here a new camp was formed, with the aim of training up *réfractaires* sent from the city. Valentine would be heavily involved from the start, helping the group as a liaison agent and providing support to the men by, for example, bringing news of the men's well-being to their parents. The group armed itself through ambushing track watch-men, several *miliciens* and a small number of Germans.

Valentine covered the whole department on her bicycle, using a letterbox behind the town hall in Périgueux. Here a Monsieur Baptiste, a cobbler, slid messages into the heels of shoes. Valentine was then able to negotiate German and French roadblocks and inspections because, according to André Danède, she was 'lovely'. In November 1943, as liaison agent, Valentine brought the regional FTP chief, Vincent Bonnetot, to the camp – a hugely dangerous job for which Valentine had volunteered in the knowledge that she would pass as less suspicious than a young man. After this she persuaded Bonnetot that she should be allowed to continue to undertake more dangerous missions and spent the following months zig-zagging around the department, connecting the major towns of Périgueux and Bergerac. She would make countless stops along the way, initially dropping off propaganda and passing on messages. After gaining the trust of 'Hercule' (Roger Ranoux of Terrasson, now one of the FTP's local leaders), she moved onto more dangerous and difficult tasks, many involving the transportation of munitions; she accepted these missions with her trademark brave certitude in the ultimate goal. In the one available photograph of her, she stares out wistfully, her dark hair pulled back and piled up into an organised bundle. She was 5ft tall and pretty, and her face carries with it an innocence that would have captivated those who came across her. She was fit and agile, despite often being buttoned up in coats and wearing woollies to protect from the cold and to partially cover her features. In service to the Resistance, she crossed many hundreds of kilometres on her bike, through countryside that undulates as much as it twists and turns. Often, she took the longer route if it meant that a more major, and so potentially problematic, road could be avoided, and she was stopped on her bicycle several times by German soldiers and GMR agents. On these occasions, she managed to distract them from a valise full of armaments by smiling, chatting and producing a performance of detached calmness. Having engaged them in conversation, she got back on her bike and ambled unhurriedly away, the luggage on the bike's pannier left unopened.

Most members of the French Resistance who joined prior to the imposition of the STO would likely claim that the Resistance came to them. Activity associated with protest against the repressive Vichy regime was highly secretive, and so finding out where to go and who to approach was often something of a challenge. Well-run Resistance networks also had to be highly suspicious of newcomers. The work of spies had to be made impossible; all too many Frenchmen and women were ready to denounce their compatriots. Information on the whereabouts of Maquis camps had to be protected, as did the names of civilian agents. Becoming a *résistant urbain* was just as dangerous as entering the Maquis, both offences carrying the same punishment. Whether a postal worker for the Postes, Télégraphes et Téléphones (PTT), gendarme, liaison agent, telephone operator, *cheminot* or shopkeeper, the prospect of deportation or death was an overriding concern. Once the Maquis was in existence, its soldiers relied heavily on men and women of extreme courage to support them who, tied to their everyday existence, were less able to relocate or flee.

Alice Barrat ran a tiny restaurant opposite the church in Saint-André-de-la-Double, a village just inside the area known as the Double Forest, 11 miles north of Mussidan. Numerous young men, *réfractaires* normally, passed through the village on the way into the woods hoping to find the Maquis. But they needed guidance, and Alice, knowing the location of the many Maquis camps in the area, served as a buffer for the group leaders. She sat the young men down, gave them a drink or something to eat, and sent messages to the camps. They would then be told to go to specific meeting points so that leaders, such as Roland Clée, could meet them and decide if they were trustworthy and suitable. Her café served as a letterbox for Maquis leaders to communicate with each other or with the regional command, and very often the young men returned for a drink when they needed reassurance. In offering her services in this way, Alice Barrat placed herself and her family in great danger, but it was her way of doing what she considered right – serve her country.[11]

Many of those who followed their principles to serve their country didn't escape unscathed, however. Saint-Jean-d'Eyraud is a village in the middle of the forest of Liorac, midway between Mussidan and Bergerac. In 1943 a 16-year-old girl called Christiane Beau managed the post office as well as serving as secretary of the town hall. In addition, her small office served as a letterbox and she worked as an liaison agent using the name 'Cricri' for both the AS and the FTP, transporting food tickets and identity cards, as well as working closely with Albert Rigoulet (Le Frisé) in organising escape routes for Allied pilots who had come down in France. In Rigoulet's words:

On 5 August 1944, when the German troops came to carry out reprisals in Saint-Jean-d'Eyraud, they burned the house of her parents, killing her father Monsieur Beau, and trashing the post office looking for the 'terrorist' manager. Cricri, having thought through her escape plan, fled and, despite the roadblocks, joined up with the Maquis group that I was commanding, serving us as an intelligence agent up to 21 August, date of the liberation of Bergerac.[12]

While it is accurate to say that Resistance was an activity of the minority, the number of people who put their lives on the line in the course of doing their job is still staggering. A 1947 report on Resistance within the PTT, the French administration of postal services and telecommunications within the Dordogne, reveals how members of the service disrupted normal working processes. The sabotage of telephone networks, rerouting or hijacking of enemy correspondence, distribution of newspapers or tracts, transmission of messages to groups in cities such as Limoges, Toulouse, Lyon or Clermont-Ferrand, movement of messages to and from those destinations to letterboxes in the area, networking around the organisation to find friends of the Resistance at different operational levels and liaison with Resistance in the railways carried with them many dangers. When carried out in the workplace, it was very difficult to deny involvement as the worker would immediately be placed at the scene of the crime. As the report, written by the director, Meynard, states:

> For this glorious combat numerous postal workers gave the best of themselves. And it is possible to say that in the course of the different phases of this historic period … the whole of the personnel of the Dordogne did his duty, each at his post, with the means at his disposal and that he put all his effort into ensuring the best possible functioning of our great public service, despite numerous difficulties.[13]

Postal workers and railway workers had to take personal risks in order to resist in their occupations. Colleagues did not discuss activities openly for obvious reasons – fellow workers who might seem friendly might equally prove otherwise. Just like postal workers, railway workers engaged in the Resistance could inflict material damage on the German effort. Their skills, their access, their knowledge and their resources were sought out.

No single PTT Resistance movement existed, and Résistance-fer was only created after the war – an association for former *résistants* who worked on the railways.[14] Even attempts to bring railways into the Noyautage des Administration Publiques (NAP), which at least contributed to cohesion in the PTT network, didn't really work for the *cheminots*.

In Périgueux a huge SNCF workshop had been a feature of the Toulon *quartier* for many years, and a significant 1920 national strike began there (allegedly triggered by the management's failure to install sinks but rooted in much wider issues).[15] A socialist movement existed there, neither a union or political party, but rather an effective ideology passed from one generation of workers to the next. A nearby school, the Lycée Professionel Albert Claveille, trained workers for jobs specific to the SNCF installation. Christian Galtié was called up to the army but let go on the dissolution of the armistice army in November 1942 to take up his position in the workshops again, now something of an arms expert as well as a trained engineer. This process created many just like him, the barracks of the 35th Artillery Regiment being less than a mile away, and the *cheminots* of Périgueux became significant numerically. Even when caught, *cheminots* were rarely fired, just relocated. So, when Galtié was caught stealing the identity documents of a co-worker who was also a *milicien* to pass on to the Resistance, he was simply moved to Brive, where he once again took up his Resistance activity.

Mouvement National Contre le Racisme

Raphael Finkler, Léon Lichtenberg and their high-school friend Georges Smolarsky, the son of Strasbourg refugees, did not know that their new friend, Willy Ibram, who had penetrated their circle of friends and acquaintances, was watching them. This young Alsatian Jew was like so many others who had come to the Dordogne and for many weeks he simply showed up at cafés and parks, where he joined discussions on politics and France's future. In fact, Ibram had been sent from the headquarters of the Resistance's newly formed Mouvement National Contre Le Racisme (MNCR) in Lyon. Travelling from town to town by bicycle, his job was to establish a new arm of the MNCR in Périgueux and the rest of the Dordogne. Only once he had worked his way into the life of Finkler and his friends did Ibram feel sure that all three had demonstrated sufficient qualities and solidity of character to offer them the chance to engage in a Resistance movement, which he offered in April 1943.

The three young men jumped at the opportunity, despite being warned of the very real dangers. The MNCR was an off-shoot of the MOI, itself under the direction of the FTP. Communist in origin therefore, the politics of the movement were less important to the young men than the overall goal of Resistance: the opposition to and removal of the Vichy government and German occupiers. Like most early networks, the MNCR was based on *la Résistance urbaine*, and its strategies reflected that. Amongst these was the provision of help to Jewish families in need, the distribution of anti-Nazi propaganda that provided information on the persecution that was taking place and recruitment into the organisation. The MNCR shared many features of other communist groups, particularly in the shape of its organisation and security arrangements.

Ibram trained the new group, along the way implementing the *système de triangle* to which the three new *responsables* and all their subsequent recruits would have to adhere. Each leader would be responsible for one of three vital areas: Lichtenberg would look after membership (*effectifs*), Finkler would be responsible for technical issues (*téchnique*) and Smolarsky would head up political affairs (*politique*). All three were to locate, survey and recruit further members separately. From each of those new recruits a further three could be taken on. In such a system, should security break down, under interrogation and torture, each recruit could only possibly give away four people. Those endangered were restricted to his or her own leader, him or herself and his or her two parallel colleagues.

This system was widely and successfully used amongst civilians of the FTP, but Finkler, Lichtenberg and Smolarsky struggled with its implementation. As soon as Ibram returned to Lyon, the three found the system's failure as it held back their drive for more recruits. Nevertheless, the MNCR was soon thriving in Périgueux, with twenty-five members in addition to the three *chefs*. As was the case with most Resistance movements, identities had to be protected and so everybody chose a *nom de guerre*. Léon became 'Phil' and Georges became 'Pierre-Louis'. Names were inspired by all manner of things: animals, history, legends or American culture (which had been permeating French society since the 1930s in the form of jazz and cinema). Finkler chose the name 'Achille', though he later changed it to 'Ralph', worried he had doomed himself to be shot in the heel. By April 1943 the MNCR was up and running despite the three young men still being at *lycée*.

The boys spent Sunday afternoons in the cinema Marignan. Fans of American movies, they had grown used to the changing nature of the programming but used the opportunity to keep abreast of news. There would be occasional public whistling at Vichy propaganda, but Finkler and Lichtenberg didn't engage with such outward protest. The SOL had begun attending the shows and circulating the screening rooms, ready to dash into the aisles and arrest troublemakers. Now that he was engaged in something bigger, Finkler didn't want to risk getting arrested so cheaply.

During one show in April 1943 Finkler's attention was drawn by the scent of rare perfume to the silhouettes of two young women who took their seats next to the boys as the lights dimmed for the second part of the show. The teenage boy, in typical cavalier fashion, engaged the girls in conversation and, surprising both Finkler and Lichtenberg, they agreed to join them for a drink at the Café de Paris after the film. Sitting around the table, it became clear that they shared similar views not just on cinema, but also on the German occupation. A lasting friendship quickly developed. The younger of the two was called Maryse Nicolas and she was accompanied by Monette Leclerq who, despite appearances and their similar ages, was her aunt. The pair had only recently moved to Périgueux, where they had rented an apartment on the rue de la Boétie, just a few minutes' walk from the city centre. Nicolas' father, Louis, was a solicitor in Pisany, in the occupied zone and just 15km away from the coastal town of Royan. Leclerq, who was the younger sister of Nicolas' mother, had a husband who was still being detained as a prisoner of war.

The women had left their homes mainly because of Nicolas' determination that the occupation was fundamentally wrong. Her father had taken on work from some of the many Germans who had come to the region to build the Atlantic wall – necessarily so, to avoid drawing unfavourable attention to the family – and became one of the best-known and -respected men in the commune in so doing. However, this displeased his daughter, and their disagreements had become heated.

One day Nicolas took it upon herself to pour a chamber pot out of her bedroom window onto the head of a German lieutenant passing on horseback below. This was the latest of a number of incidents through which the young girl, herself well known, had enthusiastically and publicly remonstrated with the occupiers. Her parents agreed that it would be best for their daughter to relocate for a while to let the situation cool down and to draw attention away from the family business. Nicolas agreed to go to Périgueux since some distant relations were already there, and her Aunt Monette agreed to accompany her.

Within a short time spent with the boys after their cinema encounter, they both offered their services to the Resistance. They were subject to a very short vetting procedure by Finkler and Lichtenberg, and from there the group became inseparable, Finkler's home being just a short walk from the girls'. Finkler told his parents, 'If you are in need of anything at all, you can call on Maryse and Monette. They are reliable friends.'[16]

The work of the MNCR was busy, varied and carried out with enthusiastic professionalism. Lacking any resources whatsoever, the group's members were forced to use whatever they could lay their hands on. The apartment on rue de la Boétie became key, providing a workshop and a hiding place, and hosting regular meetings. A key part of the group's work was the distribution of tracts, although they would do whatever their directives from Lyon instructed. To help spread the word, Finkler had the idea of making small leaflets using stamps, pads of ink and small pieces of paper. Being careful to vary who bought the letters, and purchasing individual letters several at a time to avoid arousing suspicion, they were put to use to create short, sharp messages. Slogans such as '*Vichy Source de Traitres*', '*Mort à l'envahisseur allemand*' and '*Honneur à votre armée le Maquis*' ('Vichy Source of Traitors, Death to the German invader and Honour to your army the Maquis') were left in cafés, pushed under doors or stuck onto walls. Those printed on small stickers were stuck to gutters. When sticking propaganda tracts up careful precautions were made. The time of day was chosen carefully, usually Friday at 6.30 p.m., and clocks and watches were carefully synchronised to ensure that several key places around town could be targeted at once before the tracts could be taken down. The operation was carried out by a dozen young *effectifs* – two per main street, with one pasting while the other produced the papers. Under strict instructions from their chiefs, each operation could last a maximum of one minute. If any papers remained after that time, they were to be dumped 'because a tract of that type could equate to death'.[17]

Throughout the summer 1943 the MNCR carried out a large number of important missions relating directly or indirectly to propaganda, but as its membership grew, so did its ambition. After several months, a contact called Fernand brought them other propaganda to distribute in the form of newspapers, usually no more than double-sided sheets of print under the titles *J'accuse* and *Fraternité*.

It was important for the MNCR to gain maximum publicity in whatever acts of protest they carried out. A preferred method of getting attention, causing lasting damage and creating noise – all of which helped for propaganda purposes – was to smash shop windows. Targets were chosen carefully so as to avoid incurring the wrath of otherwise pliable minds – collaborationist owners of businesses were selected. Each time a window was broken, people talked about it, and the strategy proved highly successful. Finkler and Lichtenberg were aware that this new approach was dangerous and increased the risk of being discovered.

For the two boys, their involvement in the MNCR was now finite. They set objectives and devised a final few high-profile attacks. The penultimate *vitrine* to be destroyed was that of a local *parfumerie* whose owner was the head of the newly formed local Milice. On 24 November 1943, just before curfew and when the streets were relatively busy, Finkler and another Alsatian, Maurice Burstin ('Daniel'), cycled up to the establishment. Three lookouts placed in strategic positions within sight nodded the go-ahead. With all their might, the two young men each launched a brick through the shopfront of the *Parfumerie Bleue*. Each brick was wrapped in paper that carried the message, '*Collabo, après ta vitrine viendra ton tour*' ('Collabo, after your window your turn will come') and tied with string. The operation went well, the overwhelming scent of broken perfume bottles being left in the wake of the men, who melted away from the scene. The mission was deemed a major success.

One target remained: the headquarters of Doriot's party, the PPF, on rue de la République. As a target it was ideal, and the MNCR's statement would be made loud and clear. Finkler, however, was uncomfortable about the plan. The *parfumerie* had been high profile and had rubber-stamped the group as a target for the authorities. Finkler suspected that the group was at its most vulnerable, was possibly being watched and could already have been infiltrated. He discussed the situation with Lichtenberg and they decided that they had to move on – continuing with the MNCR was now too dangerous. They both wanted to enter the Maquis, being keen to engage in real action, in a military sense.

Finding contacts to get in touch with the Maquis was not easy and Finkler assumed that his contact in Lyon, Fernand, would provide a link to the FTP – the parent group of the MNCR. However, the answer to his request was a resounding no. Afraid that letting two of its originators join the Maquis would result in a decapitated group, the MNCR direction put the brakes on any hopes the boys had to join the newly formed FTP. They were left with only one option. Through a series of interlocutors, Finkler knew of a contact that might be able to accept them into the AS. They discussed the issue with Paul Frydman ('Le Parisien' or 'Dave'), a new member of their team who had arrived in the Dordogne with his parents and two brothers when the exodus had arrived from Alsace-Lorraine, and had stayed when it was clear that, as Jews, they would be unable to return. Frydman, tall and rangy and a few years older than Finkler and Lichtenberg, had become something of an extra leader within the MNCR. He not only encouraged the men's decision to join the Maquis, but decided to go with them. To do so they would need to travel to Vergt.

Meanwhile the momentum of the MNCR was such that Maurice Burstin was determined to follow through with the attack on the PPF headquarters, despite advice from Finkler that the site would be protected by agents eager to catch the MNCR in action. Not willing to listen and benefiting from the withdrawal of three of the group's most influential leaders, Maurice led the attack. Sadly, Finkler had been right and armed civil police were ready for them. Two activists were injured by gunshots while six others were arrested. Burstin managed to flee, and through Nicolas and Leclerq, got word to Lyon that the movement was in danger. Before long, despite efforts to revive it, the MNCR in Périgueux was no more.

The group may have run its course, but it had contributed to the awakening of Périgourdin consciousness towards the persecution of the Jews, particularly in the towns. Thanks to the work of the group of civilian agents in propaganda, the fate of persecuted Jewish families began to be perceived as a wrong that transcended any pretence of national renewal:

Call to the Population of the Périgord
German atrocities have once again taken place in our town. Whole families have been deported: their sole crime was to be Jewish: elderly,

women, children, nothing was spared by the Nazi brute. Amongst them were former combatants and wives of prisoners. These unfortunates are going to be taken to Drancy and elsewhere, and so many Israelites they will be massacred.

Frenchmen! Indifference or unconsciousness before such acts would be criminal. Human consciousness and Christian charity revolts before these atrocities.

True patriots are understanding that these persecutions are just the beginning of new ... [measures] that will extend to the whole of the French population.

The Hitlerian tactic has divided the French people into Jews, into classes, into categories (deportations of women and of workers) whilst in reality it is targeting the total destruction of the French nation as Hitler took pleasure in exposing in 'Mein Kampf'.

Frenchmen! Let us unite to help our Jewish brothers. That each Frenchman knows that by protecting the Jews he is protecting himself. Thus, he will have fulfilled his duty as a man and as a Frenchman.

The liberation is near, but one last effort is asked of all in order to real-ise that union of brotherhood before which Hitlerian fury will fall apart.

Mouvement National contre le racisme.[18]

5

TURNING TIDES

Further to the round-up of 26 August 1942, the Dordogne suffered another on 8 October, when the communes of north-eastern Dordogne on the occupied side of the demarcation line saw 179 Jews deported to Drancy. They were sent to Auschwitz in convoy 40 on 4 November and 42 on 6 November. Such round-ups had proved that the Vichy government, which was fast losing support, was capable of atrocious policy in support of an occupying power. It was also becoming clear that Germany had never planned to treat France as an equal partner. Stories were spreading of the fate of Jews that had been sent to camps and deported, just as they had of deportations of other undesirables such as communists, gypsies, masons and *résistants*. However, the idea of such large groups of people being systematically murdered still seemed a little far-fetched. While German propaganda blaming the Resistance and all ills on the Jews and communists was rejected, talk of death camps was just as easily dismissed.

The landing of American troops in North Africa in November 1942 pushed the German decision to undertake Operation Attila – the full occupation of the southern zone – but it had consequences. Chief of police René Bousquet, concerned that prefects were losing track of Jews who had begun to scatter and go into hiding to escape the Nazis, ordered the prefects to rigorously apply a November law prohibiting foreign Jews from moving freely beyond their commune of residence without police permission. These foreign Jews were placed at the front of the queue for the next round of deportations. On 10 December, Hitler ordered the arrest and deportation of all Jews, as well as other enemies of the Reich such as communists and Gaullists, from France. The proximity of the advancing Allies to the south also suggested a real possibility of support being whipped up in the event of an invasion.

A new wave of deportations was prepared for the first quarter of 1943. The Judenreferat ensured that trains were available to carry deportees from Drancy, and all deportable Jews were prepared for transit east in mid-February. Meanwhile in the southern zone more and more Jewish papers and ration cards had been stamped with the word '*Juif*', increasing the number of registered Jews in the south from 110,000, as per the census of March 1942, to 140,000 stamped by February 1943.[1] The stamping of the ration cards was damaging for those Jewish families unable or unwilling to use false documentation – it meant they were easily identifiable and resisting identification opened them up to immediate arrest. Then, on 13 February 1943, two German officers were assassinated in Paris and 2,000 more Jews were demanded for deportation as a reprisal.

Regional prefects were instructed on 18 February to round up foreign Jews and send them to the French concentration camp at Gurs, on the foothills of the Pyrenées. Round-ups took place in the Dordogne between 23 and 27 February 1943. The Gymnasium Secresat was requisitioned on 20 February by the prefecture and used to hold those arrested. According to a plaque on the site, of the 'foreign Jews of the department, victims of the round-ups carried out by the Vichy government, more than 70 were deported to the extermination camps of Maïdanek and Sobibor'. Local historian Bernard Reviriego has since revised the figures to 'at least 110 men interned ... deported, via Drancy, by the convoys numbered 50 and 51 of between the 4 and 6 March 1943'. According to a report from the prefect of Limoges, 509 Jews were sent to Gurs from the region in the period 24–27 February.[2]

The arrest of Jews may have helped fulfil quotas, but it was turning public opinion even further away from the Vichy government, feeding a singularly unexpected base of support for the Jews in the region of Limoges, including the Dordogne. More and more members of the French public saw their lives being affected by the disappearance of human beings who they had come to know. In addition, people considered French were being arrested and sent to an unknown destiny. The clergy had taken note of the persecution of the Jews and had begun to condemn it. In August 1942 Jules-Géraud Saliège, Archbishop of

Toulouse, wrote a letter of condemnation that was circulated by the Resistance. Holding nothing back, he wrote of events in his parish saying, 'Jews are men, Jews are women. All of this is not permitted against them, against those men, those women, against those fathers and mothers of families. They are part of the human race. They are our brothers like so many others.'[3] Copies of the letter were posted throughout the southern zone and a copy was handed to the chief of the Service de Renseignements Généraux (RG) by a policeman who had been handed one on 19 September. In the accompanying letter, the policeman wrote that he was trying to establish how many copies had been distributed.

The round-ups led not just to an arousal of public opinion in favour of the Jews, but also a 'movement of compassion'.[4] More militia on the ground, more martyrs in the countryside, more controls for all to have to deal with, and more arrests throughout 1943 and 1944 built on the discussions raised by the clergy. The public were beginning to show pity to the families being forced to move around and hide, and this despite the 'congestion' caused by the extra people in towns that needed feeding and accommodating.[5] Everywhere, whether in the countryside where these issues were felt less keenly or in the towns, the population of the Dordogne was becoming aware of the hardships forced on their fellow humans. The prefects became acutely aware that the people wanted, at the very least, women and children to be afforded protection. The CGQJ was furious: it had worked so hard to paint the Jews as the cause of all the French public's ills, yet public opinion was swaying towards supporting them. Propaganda was subsequently stepped up both on the air and in print, the Légion leading the way. It insisted that sanctions be increased not just against Jews, but against those who helped to protect them. Surveillance measures were also escalated, with schools and even churches targeted.

Within the Limoges region, differences of opinion in politics and religion had always existed. Departments that were home to larger cities and industry, such as the Corrèze and Haute-Vienne, were strongly leftist and anti-cleric. The Dordogne had an 'old radical and republican heritage' which, like the Limousin, did not favour the ideas of National Revolution. However, certain characteristics were shared throughout. Self-sufficient and rural, this part of France was used to solidarity in work and in suffering during hard times. Fortunately for Jewish families who became dependent on goodwill to survive, these were qualities shared in their hosts. The area also had a strong tradition of helping – even saving – those in peril, Christian or otherwise, who had come to the area in need. But perhaps the most important characteristic of the people of the Dordogne for the Jews was their willingness to engage in civil disobedience in order to protect them. This may not have been card-carrying resistance, but it was vital nonetheless.

In 1940 Bertrand Lévy was one of many children yet to find out what being Jewish had come to mean. On 4 October that year, he noticed a poster on a wall as he walked to school along rue Gambetta in his home town of Brive. He was 10 years old and asked his parents what the poster meant that was drawing lots of attention from passers-by. It was titled '*Dispositions concernant les juifs*'. On that day, he began to understand a little about what is was like to be a 'rabbit rather than a hunter': 'I discovered that day that I was Jewish, I didn't know. It didn't have anything to do with my culture … I knew something of the human values it represented … but when it comes to racial or religious matters, I had no idea.'[6]

Three years later, on a sunny winter's day, he was in class in the same school, the Collège Cabanis, when the general supervisor, a figure of immense authority in schools at the time, came to the classroom looking for him and said, 'You, pick up your schoolbag and come with me.' Bertrand had no idea what he had done wrong but did as instructed.

'You know that little door over there?' said the supervisor. Bertrand, a small child, told the supervisor that he knew of it but had never been through as it was not allowed. The supervisor continued, 'Go out of it quickly, run home and tell your parents to get away quickly, quickly, quickly.'

Bertrand later found out that the Gestapo was already in the school, looking for him: 'I never had time to say thank you. It was like that, we were living in fear.'[7]

Hidden Heroes

Throughout the Dordogne more and more Périgourdins were willing to help people living in peril. In Brantôme Pierre Bouty – who had been recognised for bravery during the First World War – was the director of the Preventorium Les Fougères. He had established it with his wife Marguerite when he returned from active duty, and its purpose was to take in children who had the tuberculosis virus but were yet to display outward symptoms, in a bid to eradicate the disease through isolation and treatment. Prior to the outbreak of war, the establishment had dealt with a large number of children from the Paris region who came to Brantôme for the healthy country air.

In 1942 Bouty went down another branch of heroism when he joined the Resistance, serving in the AS's Groupe Valmy. However, the unofficial activities the couple carried out, which they kept secret into later life, really marked them out as true heroes of the Resistance. Only one of many examples of this heroism in shown in the case of the Braun family. In 1939 Alice Braun travelled to Périgueux from Bitche in the Moselle with her children, Armand who was 2 and Denise who had been born the previous year. Her husband, Mirtil, had fought against the Germans but joined his young family in Périgueux once the fight was lost. In 1943 the round-ups of Jews caused the Braun family more anxiety than they could bear. Hearing that several Jewish children had been accepted into Les Fougères, they took their children to Brantôme where they were taken in under a false name. There they stayed, in safety, until their parents collected them in August 1944, after which they returned to Moselle. The parents were never asked for any payment whatsoever.

Following the war Pierre Bouty never accepted that he had done anything beyond his duty. But the veil of secrecy with which he had surrounded his establishment saved around fifty Jewish children from deportation and, given that no children deported from the Dordogne ever returned, certain death. Bouty never spoke of the children he saved, and Les Fougères doesn't feature in any official commission lists to recognise establishments that hid Jewish children. Perhaps that was the key to the success of this remarkable *résistant* and his equally remarkable wife: total secrecy kept the children alive. Only when Armand Braun and his wife published a book in 2008 did the story of the Bouty rescues in the quiet town of Brantôme, full of tourists for a few months of each summer, become known beyond the locality.

Other Jewish children were saved at Château de la Juvénie near Payzac. The medieval structure had served as agricultural buildings in the nineteenth and twentieth centuries, but it was requisitioned by the Croix Rouge Alsacienne during the evacuation of September 1939. Initially it was used to house nuns – Bon-Secours sisters from Strasbourg – then the majority of the building was taken over to house the École Normale de Colmar. Around 100 children attended this orphanage, including many Jewish children listed under false names. The establishment was managed by the nuns who, along with the school's teachers, helped guard the children from the dangers that surrounded them. The parish priest, L'Abbé Henri Galice, along with neighbouring farms, helped to look after the children, some of whom were placed at the school by Resistance networks. On 10 May 1944 several teachers, including the *directeur* Jacques Lagaude, were arrested by the Milice during a round-up and taken to the internment camp at Saint-Paul-d'Eyjeaux. Remarkably none of the children were taken and all were protected during the whole war.

Meanwhile, in Sarlat, a little girl called Paulette was thought by many of the workers in the small artisanal jar factory to be the granddaughter of their boss. They made her little toys and Paulette was well loved by all. Boss Paul Berthoumeyrou and his wife Jeanne had lived in Sarlat all their lives, and their own daughter Colette was 21 years of age. To those didn't know the family well, Paulette was assumed to be Colette's daughter, and Colette looked after her just as she would her own. In fact, Paulette had arrived with the family only in the summer of 1943, when her parents, a Jewish Czech couple by the name of Bergman who had been evacuated from Metz to Saint-Cère in the Lot in 1939, were at their lowest point, no longer able to support their daughter. The Berthoumeyrous had come to know the family and recognised that they needed to help them, such was the level of their deprivation. They duly offered to look after the child, and until Paulette returned to her parents in 1945, the Berthoumeyrou family loved and spoiled her. The young girl learned to answer to any that asked that her parents had been killed during a bombing raid, so anybody who didn't simply presume her to be Colette's daughter instead believed her to be the orphan of a Christian family. The Berthoumeyrous did all they could to make the ordeal easier for both Paulette and her parents. They sent photographs of Paulette to her parents, who were living so frustratingly nearby but were unwilling to place their daughter in danger or disrupt the arrangement by meeting with her. When they discovered that Paulette's aunts had managed to find shelter in Sarlat they very carefully arranged limited visits in the hairdressers.

Breaking Networks

Whereas individuals were beginning to take risks to protect Jews, their support networks were generally localised. The Jewish question was not at the forefront of the priorities of the bigger networks. Throughout 1943 these movements were beginning to gain some notoriety with the German and French police forces on the ground. Security within the networks was creaking as activities diversified, and Gestapo agents were appointed to break them down by building a web of informants. Joseph Meyer, also known as Barry, was in his early thirties and was a student at a theological college on the outbreak of the Second World War. In 1941, when the Moselle and Alsace regions were incorporated into the Gau Westmark,★ citizens from the area were drafted into the Wehrmacht. Meyer joined the SS and by 1943 was attached to the Limoges section of the Gestapo, headed by Erik Berhels. The Gestapo was part of the overall German police system, the SD. Since November 1942 the SD base in Limoges covered the whole R5 region and numbered around 100 agents. It was taken over in June 1943 by Leutnant August Meier, member of the SS since 1933, who had overseen massacres of Jews and opponents of Nazism while leading a commando unit in the Ukraine between 1941 and 1942. The Limoges Gestapo, under Berhels, had an anti-Jewish section and an information section led by Jachim Kleist. Frenchmen René Ohl, from Alsace, and Joseph Meyer worked under Kleist, often travelling to Périgueux where agents had set up in the Hôtel du Commerce in November 1942, with the regional office made official in January 1943.

In a document dated 10 June 1943 SS-Oberscharführer Meyer reported on a series of investigations and arrests over a period of several months. The report summarised an operation that aimed to close the Resistance groups Combat, Francs-Tireurs, Libération and AS.[8] Meyer began his investigation by picking apart a group that were enabling an escape route into Spain and onwards to North Africa, where members could join the Free French army. His investigation led him from Limoges to Périgueux, where a Jewish man named Albert Amsallem was preparing to leave with a group of five or six young people. From that arrest and interrogation came a supply of names

---

★ The Gau Westmark was an administrative division of Nazi Germany so named when these French departments were added in December 1940.

including police officers, clergymen, chemists, prison guards, teachers and the husband and wife directors of a school who also ran an agency of *passeurs* for the FTP. Under intense interrogation and probably torture, some of those arrested tried to reveal limited information and hold important details back, whereas others in the chain revealed a great deal more that led the deck of cards to tumble. Letterboxes were uncovered in a local bookshop and newspaper seller, and another in a patisserie. One by one, men and young women were discovered to be liaison agents. Through these *légaux*, a link was found to Maurice Schmidt, known as Simonin or Savil, based in Limoges, who was understood to be the departmental chief of the newly formed AS.

The situation worsened as the leader of the AS for the Haute-Vienne, Corrèze, Dordogne and Creuse was discovered to be someone called Clery, formerly known as Hermant and known to be a member of the Combat network. This information was apparently revealed by Schmidt who also revealed details of a meeting that took place bringing together leaders of all three main movements. Names were forthcoming as was, unfortunately, a host of papers that Schmidt had left at his home, which was thoroughly searched. The papers revealed all sorts of details about the structure of the new AS, as well as names of police officers and professional army officers involved. This willingness to keep documentation was perhaps a sign of weakness of the early AS. Meyer found plans that outlined the steps that the AS would take in preparation for the Allied invasion, undoubtedly drawn up by a professional soldier. A police officer whose name appeared a number of times was arrested, and he in turn was found to be in possession of a list of members of the AS.

Arrest after arrest and interrogation after interrogation followed, leading to the interception of Jean-Baptiste Lemoine, a member of Libération who had been given the role of provisional departmental chief of the AS. As further names emerged, Meyer learned of the AS recruitment methods, by which lists were drawn up of young men who were due to be sent to Germany under the STO. Trusted civilians were appointed and paid to find these men and direct them towards the AS. He learned of the preparations that needed to take place in order to locate and use appropriate parachute landing sites, as well as what might be contained in such drops, including a supply of newspaper for printing clandestine propaganda. Finally, the regional chief of the AS was tracked down too.

Known as Clery, or Hermant, Charles Hinstein was a 40-year-old divorcee in the manufacturing industry who had been born in Paris and one of whose parents was Jewish. Since Hinstein had also insisted on keeping papers in his home, his arrest was disastrous for the whole R5 region. It led to arrests throughout the southern zone in Tulle, Clermont-Ferrand, Lyon, Montpellier, Toulon and Toulouse. From an interrogation 'which was pursued throughout the night' Hinstein 'gave all the names of the personnel leading the AS in the 5th region (Limoges), including the letter boxes in Limoges, Périgueux and Tulle as well as the liaison agents who were working for the AS'.[9]

Amongst others named were Raymond Berggren, chief of the AS for the Dordogne and known as Bordeaux 48, who was arrested in Bergerac. André Boissière, the teacher from Périgueux known as Berthou, was also arrested in Périgueux in front of his students. Boissière did his best to minimise his interest in the AS, saying that he didn't take his role particularly seriously but, according to Meyer's report, at the time of his arrest he too was found to be in possession of an incriminating document detailing units under his command. Whether this was actually the case is not possible to verify. While it would have been a rather ridiculous oversight of security, Meyer had no real reason to lie in the document given all the evidence that pointed his way. Berggren's arrest was hard-hitting, as he had been head of the AS in the Dordogne since its creation in 1942. Even he was not immune to talking during interrogation. Names that he appears to have given away during interrogation include Maurice Loupias (Bergeret), leader of the AS for Dordogne-sud.

Berggren later died in deportation, while André Boissière was interned in Périgueux and then sent to Limoges, followed by Romainville. As well as being a member of Combat, Boissière's role within the NAP network should not be underestimated. Without him, the placement of many Resistance agents in public services, such as the postal service and town halls, might not have happened. On 5 October 1943 he was shot at Mont-Valérien, as one of fifty hostages executed in reprisal for the assassination of SS officer Julius Ritter by the FTP-MOI in Paris.

Overall, the Maquis could no longer allow information to be so widely available, and security and strategies had to be tightened up if the AS was to survive and grow. Throughout 1943 significant arrests had been made following either carelessness or individuals holding too much documentation at the time of interception. This was not the case with the FTP, which ring-fenced knowledge into teams of three amongst their non-Maquis members, who only ever had contacts while similar arrangements existed for the upper echelons of the leadership. This was not the case in the AS or ORA.

At the beginning of 1943, members of the public, politicians and activists who had chosen to support the Vichy cause felt happy with the way things were going. Following the Allied landings in North Africa, and the subsequent implementation of Operation Attila that rendered the demarcation line meaningless, German troops were scattered widely around the R5 sector. As a result, denunciators and collaborators of all types felt encouraged, protected by the presence of the '*Boches*'. Arrests followed throughout the year.

Arrests

In late January 1943, Raymond Terrenq took a deep breath as a convoy of military vehicles flanked by German motorcycles pulled up outside the Collège de la Boétie, the school in Sarlat of which he was principal. The Germans had arrived two weeks earlier, setting up in the Hôtel de la Madeleine, where fifteen officers were stationed, and around forty troops were billeted nearby. When they arrived, Terrenq and Pierre Vialle knew they had to clear the school of any signs that many Resistance meetings had been hosted here. They also had to remove stocks that they had held there. So, when the Germans burst in on 21 January demanding the arms they knew were hidden there, Terrenq was able to deny all knowledge. The troops searched with spades and pick axes but found nothing. Whoever had denounced Terrenq had known a lot more than he had thought possible. It was a warning.

Arrests followed as denunciations flooded onto the desks of the Gestapo and gendarmeries. Lt Col Kauffmann was in Tulle when he heard that his wife had been arrested in his place. Fleeing to Lyon, he decided that if he wanted to carry on transmitting messages he would need to find somewhere quiet, far from the possibility of being found by agents of the R5 region, where he was being actively sought. He settled in a village called Pougnat, near Volvic in the Puy de Dôme, and re-established his base.[10]

Although successful in remaining unnoticed by the authorities, even Edmond Michelet's luck ran out. The credibility of the official cover had worn thin. A friend said of him:

> He did not represent the type of person ideal for Resistance, those who sink into the background. I have the impression that in Brive if you had asked in the street: 'Who is the leader of the Resistance please?' you would have been directed there and then to Michelet's big house.[11]

Michelet had first roused the suspicions of the Vichy police in June 1942, when he had been arrested and implicated in relation to a large investigation into Combat, but his case had been dismissed. Under cover of his work for Secours National, he continued thereafter to travel up and down the roads of southern France, helping to implement Combat's aims wherever he went. He even welcomed to his home huge Resistance figures such as Berty Albrecht and Pierre Brossolette. He may have gone a step too far when, following the crossing of the demarcation line by the Germans on 11 November, his entourage organised a mass demonstration of thousands of people. Even London warned against the planned event, fearing for the safety of those involved, but it went ahead, and the authorities decided against taking action.

But 'the worm was in the fruit',[12] and a refugee who had been recruited by the Gestapo infiltrated the network. He never actually met Michelet, but on 29 January 1943 the local leaders of Combat were arrested, Michelet included. Using his manifold contacts, including the Mayor of Brive who attested to his 'good faith', he was set free. He was advised to go into hiding in Montpellier by the leaders of Combat, but Michelet refused to leave his large family, fearing that if he abandoned them they would be arrested and used as hostages. On 25 February he was again arrested and this time he was not released. Having always preached the need for prudence to others, he had not followed the sound advice himself. After interrogations in Limoges, he was interned in Fresnes for six months. On 15 September 1943 he was taken to Dachau, prisoner 52,579, where he would mix with STO resisters and black-market merchants; he was determined that his Christianity and Gaullist beliefs would benefit and unify all of those around him.

Around Sarlat, in the south-east of the Dordogne, the net was growing even tighter around the Resistance and its leaders. Near Groléjac, Lucien

Dubois discovered that he was being subject to tight surveillance. The time had come for him to disappear and so he 'took to the Maquis' – a term that was becoming widely used. Lt Col Kauffmann's 17-year-old liaison agent Lucien Bitarelle (Lulu) was intercepted and interrogated by the Gestapo. Deciding his best chance would come from acting as a simpleton, the exasperated agents put him under watch in a local barn. Waiting for an opportunity and knowing the area well, he managed to escape when the attention of his guardians lacked for a few seconds by jumping through a window and into a small stream called the Cuze. Soon he was gone. But the denunciations kept coming. *Réfractaires* in woodland around Beynac were hunted down, as were those suspected of supporting them.

The Arrest of Goldman

Mieczyslav 'Marc' Goldman ('Mireille') established Maquis group Sanglier in the forest of Liorac in June 1943. As a Czech and a Jew, he was able to establish a group from young men drawn to him. He was brave, dynamic and seemingly unaffected by fear. The group, containing a company run by Roland Clée, soon became unwieldy and moved location, settling at Durestal, near Sainte-Alvère, 20 miles south of Périgueux. Six days after a minor clash with a German company, it was surrounded on 17 September by several hundred *miliciens* and GMR. Not wishing to see blood shed between Frenchmen, a truce was called and the men were told to disperse, which they did. Goldman and his men simply relocated further north, near Neuvic-sur-l'Isle. Denounced once more, Goldman recognised the need to break up into smaller units around the Double Forest, north of Mussidan and west of Périgueux.

Goldman was planning greater things and, if incredibly resourceful and widely respected, he was known occasionally to take too many risks. On 12 October nine Georgians deserted their Wehrmacht unit, Ost-Bataillon 799, which was stationed in Périgueux. These men had been recruited by the Nazis and felt no affinity to their German uniform. Instead they felt for the Maquis, and the men rising up against the Nazi invaders. In this, Goldman saw an opportunity. These genuine, hardworking and incredibly tough soldiers were examples of auxiliary troops who, given a prod in the right direction, might just tip towards the Maquis. His idea was forward-thinking, as further Georgian troops would later join the Maquis and fight superbly under the banner of the AS and FTP. Goldman used contacts to communicate with several officers of the 799 and arranged a meeting for 30 October 1943 at Place Francheville, Périgueux.

It was a trap, set up expertly by Gestapo chief SS-Untersturmführer Michaël Hambrecht. Goldman and his two deputies were both arrested after a short struggle, and the Germans didn't delay in publishing details of the arrests in the departmental newspapers:

'Patriots'
Recently the main leaders of the Maquis of the Dordogne were arrested and this is their civil status:
GOLDMAN Mejezyslaw
JEW, Czechoslovakia.
BAUM Alexandre
JEW, born in Petrograd.
JEZEKIEL, Jacques
JEW, born in Vilnius
Are they French? NO. What have they done for France? NOTHING, and they are destroying the country.
JEWS too are those in London who launch stirring calls for fighting and murder in the name of patriotism. Ah! They really do understand the level of their audience. After all they convinced everyone! That the soldier far from the front is a patriot, and that the fighter, the real fighter, is a traitor.[13]

On 3 November a 'clean-up' was carried out around Le Maine-du-Puy, the location of Goldman's camp. Once again negotiations were started, but this time a shot was fired and a twenty-minute battle raged. While two GMR were injured, three *maquisards* were hurt and one killed. Thirty-two arrests were made, and paperwork was found on the site that detailed AS units. Included amongst the arrests were five of the Georgians who defected, and they were given back to the Germans who had them shot on 10 December.

The events at Maine-du-Puy had two major consequences. From that moment on, as far as the AS Maquis were concerned, there no longer existed any distinction between enemies that were French or enemies who were German. Whoever attacked the Maquis would be considered traitorous and probably killed. In the coming weeks three local collaborators were eradicated. Secondly, Gontran Royer, at the time leader of the AS for the R5 region, discovered in the course of a meeting with friends in Limoges that a message had been left at a letterbox by two young *maquisards*. They told of an attack on their Maquis, the group Mireille, and begged for help. Some units had survived, they said, and had dispersed, managing to bury and camouflage weapons and materials. As requested, Royer acted quickly, choosing to travel to the Dordogne himself in order to help. On arriving at his rendezvous he was met by the Gestapo. Once again, a trap had led to the arrest of a major figure. Royer was deported to Buchenwald.

Deportation

Arrests leading to deportation became all too familiar a fate for agents and leaders during the difficult days of 1943. On 21 December liaison agent Vincent García Riestra watched from the bus he had been boarded onto as yet another arrest was carried out in a town square restaurant. That man, too, was brought aboard the bus, which then called at various spots where Gestapo agents jumped out of cars, banged on doors and collected further prisoners. García noticed that the agents knew where they were going and who they were looking for. The two contacts with whom he was regularly in contact were also boarded onto the bus.

FTP agents were restricted to having contact with only two or three other people in a chain or team. The idea was to keep everybody safe. If one person was arrested, and they could only betray two or three others, then the network could remain intact. But in García's case an insider had sold out a whole network. The Gestapo agents were even carrying names and addresses – they did not have to ask around to find anybody: 'they did not round us up randomly, they knew who and where we were.'[14] Thirty arrests were made.

When they reached Sarlat, García recognised another face. Though he had never been treated by him personally García knew of Dr Victor Nessmann. He didn't know of his vital role in setting up the Resistance in the area, but he knew that he was a doctor who treated the Maquis. The prisoners were taken to Bergerac, Périgueux, then on to Limoges prison, seat of the local Gestapo headquarters, where they were held for three weeks. They were put in groups of six per cell designed for two prisoners at a time, so beds were removed and straw was thrown on the ground. García was interrogated, beaten and tortured, as were all of his fellow prisoners. One of his cell mates returned from an interrogation with broken arms, having been suspended by the wrists with his hands behind his back. Nessmann was seen being led away from his cell one day, never to return. It is believed that he died under the strain of the severe beatings he endured. His body was never found.

Vincent García Riestra was born on 20 January 1925 at Pola de Siero, part of a large family. His father, Gregorio García Lavilla, was employed in public works while his mother, Aurea Riestra Morilla, worked in the shoe-making industry. Vincent's father belonged to no political party, but believed in the Republic, opposed fascism and was a trade unionist. When the Spanish Popular Front was victorious in 1936, the whole family rejoiced, and Vincent's father helped the Republican cause by being in charge of supplies, never on the front line, and ensuring that they reached those supporting Franco as well as those fighting for the survival of the Republic. His was a humanitarian cause, not a political one.[15] However, his youngest brother, at 18 years old, actively fought for the Republic.

When the Republic looked likely to fall, and with Franco's forces fast approaching, the region's women and children were evacuated. Vincent's mother was advised to flee to the Soviet Union, but she refused, opting instead to go to Barcelona. Twelve-year-old Vincent was separated from his mother and placed in a military school in the Barcelona suburbs. However, on 22 January 1939, the then 14-year-old Vincent was forced to flee as Franco's troops approached the city. He managed to get over the border on 2 February 1939, travelling within one of the communist Brigadas Internacionales after having suffered an injury to the left foot from a grenade explosion.

Once in France he was considered a 'casualty of war' and transported to a hospital in Le Mans, where a nurse took him under her wing and helped him track down the rest of his family. They learned that his mother, brother and sisters were in the Dordogne, having found their way to the Centre Hospitalier de Lanmary, several kilometres north-west of Périgueux. Several Spanish families were lodged in terrible conditions in a barn nearby, and Vincent managed to join them. However happy he was to see his mother and siblings, the meeting was tinged with awful sadness. Vincent learned that, following the defeat of the Republic, his father had been arrested at the end of January 1938. He had been tried on 3 February and shot on 4 March. His body had been thrown into a mass grave with 1,600 others.

The 1940 defeat of France was a further blow to the Spanish who had fled to France, fascism seemingly closing in around them. Most were not surprised, however, given the decisive intervention of Göring's Condor Legion in Spain.* The García family managed to find their way to Bourrou, a tiny village in a hilly and heavily forested area halfway between Périgueux and Bergerac. Here Vincent's mother found employment, and Vincent also found work as a farm hand. For the Spanish who had come to France, 'our enemy changed name. Before it was Franco, then it became Germany.'[16] It was an opportunity for vengeance and eventually the majority of young men who came to France joined the Resistance in some way or another.

Vincent's own involvement began when he was 15 years old. Then living near Cadouin and working in Le Buisson – a 6km cycle journey away – Vincent often met with friends at a local café in Cadouin and discussed everyday matters and the ongoing civil war in Spain. No alcohol was ever available – all Vincent and his friends would ever consume was a single café au lait. A local French man who, Vincent learned, was a teacher began mixing with the group, eager to discuss the Spanish war. One evening he asked Vincent, the youngest of the group of Spaniards, if he could talk to him alone and asked whether he would like to be able to speak French properly (*'comme il faut'*). Vincent was enthusiastic and began to attend French classes at the teacher's home on a semi-regular basis. The teacher, a Spanish speaker, got to know the young man well and trust developed between them. The teacher's name was Lucien Dutard.

A communist as well as secretary at the town hall, the keen *rugbyman* (he captained the Le Buisson club for five years between 1934 and 1939) had been involved with communist elements of the Resistance after being decommissioned from the army in 1940. Meetings took place at his mother's home in Le Buisson and Dutard arranged for clandestine travellers to receive shelter while passing through the area. He had married in 1937 and fathered two children, but his wife died in 1942. Because of his family situation, he did not enter the Maquis but acted as a civilian resister, organising

---

* A military unit composed from the air force and army of Nazi Germany, which served with the Nationalists during the Spanish Civil War of July 1936 to March 1939.

liaison agents, distributing propaganda and helping to recruit and direct young men called up to the STO towards the Maquis. He was not closed to the idea of a unified Resistance so helped AS groups as well as the FTP, but entered politics as a communist after the war, following a similar path to another communist politician heavily involved in the FTP, Jeanne Vigier.★★

Vincent García Riestra's French lessons slowly led to his involvement with the Resistance when, during several conversations, Dutard asked Vincent questions about the war. In time, Dutard asked Vincent if he would like to earn a small commission on his daily trips to and from Le Buisson; so, ignorant that his messages had anything to do with the Resistance, he would visit a female contact in Le Buisson and she would send messages back with him that he would have to remember without always understanding the words. Over time Vincent suspected what was going on and eventually Dutard revealed that he was part of a Resistance network. He asked Vincent whether he would like to work for the Resistance in a more official capacity. Young Vincent agreed and at the end of 1942 he was properly engaged as liaison agent for the FTP, Dordogne-nord.

As a civilian agent in Dutard's network, Vincent's job changed, becoming much more involved. He now worked in '*espionnage*' – as he liked to describe it – and as such carried on life as normal, all the while carrying messages between the two other people he had been given access to within the network. This part of his role involved travelling from one to the other by bicycle or train, waiting for a response and, if one was forthcoming, returning with it. Alternatively, he might pass it on to the next person in the chain. It was vital work and very dangerous. He was also tasked with providing information on the movement of troops to his contacts, which he would procure by contacting the right person or observing the troop movements himself. There were relatively few troops in Périgueux, where the German presence was primarily Gestapo and other police forces, but there was a large military presence in and around Bergerac. Just 72 miles

---

★★Jeanne Vigier was a grower from Le Buisson, who during the 1930s was active with the Communist Party, in which she defended the interests of the farming community. She became a very well-known figure of the Resistance in the Dordogne, actively opposing the 'Corporation paysanne' of the Vichy government. She founded the Comités de Défense et d'Action Paysanne throughout the south of the Dordogne and went on to serve as a senator in the Assemblée Nationale.

east of Bordeaux, this was a vital staging post for troops going to and from the Atlantic wall and passing in and out of the southern zone.

Vincent's work as liaison agent carried on until late December 1943. Each day at midday Vincent would walk or cycle to his mother's home in Cadouin, where he would lunch with her. One December day, as he approached his mother's home, he saw someone standing at the door. The 'dark clothing' gave the figure away immediately as Gestapo.★ Vincent's heart sank, and time stood still for him. He knew that if he turned to run he would be shot in the back. His only hope was to continue to the door and try his best to appear confused. When he reached the door, he was roughly grabbed by the arms, searched and told to produce his papers. As his mother looked on through the window, Vincent was marched to the central square in Cadouin where a bus was waiting. He was boarded onto the bus by armed guards that he was sure were Georgian conscripts. Eventually, on 18 January 1944, Vincent was taken to the concentration camp at Compiègne, where prisoners were sorted depending on the crimes they were accused of. Here he learned he was to be deported to Germany, and on 22 January he set off, part of a convoy of 2,000 people. He had no idea what awaited him. Nobody could know what awaited him because it was unimaginable. On 24 January 1944 he arrived in Buchenwald.

Power in the Countryside

In August 1943 the prefect of the Dordogne received a letter from the commander of the territories of the south of France, signed by General Niehof, complaining of 'attacks carried out against members of the occupation army, against buildings occupied by them, against communication paths, high voltage power lines, means of transport ...'[17] The letter went on to warn that measures would be taken against any official deemed to be failing in his duty and responsibilities. At that time the nature of Resistance in the area was about to change considerably. Up to the end of 1943 such disturbance was, according to the chief of the Gestapo in the area, Michaël Hambrecht:

★ This is Vincent García Riestra's description, by which I believe he was describing the long leather coat.

confined to the actions of isolated individuals against members of the occupation troops and their facilities … armed attacks on isolated soldiers, railway sabotages, especially on trains transporting troops and German materials, on German cars and lorries and on buildings occupied by German services … The repression of such activity could still be effectively carried out by means of police work and with the help of my own limited forces. But even at this time I was unable to complete my task one hundred percent because of a lack of numbers.

Monthly reports by the prefect of the Dordogne, Jean Popineau, tell of a growing concern by the French police forces and provide valuable insights into the gradual shift in public opinion. Based, amongst other sources, on the contents of thousands of opened letters, these reports outline the prefect's understanding of the fine balance between the population's acceptance of the Maquis, which would make tracking down the groups far more difficult, and the opposing view that the men in the woods were little more than troublemakers. Reporting on the state of the department in autumn 1943, Popineau hinted at a state of anarchy in the countryside where 'no one trusts anyone or anything any longer'.[18] This was partially due to the geographical and topological nature of the Dordogne, with its relatively small towns and large peasantry. Things were more developed in nearby Corrèze, just a few miles further east. There, Brive was a cradle for active resistance, ever since Edmond Michelet had set the ball rolling in June 1940. A prefect report from that department written at a similar time intimated that 'the population in the countryside is living in an atmosphere of fear and has lost all confidence in the police forces. Nevertheless, it is certain that the majority of the bandits known as "Maquis" have the sympathy of the biggest part of the population.'[19] The prefecture in Périgueux developed a deeper understanding of the situation and came to recognise that, in the two or three months that followed, a significant shift in power was taking place: from Vichy to the Maquis.[20]

At the end of September 1943, Popineau noticed that public opinion had become 'worse and worse'. In particular, it had changed 'from passive, as it was' and was becoming 'active in an anti-governmental direction'.[21] The public were beginning to say out loud what they might have only whispered before, believing this was a regime that was unlikely to last. By the following month, Popineau claimed that the police forces, despite their best efforts, were 'no longer able to effectively maintain public order'. There had been a series of explosions at the Gestapo headquarters in Périgueux and kidnappings of known Vichy sympathisers, such as a former militant of La Cagoule in Vergt and others in Bergerac. Two PPF militants had been killed near Sarlat, while in Excideuil a young man suspected of being an agent of the Gestapo had been murdered. On 23 October, the first German soldier was killed in the department when on patrol with another officer. They had come across two members of the AS Groupe Roland, Robert Mathé and Robert Chalon, and while both *résistants* managed to flee, Mathé's father was deported along with his friend, Fernand Besse. Armed attacks had taken place at the Chantiers de la Jeunesse, tobacconists and town halls where *cartes d'alimentation* were being delivered, while the Service de Renseignements Généraux had reported the existence of companies of '*réfractaires* grouped by "Maquis" of twenty to thirty individuals who are incontestably at the root of most of these incidents'. Notably, 'there is no doubt that many of these people are favourable to the "outlaws" in as much as they consider them as opposed to the occupation and the demands of the Germans'. In November, in the north-west of the Dordogne, in Angoisse, a letter was pushed under the door of a home, addressed to the gendarmerie. It warned them not to interfere in operations, threatening them with article 75 of the penal code. It was signed *l'Armée française de la libération*.[22]

Operations carried out by the French police followed throughout November, leading to the arrest of around fifty *réfractaires*, but this was nothing compared to the number of young men who had taken to the Maquis. Armed attacks, kidnappings and killings continued through December, to the point that the prefect claimed as more necessary than ever 'new police operations if we want to avoid the situation worsening'. The groups were not only organising and reinforcing themselves but, according to Popineau, 'they are operating with an audacity and with an increasing impunity'.[23] By the end of January 1944, this audacity was such that 'they claim every day that the small number of police is so insignificant that they are not worried by them'.[24] Quite how these claims might have been communicated by the *maquisards* to the prefect is unclear.

In addition, 'the population, sometimes terrorised, but often favourable to this "Maquis" sometimes openly demonstrates its approval.' That loyalty had begun to manifest itself in a number of ways. Firstly, the *maquisards* had begun to make raids on town halls, taking food ration tickets with them.

In La Coquille on the north-west of the department, members of the public not only stood and watched such a raid, but actually applauded. In Terrasson a total of 150 people witnessed a similar raid, but none gave any information, such as a description of a vehicle or sightings of known faces, to the local gendarmerie. There are several reasons for this, all of which might have played some part. Certainly, there was a fear of the *maquisards*, especially for those already concerned that their number had been marked. Secondly, the local gendarmeries had become very hit and miss in their support of the Vichy regime, and reports of crimes, misdemeanours or infractions blamed on the Resistance may not always have been pursued with the vigour that might have been expected by the prefecture and Gestapo. Thirdly, there was a closing of the ranks – a 'popular protective action' – that was becoming increasingly and worryingly evident in the minds of the Vichy officials, its followers and the German occupiers. As Popineau points out in the 31 January report, 'These are two attitudes that appear to me to be very serious: they are an indicator of a deep chasm between a large part of the population and the public powers'.[25]

Throughout the winter of 1943 and into the early months of 1944, the power and influence of the armed Resistance grew steadily. From a worrying but manageable minority rose a movement that began to seize control of the minds and hearts of an ever-increasing proportion of the population. From its beginnings as a low-level propaganda and information machine – still the case in late 1942 – Laval's STO had contributed to the change in its nature. The influx of young *réfractaires* into the AS, FTP or even in the ORA was not the result of political choices but rather circumstances and a wish to remain in France and, notionally at least, free. Life was tough, and, if not for their youth and spirit of adventure, it would have overwhelmed those whose backgrounds were at least modest. Living in covered trenches, abandoned farm buildings or hunting cabins – and later in tents made from parachutes – there was little in the way of hygiene, and no comfort. Sleeping on straw led to lice infestations. In such circumstances the experience of Spanish republicans helped those new to such issues. Raphael Finkler recalled a Spanish comrade ordering him and 'Phil' Lichtenberg to strip naked in the freezing cold; he boiled their clothes and covered every inch of their bodies with engine grease and industrial insecticide while their only set of clothes dried over the fire. It was a horrible experience, but at least it helped with the lice.[26]

Maquis units in the countryside needed food, clothing, information and armaments. Supplies and subsistence primarily came from the populace, the majority of whom – peasantry and farm owners at least – looked favourably on them. These 'visible' resisters, often women or vulnerable older people, played a vital role in allowing the Maquis – mostly young men – to develop and later engage in direct action. They often risked their own lives and livelihoods to do so. Those *paysans* who sheltered the Maquis or brought them food risked the destruction of their homes and livelihoods, as well as a bullet to the back of the head. The Vichy authorities were also happy to provide the Germans with workers, so deportation to work camps elsewhere in the Reich as well as concentration camps was just as feared. Any suspected *résistant*, whether *légal* or Maquis was a potential source of information for those authorities whose purpose was to destroy the Resistance movement. Therefore, torture became more and more commonplace as Gestapo methods were passed on to French police inspectors, and subsequently to French natives recruited to work for the Gestapo.

Those targeted by the Maquis tended to be people or institutions directly associated with opposition to the Resistance or sympathy for the Vichy regime. They targeted the many Chantiers de la Jeunesse for uniforms or supplies, and town halls for ration tickets; frustratingly for the prefect, they rarely met with any difficulties in these operations. Throughout that winter of 1943, the growth of the Maquis led to changes in what French society could consider acceptable behaviour. Some of these changes included turning a blind eye to criminality, or the acceptance that theft or even murder could be a necessary evil. While these changes fed into mistrust of the *maquisards* by some law-abiding members of the local population, for others the Maquis were demonstrating a clarity of their intentions that propagated a burgeoning support.

Those who supported Vichy shifted uncomfortably because the tide of the war was also turning. Once an informer, the choice was to side with the Resistance – while hoping previous allegiances would go unnoticed – or help the German and Vichy authorities eliminate the Maquis. Some of those who had already chosen to side with Vichy continued their denunciations, but others began to look at ways to cover their tracks.

Vichy's Response

The Vichy propaganda machine, led by Philippe Henriot, worked to suggest an intrinsic link between the Maquis and the Communist Party. A Jewish-influenced Bolshevik uprising was promoted as their ultimate aim. Furthermore, links between de Gaulle and Bolshevism were fabricated – in reality non-existent – suggesting that Gaullism was a column in the perceived Bolshevik takeover of France. Those tempted by Gaullism, the propaganda pointed out, should remember that national unity could only be achieved through patience, effort and sacrifice, and above all loyalty to the 'Leader who … commanded in Verdun'.[27] The campaigns sought to drive a wedge between the peasantry and the Maquis. They screamed of bands of Maquis criminals terrorising the peasantry in order to make them the primary objects for their revolutionary intentions and were designed to provide 'persuasive misinformation'. But the peasantry, the *ouvrier* and even the bourgeois classes didn't really buy into it – at least not wholesale. In January 1944 the railway station at Périgueux bore witness to a large-scale 'attack' from an armed group that took away vehicle loads of livestock and vegetables. This happened at 7.30 p.m., and with a large number of witnesses, but the affair was never fully pursued. It was just what the Maquis did. Repressive measures were therefore going to be necessary because all other means were not having the expected destabilising effect.

Joseph Darnand engaged in a quest to lead the Milice forward in ridding the countryside of the Maquis scourge. Having already requested an expanded fighting force from General Oberg, head of the police forces in France, and been declined, as the Milice had not shown enough discipline yet to merit expansion, Darnand was hungry to demonstrate the effectiveness of Vichy's tools in disposing of the Maquis. In fact, he wanted the destruction of the Maquis to be a task carried out solely by Vichy authorities.

German attempts at repression had so far been relatively ineffective. On 12 November 1943, following information provided to the Germans by a spy who had managed to infiltrate a group of *maquisards*, a detachment of Georgians led by Gestapo agents made their way to an FTP camp near Montignac to launch an assault. By the time they got there, the *maquisards* had received word and fled. On a foggy Sunday, 16 January 1944, between 500 and 600 Germans, led by Gestapo agents from Limoges and Périgueux, circled Mussidan. Eight days earlier a local man named Jacques Binger, known to be a close friend of well-known *miliciens* and suspected of acting as an agent to the Gestapo, had arranged for his contacts to arrest a member of the Resistance. The following day, on leaving Hôtel Andanson where he often went to drink an aperitif, Binger was killed in the street. The following encirclement of the town and its surrounding areas were a result of a complaint made by the *miliciens*, who had used all their resources to produce a full, accurate list of those in Mussidan suspected of being in the Resistance, helping the Resistance or being hostile to the Vichy regime. The people were told to stay in their homes while arrests were carried out. However, most of the those deemed important to the Resistance managed to escape detection, including Marcel Arnault, who hid on the roof of his home. Cruelly, however, the wives of two of those sought were arrested in their husbands' place and sent to Ravensbrück, leaving behind three young children. Passers-by were also arrested in order to make up the numbers to the expected figure.

Those who managed to escape the clutches of the Gestapo that day were forced to take to the Maquis and clandestine life but thirty-six people were detained. They were held briefly in Limoges where many were subjected to violent interrogation and torture. Next, they were sent to the internment camp in Royallieu, Compiègne, before the men were sent to Buchenwald and Mauthausen, while the women went to Ravensbrück. Only around half of those seized that day returned at the end of the war. The round-up was intended to dissuade the Resistance and those who helped provide for it. The overall aim was to represent the Resistance as the root of all the populace's troubles. It no doubt took a great deal of courage to continue to resist. This was perhaps one of the first moments that a collective solidarity against the trials of occupation was demonstrated. A message was being sent to those who, as yet, were not involved with the Resistance: the arrest of people uninvolved with Resistance activity would be pursued as policy. Nobody was safe from repression as long as the collective cover was maintained through silence. Following that day, Resistance around Mussidan not only carried on, but it strengthened to such an extent that the town would be visited by the forces of law and order, either German or French, a further three times before mid June 1944.

Infiltration

Prior to the periods of severe repression that were to follow, the single biggest concern for the majority of the non-Jewish Périgourdin population was putting food on the table. According to the commissioner's report of 7 April 1944 that gave an overview of recent months, it was the *ouvriers* (manual workers) who suffered most, being unable to afford the products being sold at an unrealistic price by the *paysans*.[28] The bourgeoisie were also complaining of the elevated cost of life for similar reasons. The *paysans*, on the other hand, were not so badly affected as they were living on a basis of product swapping. In this sphere the Maquis have been rounded upon as having compounded matters, but the situation was complicated. The programme of *ravitaillement général* (general food supplies) was leading to a shortage for those who needed to buy their food. It had not taken long for the peasantry to claim rightly that most of the imposition orders made for low authorised costs were intended for transportation to Germany. As a result, prices in the open market rose, compounded by the low value of the franc imposed by the Germans, in turn giving the Germans tremendous spending power. Even the prefect himself announced he was stopping the export of potatoes to other departments, hinting at a little sympathy for popular protective action. The fact was that only 5,000 of the 14,000 tonnes due according to the imposition order had been collected. Stubbornness on the part of the *Corporation Paysanne* combined with threats made to collectors and a weak crop had all contributed to the shortfall, but this did demonstrate that the peasantry was actually undermining and disrupting the running of the *ravitaillement général*.

Was this due to threats from the *maquisards* – an accusation levied both at the time and in subsequent decades? The answer is that no data exists that could possibly quantify the extent to which this was the case. Certainly, the Maquis would have had some influence, but mostly it would have been a result of non-co-operation with the Vichy regime. The Maquis did, however, have direct influence on the sale of goods.

Any Maquis group was a haven for the odd criminal, and as such some unforgivable crimes took place directly attributable to Maquis members. An October 1943 report by the Service de Renseignements Généraux (RG) on the Durestal Maquis listed crimes committed during the previous year as including theft of food ration tickets, petrol and tobacco, as well as three kidnappings and an armed robbery.[29] The Maquis of the area 'acting under the Gaullist banner' consisted of, according to the report, 'former army officers, illegal aliens, outlaws and those wishing to evade the police (notably communist elements), réfractaires from other regions'. However, most *maquisards*, particularly those from the FTP, recognised their responsibilities, both social and socialist. Often where Maquis requisitions took place payment would follow, though not always immediately. Maquis leaders also considered what they were doing a service to their country for which they should be recognised, so some element of theft was considered acceptable. Whereas requisition orders were often left for vehicles, goods were usually, according to the report, paid for generously. Despite this, the report claims that the people of the countryside were scared of the *maquisards*, and afraid of denouncing them. This is something of an exaggeration as the majority of the rural population co-existed alongside and supported them. What the *maquisards* were able and willing to do was have some effect on the fixing of non-official prices, and this benefited the *paysans* in particular.

Lists were drawn up of prices that were considered fair given the market forces at play. Farmers found to be inflating prices unfairly would be punished through a taxation – normally a requisition to be taken to Maquis camps to help feed the group. Repeat offenders might be more seriously dealt with. Farmers founded to be hoarding stock – particularly meat – would simply have that requisitioned. Sometimes *maquisards* would be present in town and village markets, keeping an eye on the prices. If a farmer was found to be overcharging, his stock might be removed in waiting vans and whisked away to help feed the hungry young paramilitaries. The Maquis was, in effect, policing in plain sight of the Germans. For those in the towns that feared communism, the FTP's methodologies probably benefited them too in the short term.

Reports of the time describe the response of inhabitants of smaller towns and the peasantry to Maquis threats and intimidation as a mixture of fear, respect and enthusiasm. Accounts given to local police of Maquis incidents were often generalised and vague, especially when it came to enabling the pursuant or even recognising particular groups of *résistants*. Vichy tried to drive a wedge between the local population and the armed Resistance groups, but local authorities were often faced with general unhelpfulness. Some gendarmeries, though, worried and irked by attacks carried out by the Maquis, will no doubt have recognised the necessity for such events in order for the groups to survive.

The report to the prefect of 7 April claimed that traders and industrialists were working at a slow pace, having been deprived of certain raw materials to use or sell on. Local government officers and administrators in the town halls were, it also claimed, doing their jobs without issue. Did the writer have any clue that it was here that a growing number was carrying out clandestine tasks such as producing false identity cards and food tickets for *réfractaires*? These people, though small in number, were well placed and willing to put themselves in great danger, all the while continuing to appear utterly on the side of Vichy.

Soeur Marie-Philomène

It was not unknown for postal workers to intervene in Resistance matters at crucial moments. One such occasion occurred in the north-east of the Dordogne at the end of 1943. Christmas was just weeks away when a postal worker at the Thiviers sorting office, recruited as a civilian agent by the Résistance-PTT, opened a letter addressed to the Gestapo in Périgueux. Denunciations were at an all-time high and some method of curbing this danger for the Resistance had to be found. Seemingly no one was safe: Jewish families, those suspected of harbouring communists or other undesirables, people suspected of providing shelter or supplies to the Maquis. Not all the denunciation letters could be intercepted – there were simply too many of them. Indeed, some were traceable to old family or business disputes and founded on nothing but hot air and venom. Others had to be allowed to slip through the net to draw attention away from the brave work of the PTT workers risking their lives. Certain handwriting styles and stationery were clues to suspected collaborators, who sent letters to Vichy or German authorities.

The letter opened that day in Thiviers was addressed to the office of the Gestapo HQ in Périgueux. Contained within were the names of a dozen or so members of the AS, including that of chief of the sector Rodolphe Cézard, known as 'Rac'. Cézard was particularly vehemently targeted. The letter denounced 'bad Frenchman who are working for the English and against Marshal Pétain'. Further missives followed – a dozen or so, all well informed and providing information that could only have come from an insider. Thiviers had become such a crossroads of Maquis activity and information flow that the Milice had set up a headquarters in the Hôtel des Voyageurs. The naming of such important leaders sparked panic amongst the angry *maquisards*, and Cézard and his men met to discuss what to do next. Not only had Cézard been named, but so had René Tallet ('Violette'), and others. If the information slipped through the AS in the northern region could be decimated and its strength – of its leaders with military experience – could be eradicated.

The problem was mulled over between Cézard and Tallet but both men knew that something needed to happen soon. Infiltrating the sorting office further was too risky, and there remained the issue of further potential letters. Tallet came up with an idea that was simple but by no means guaranteed to work. All of the letters had been posted in and around Thiviers itself. The owners of the two *librairies* (book and stationery sellers) in the small town were known to be sympathisers to the Maquis cause, and they were told to carry out a task. Whenever a pen was bought from their shops, they were to ask the client to write a couple of lines on the pretext of checking whether the pen worked. Two examples of one of the letters were provided to each of the shopkeepers for comparison. The plan would fail if the author of the letters was well equipped with stationery, just as it would if the request for a writing sample was questioned. Weeks passed, and further letters were intercepted with no clue as to the identity of the informer, until one afternoon, six weeks later in January 1944, a shocked shopkeeper arrived with news for Cézard. On selling a pen, a piece of paper had been handed over to the customer, who had duly obliged. What was written was strange enough: '*Je suis folle. Il faudrait m'enfermer*' ('I am mad. I should have been locked away'). This woman – the adjectival agreement of the word '*fou*' demonstrated her femininity – didn't, it seemed, like what she was doing but she was powerless to stop.

The leaders of the Maquis – young and religious – were told that this had come from the hand of a nun. Her name was Luce Million, and she was known as Soeur Marie-Philomène. She lived and worked in the small Thiviers hospital, spending most of her time looking after the elderly. Born in 1904 near Saint-Foy-la-Grande, a few steps over the Dordogne border, in the Gironde, she was nearly 40 years of age. She had lived in the Thiviers area since 1940, before which she had worked in the Francheville clinic in Périgueux without ever displaying any outward zeal towards Vichy or distaste for resistance. In fact, she was not unknown to several members of the group and had been thought to be supportive of their cause.

Disaster had been averted for the time being, but unless Cézard knew where she was getting her information, the leak would likely spring again. That she was a *réligieuse* made no difference, no matter how Cézard felt about the matter: she had to be arrested and brought to account. Cézard picked up the telephone and was passed through the sympathetic PTT operator to number two in Queyroi de Sarlande, and Tallet was informed of the news. A commando unit was assigned and, as was often the case when collaborators needed to be dealt with, Tallet's Sarlande-originated Bataillon Violette was given the task of bringing her in. Raoul Audrerie was assigned to approach and, if necessary, drag her in. He was accompanied by another three members of the *bataillon*, including Raymond Pivert. Cézard went to the hospital and spoke with the director, discovering that the sister had been granted two days' leave. She was staying with her parents, who were celebrating their golden wedding anniversary, in Bergerac. With the potential for letters now to be posted and sorted outside of Thiviers, the operation became urgent. She would have to picked up from her parents' home.

On 22 January the team, including Audrerie and Pivert, went to Bergerac by car, followed by another vehicle close behind. They hoped to pick up Luce Million and bring her back to the Thiviers countryside for the next part of the operation. The plan had taken considerable preparation and Cézard had been helped in the more practical elements by Lieutenant Raoul Christophe, Krikri of the ORA. Audrerie and Pivert wore German uniforms and carried false papers identifying them as German police, despite neither actually being able to speak German. Christophe had managed to secure, at very short notice, a suitable car, German uniforms and weapons, and paperwork. His planning skills would become evident elsewhere, later that year, when he planned a train robbery in Neuvic-sur-l'Isle that was, and still is, the biggest such haul ever. As a member of the ORA, his support network and ability to acquire material or information reached as far as Vichy itself.

Audrerie, Pivert and two further *maquisards* also dressed in German uniform were met at the door by Luce Million's mother, who informed them that she was attending a special Mass in town. It was just after eight o'clock in the morning. The men entered the church and waited near a chapel at the rear until the service was finished. They identified and approached Soeur Marie-Philomène and showed her the letters she had sent. Knowing nothing of their deception, she confirmed that it was she who had sent them and confirmed her belief that the denunciations were all correct and in good order. Invited to follow the two men, she was told that arrests had been made and she was required to help identify the suspects. She climbed into the car for her journey into the countryside, stopping briefly for her to collect some items from her parents' home. The second car contained a further four men. These included Raoul Christophe and Jean Delage, one of the older and more experienced *maquisards* based at Pont Lasveyras. He was 21 years of age.

In a hamlet near Thiviers, Christophe had organised the final part of the deception. It seemed from the letters that while she would be able to identify some of the men by sight, including the leader Cézard, she might not be able to recognise all of them. She was taken to a run-down house where, she was told, those arrested were being held under armed guard. Tallet played the role of another German officer and presented her with Cézard, complete with ripped clothes, ruffled hair and bloodied face. It was not unusual for French police to operate in German uniform, but it was fortunate for the sake of the operation that she did not recognise Tallet. They asked her to identify him by name, which she did, accurately, claiming that she knew he arranged parachute drops and plotted against the Vichy regime. '*C'est lui, c'est bien lui*,' ('That is him, that's definitely him') she said. In the dark, damp building Cézard revealed his identity and Soeur Marie-Philomène's betrayal of the *maquisards* was confirmed. Cézard asked her why she had denounced him to the Germans – the enemies of the state. '*C'est mon secret*' was her reported response.

With the benefit of hindsight, it is all too easy to condemn those who informed against the Resistance as conniving or selfish, but this was not always the case. Some were following their instincts, some were misguided and some were just trying to ensure that their families survived. The case of Soeur Marie-Philomène was, however, different. She had been described as friendly to the Resistance cause by several who knew her. Spite conflicted with her religious training and, apolitical as it officially was, some in the Catholic Church had declared support for those who stood up to occupation and condemned

Raphael Finkler, who began his resistance journey while still at *lycée* as a *légal* before experiencing life in the AS and then the FTP-MOI. (Ralph Finkler)

Marshal Philippe Pétain meets German Chancellor Adolf Hitler at Montoire in October 1940.

An iconic photograph of Jean Moulin a former prefect of Eure-et-Loir sent back to France by De Gaulle to help unify the various factions of the Resistance. (Marcel Bernard © Legs Antoinette Sasse, Musée du Général Leclerc et de la Libération de Paris/Musée Jean Moulin (Paris Musées))

A painting of Raphael Finkler attacking the Parfumerie Bleue in Périgueux at 6.40 p.m. on 24 November 1943, commissioned for his birthday and painted by Marcel Pajot. (Ralph Finkler)

One of the false identities used by Louis de la Bardonnie. (Collection de la Bardonnie family)

Château Laroque, the home of Louis de la Bardonnie in Saint-Antoine-de-Breuilh. De Gaulle stayed there during his visit to the Dordogne after the war. (Author's collection)

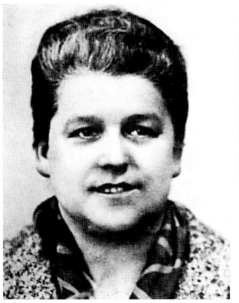

Hélène Dupuy, responsable for the Service Social de la Résistance en Dordogne. She found schools and homes for Jewish children and protected *maquisards* sent into town on missions. (Collection Guy Penaud)

Roger Ranoux (Hercule) and his brother Guy (Mickey). Both became important leaders in the Maquis, Roger rising to *état-major* of the departmental FFI. (Collection Guy Penaud)

Laure Gatet, the young scientist who joined Confrérie Notre Dame (CND), one of the earliest Resistance networks in France. This picture was taken in 1940. (Private collection, All Rights Reserved)

Vincent García, who arrived in France as a 15-year-old, having fled the Spanish Civil War. (Collection Vincent García)

The *groupe franc* Roland. Standing in the centre of the picture holding the tricolour flag with the Croix de Lorraine on it is Charles Mangold, regional chief of the AS. To the right of him is Roland Clée. (Collection Guy Penaud)

The small restaurant in Saint-André de la Double where Alice Barrat provided a vital link between the outside world and the Maquis groups of the forest. A yellow plaque marks her contribution. (Author's collection)

Claudette Négrier whose father owned a café in Vergt that served as home to many Resistance gatherings. Claudette became a liaison agent. (Collection Claudette Hauswirth)

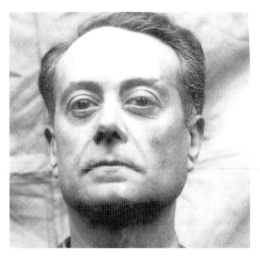

Paul Lapuyarde, agent PX 301 and 'Homme de confiance' of the Gestapo in the Dordogne. (Collection Guy Penaud)

A train on the Bordeaux–Périgueux line following a sabotage. (Collection Guy Penaud)

A *maquisard* of AS Dordogne-nord, which became Brigade Rac, preparing for an ambush. This photograph was taken by André Léonard, photographer of Brigade Rac. (Collection Alan Latter)

Valentine Bussière, the legendary FTP fighter who met the 'Das Reich' division head on. (Collection ANACR)

Gestapo chief SS-Untersturmführer Michael Hambrecht during an operation in Brântome, April 1944. Behind him is Charles Schmidtt, an Alsatian. (Collection Guy Penaud)

Jacob Rauen poses in front of the Gestapo's regional HQ with a flag taken from the groupe Roland in June 1944. François Collin looks on. (Collection Patrice Rolli)

A ceremony on the steps of the *palais de justice* in Périgueux, celebrating the new recruits to the local police. Jean Popineau, prefect of the Dordogne, is on the far right and second from the left is René Bousquet, secrétaire general de police within the Vichy government. (Archives Départementales de la Dordogne 1Num 19)

Miliciens march through the streets of Ribérac. (Archives Départementales de la Dordogne 5 W 5)

François Collin at the time of his arrest. (Archives Départementales de la Dordogne 14 J 7)

On the left, Victor Denoix (sometimes known as Adolphe Denoix), head of the Milice in the Dordogne. (Collection Patrice Rolli/Frédéric Dumait)

Vichy propaganda against Jews and Francs-maçons. (Archives Départementales de la Dordogne 14 J 25)

General Walter Brehmer, commander of the division that terrorised the region in March and April 1944. (Collection Guy Penaud)

René Cousteiller ('Soleil') in Siorac-en-Périgord in June 1944. (Photo by Michel Carcenac, Collection Guy Penaud)

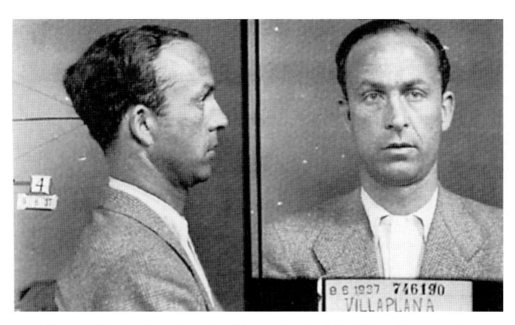

Alexandre Villaplane, formerly captain of the French national football team, later a member of the Gestapo Française and a leader of the Brigade Nord-Africaine. (Collection Patrice Rolli/Archives Nationales)

Members of the Brigade Nord-Africaine (La Phalange) and of the Gestapo at the start of the Brehmer operations, late March 1944. (Collection Patrice Rolli/Archives Départementales de la Haute-Vienne)

Hostages gathered in front of the *mairie* in Mussidan on 11 June 1944. Those on the left would be released. Those on the right with their hands in the air would be shot that evening. (Collection Patrice Rolli)

Jacques Poirier (Captain Jack, left) and Robert Brouillet (Charles le Bolchévique).
(Collection Guy Penaud)

The *préfecture du maquis* formed in June 1944. Maxime Roux is second row back on the left.
(Collection Guy Penaud)

The village of Mouleydier, entirely destroyed by soldiers of the 11th Panzer Division on 21 June 1944, following the execution of twenty-two *maquisards*. (Collection Patrice Rolli)

Skorpion West propaganda – the tract distributed following the destruction of Mouleydier. (Collection Patrice Rolli)

General Charles de Gaulle visits Rouffignac, 5 March 1944. (Collection Patrice Rolli)

Above: The Schenkel children of La Bachellerie, all of whom would be aboard the train that left for Drancy. (Private collection, All Rights Reserved)

Left: Bags containing the 2.3 billion francs stolen from the Neuvic train. This is the only known photograph. (Collection Guy Penaud)

FTP-MOI *maquisards* in Brântome prior to their departure for Angoulème. (Collection Ralph Finkler)

A detachment of the Soleil group during the liberation parade in Périgueux. (Collection ANACR)

A group of Resistance leaders in front of the Hôtel Domino in Périgueux, August 1944. On the far left is Roger Ranoux (Hercule). Central is Jacques Poirier whose father Robert Poirier is to his left, looking at the camera. (Collection Guy Penaud/Musée Militaire de Périgueux)

Several members of Groupe Paul Frydman, the Jewish group led by Raphael Finkler and Léon Lichtenberg. The boy is 7-year-old Lazare Frydman, the only survivor of the Frydman family, who escaped the massacre by hiding in a barrel. (Collection Ralph Finkler)

collaboration. Soeur Marie-Philomène had acted, it seemed, not through a belief in political or religious doctrine. What she had done – and she denied none of it – she seemed to have done for purely personal reasons.

Mystery will always surround the exact details of the affair. Several local historians have, however, worked hard at piecing together written evidence – practically non-existent but for prefectural police reports and witness statements.[30] Further details can be drawn from a number of books written about Brigade RAC,[31] but inconsistencies are rife. Michel Maureau did more than anyone in trying to unpick the exact details of the case over a thirty-year period but found himself up against a brick wall of silence on the part of some who were probably there. It is possible, probable even, that what happened next was covered up by at least some members of the Maquis. Decisions that were made and actions that were taken were not done illegally in the context of war, but it would be a surprise if they did not haunt those involved.

Contrary to what she might have believed, it is unlikely that Soeur Marie-Philomène's secret was unknown to Cézard for very long after her arrest. She had fallen in love with a local priest: a chaplain to the Resistance named L'Abbé Jules Ferry. Their relationship had become real, illicit and physical. But when Ferry rejected her for another nurse named Jeanne Lognon, like Ferry attached to the Maquis and at the same hospital as Soeur Marie-Philomène, her reaction was one of vengeance. Jules Ferry, whose name was almost comical in a French religious setting,★ had arrived in the Périgord from Lorraine in 1939 with his mother. His family was close to the Cézards and he was an intimate friend of the man who was to become leader of the local Maquis. Regarded as a potential future priest, Ferry engaged in the Resistance alongside his friend. Brigade Rac did all it could to retain a religious soul and several chaplains served therein, including Ferry. It appears unlikely that Ferry, on discovering the identity of the letter's author, would have kept his affair secret from Cézard. It seems that the young, handsome chaplain had a way with the opposite sex and that the nun had fallen for his charms in a fashion that was not fully reciprocated.

Whatever the circumstances, death was the punishment for traitors who denounced the Maquis. The Resistance story is full of executions that were carried out for such 'crimes'. For decades following the war, historians

---

★ Jules Ferry was a famous French statesman – a republican and avid promoter of laicism. He was assassinated in 1893.

debated the actions of certain overzealous *maquisards*, and one of the tragedies of the STO was an increased possibility for young men with criminal
tendencies to infiltrate the Maquis and, for want of a better term, commit
crime. But the settling of the fate of Soeur Marie-Philomène transcended
that. The operation to bring her in was carried out by leaders, and Audrerie,
Cézard and Tallet were all military men with morals, saturated with military discipline and clarity of thought. The sister was incarcerated while the
men decided what to do. Despite her admission of guilt, she showed little
or no remorse. Initially they offered her a position with her order in Spain
– something that would have required a significant amount of organisation
through channels outside of the Maquis group – but she refused to even
consider it. Cézard, a Catholic who like so many others had come to the
Dordogne from the north-east of the country at the outbreak of war, found
that he could not simply condemn her to death. His only course of action
was to take advice on what to do. Monseigneur Ruch, the Archbishop of
Strasbourg, was another who had come to Périgueux when his city was
evacuated. A veteran of the First World War, he represented, for Cézard,
an authority qualified to make the decision. Cézard and Tallet travelled to
Périgueux and spoke to him, after which he requested a little time to think.
When he finally replied his answer was: 'This is a woman who has betrayed
her country. If the Resistance is going to survive, it has to defend itself. I do
not have to tell you what to do. But, if she is condemned to death, I will
send a priest for her to confess, and to be present.'[32] In doing so, for those
involved the Church had fulfilled its responsibilities. The decision was left
to Cézard and Tallet, who now believed that the Church did not formally
object to the execution.

At the beginning of February 1944, Soeur Marie-Philomène was driven to
Pont Lasveyras, where the ever-expanding AS Maquis of the northern sector
had set up a base at the Moulin de la Forge-de-Pissac, close to Beyssenac
in the Corrèze and Payzac in the Dordogne. Here, the Pont Lasveyras mill
was chosen as an ideal set-up for an *école de cadres*: it was remote and located
alongside the River Auvézère. A beautiful stone structure hundreds of years
old, its owner had not been seen in the area for years. To get to it only one
main pathway could be followed, and that was slippery and treacherous. The
bataillon decided to hold Soeur Marie-Philomène in that isolated spot, having
failed to find an alternative holding area that was suitable for a non-enemy
prisoner. Here the situation could be dealt with securely and sensitively.

On the evening following her arrival at the camp, Soeur Marie-Philomène faced a tribunal composed of several local leaders of the AS. Cézard and Tallet were not, it appears, present. She persisted in her beliefs and lack of remorse for her actions, and there is little to support the theory that what she did was purely the consequence of a broken heart, though it is possible that she simply could not forgive the man she still loved. She was, however, given ample opportunity to escape death, to declare remorse and recant her reasoning. Keeping her as a prisoner was not possible as the need to guard her was a waste of resources but, had she been at least part willing, she might have been detained as a nurse to the Maquis. There is no record of this option having been refused or offered. Perhaps her infidelity to the Church was the transgression for which she felt death was the only proper punishment. She was, she said, not afraid of death and she was so condemned. Ruch, on being alerted of the news, sent his secretary Canon Sharneberger, who spent the evening praying with the sister, heavily guarded by *maquisards*. In the absence of Cézard, the running of the following day was left to young Jean Delage, who had been in the car that followed the men who arrested her. Sharneberger left her alone to pray through the night. When daylight came she was led out towards a firing squad composed of seven men whose names had been chosen at random by drawing lots. Delage ensured that the event was efficient, well run and respectful. The firing squad knew that one of them had a weapon with a blank shell. This way nobody could know for certain who had delivered the mortal wound.

The path leading up to the flattish spot on the edge of woodland where the execution was to take place was slippery due to recently melted snow. Soeur Marie-Philomène was accompanied by a young *maquisard*, who in all likelihood was also chosen at random. His name was Georges Lachaud. He was 21 years old and had only recently joined the Maquis; he had been given the additional role of waking her up, though he found her ready for her destiny. Soeur Marie-Philomène refused the offer of his arm for support, only grabbing his hand once when she almost fell: 'It was on a steep bit of ground, but she did not want to take my arm. She was very strong. She did not even want a blindfold.' She asked to be allowed to kneel in front of the post, and she was not secured to it. She made no sound, refusing to speak, and offered up no audible prayers. 'Then, I stood back and the firing squad fired on her.'[33]

Details of what happened to Soeur Marie-Philomène emerged slowly. When she did not return to the hospital in Thiviers the sister in charge contacted her parents. They reported her missing to the police and an inquest was launched. Over a period of a week at the end of January, when Soeur Marie-Philomène was still alive, messages were passed to and from the French and German police. The prefect was, it seems, convinced that the sister had been arrested by the German police, especially as she was known to be associated with L'Abbé Ferry, who had recently been identified by the Germans as wanted for arrest, alongside Rodolphe Cézard. Herein lay the clever consequence, intentional or otherwise, of Raoul Christophe's plan. Neither police force seemed to know of each other's operations, or indeed trust each other enough to be convinced of the other's non-involvement. Witness statements that at least one of the policemen spoke excellent French, and that another spoke in local patois, convinced the German police that the Resistance had probably picked her up when Cézard and Ferry fled into obscurity, organising for her to serve as a nurse clandestinely. Archival letters suggest that at the time Luce Million was being led to her Calvary the blame was still being passed to and from the police agencies. The letters state that '*les motifs de l'arrestation sont inconnus*' ('the reasons for the arrest are unknown'). Only one small handwritten note suggesting Maquis culpability was found, archived with those letters undated and unsigned:

Information from Limoges: Could have been kidnapped and killed by the Maquis of Beyssenac. J.P.[34]

The Maquis and Sabotage

As a civilian agent for the FTP, Lucien Cournil continued his work in propaganda dissemination, as well as recruitment. However, the focus of that role changed in the early months of 1944 when he was told he should now channel newcomers as there were too many men in the Maquis for them to be effective. He began a process of signing up interested parties and sending some to safe houses or training camps, telling others that they were not needed at that time. Like many other non-Maquis-based *résistants*, he also took part in small, armed night-time operations in and around his home commune of Terrasson. He was in close contact with Dr Pierre Daunois, a leader of one of the very first Maquis groups in the *Terrassonais*. Cournil's operations often consisted of minor sabotage, further distribution of tracts or simply passing necessary information along the line. Those who chose to become a *légal* usually held down full-time employment during the day while carrying out dangerous operations at night.

On one of Cournil's missions, on the evening of 9 March 1944, he received a bullet to the leg. He didn't see who fired it, nor whether it was one of Adolphe Denoix's local *miliciens*.[35] In a serious condition, he was hidden for several days then transported to the hospital in Clairvivre, where he was cared for by Dr Fontaine and his team. René Fontaine (alias Colonel Elliott) was part of the hospital staff from Strasbourg that had relocated to Périgueux in 1939 and his – and his team's – medical expertise saved many Maquis lives. Once partially recovered, Cournil returned home to continue his work but in the last week of March his mother was visited by a local gendarme: 'I don't know what your boy is doing but take my word for it he had better stop it and get out of here.'[36] At the end of the week the dreadful events of the Brehmer operation took place in which Resistance members and Jewish families were killed or deported. Cournil's activities were obviously known about – at least by the gendarmerie – so he was forced to flee, spending several weeks hiding on a farm in nearby Villac while continuing his Resistance work.

Cournil's childhood friend, four years his senior, Roger Ranoux ('Hercule') returned to the Dordogne in December 1943, having sought permission to bring his Lucien Sampaix group with him. A banquet was served in his honour in fields not far from the main Périgueux–Terrasson road and the Ranoux family home in Tranche, near Le Lardin. Not only were the *maquisards* present for a meal that included a stuffed pig, but so too were the many *légaux* supporting the Maquis of both the FTP and AS, for whom Ranoux had developed huge admiration.[37] A gathering of more than 100[38] was not advisable given the climate, especially so near the main road between Périgueux and Brive, where Germans and *miliciens* were routinely patrolling, but it was a memorable evening for all involved. Following the meal, in the early hours of the morning, Ranoux and his team, as well as a number of FTP civilians, travelled the short distance to the Progil paper and chemical factory in Condat-de-Lardin. There they set plastic explosives and rendered parts of the factory unusable, having had inside knowledge on what needed to be destroyed in advance. In the early hours of the morning 1 January 1944 – a Saturday – Jean Rouby called up several of his volunteer firefighters and they spent the morning putting out a fire that some of them had helped start.[39] After they were treated to lunch at a nearby hotel by some of the factory's management. That same December night sabotages were carried out on locomotives in Bergerac, Le Buisson and Eymet, organised by Philippe de Gunzbourg and AS groups in the Bergeracois. In Périgueux, Roland Clée and members of Groupe Franc Roland attempted to kill Paul Lapuyarde, but the operation went wrong, and he got away.

January 1944 saw a concerted attack on the railways of the region. All lines around the region – especially that between Périgueux and Limoges – were put out of action on an almost daily basis by some attack or another. Trains carrying men or materials towards Germany were derailed. Some attacks brought down bridges or collapsed tunnels. One line remained relatively uninterrupted, between Périgueux and Coutras, just outside Bordeaux – the Germans ran an armoured train for protection along this route. The ORA, based primarily around Périgueux, were also active in railway sabotage, including the lighting of wagons of straw at La Coquille on 30 January that turned a train into a furnace.

The involvement of *cheminots* was often central to the sabotage of rolling stock. Sometimes trains were stopped just outside a station – the signaller being in on an operation – and other *cheminots* detached the train and helped move it away from its carriages before explosive charges were set off, ensuring the train was incapable of continuing. Sometimes charges were set on tracks with more devastating effects, though this required a high degree of training with plastic explosives, fusers and timers. Targets were sometimes static too. An attack on 12 December 1943 on the SNCF depot in Périgueux saw a 50-tonne crane, which was vital to repair railway lines throughout the region, put out of action. The damage was limited, delaying repairs by two weeks, but it was enough to have a knock-on effect around the train networks.

A further attack on the SNCF workshops was carried out on 16 January. Detachments from FTP groups Gardette and Lucien Sampaix, which included Roger Ranoux, were instructed to sabotage the engines stored in the workshops. Around 10.30 p.m. the *maquisards* sounded a bell, after which a complicit worker released the opening mechanism of the doors. Some of the *maquisards* subdued the workers present, while others posted themselves around the huge structure. Before a third group could begin laying the explosives, a detachment of Nazis arrived (in fact Georgian) and a brief firefight ensued. The mission was a failure and was reorganised for the last day of the month under the stewardship of Albert Thomas (Jacky), who had been sent to the area from Tulle. This time three groups were involved – Gardette, Gabrielli and Lucien Sampaix – and most men participated in this second attempt. The saboteurs met no resistance. Only one terrified German guard was present, and he was made prisoner. Pierre Michaud (Normand), Ranoux's deputy, ripped down the posters of Pétain and Hitler from the walls of the office, while paperwork was burned, and *Vive de Gaulle* was scrawled in blue pencil. During that time twenty-four charges were set on machines and several locomotives in the workshops. Word had been passed around that employees should be several hundred metres away from the workshop that evening, and some minutes later the *résistants* were themselves at a safe distance when a series of large explosions lit up the night sky. The Germans were unable to survey the damage until the following morning, when it became clear that, despite only fourteen out of twenty-four charges successfully detonating, a significant amount of damage had been done.

The following month, on the night of 12 February 1944, two FTP groups worked in tandem, simultaneously attacking two electricity stations. These installations supplied the Dordogne, the Gironde (in the occupied zone and home to factories around the Bordeaux area as well as the city's submarine base), the Lot-et-Garonne and parts of the Charente. Ranoux's Lucien Sampaix group and the Gardette group targeted the Mauzac installation while the FTP Ricco group moved on the factory at Tuilières, a little further west and closer to Bergerac. The sabotage operation was ordered at an inter-regional level by the FTP and resulted in the Société Énergie Électrique du Sud-ouest being robbed of 40 per cent of its overall production capacity.

Finding the Maquis

On 1 January 1944, following a New Year's party with friends in Mussidan, Raphael Finkler and Léon Lichtenberg met Paul Frydman in Périgueux and took the small steam train towards Vergt. Only knowing that they needed to find the local butcher, they took their seats together, each carrying a small cardboard suitcase. They had told their parents that they were going, along with Maryse Nicolas and Monette Leclerq, but nobody else. The underpowered train, known as the *tacot departmental*, was slow and followed the main route as far as Vergt. Throughout the journey, during which it sometimes seemed as if the passengers would need to get out and push when climbing the most minor of undulations, Finkler noticed two men watching them. They were wearing sheepskin coats and leaned on railings out the back of the rearmost carriage. When the train finally reached Vergt, the group headed to the village centre by foot, but before they could locate their contact Finkler felt a pistol pushed into his back. Glancing over his shoulder he saw the men who had been watching them on the train, both with pistols.

The young men explained their intentions and told them of their journey in the Resistance so far. After a long conversation they were led, on foot, to woodland nearby. They followed a trail for what seemed an eternity until eventually they heard voices and were allowed past an armed sentry. A few hundred metres further on, they saw the small clearing. A multitude of men were chatting and busying themselves around large wooden benches, raised branches that they soon discovered to be shelters and several vehicles gleaming amongst the greenery. Cigarette smoke and chatter were everywhere, and ahead stood a barn into which the three men were led. There were several rooms: two for the officers and another larger room covered in straw, which evidently was where most of the men slept. They were introduced to the group's leader, Commandant Roland, as 'three Bolsheviks'. They had arrived in the Maquis, but rather than being in the FTP as they had wanted they were in the AS. Their request for an FTP contact had been refused by their MNCR contacts, so the AS was their only known way into an armed Resistance group. That they had little in common politically with de Gaulle was not a problem. What they didn't know was quite the extent to which the *strategy* of the AS was unsuitable for them.

There were plenty of young men at the camp, but the consequence of STO was that not all had the same appetite for action as the three friends. Whereas AS leaders had partially budged away from pure *attentisme*, central to the existence of the AS was military discipline. AS Maquis camps were barracks, not moveable bases for assaults. Despite now engaging in some sabotages and raids, AS leaders had been guided towards setting up *corps-francs* (commando units) – small groups of men, often former soldiers, who were particularly suited to short, sharp operations that rarely involved engaging the enemy in combat. Before the Allied landings in Normandy, *corps-francs* operations carried out by the AS aimed at disrupting infrastructure, transport of goods to Germany or securing equipment. Few AS were sufficiently armed; AS Groupe Roland, for example, armed its *corps-franc* well, but for the rest of the camp only the sentries on duty were ever fully armed during January 1944. If there was sufficient armament to defend the camp in case of attack, it was not distributed amongst the men. For the Allied leaders – Eisenhower in particular – arming the French Resistance was not a priority: finite resources were better directed towards preparation for invasion beyond France's borders. President Franklin D. Roosevelt placed little faith in the military capabilities of an interior army against the might of the German Wehrmacht. Even in the lead-up to D-Day, materiel sent to France for use by the Resistance rarely ever surpassed the relative status of breadcrumbs.

The AS, whose leaders had no desire to see the French army flooded with communism, kept the FTP at arm's length, and in most of the Dordogne partnerships were never developed. Feelings ran deep and were reciprocated: the FTP accused the AS of 'wasteful' *attentisme*. They questioned whether resources and arms were being hoarded, needlessly waiting for Jour-J, when they could have been used directly against the enemy. The stockpiling of weapons and munitions may not have been as widespread as claimed by some FTP *maquisards,* but parachuted material was sent primarily by de Gaulle and the Allies to the AS rather than the FTP – de Gaulle himself mistrusted both the conviction and aptitudes of the largely non-military FTP. This led to resentment, and some FTP groups carried out raids on AS camps to secure equipment. Information on parachute drops were kept away from the FTP and in some areas of the Dordogne – and throughout France – the proximity of FTP Maquis to the AS could lead to serious issues, even after agents from England were sent to add cohesion to the burgeoning military potential. AS leaders argued that the FTP was guilty of provoking the occupying forces and police by engaging in ambush and other forms of direct action which unnecessarily endangered the local population. Certainly, most of the small-scale attacks on German soldiers themselves could be attributed to FTP Maquis. Defenders of FTP strategies, which included targeting German soldiers and thereby spreading the ripples created by the Châteaubriand martyrdom, spoke of patriotism. Leaders of FTP groups believed in the need for Frenchmen and women to make sacrifices for the greater good, just as they were doing.

De Gaulle didn't want the FTP armed, which caused resentment and infighting between Maquis factions, and while SOE's policy was to deal with the AS, it took the more open-minded agents on the ground in France to recognise the potential of the numbers offered up by the FTP. Ironically it was Colonel Passy's BCRA – de Gaulle's London-based intelligence agency – that recognised the potential of the FTP, due to the sheer numbers. For SOE agents such as Jacques Poirier, who approached the problem on the ground with an open mind, the Maquis was as good as its leaders, its intentions and its courage. It had taken visionaries such as Jean Moulin to recognise the full potential of bringing all of the potential firepower and talent under one umbrella, but he had been arrested near Lyon in late 1943 and died as the result of horrendous torture.

In the agricultural south-west of France and amongst its larger towns, the working class *cheminots* and *ouvriers* were joining the FTP in large numbers, and FTP chiefs rounded on the AS for surrendering the initiative to British, Gaullist and American agents. Certainly, when Maurice Buckmaster first sent agents to France from his F Section of SOE, he was only interested in contact with the AS. However, when the STO swelled Maquis numbers across the board, some of the idealism of the core members diluted and original strategies were adapted. Most young men fleeing as *réfractaires* didn't choose their groups through political tastes – as was the case with Finkler and Lichtenberg, many men found it hard to find a group at all. In their case they wanted to join the FTP because it fitted with their desire to fight rather than wait, not because either were overtly political. A large number of *maquisards* only discovered after the war that they were classified as FTP fighters, and some were astounded to be described as communists.

A further criticism of AS methods by the FTP related to the young recruits who were eager for action but were held back in a state of inactivity and frustration. Perhaps the FTP's attitude was idealistic while the AS was realistic. A non-professional army with extremely limited resources could only disrupt the German military might for short periods. However, for all its over-exuberance and sometimes misguided reliance on patriotic spirit over proper planning, the leaders of the FTP knew full well that their role would only ever be limited to disruption of the German war machine. Ensuring that their enthusiastic charges drawn from all walks of life, often with little or no military service to their name, understood this was another matter. There were too many examples of loss of life of FTP fighters in battle, or as a result of reprisals following spontaneous decisions to change plans or add operations following successes instead of withdrawing and taking stock of their situation.

Finkler and Lichtenberg found that once they were in the AS it was very difficult to get out. They quickly grew tired of sleeping in the same lice-infested barns waiting for something to happen. When the *corps-franc* was formed in their AS group, they felt they were no longer needed, and were further frustrated at the lack of action. They passed on their feelings to their leader Roland Clée, who arranged for them to accompany him on an operation. Finkler and Lichtenberg's hearts sank, however, when they realised that the operation to steal uniforms from a nearby Chantier de la Jeunesse was pre-arranged. Clée had organised a meeting with the camp's leader who, being sympathetic to the Maquis cause, was happy to hand the uniforms over while Finkler and Lichtenberg carried out sentry duty. Finkler appreciated Clée's effort at getting them involved with an operation of sorts but felt that their involvement in the task was only engineered to divert them.[40] Indeed, in camp they were known as *les Bolsheviks*, which neither of them particularly liked. They explained to their captain again that they just wanted to fight.

During Finkler's time at the camp, the *corps-franc* – a dozen or so of Clée's best men – moved out in order to become a more mobile unit. Clée went with them as part of the commando. His replacement, Capitaine Marcel, ran the unit differently to Clée, placing even more emphasis on military preparation for D-Day. Finkler and Lichtenberg were unimpressed by him,[41] and were unenthused by the marching and cleaning duties that, for them, belonged in the barracks, not on what they considered to be a battleground. Marcel was unhappy at having 'communists' amongst the ranks and when Finkler, Lichtenberg and Paul Frydman mischievously sang the

Internationale one evening, the three men were locked in a single wardrobe for thirty-six hours as punishment. The men were desperate to transfer to the FTP and their requests were eventually passed on to the inter-regional leadership who contacted Charles Mangold. Mangold was originally from Alsace-Lorraine and had involved himself in the early days of AS Roland, rising to become leader of the AS in the Dordogne when Marc Goldman ('Mireille') was arrested. Mangold agreed that the three men could transfer to the FTP on the understanding that he passed the case on to Vincent Bonnetot, now responsible for the FTP in the R5 district, and based in Limoges. The transfer was arranged, with the utmost respect for security: one man could leave at a time, and only when the camp changed its location. 'Phil' (Lichtenberg) was the first to move out and within weeks all three were ready for incorporation into their new setting.

Bonnetot's choice of group was surprising to the three young Frenchmen, as he assigned them to the FTP-MOI. At the same time as Finkler, Lichtenberg and Frydman were being assigned to the recently formed Dordogne group, all of those arrested from the Manouchian group were sentenced to death, most being shot immediately at Mont-Valérien in Paris in February 1944. When the Manouchian group were executed the Germans used it as a propaganda opportunity, printing a red poster carrying the photos of the condemned prior to death. On this famous '*Affiche Rouge*' the message was clear: the Maquis were foreign communists and Jewish terrorists.[42] The FTP-MOI certainly were more directly influenced from Moscow, but it had been formed under the same terms as the FTP, without any additional motivation. The Paris group was a mix of nationalities: foreign communists who had never been members of the French Communist Party. It also contained intellectuals and a number, if only a minority, of Frenchmen and women. The same was the case in Marseille, Lyon and Toulouse. One small FTP-MOI team from the Toulouse brigade carried out one of the earliest attacks on the Germans in the Dordogne, by managing to blow up machinery at the Gestapo headquarters, based in the theatre near the Palais de Justice in the centre of Périgueux. More than 80 per cent of the MOI were killed or taken prisoner.

The southern FTP-MOI's foreign constitution differed to the Parisian groups in that, while it too was made up of a variety of nationalities who had fled to southern France including Italians and Eastern Europeans, a significant proportion were Spanish. These Republicans had crossed the

Pyrenées to escape Franco's regime in the mid and late 1930s. Many of those who had arrived came with no papers, and as such were considered illegal aliens. On arriving in France many were immediately arrested and put into holding camps at locations along the Mediterranean coastline such as Rivesalte and Argelès. These were amongst the first 'concentration camps' that Europe had seen and would serve again, less than a decade later, as holding camps for Jewish families arrested prior to departure for Germany. In 1940 work camps were set up around the country to hold foreign workers who were surplus to the overall requirement in France. Known as *groupements de travailleurs étrangers* (GTE), these were often forestry based, or may have involved mining; both of these occupations were exploited in this way in the Dordogne.

The FTP-MOI had, by the end of 1943, organised into seven divisions throughout the southern zone. One of them, the 15th, under the command of Vicente López Tovar (Alberto), was composed of three brigades: A (Dordogne), B (Lot) and (C) Corrèze. Brigades B and C were absorbed into local FTP groups, whereas Brigade A retained a proper MOI name, controlled by the État-major Departmental (Departmental General Staff) of the FTP. While that group had begun life in the area around Domme with only about eight members, it carried out a number of impressive attacks on railway lines, pylons and tunnels, bringing the Paris–Toulouse line to a standstill on numerous occasions. Explosives were supplied by fellow countrymen based in GTE camps and given work in the small mines of the south of the department. Their first objective was the acquisition of arms.

In Autumn 1944 a second, larger group was established near Got, in the south-east of the Dordogne, led by Juan Jimenez, and the MOI of the Dordogne was becoming known after its inter-regional boss, Charles Henri Ordeig ('Carlos'). It was to this group that both Finkler and Lichtenberg were assigned. Since Vincent Bonnetot didn't know the young men personally, he may well have seen their names, seen that they were Jewish and therefore assumed they were foreign.[43] But it mattered little to them. They were happy in their new surroundings. The FTP-MOI was primarily composed of foreign fighters whose overall shared goal – whether they came from Eastern Europe, Italy, Germany or Spain – was to fight fascism. The Spanish brought with them experience of guerrilla warfare that served the Maquis very well. Throughout the various movements and alongside the French and Spanish could be found Bulgarians, Yugoslavs,

Italians, Romanians, Poles, Czechoslovakians, Africans and Indochinese. Added to that were British agents sent to operate within France, as well as the odd American and Canadian who may have been shot down in the skies over the country, or who possessed linguistic skills that enabled them to remain undetected.

One of the most well known of the early AS Maquis leaders in the area was Mieczyslav 'Marc' Goldman ('Mireille'), a Czech of Jewish background. One of his two deputies was Lithuanian; another, Angelo Ricco, was an Italian who opposed Mussolini's Fascist regime and led the 3rd Bataillon FTP in Excideuil, while the head of the 2nd Bataillon was a Spanish Republican called Emilio Álvarez Canosa ('Pinocho'). In the north of the department the FTP in Sarlande was soon led by 'Petit-Pierre', an officer of the Spanish Republican army whose real name was José Gonzalvo Ùson. In Fanlac, the FTP *école de cadres* (training school) was run by a Spaniard too, as passing on Spanish-style guerrilla tactics was key to the survival of the FTP. His name was François Coy, and his two second-in-commands were also Spanish. When he was injured on 15 March 1944, his replacement also came from Spain. The Spanish were well regarded and trusted. When André Malraux assumed 'command' of the Dordogne Maquis in 1944, he insisted that the security detail for important gatherings of leaders was carried out by the Spanish, and the MOI was employed on several occasions for that purpose. Malraux was himself a veteran of the Spanish Civil War and trusted them implicitly. René Cousteiller ('Soleil') – one of the most incendiary characters of the region's FTP groups and a difficult man to win over – relied heavily on his Spanish contacts.

Elsewhere in the Resistance other nationalities shone through too. During 1944 a significant proportion of the Nazi army was made up of forced conscripts from the wider German Reich. Georgia in particular supplied many to the various divisions that passed through the area, and several hundred of these men risked their lives by deserting and joining the Maquis. Tamara Wolkonski, born in Petrograd in 1895, was nicknamed '*la princesse rouge*' because she had married Prince Alexis Wolkonski – an officer who had been killed in Russia in the civil war. She arrived in France in 1930 and made her way to the Dordogne via Marseille and Paris, crossing the demarcation line with two Russian–Jewish children[44] and taking up work with the Resistance as a senior nurse, as well as later acting as an interpreter for the Georgian troops who deserted the Germans and joined the Maquis. After following the FTP to their later battles in the west of France, she kept her Russian nationality but stayed in the Dordogne until her death in 1967, having been awarded the Croix de Guerre Française and the Médaille des Services Volontaires.[45]

The FTP-MOI benefited from support networks, comprising civilian agents including the likes of *légal* Georges Marty of the AS near Belvès and one of the characters of the Resistance in the Dordogne, Robert Brouillet. Known as 'Charles le Bolshevik', this carpenter in his forties had three children and a wife named Marguerite. They lived in a large house in the middle of Siorac-le-Périgord known locally as 'Le Château'. The building was divided into two establishments: Robert Brouillet's home and small workshop, and the presbytery that housed the town's priest. Brouillet was a true Bolshevik and ensured that those he came into contact with knew as much. On first meeting SOE agent Jacques Poirier in his large communal kitchen early in 1944, he said to the newcomer, 'I don't know you … but I'd better tell you, whether you like it or not, that I'm a Bolshevik and always will be … Well do you think you'll care to work with a Bolshevik?' When Poirier responded that he cared little about Brouillet's political leanings, and only that he was a soldier who wanted to fight the '*Boches*', Brouillet accepted Poirier over copious generous bowls of *chabrol* (wine mixed with soup and drunk straight from the bowl).

Poirier described Brouillet as the soul of integrity and discretion while Siorac was a hive of Resistance built around the effective network created by this one man. Systems were in place to alert the town's population of approaching strangers or Germans before they entered, achieved by using a telephone line to Le Château from the local postmistress. He was a pragmatist who maintained strong friendships with local clergy – Brouillet's Bolshevism never stood in the way of friendships – such that he was able to use churches for hiding weapons. He was able to locate men with the right skills, arms from hidden caches, information on landing sites and obtain accommodation for airmen or indeed any *résistant* requiring it – he was that resourceful. This on top of leading his own combat unit, the Castelréal group. He and Marguerite kept an open house at Le Château and genuine *résistants* could always rely on them for a bed and a meal when in need. Brouillet proved to be a vital source of support for the FTP-MOI.

This was also the case for Pierre Vorms ('Claude'), an art critic and refugee who was based in Belvès, which also had a strong Resistance presence.

Vorms was at the heart of the organisation of a very efficient information network known as Service B de Renseignements. Created for the FTP, the service was a tight network that managed to weave an effective web of informers: people within municipal administration, communication networks and even the local police forces who readily supplied information beneficial to the Resistance.

6

COLLABORATION AND REPRESSION

As the war on the Eastern Front devoured German manpower, the arrests and round-ups that characterised German responses to attacks in France intensified. It seemed that whatever the German machine tried, ably assisted by its Vichy resources, it had little or no effect on the snowballing numbers of men and women who chose to resist. But this was a dangerous time for the Resistance, Maquis or networks of civilian agents. The FTP in particular, keen to press ahead, made mistakes that were costly.

Having reached a new level of direct confrontation with the Germans, the FTP leadership encouraged ambushes. On 14 February, near a place known as Les Rivières Basses in Sainte-Marie-de-Chignac, a German column return-ing from operations in Rouffignac and Peyzac was set upon by *maquisards* of Groupe Gardette, commanded by Samson Roche ('Coco'). Two German soldiers were injured, with one dying later in hospital. The local head of the Gestapo, Michaël Hambrecht, was himself injured on the left arm, though not seriously. It was not something that he would forget.

Groupe Gardette followed up the assault when, on 4 March, it learned that a German column, again including Gestapo agents, would be passing near Saint-Pierre-de-Chignac, just kilometres from the previous attack. This time commanded by Paul Barataud ('Julot'), a group decided to attempt a similar assault to that of 14 February. Setting up their ambush, they were surprised by a separate German convoy approaching from the other direction. After a fire fight that lasted almost two hours, three *résistants* including Barataud were killed, and three others were taken prisoner; two escaped the battle. However, a nearby farm that the *maquisards* had used for shelter during the conflict was burned down and another six nearby were pillaged by the angry Germans.[1]

On 16 March, following a further attack by the FTP, led by Jean Mignon (Groupe Kléber), on a caterpillar truck at Servanches, the prefect Jean Popineau wrote a special report, destined for the top level of government, in which he outlined his alarm:

> On several occasions I have drawn your attention to the terrorism that is hitting the department … Unfortunately, events are confirming my misgivings. The situation is becoming more and more worrying. Burglaries, thefts and attacks of all sorts are multiplying … In almost the entire expanse of the department, the outlaws are acting as masters in gangs of 20, 30, 40 individuals, under the powerless watch of the gendarmes. Their audacity is becoming greater and greater.[2]

Throughout the department this meant armed roadblocks, interruption of supply convoys and the arrest (and an increasing number of kidnaps and murder) of those French citizens openly supporting the Vichy regime. In the report, an exasperated Popineau claims to be unable to call on gendarmeries for the purposes of repression because of 'their dispersion and their lack of armaments'. In any case, 'I have no confidence whatsoever in them for the repression of terrorism.'[3] This may have been because of sympathy on the part of the gendarmeries towards the *maquisards* or, just as likely, because 'the Maquis' endogenous guerrilla warfare literally suffocated the gendarmes'.[4]

Popineau estimated the strength of the 'outlaws' at that moment at several thousand. He claimed that 'there are lots of Spanish' but estimated that the majority were communist FTP. He seemed unaware, or unwilling to say that there were a great many *maquisards* at that time who were formerly military men with no communist influence who were attracting hordes of disaffected youngsters kicking back at the prospect of deportation to Germany. Popineau was clear in what he wanted, however:

> I strongly insist on the gravity of a situation that each day is becoming more and more alarming. The picture that I have just painted is not darkened for effect. It is no longer any less than the strict reality. If we wait too long to take the necessary measures the outlaws and the communist gangs will end up becoming entirely the masters of the land.

Popineau claimed that 'in order to … become a true business of war, it is absolutely necessary to send to the Dordogne many men, at least 2,000 of them and well-armed.'

While Popineau's police forces were becoming less and less able to contain the Maquis, the German occupiers were finding that their troops were similarly unable to cope. Michaël Hambrecht claimed the situation had entirely changed by spring 1944, and that the numbers of *maquisards* almost everywhere in the department now far outnumbered the number of German troops on the ground. More frustrating for him was that the German troops present in the Dordogne were largely inexperienced in any sort of warfare, especially the very specialised task of combating guerrilla fighters – and those *maquisards* were having a lot of success.

The Germans and the Vichy police were becoming powerless to prevent the sabotage of military installations, as well as the raids and attacks on the civilian administrative installations that were feeding the German war machine. Fuel depots, gunpowder factories, forestry and wood preparation installations were all being targeted. The occupying troops were no longer sufficiently armed or manned to control the Maquis. Hambrecht did not pretend to have tried to eradicate the Resistance, which had out-grown the abilities of the German powers and which now could only be combatted through a vastly different approach. The solution, a short-term 'cleaning out' of the Dordogne and Limousin regions by trained combat forces, arrived in late March 1944, around the same time as the arrival of a mercenary group formed from the Paris underworld.

The Brigade Nord-Africaine (BNA) was formed as an auxiliary of the German police in areas of France where the Gestapo and French police were struggling to contain or reduce the increasingly violent and effective attacks by the French Resistance on German military units. The Dordogne had been identified by the Abwehr as one such department. Other BNA units targeted the Corrèze while further units were sent to Montbéliard in the east of France.

Despite a small amount of military training while stationed in Paris, the BNA's involvement in combat with the Maquis was minimal. The BNA, or 'Phalange' as it became known, was made up primarily of non-military men, many of whom had criminal backgrounds. Locals in the Dordogne came to know them as '*les bicots*', a pejorative term originating in France's dark colonial past. The group originated in Paris, where Henri Lafont, a career petty criminal, and Pierre Bonny, once a famous police officer until disgraced and jailed for corruption, struck up a business relationship. They began to deal heavily with high-ranking Nazis, procuring whatever the officers required through a vast range of mainly illegal means. Lafont envisaged that those 1940 prisoners of war who were of North African origin could be freed to form an army of some 50,000 men. These, he argued, could ensure the annihilation of the Resistance in the provinces.

Lafont and Bonny's vision was moderated by SS Colonel Helmut Knochen, Chief of the Gestapo in France, and a force of some 300 men was authorised. El-Maadi was put to work recruiting men who were readily available and attracted by the 5,000 francs per month salary, which was more than the going rate at the time.

Born in Algeria in 1905, Alexandre Villaplane led the French national football team against Mexico in the inaugural FIFA World Cup and has since been described as the 'Platini of the late 1920s'. At the height of his sporting powers, Villaplane had been well paid, and was well known in the social circles of Paris and the Côte d'Azur, where he lived the high life but developed a dangerous love of gambling. Soon becoming disinterested in the game of football, he ended his career in the lower divisions and in 1935 he was imprisoned for his involvement in a horse-racing scandal.

Villaplane's involvement in racketeering took on new dimensions just as Paris was occupied in June 1940. Profiting from the misfortune of Jews, he was amongst those in the Paris underground who saw the occupation as a wonderful business opportunity. A well-connected gold dealer, he also involved himself with rackets carried out by a network of false policemen.

Lafont, Bonny and Villaplane formed a gang dubbed the 'French Gestapo' and their base in Paris at 93 rue Lauriston became one of the most notorious addresses in the capital. The Gestapo handed certain responsibilities over to their new allies, including arrest and torture. Villaplane was given the SS rank of Untersturmführer and wore a German uniform, as did Lafont.

A fifty or so strong division commanded by Villaplane arrived in Périgueux in March 1944. Dressed in a combination of sheepskin jackets with baggy blue boiler suits and berets, they wore thick leather belts with a Waffen SS buckle and were armed with machine guns and grenades. During the six months that they were in the Dordogne, Michaël Hambrecht turned a blind eye to the violence and crime committed by these men, many of whom were hardened criminals who had been given police roles. Hambrecht tasked them to become enforcers for the various German units in the area, serving the Wehrmacht who were intent on crushing the Périgordin Maquis. Official records, as well as the many eyewitness accounts and reports by the *police judiciare*, tell of pillage, rape, plundering and burning of property, extortion and profiteering. However, that was just the tip of the iceberg; arrests, deportation or summary murder of civilians and the execution of suspects became the speciality of this unique auxiliary police force to the Gestapo.

While the BNA was formed for a specific purpose, other French people chose to side with the occupiers to progress their own lot or because it seemed like the best course of action at that moment. Others fell in with the Germans through circumstances beyond their control. However, François Collin was one of the small group of Frenchmen who sold themselves heart and soul to the German occupiers. Tall and rangy, with dirty blonde receding hair, he became known and feared throughout Périgueux and its surrounding towns and villages. His limited skills were exploited by those in the headquarters of the Gestapo in Périgueux, and he was present during their most distasteful operations.

Born in Strasbourg, he was a fluent speaker of German and French who came to Périgueux in 1940 as a refugee and a married man. He worked a number of jobs as a cook in several restaurants in the town, before procuring a bank loan of 52,000 francs to set up his own business, Aux Trois Alsasciennes, struggling to pay a rent of 2,000 francs per month.[5] His clientele, primarily Alsatians, were soon ousted by the German military and consequently Gestapo agents found Collin to be entirely of their thinking and a German speaker who could prove useful to them.

Collin found himself arrested in June 1943, possibly following a disagreement over a woman named Paulette Rey who had become the mistress of one of the Gestapo's interpreters. Collin had left his wife and was busily building up a profile of mistresses of his own but had upset someone in the Gestapo and was brought in for questioning. As often happened in such cases, on his release Collin began working for the Gestapo, firstly on an ad hoc basis as a cook and then a driver. Whether it was part of the deal for his release or not, Collin's new-found association with the German agents of the vicinity, as well as others like him, suited his beliefs and personality well. He began to make good money for his work and before long gave over the running of his business to a partner, Christian Loucher.

Over time Collin began to appear in German uniform and carried a pistol with him constantly. He frequented local bars and developed a reputation for violence, more often than not carried out in a state of drunkenness. Much of his time was spent with members of the BNA and the witness testimonies prepared for his trial spoke of a man who began by bullying fellow citizens but quickly turned to far more sinister dealings. There were so many testimonies at his trial that he could confidently be convicted of having not only been involved in beatings of prisoners, but in their arrests and in some cases in murders. He participated in operations against Jews, *résistants* and other 'anti-French'. He also spied on, threatened and, along with members of the BNA, pillaged the property of whoever he so chose.

Following his relationship with another mistress called Marlène Metout (who, like Paulette Rey, was later executed by the Resistance), Collin began to see a 19-year-old girl called Georgette Peynaud who, at the time, still lived with her parents. Contemporary police reports paint the picture of a young girl who became intensely infatuated with Collin, telling friends and colleagues that they were to be married.[6] Through her parents' contacts she had been employed by at the Préfecture de la Dordogne, in an auxiliary capacity working for the Service des réfugiés.

Whether due to the influence of Collin, or her own innate character, she was not well liked. She began to appear in expensive clothes and jewellery which, she was happy to admit, were the bounty of the deportations and confiscations carried out by her boyfriend and the North Africans with whom she boasted of spending her time. One day she wore an expensive jewel and told colleagues that it was her engagement ring – no doubt another confiscation. On finding herself isolated in her job, she boasted of her exploits and threatened to arrange for the arrest of one colleague, who happened to be Jewish, though this never happened. As the months went on she began to miss work, sometimes without explanation other than that she was involved with the Gestapo, which was more important by far.

Both François Collin and Georgette Peynaud became known to the Maquis, and Collin no doubt knew that they were in danger because he moved her into the Gestapo 'barracks' in the town theatre and surrounding buildings in the centre of Périgueux. The pair felt protected and Collin's crimes began to intensify until he became an undeniable criminal of the war. Over fifty witness testimonies gathered in preparation for his trial place him at the site of several killings and round-ups:

> On the 4 March last year Collin, accompanied by two German soldiers in uniform and four north-Africans, made the arrest of around thirty Israelites who were living along the route de Lyon.
> Rose Meyer, 51, 141 route de Lyon Périgueux

> I must tell you that all the people of the Lespinasse quarter are without news of the Israelites arrested last March.
> Pierre Wack, 40, Carpenter, 5 Cité Lespinasse in Périgueux[7]

★★★

Within the ranks of the Maquis throughout south-west France times were nervous and uncertain. Aversion to the Maquis was growing too rapidly, though support for it also appeared to be strengthening. Structures were tightening up and strategies were becoming more co-ordinated, but rivalries were at their height during the winter of 1943 and spring of 1944. Chinese whispers, conflict of ideology and misinformation perpetuated myths that continued after the war.[8] The FTP were accused of widespread crimes, such as banditry and piracy of men, arms and ammunition from AS camps.

Exceptionally, some of these petty rivalries between Resistance groups escalated. The FTP was also accused of attempting to indoctrinate the population into the politics of the Communist Party and, while some of this undoubtedly took place, it was not the aim of the FTP. Some *maquisards* found their way into action through the efforts of local recruiters for *Jeunesse Communiste*, but most who entered the Maquis did not do so for political reasons.

Two weeks after the burial of Soeur Marie-Philomène in an unmarked grave at Pont Lasveyras, the ice and snows of the cruel winter of 1943–44 were making those who had been sent there glad of the shelter of the old building. The mill's proper name, Moulin de la Forge-de-Pissac, was rarely used, locals referring to it as Pont Lasveyras after the nearby stone bridge that dated from the middle ages. The buildings, next to the Auvezère river, were separated by a courtyard, with an old house on one side and the mill itself, unused since the First World War, on the other. Its owner, a Doctor Dutheil, had bought it as a summer retreat but rarely visited. He had not been there for two years and was based in Limoges. The abandoned buildings were therefore a prime location for a number of groups from the ever-expanding AS Maquis around the north-eastern edge of the Dordogne. Near enough to Payzac, it had been chosen because of its isolation and the ease with which it could be guarded. As had been the case when Soeur Marie-Philomène had been brought there, its two steep pathways, only one of which was passable by anything other than on foot, could be well guarded by two sentries.

The mill had been suggested to René Tallet by Raoul Audrerie, who knew that Doctor Dutheil was not only an absent landlord but was also in favour of the Vichy regime. Parachute drops were arriving, so weapons had to be stored, and young recruits needed to be trained. The STO had brought in numbers above and beyond what the existing camps could hold. Several hundred military uniforms stolen from a nearby depot were taken to the new camp, as were materials including a good number of weapons. There was very little in the way of ammunition but Audrerie, known to all the men as 'Le Crapaud', planned for the camp to be supplied as and when it arrived.

By mid February, two complete Maquis groups were based at the mill, one led by Jean Delage ('Jeantou') and one by Raymond Pivert, nephew of Raoul Audrerie and using the *nom de guerre* 'Guy Lachau'. Typically for AS camps in early 1944, the day was filled with patrols and the search for armaments. The young men would each try to source ammunition and weaponry from wherever they could, including all the local farms.

Roger Delon joined the Maquis in December 1943 and, after staying at a farm near Payzac, was sent to the mill at the beginning of the new year. Audrerie often visited the mill as, occasionally, did René Tallet. Delon found life there passable, 'During the day we practised military operations and we often went out on expeditions,' while, importantly, 'the food was perfect, we made an excellent vegetable soup, we never lacked meat or bread.'[9]

Though the isolation and steep descent to the mill enabled a secret existence for its new inhabitants, it did rather limit the escape routes. With the fast-flowing river blocking off escape up into the trees of the opposite valley, a well-organised and well-co-ordinated operation could, in theory, trap the *résistants* in a position where they could be soon overwhelmed. However, a significant number of *miliciens* would be required, and it would be unlikely that the German Army would carry out such an attack. The well-placed sentries would also be able to get news of any potential intruders to the mill in sufficient time for its inhabitants to flee.

On the evening of 15 February the weather was particularly cruel, with strong winds and snow forcing most of the men indoors as the night fell. Several men were absent, some with flu while others had been unable to get back to the mill that night. Raymond Pivert was being treated at the Clairvivre Hospital in Périgueux by Professor Fontaine; Roger Delon had been on patrol until two o'clock in the morning, after which he climbed up into attic above the kitchen and managed to get to sleep; and 20-year-old André Cubertafon had also been on guard duty between one and two o'clock. On being relieved of duty, he went indoors to try and find a space to lie down and sleep upstairs in the farmhouse but could find no room, so he set to drinking coffee and preparing beans for the coming day.

Day was breaking when Cubertafon saw and heard a bullet crash through the upper part of the kitchen window. Roger Delon and everyone else in the mill awoke to machine-gun shots. Looking outside, Delon could not make out who was shooting, GMR or Milice. Some of the men called out that they were sure it was the Germans, and looking out across the river, Cubertafon saw German helmets. Both Cubertafon and Delon fired shots, but they knew that they had hardly any bullets to spare. Outside the mill were German troops who had arrived from their Limoges base.

The attack was well planned, with the troops divided into four companies, which had set off during the night. One of them made their way upriver, while another came south from Payzac. A further two companies had surrounded the area and closed in on the mill ensuring that no *maquisards* could escape. The sentry guards had not been able to ring their bells to warn the men at the mill, and one was later found with his throat cut. There was no doubt that the operation had required local knowledge, and several locals were later identified as having helped the Germans. The position of the sentries had to be known beforehand, as did the potential escape routes. The buildings were not badly damaged and certainly not burned to the ground as would normally be the case in such circumstances. The owner of the mill was never seen again. It was later discovered that he had fled to South America.

That morning, the buildings were surrounded and fired upon until the men were forced to surrender. Some, such as Albert Brun, were killed straight away, executed when a German discovered that he was disabled, having been born with a deformed hand. As the men emerged from the mill with their hands behind their heads they were struck with rifle butts. German soldiers then entered the mill and shot the injured. Those who surrendered were made to lie down flat in the muddy grass with their hands behind their heads, in three groups. The German soldiers killed several *maquisards* who had merely looked up or moved their heads.

They demanded to know the man in charge and Jean Delage gave himself up. He was taken to the top of the valley and put into a van. A small group containing Roger Delon was told to carry the Germans' equipment up the slope to the road to be loaded onto lorries, and as they were being herded onto trucks themselves they heard firing from the valley floor. The men who were left behind were all being shot.

André Cubertafon, who had already received a bullet to the leg and shoulder in the fracas, was shot in the nape of the neck. The only audible cries from the young men, most of whom were between 20 and 22 years of age, were 'Maman!' and 'Adieu Maman!'. Delon, Delage and eleven others were loaded onto trucks and taken to Limoges. By the end of April they had arrived at Auschwitz, and eight were eventually liberated at the end of the war.[10]

Raoul Audrerie and René Tallet, neither of whom had been at the mill, managed to round some *maquisards* together but could not get close to the mill, where the Germans remained until mid afternoon. On spotting a truck in a nearby meadow, they succeeded in getting some shots in, injuring some German troops, but they could have no real influence on events at the mill. By the time dusk came, the Germans had withdrawn and a small group from Payzac, including a doctor who had been refused access earlier in the day and another *résistant* from the village, Raoul Nouaille, found their way down the ravine to the mill. Over thirty bodies lay there, 'shot like rabbits'[11]. Paul Chartrain, a local gendarme fully sympathetic to the Maquis, was also amongst the group, as were Monsieur and Madame Gardes, parents of 19-year-old Jean. Earlier that day they had received word from the post mistress at nearby Angoisse that trucks full of Germans had driven by on the Route Nationale towards the area in which the mill was found. It was they who had contacted Chartrain, who had not only witnessed much of the killing but had helped guide Tallet and Audrerie to the correct spot to fire at the Germans. On arriving at the mill, Monsieur and Madame Gardes were desperate to find their son, and eventually came across his body face down near the river. Thirty-three bodies were found alongside a large fire, on which camp materials and weapons were burning. A month later, a thirty-fourth body was found in silt further downstream. Just two *maquisards* had managed to get away to safety, one of whom had escaped the bullets and leapt into the river to be swept away by the current.

Raoul Nouaille and Paul Chartrain slowly examined the bodies in a bid to identify each one. Nouaille called over to Chartrain when he came across one that was not as cold as the others, despite being face down and not moving. Gently, Nouaille turned him over and sat him up and in doing so noticed a quiet sigh. 'Don't worry, we are French, and we are here to help,' said Nouaille in patois. The boy had injuries all over his body, a mouth full of blood and a smashed jaw; blood was escaping from a shoulder wound. It was André Cubertafon. Nouaille and Chartrain carried the young man to the top of the ravine and loaded him into a car. They took him to a nearby *cabinet médicale* where initial assumptions were that he would not survive.

Chartrain insisted that everything possible must be done to prolong his life because he was the only known witness to events at Pont Lasveyras. It was dark, and it was already a miracle that he had survived for so long, but he was taken to Clairvivre Hospital in Périgueux where Doctor Fontaine operated on him. Unable to guarantee his safety, they moved him to the home of an elderly farming couple near Payzac, and over the coming weeks he was moved several times to new locations. Miraculously, André Cubertafon survived.

Things could have been very different for him. He was taken from Clairvivre at four o'clock in the morning, and at six o'clock Doctor Fontaine was a paid a visit by the Gestapo. They had been informed that a surviving terrorist was there and they needed to take him away. Doctor Fontaine informed them 'that I treat terrorists in the same way that I treat Germans, but that the terrorist that they were looking for was no longer at the hospital, that he had left. If they wanted him, they would just have to look for him.'[12]

The events at Pont Lasveyras, as devastating as they were for the Maquis, could only be deemed a partial success for the Germans. The arrest and killing of a comparatively small number of young *maquisards* had not led to the arrest and detention of the leaders they were looking for. René Tallet was still at large.

Two days after the attack, a Citroën 301 pulled up outside the garage in Sarlande owned by René Ségui, formerly known as 'Violette' before he had handed on the *nom de guerre* to his friend, Tallet. Those within the vehicle did not know that their vehicle had been spotted travelling with the German convoy on the day of the massacre and had also been seen circulating around the region, presumably gathering information on Resistance activity and probably for a financial reward. The two men inside wore civilian clothing and were accompanied by a pretty blonde woman. The men were French informants and, it later emerged, the woman was a prostitute.

The men approached René Ségui's wife and asked if they could speak to her husband. Hypersensitive to any such threat, she managed to play for time while she informed Ségui, who in turn ensured that a message be passed along to friends nearby. Ségui eventually emerged and was pounced upon by the two men while the young woman watched. As they battled to subdue him, a group of *maquisards*, including the current 'Violette', emerged from their hiding place. The two men were shot as they tried to flee. The woman was made to talk, then she too was executed.

On 4 March, an article appeared in the official local press informing the public of the events. Having emerged from the Vichy-controlled press rooms, the articles in both *L'Argus du Périgord* and *Le Courrier du Centre* were practically identical and demonstrate the occupiers' handle on local propaganda. The title, 'A band of dangerous terrorists is put out of harm's way – Forty bandits killed during the battle – Thirteen others taken prisoner', shows the typical vocabulary used to stoke up emotion amongst the population. The short article claimed that the leader had been found, though of course neither Tallet nor Audrerie were at the mill. The leader mentioned was Jean Delage, who, when questioned in Limoges, supplied some information about what had happened several weeks earlier to Soeur Marie-Philomène at the mill. This was too good a propaganda opportunity for the German press officers to pass up:

His interrogation threw light on a great number of armed attacks that have recently taken place in the Dordogne. The boss admitted, amongst other things, to the murder of a nun, accused of denunciation to the

French police. The band, who claimed to be part of the Armée Secrète group and certainly wished to outdo the communists, ordered through the district chief, that a priest be brought to the camp in order for the nun to confess and take communion on the eve of her execution.

Communist gangs (FTP) came to the rescue of the bandits armed with machine guns and grenades just as the German police were leaving. This proves that the secret army of de Gaulle collaborates directly with communist gangs.[13]

Of course, many details are correct and even if the Soeur Marie-Philomène story had not come from Delage it could have come from any other of the men arrested.

The security of information following arrests was never as secure with the AS as with the FTP and their triangle system, but information leaks were acceptable as long as they related to past events. Even the SOE did not expect an agent to withhold all information until death. The expectation was that agents under such stress should hold on as long as possible to enable infiltrated networks to disassemble in order to lie low and reassemble at a later date. In the case of those AS men arrested at Pont Lasveyras, there is little to suggest that much useful information was gleaned from the arrests.

The newspaper report does make a surprising link between the very limited counter-attack carried out by Tallet, Audrerie and the small number of men they had been able to gather as the Germans were about to withdraw, and 'communist gangs' who came to their rescue with machine guns and grenades. Such an attempt to band Gaullist resistance with communism is cynical with the benefit of hindsight, but in 1944 played to the fears of a public unclear as to who the Maquis were or what their ultimate goals could be. For those citizens torn between patriotism and a fear of Bolshevism, it was an early example of a clever piece of press-based propaganda.

A large monument today stands on the spot where the massacre of Pont Lasveyras took place on 16 March 1944. In March 2012 a further monument to all those who died in the name of France was erected in the centre of the nearby town of Payzac. In particular, the plaque pays homage to those who died at the mill. A second plaque below lists the names of three further men '*morts pour la France*'. These three men are listed as having died in tragic circumstances in Payzac on 31 March 1944, just a fortnight after the massacre. One of those is Raoul Nouaille, one of the first to arrive at the scene on 16 March and who found André Cubertafon alive, taking him to safety. Official documentation list him and the two other men killed, Baptiste Aumaitre and Louis Pelisson, as having been 'shot/executed'.

Little is known about what happened on that day. One local historian suggests disagreements over AS reorganisation in the area,[14] other sources link the murders to another Maquis from outside the area, perhaps reaffirming that this was an assassination within the clandestine networks. Sadly, such events were not unknown, petty jealousies over rank, supplies and territory could rise to the surface and did so. In this case, unusual action was taken by Raoul Audrerie and two other Marquis leaders, Gaston Devaux and Doctor Lacôte, the day after the deaths, declaring in writing that the three men had belonged to their network. They were finally recognised as '*Morts pour la France*' in 1949.[15]

A number of theories emerged after the war as to whether the death of Soeur Marie-Philomène was linked to the massacre at Pont Lasveyras. It seems unlikely. While the story was useful propaganda, even the prefect who conducted the investigation into her disappearance made no assertion that the Maquis could have been involved and so there would have been nothing to gain through 'reprisals'. Either way, her death would be unlikely to have registered on the level at which the Gestapo were working. They were more interested in the location of *maquisards* and Jews. They would probably have conducted their visit to Pont Lasveyras in exactly the same way whether they knew about the kidnapping or not. Just days after the appearance of the newspaper report informing the public of the execution of the *religieuse*, the famous pro-German voice of Vichy's finest propaganda merchant, Philippe Henriot, condemned the killing on Radio Paris. He condemned the '*terroristes français*' who had 'surpassed in cruelty even the red torturers of the Spanish War'. The event was indeed a propaganda coup for Vichy. The killing of a nun was previously unimaginable, yet unavoidable for the Maquis. For the German occupiers, the Gestapo and Vichy police, it was the kind of event that could only help to drive a wedge between the public and the Resistance.

★★★

Roger Meyer's father felt sure that his family would be safe from persecution in the Lorraine capital, Nancy, despite being Jewish. Having served in the German Army during the Great War, albeit as a tailor, his business was a thriving one in the city. With clients who included any number of high-ranking officials, Roger's father was convinced that he would be safe from persecution so the family did not head south during the exodus of 1939. Nor did they head south when the statutes prohibited the Meyer family from owning and running the business that they had built up. Even when a *gérant* was appointed to take over the administration of the shop, Monsieur Meyer, annoyed and aware that the situation had become serious, still did not think that things could become *that* bad for them. He was well known to the local military and police, many of whom were customers. He felt that the family was protected by his past.

By 1942, Roger, then 16 years of age, thought differently. Feeling that he had to do something to get away from the ever-approaching Nazi trap, he decided to travel south, cross the demarcation line and join his uncle who had settled in Périgueux. This he did in October 1942. Less than a month later, the Germans followed, crossing the demarcation line to occupy France in its entirety.

Roger soon made friends and joined a Scout group, having met with Raymond Kinver, an employee of the *prefecture*, who encouraged his involvement. Despite the closeness of his new friendship, Roger knew nothing of Raymond's involvement in the Resistance until later learning that he had been shot.

In late 1943 Roger Meyer became a liaison agent himself and, being a Scout, was very good at moving around the countryside, finding good places to hide items and setting up routes through the countryside to carry messages. One of his first missions was to deliver a number of medicines to the camp at Pont Lasveyras. This he did, and after a long journey to get there he was offered some space for the night. Roger told the *maquisards* that he was concerned by noises that he had heard on the way – these were quite nearby, or so it seemed to him. They told him not to be concerned, there was nowhere safer than their current protected hideout. However, Roger was unconvinced and told the *maquisards* that he preferred to head back in the direction of Périgueux, as he had a long way to travel by foot. He spent that February night in the open, using his Scouting knowledge to camp in the wild. He later learned that had he stayed in the mill that night he would have been amongst the men who had been massacred there.

Not all 'cleansing' operations were carried out by German soldiers; Vichy police forces also carried out countless operations. The GMR was particularly active in finding and wiping out small groups of *maquisards*. By mid March 1944, Raphael Finkler and 'Phil' Lichtenberg were fully integrated into the FTP-MOI. When they arrived at the camp in La Trappe Forest, near Le Got, they were accompanied by Paul Frydman ('Dave') and placed under the command of Juan Gimenez. Shortly afterwards, José Flores came to the camp asking for a Frenchman for his group. This *groupe special motorisé* was based in a forest near Veyrines-de-Domme, 13 miles south-west of Sarlat, in the south-east of the department. Established at the beginning of 1944 and limited to just twelve men, this group took its name because it had access to a front-wheel-drive Citroën and a motorbike. This meant that the small unit could get around quicker than other units whose main form of transport was bicycle. Finkler and Lichtenberg had no wish to be separated and so Flores agreed to take them both, with Frydman agreeing to stay on with Juan and the rest of the FTP-MOI.

The *groupe motorisé* carried out missions that were short and sharp, throughout the region. During the night of 15 March 1944, half of the group, including Finkler, returned from a mission at half past two in the morning, and soon afterwards another group of five set off in the still-warm Citroën. All was quiet in the small abandoned farm house that the group had been allowed to use. Located near Veyrines, 60km away from Périgueux, it was known as Le Canadier. The farm was surrounded by the woodland which was accessible by several footpaths leading to the route de Veyrines to the north and La Chapelle-Péchaud to the east; the hamlet of La Raze was nearby.

Finkler and Lichtenberg were already uncomfortable about the number of nights the group had spent at the farmhouse; one of the key principals of the Spanish Republicans' method of conducting clandestine warfare was to move often, as staying still was too perilous. It was time to move on, to find another roof.

The room in which the men were sleeping during the early hours of 16 March was square, the same dimensions as the outer walls, around 7m by 7m. Below that main room was a cellar at ground level, meaning the main living area was elevated, accessible by seven or eight stone steps. In the middle of one wall was the chimney, and around the floor were scattered blankets where several men slept. There was a single luxury, a mattress between the door and the chimney on which slept Flores and Finkler who were trying to keep warm from the cinders of the long-extinguished fire. The oil lamp was out and the snoring of sleeping men was the only sound that broke the silence.

As the first suggestions of light appeared through the window that looked out onto a vineyard below, the church bell at La Chapelle-Péchaud sounded five times – it was time for a change of guard. One of the men, known as Antonio, pulled his boots on. Lichtenberg offered to take his sleeping friend Finkler's place. After all, Finkler had been part of the team that had only arrived two and a half hours previously.

The two guards had a large area to cover, and they made their way north towards the Veyrines road. Finkler continued to sleep, unaware of the small sacrifice made by his friend on his behalf. When the first shot rang out – a signal only – Finkler did not wake. Flores rose with a start, pulling on his boots, grabbing his weapon and moving towards the window. The machine-gun fire that whipped through him, throwing him to the ground, woke everybody. A voice could be heard after several seconds of repeated machine-gun fire. It was a French voice, 'Give yourselves up, you are surrounded.'[16]

Finkler rolled to his right, pulled on his boots and grabbed his Sten machine gun, his belt on which his Lama 9mm pistol was holstered, and his leather satchel containing ammunition and grenades. Shots rained in from two machine guns, as well as the hand guns of around fifty *miliciens*. Flores, mortally wounded, called out for his mother.

In the dark, and with so much activity during the night, the men were not even sure who was in the farmhouse. They each called out their names. As well as Flores there were four of them left. Finkler, who had been sure that he would never see his 20th birthday, knew for sure that his time had come. He prepared his Lama pistol knowing that, should the time come, he would not be taken alive – this bullet was for himself. One of the *maquisards*, who Finkler knew as '*El Chaúfer*', or 'Madriles', and who had only joined the group days earlier, shouted, '*Bueno! adios hombres y fuego*'. He pushed open the door and began firing while Finkler and the other man present, Luis, took up positions at windows either side of the door also shooting at whatever they could. 'Madriles' moved forward and was cut down on the steps. Injured and refusing to be taken alive, he finished himself off with a bullet to the head.

Some calm followed, and the remaining men could hear the cries of Flores. They decided that the only means of escape was a window that looked over the vineyard. Luis suggested that they try the window and he had barely finished his suggestion when the group's cook, '*El Cocinero*', leapt straight out. He managed to run a short distance into the vines before he was dropped by a volley of bullets.

Finkler decided that he had to try to escape. He too leapt from a window, falling several metres into a ditch containing stones, pieces of bottles and brambles. He was spotted and fired at but managed to evade the bullets until he was able to lie flat in long grass. Then, launching a grenade towards the enemy, he sprinted downhill towards a thicket that led into wood-land. The undulating ground helped him, the bullets flying overhead. As he rushed through brambles and overgrowth his skin and clothes were torn but he eventually found a farmhouse from where he was directed to rela-tive safety at a 'canteen' in nearby Veyrines. He was shut in a kennel with a dog until it was safe for him to move. That night, a contact collected him and took him to rejoin Antonio and Lichtenberg.

Raphael Finkler was the only survivor of the five men who were in the farmhouse when the French police arrived. For months afterwards Finkler not only suffered nightmares but refused to sleep indoors. Luis, who had been left behind, was injured by gunfire and unable to escape. He was taken prisoner, transported to Limoges and executed on 25 April 1944.

In a carefully planned operation, the farmhouse had been raided in the night and the owner taken in his night shirt and bare feet and forced at gunpoint to lead one of the units towards the farmhouse. Another unit had descended upon the village looking for a baker who had been denounced for supplying bread to the Maquis. Luckily, he was not there, but another young man named Pierre Godefroy was commanded to lead them to the Maquis. A friend of the Maquis himself, Godefroy cleverly chose minor pathways to try to buy them some time. 'Phil' Lichtenberg and Antonio were too far away to be able to do anything to save those in the farm and instead searched for help for when the battle died down. Finkler, Lichtenberg and Antonio rejoined the rest of the group.

A police report of 18 March, which was destined for the prefect, detailed the injuries to the '*éléments de la escadron de la garde de Bergerac*' – the Bergerac

Milice – who had carried out the attack. The captain commanding operations had received a bullet to the stomach, the lieutenant a similar injury to
a thigh, while a further garde had received a bullet wound.[17] Considerable
material had been recovered, according to the report, including an automobile. Funerals were held on 17 March for the three Spanish men whose
bodies were recovered from Le Canadier 'in the name of the fight against
fascism'. Most of the population of Veyrines and the surrounding areas
attended and representatives of the gendarmerie of Domme were also present 'to ensure order'.[18].

A short report of the incident appeared in the newspaper *L'Avenir de la
Dordogne* on 27 March 1944 under a front-page subsection titled '*Le ban-
ditisme et sa répression*'.[19] The minor rubric, 'A den of terrorists destroyed
in the Dordogne', outlined the success of the 4th Squadron of the
5th Regiment of La Garde in killing four terrorists, with three injuries to
the 'forces of order'. The subsection featured another story of an attack on
a detachment of ten '*Francs-gardes de la milice française*' commanded by their
chief, Tomasi. Nine assailants had leapt from a lorry and attacked the *miliciens* using guns and grenades. Although the *miliciens* had regained control
of the situation by responding 'energetically', one *Franc-garde* was killed.
Five 'bandits' were killed while the other four fled, proclaimed the article.
The attack had happened as the detachment were on their way to attend
the funeral of Madame Rose Denoix, wife of the chief of the Dordogne
Milice, whose body had been found.[20] Whatever the papers were saying,
the situation *was* becoming critical.

The attack on the FTP-MOI at Le Canadier hit the group hard and
when Finkler and Lichtenberg met with Charles Henri Ordeig, MOI chief
in Dordogne ('Carlos'), they were asked if they could help. Ordeig needed
someone to act as liaison between the group and Limoges, where the management triangle for the MOI in the Aquitaine was based. Finkler and
Lichtenberg instantly suggested Maryse Nicolas and Monette Leclerq, who
had proved to be excellent support as part of the MNCR. Ordeig trusted
their judgement. He told them to make the necessary arrangements the
following day, while using the opportunity to pick up some clothes.

Finkler and Lichtenberg took a taxi, the only one in Belvès, to
Périgueux. Ordeig had forbidden them to carry any weapons so the sight
of a Périgueux filled with Germans and barbed wire made them very
nervous. The atmosphere was 'threatening'. The boys made their way to the

apartment on the rue de la Boétie where they found Maryse and Monette, who agreed to become the new liaison agents for the FTP-MOI. Maryse was sent to find Finkler's mother, and Monette to find Lichtenberg's mother. This was the first time they had been reunited for several months, as Finkler and Lichtenberg had left on New Year's Day 1944. Tears were shed, and long hugs exchanged, but the meeting had to be brief. The girls had returned with suitcases filled with clean garments and some food supplies. Then they had to leave, exchanging emotional farewells before taking the taxi back to Belvès.

The girls became agents of the very highest order. Maryse took the *nom de guerre* 'Michel', a boy's name in France and her aunt, Monette, became 'Lina'. For months to come they travelled regularly between Limoges and Périgueux carrying orders, materials such as identity cards, unidentified parcels and small arms, all of which, if discovered, could have got them killed. In the same way as many liaison agents they put their lives at risk every day, working for the Resistance in plain sight. As pretty women they sometimes used their charm to try to dissuade police officers or German soldiers from approaching or stopping them, perhaps by smiling at them, while inside they were terrified that at any moment they might be discovered.

These were extraordinary people —men and women, old and young. The *maquisards* in the forests were brave, but the civilians, known locally as *légaux*, or *résistants urbains*, who were supporting the networks while working and living two separate lives, could be uncovered at any time. Their courageous exploits should be equally recognised.

As well as going to Limoges, Maryse and Monette also travelled by train to Siorac-en-Périgord, the home town of Robert Brouillet (Charles Le Bolshevik) and an oasis of Resistance activity. There they met a figure known as 'Crespo', the *commissaire politique* of the Spanish group, again exchanging orders, passing on money and material. They developed links with a Maquis group, 'Mercedes', based in Bassillac, just east of the city and where there was an airfield. These links were vital in the process of the liberation that, it was hoped, would follow. They even hid an English airman. But their most important task, at least as far as Finkler and Lichtenberg were concerned, was still to come.

In a similar vein to Maryse and Monette, who had found their way into helping the Resistance primarily through circumstance, Claudette Négrier's involvement with the Maquis had progressed in Vergt as she had come to know AS leader, Charles Mangold and his son, Jean-Paul Seret-Mangold who had found lodgings at the home of the town chemists, Alice and André Boubaud, who were themselves involved in the chain between civilian life and the nearby Roland group.

Claudette began to work as a liaison agent and became a vital link between Vergt, '*petit capital cache du* maquis', and the Maquis groups in the nearby Durestal Forest. Charles Mangold came to the village often to gather information or give orders. Others in the town, such as the baker Roger Gervais, were involved with the provision of food to the Maquis, and Claudette, now known as 'Coco', transported goods and food tickets as well as false documents and radio messages. Her father, as well as running the café where many *maquisards* from the Mireille and, later, Roland groups sometimes gathered, was also a seller of guns. At times, Claudette transported arms to her father for storage or repair. She worked with the *corps-franc* Roland and the likes of Jacques Poirier and Peter Lake of the SOE when they also came to the area.

Claudette's friend Antoine Cloup moved to Périgueux where he became vital to the cause, infiltrating the Milice and providing information from within. Mangold often visited him at 43, rue Pierre Magne, as well as his former neighbour, Hélène Dupuy, by then considered '*la Maman du Groupe Franc Roland*'. Claudette also kept in touch with Alice Garrigou, whose home for orphans became a meeting place for many of Mangold's secret meetings.

Despite his near miss during his first mission to the mill at Pont Lasveyras, Roger Meyer continued his work as a liaison agent while at *lycée* working towards the final year of his baccalaureate. He had agreed to help distribute propaganda and this he did as well as actively trying to encourage others to distribute tracts and information sheets for him. One day he was called to the office of the head teacher for a disciplinary meeting. He learned that he had been denounced for his work, not by a fellow pupil but by a teacher of *physique-chimie* (chemical physics) who was known to be a member of the Légion des Volontaires Français (LVF). The headteacher could do nothing other than exclude him from school. As Meyer was leaving, however, the headteacher caught up, and took him aside for a private chat. His name was Maxime Roux and, as well as being inspector for the educational authority in Périgueux, he was also the leader of a Maquis group. Roux scolded Meyer for his lack of prudence, telling him that it was a good job the teacher had directed his denunciation to him rather than to the police or the Gestapo.

Roux immediately sent Meyer to a Maquis, and the 18-year-old disappeared into the woods. Several weeks later, a letter arrived for Roger Meyer via a liaison agent. It was a hastily composed note in scribbled handwriting from his mother in Nancy:

> I have just received a terrible letter from your Aunt Alice. It seems that you have broken the promises to cease all relations with your friends and that you have lied. It seems that you have committed some serious imprudence of the sort that while with Alice are impossible. It is going to make us unhappy and your father who was so well here, you are going to throw him into a serious state. We are very unhappy because of your bad conduct. The studies that you are neglecting, what do you want to do now? If you can come, come immediately.
>
> Maman[21]

Of course, Roger Meyer could not return. He had committed himself to the Maquis and had every intention of continuing the fight. One evening in Nancy, Roger's father, Lucien Meyer, did not return home. His mother, believing what her husband had told her of being too well known and liked by the local Germans to be troubled by the disturbances, stayed and waited for him for several days, along with Roger's three sisters. Then, one day French police arrived at the workshop. The inspector told them that they had one hour to pack suitcases and then they would be collected. They turned and left.

The inspector had given them something that few were given. He had provided them with time to escape. Sadly, Roger's mother still did not believe that anything bad was going to happen nor that Jews were being deported. She made the decision to stay and wait for the return of her husband. One hour later the police returned, and Roger's mother and three sisters were arrested.

In September 1944 Roger Meyer wrote to the neighbours of his parents in Nancy, asking if they knew what had become of them. In a heartbreaking response written on 31 October 1944 they told him they did not know where they were — some thought they were in Poland while others said they were in Silesia. They told Roger that they believed his father had made a mistake by not fleeing to the unoccupied zone when they had been presented with the chance in 1942, and it is always afterwards that one becomes aware of one's mistakes. They told him what had become of the family home. They had saved what they could out of the living room, the dining room and some bits and pieces, but the Germans had taken all that was in the kitchen, along with the piano, beds, mattresses, and the contents of the workshop, cellar and attic. The neighbour closed by telling Roger that he had sent him 1,200 francs by the postal service.[22]

★★★

At 5 o'clock on the morning of 17 March 1944 Adolphe Denoix, departmental chief of the Milice, descended the steps from the night train onto the platform at Périgueux having just travelled from Vichy. Denoix had spent the previous day with Joseph Darnand planning the development of the Milice from Bordeaux south to the Pyrenées. Waiting for him on the platform was Georges Breton with news that rocked him. The previous afternoon, Denoix's wife Rose had been kidnapped from their home in La Bachellerie. She had not been the only one taken.

Earlier on that same afternoon, two of Denoix's *miliciens* had been forced into a Citroën in the Place de la Bascule in the village. Four *maquisards*, armed with machine guns, had then visited the Denoix home. Having been unable to locate Adolphe Denoix, known sometimes by his other name Victor, they searched the property, collecting a hunting rifle and some grenades. They sprayed bullets into picture frames and the TSF radio set. Once they had taken two agents into Maquis custody, they returned later in the day having decided to pick up Madame Rose Denoix in place of her husband.

Denoix rallied his troops, bringing a unit to his farm where a search base was set up. Through the prefecture he published a communiqué: 'Madame Denoix, wife of the departmental chief of the French Milice, has been taken from her home. If this person is not returned in the shortest time, serious sanctions will be taken against the population.'[23]

Town criers were told to spread the message to the population.[24] However, for several days nobody came forward with any information. On 21 March the body of Denoix's wife was found by a farm worker near Breuilh. Her face was swollen, and her left temple had been torn out by several bullets fired at close range. A shocked Denoix, on finding out the fate of his wife proclaimed to Georges Labarthe, Mayor of nearby Terrasson, 'I've been in Vichy where I saw Darnand. You will see in several days what is going to happen.'[25]

★★★

Soldiers and officers of the Wehrmacht had nicknamed the Dordogne of early 1944 'little Russia' because of the problems they were having with subduing the Maquis groups, which were growing in size and influence. Favourable public opinion was crucial in order for the Germans and the pro-Vichy factions to seek out and destroy the Maquis. If the Germans were to eliminate the Resistance network to a sufficient degree, they had to create a climate in which the public shared their view of the Maquis as 'terrorists'. These outlaws had to be painted as criminals and bandits, willing to risk the lives of their countrymen and families in order to achieve sporadic and insignificant military wins which were only sufficient to advance the road to a Soviet French State. Thus inspired, informants would emerge to help track down the Maquis leaders, leaving the large numbers of gathered fighters rudderless.

Public opinion was, however, balanced on a knife edge, and the leadership of Pétain was being questioned even by his most committed proponents. Belief in his double game had been blown apart. The reputation of the Vichy government was already mortally wounded, and even those who had held on to hopes that Pétain still had fight in him were seeing a much older man on cinema screens, while those in contact with him saw a decline in his ability to lead and inspire. France had been sold out and liberation from the German occupiers seemed, for those uninvolved with active Resistance, a distant dream.

Cracks were appearing in the Vichy administration with the turning of the tide. In order to finish the occupation in credit rather than debit, some officials rallied behind the 'struggle'. The forces of order began to shift too, the gendarmeries in particular. The majority of stations were based in towns around the region, employing local officers who were stepping up their help of the Resistance through existing and well-developed contacts. When the time came, a significant proportion of the region's gendarmes took to the Maquis or contributed to the liberation of towns and villages.

For those in towns, prices were high and provisions short, but a departure from the policies of Vichy, which continued to strip the country of much of its best produce as well as deporting ordinary Frenchmen, seemed unlikely. The arrests of those suspected of anti-French activity were commonplace and deportations of Jewish families, proven *Francs-maçons*, and other minorities, had become the norm. There was talk of something beyond the awful labour camps of the Reich, with the fate of those sent further east being questioned. While the extermination of minorities was still beyond the imagination of most, rumours had begun to spread. When Jews were being taken away, many who had promised to let friends know of their plight simply disappeared. The policy of forced labour was in full swing and even the STO was beginning to feel minor in comparison to the arrests of French men to be fed straight into the jaws of German industry on the other side of the Rhine.

Many confused, scared and angry people who dared to look beyond their own walls, whether *paysan, bourgeois, ouvrier, cheminot* or *commerçant*, were keen to do what they could to support the idea of Resistance. Georges Lassalle wrote, following a meeting of FTP leaders at Limoges on 16 March 1944, 'The population, in its majority is turning away from the collaborationist government and bringing its support to the Resistance'.[26] He also claimed that cracks were appearing in the Vichy administration, where certain members were feeling 'the wind turning'. He wrote that the forces of law and order were beginning to demonstrate an unwillingness to pursue Resistance groups, even sometimes co-operating with them.*

In his monthly reports to his superior, the Prefect Régional de Limoges, Prefect of the Dordogne Popineau told of the 'growing activity of the Resistance' and the ineffectiveness of the gendarmerie in dealing with it. Further means of control were constantly demanded, and he drew attention to 'a fresh outbreak of activity by the Resistance and a lack of eagerness by the gendarmerie to put its foot down'. He claimed 'complicity of the population' and begged for further means of suppression. Not only had the Resistance become particularly active, but it was being insufficiently punished by the Vichy security forces, and even Hambrecht bemoaned the 'pathetic' number of police available to him.[27]

---

* Lassalle would be arrested just days after producing the report and he was shot at Brantôme on 26 March 1944.

Propaganda was deemed insufficient in the climate that had evolved, although it could perhaps complement more direct action. Recognised by German High Command as being in an area of central southern France where the rise of the Resistance needed to be curbed using far more direct force, the Dordogne, Lot and Haute-Vienne had to be hit hard where it hurt – amongst its people. Hunting down the groups of fighters on their own territory would be difficult, dangerous and unlikely to succeed, as networks of civilians and trained liaison agents were now well-established. The local Milice, gendarmeries, French Gestapo and Groupes Mobiles de Réserve (GMR) could take on this type of work where local knowledge and linguistic ability would be paramount in following leads.

A more heavy-handed approach was required to lead the way and demonstrate the ends to which the Reich would go to ensure discipline. A 'flushing out' of the Maquis and their support networks, thereby 'purifying' the local population, was favoured, For this, the Germans would target those members of the population who were troublesome or in need of elimination. For example, those thought to be militants or Jews could be 'legitimately' persecuted anyway, and the 'show' would send a message to others who might be thinking of talking. During their search for the Maquis, those who did not co-operate would face execution or deportation, either to work for the Reich or to concentration camps. The action would be short, sharp and terrible. The method of extreme repression would, it was believed, work as it did elsewhere, given that under such pressure popular opinion would turn and the Maquis would be forced to desist and disperse.

'*L'ordonnance Sperrle*' of 12 February 1944 officially rendered corporal punishment on the ground acceptable. From that date on, the massacres of *résistants* and civilians that were already under way in eastern and central Europe became more commonplace. France had become a battleground.

In the Ain and Haut Jura, massacres took place in February and the Brehmer operation would now refer to the new rulings stating that the response to terrorists should now take place immediately 'by fire'. If civilians were caught up and involved in reprisals that would be 'regrettable, but exclusively the fault of the terrorists'. If, for example, shots were fired from a building, it should be burned down, and there was no longer any reason to punish the commander of a unit for being too severe in the measures he imposed. In fact, an officer could be punished if the measures were not severe enough, as this would put his soldiers in danger.

A further order was issued on 4 March by Field Marshal Keitel, which stated that '*francs-tireurs* captured with a firearm had to be shot and no longer given over to military tribunals'.[28] The stage was set for bloodshed, and the German division sent to the area to eliminate the Maquis and empty the region of its remaining Jews was given free rein to do so.

Hambrecht later wrote that he had not pursued orders to arrest all Jews in the sector with any real vigour until 23 March, the date on which the 325th Security Division (Sicherungs-Division) arrived. This unit, a heterogeneous group of troops, was led by General Walter Brehmer, a 50-year-old former combatant of the Great War originally from Nordhausen. Brehmer had been made general in March 1943 and was appointed to General von Stulpnagel's Wehrmacht section responsible for security in France. His 6,000-strong division, sent from the Paris region, possessed its own Gestapo attachment and included a significant number of Georgian recruits as well as Soviet prisoners of war. It became widely known as the 'Division Brehmer' or 'Division B'.

By the time Brehmer arrived, a large amount of preparation had already been done by both German and French police forces to enable the unit to get straight to work. Officers were provided with lists of targets. People who had hidden any *réfractaires* or those who had been suspected of sheltering members of the Resistance would have their houses burned down.

Further lists had been prepared well in advance detailing registered Jews and much of the work for these documents was carried out at town halls following recent censuses. Despite official sanctions recommending arrests, for Brehmer's troops most men were to be shot summarily and women and children arrested and deported, most to their deaths in Eastern Europe. (It is unlikely that French authorities were fully aware of that consequence.) High-quality preparation, however, meant that repression and punishment could be meted out swiftly, following a carefully planned formula.

Hambrecht's diary described the Brehmer Division as 'a unit specialised in the battle against the Maquis', but this description is misleading. The week or so of 'action Brehmer', which began in earnest on 26 March and lasted until 2 April 1944, was characterised by planned operations against civilians rather than against military or paramilitary fighting units.

Arriving on 24 March, the Brehmer Division installed its headquarters at the Hôtel Domino at the wide, central place Francheville in Périgueux. From here, Brehmer published a warning to the region's inhabitants through various departmental town halls. It demanded that every terrorist or group of terrorists should be immediately reported to the French or German authorities. The provision of accommodation to members of the Maquis, or helping them in any way, was a transgression for which any person could expect to see their home burned down. Similarly, any person with knowledge of Maquis encampments that had not been notified to French of German authorities ran the risk of severe punishment.

Once the warning had been made, the Brehmer Division, with full support of the local Gestapo unit headed by Hambrecht, could proceed to carry out its aims. Its tactics were precise and unchanging each day. A new region was encircled, in which a local temporary headquarters was set up in the biggest village. Small groups of men, four of five at a time, were dispatched in light vehicles and the region was methodically shut down so that each and every village and hamlet was visited.[29] Invariably the Germans interviewed the mayor and his deputy and then ordinary inhabitants about the presence of the Maquis in the area. Usually the responses gave very little away.

Adolphe Denoix had done his work in preparing lists that were detailed and comprehensive, containing information from collaborators, informants, spies and, no doubt, people who were simply scared. Plenty of potential agents were ready to be appointed by the German police during its preparation for a 'muscular repression' of the region's inhabitants. A list in the archives of the Gironde names 107 of these agents. The PPF also had a particularly strong presence in the department with its 240 members, while around 1,000 members of the Milice had already been established.[30]

Woodland and forestry were targeted as areas known to contain Maquis encampments, and these were to be systematically set alight with a view to flushing the Maquis into the hands of the waiting German and French police. Huge areas of forest were set on fire and the night sky around the Double Forest was characterised by an orange glow throughout the period. Elsewhere in the region fires were set, hundreds of hectares at a time, by firing incendiary devices into woodland, with no clear result. The Maquis were mobile enough to find alternative encampments and this aspect of the Brehmer occupation gave rise to very limited success.

The use of fire in towns and villages was also central to the Brehmer Division's actions as it combed the Dordogne. Not least because bodies could be thrown into the flames, rendering the corpses impossible to identify. Within a week, 143 communes were covered, and many thousands of buildings gutted by fire.

Planned searches were only part of the operation; rape and theft were reported, and local people were fired at indiscriminately, sometimes while working in fields or gardens. During the week of Brehmer's action in the Dordogne, before moving into the Corrèze, only one Maquis was attacked by the division. All members of that group – the Maurice Dujarric Group near Terrasson – got away safely and the group dispersed for a short while, most members finding their way to other groups later.

On 25 March, the historic and beautiful town of Brantôme, 15 miles north of Périgueux, was the first to be submitted to Brehmer's brand of terror following several days of sustained Maquis action in the town. The FTP Daniel Lager Group, led by Alphonse Puybaraud ('Marius'), had visited a married couple in the town who were suspected of being agents to the Germans. The couple were put into a car and executed. The following morning, members of the same group attacked the town hall and demanded food tickets. They were directed to the gendarmerie where the policemen present handed over fifty bread tickets. This was just the sort of 'favourable' behaviour that Brehmer was determined to eliminate.

Once the incursion into town was complete, 'Marius' decided to set an ambush and requisition a vehicle. His men, in groups, hid in the grass verges several hundred yards outside the northern perimeter of Brantôme. After a long wait, an opportunity emerged. Puybaraud later wrote, 'The hatred, the desire for vengeance, so long contained, suddenly broke out and our young men decided to attack the first enemy vehicle to pass.' At three o'clock, a Citroën was fired upon and it swerved into a field. The car contained three officers, two of whom were killed. 'Marius' claimed in his account that one of them asked to be shot in the head rather than be taken prisoner, which was granted. The second officer was shot at the wheel of the car. The third officer, despite his injuries, managed to flee towards Nontron, negating claims by 'Marius' that he was shot by a group of his men. The officers, who were on their way from Périgueux to Angoulême, were members of the Gestapo on an advance reconnaissance mission for Brehmer and were returning to their headquarters before the imminent arrival of their division. Most accounts agree that they were carrying maps of the region, including a great deal of information about the location of Resistance camps.

On hearing of the incident while at the gendarmerie where he had gone with his deputies to discuss the food ticket theft, Mayor André Devillard travelled to the site of the ambush with his deputies. They picked up the bodies of the soldiers and took them to the town's hospital. That evening, at nine o'clock German troops arrived from Périgueux. An ambulance and its driver were requisitioned to return the dead officers to the city and shots were fired into the hospital window. An orderly was insulted and shaken up. Mayor Devillard, almost 80 years of age, was punched and kicked, and his clothes torn as his hands were tied behind his back while Walter Brehmer himself stood by. Before being bundled into a vehicle to be taken to Périgueux for questioning, he was struck several times in the face with the butt of a machine gun 'without even having the time to receive any treatment nor to say his goodbyes to his family'.[31]

Dr André Devillard was a true man of Brantôme, who 'seemed to be a part of Brantôme just as did its river and bell tower'.* On the afternoon of 26 March he was taken back there, having been told that he had seen his last dawn. It was a beautiful spring day, the Sunday of the Passion, and the floral gardens looked perfect in the stunning town that straddled the two arms of the River Dronne. Walkers were enjoying the Sunday sun and a football match was taking place on nearby playing fields.

This first punitive expedition had been assembled at Périgueux and was led by Brehmer himself, also including Michaël Hambrecht of the Gestapo and men of the BNA led by Alexandre Villaplane. The town drums beat out, and announcements were made that the population had ten minutes to clear the streets under pain of death. Shots rang out and an 18-year-old boy was injured in the ankle.

Soon, the soldiers and auxiliaries began firing in all directions, breaking down doors and ransacking houses, helping themselves to money, jewellery and whatever useful provisions they could find. Next, the population was called to assemble in the Faubourg des Reclus, just outside the main town centre, where they were told to stand in lines in ditches on either side of the road, the men opposite the women and children. One man, a 47-year-old

---

* Writing in *Le Figaro* on 3 October 1945, Jérome and Jean Tharaud described their old college friend, who became mayor in his 30s and had served in the role for forty years. He had worked tirelessly to restore his home town to its medieval glory by planning gardens and repairing rundown structures, as well as bringing the quality of the restoration into the twentieth century.

Jewish refugee from Strasbourg, rested a leg on the side of the ditch and was immediately shot. He took two hours to die in agony, during which time it was forbidden to approach or help him. When he finally died, it was also forbidden to touch his corpse.

A coach arrived carrying twenty-five hostages who had been selected from those arrested and held at the Limoges prison, and another vehicle loaded with four German machine guns pulled up alongside. The men in the coach were either Jewish who had been arrested during round-ups, or Resistance members, proven or otherwise. Dressed in civilian clothing, they were led single file up a stony pathway along the side of a steep valley to an area known as Besse-des-Courrières. Here, amongst newly worked ground and surrounded by hawthorn bushes, overlooking the red-tiled roofs of nearby Saint-Pardoux-de-Feix, they were executed by men of the BNA. Some were finished off with a 6mm bullet to the head, as their smashed skulls would later attest.

The bodies were delivered the following morning to the Salle des Conciliations de la Justice de la Paix, and the locals were told to bury them in Brantôme. They carried no means of identification and, on leaving town, the German officer informed the town authorities that their identities would be released through the prefect at a later date.

One of those executed was Georges Lassalle, 43 (otherwise known as 'Félix'), who had written of the turning tide in the department only nine days earlier. He was arrested shortly after writing and, being an active FTP leader as well as a regional director of the forbidden Communist Party, met his end on that sunny March day in Brantôme.

An unexpected body was found amongst the dead prisoners, that of a young local farm worker called Émile Henri. Returning from a game of football that afternoon he had stumbled too near the place of execution and been immediately arrested and killed with the others. He was 21 years of age and had committed no crime, perceived or otherwise, not even that of being a Jew. Curiously, Doctor André Devillard was spared and set free, battered and bruised, but ready to carry on in his life's work helping the people of Brantôme.

On the same day, a detachment arrived in the west of the department, basing themselves in Ribérac. Here, four garage owners, apparently denounced as having offered assistance and fuel to the Maquis, were arrested, their businesses emptied of useful materials and even food and wine. Having drawn a blank on finding Maquis elsewhere in the town, soldiers took these men to nearby Saint-Martin-de-Ribérac where they were joined by Robert Dubois, who had been arrested two days earlier in an identity check in a hotel in Neuvic-sur-l'Isle. Dubois had been held at the Daumesnil Barracks in Périgueux and, having managed to escape, was rearrested on 26 March and brought firstly to the Hôtel de Ville at Ribérac for questioning, then onto Saint-Martin-de-Ribérac.

All five men were shot in the back on a narrow pathway just outside the town and, according to witnesses, 'all the bodies were lying on their stomachs, faces down'.[32] Several local farmers, as well as the mayor's secretary, were made to quickly dig a grave for the bodies. That same morning, a farm owner and his tenant farmer were questioned and then shot in the basement of their farm. The soldiers set fire to the farm having emptied oil and *eau de vie* (brandy) everywhere.

Throughout the violent days to come, similar patterns of behaviour emerged as Brehmer splintered out his operations. Sometimes farm owners were arrested and taken to Périgueux, and usually it followed that their property was burned to the ground. Others, such as Henri Gilaude who was arrested in Saint-Sulpice de Roumagnac, were led away and executed on the spot, he with a machine gun, others with a single bullet to the back of the head. It is not known how much, if anything, these local people knew about Maquis activity, but it is probable that their names featured on lists provided by informants due to illegal activities, local rivalries, or simply because they were wrongly suspected of engaging in Maquis activity. On that same day, 26 March, a farmer from Siorac was arrested and taken for questioning while another, who happened to be gathering artichokes when he saw the arrival of the Germans and ran, was gunned down there and then.

In some cases, those who had been particularly active in the Maquis were, it seems, living on borrowed time. André Lamaud of Champagnac-de-Belair was a prominent Resistance member specialising in producing false identity papers. He was hanged. When two trucks carrying around forty Germans arrived at the Château Dagnac-Haut, its owner, René Mazaudois, a patriotic *résistant de la première heure*, simply abandoned his plough and walked towards his destiny.

To his horror, the Germans also gathered together all the residents of a property on the castle grounds. Monsieur Larue, an old man whose son-in-law and great-son-in-law lived with him, was called into the courtyard of the château together with both men and their wives and children. After interviewing each man individually out of earshot of each other, the old man, women and children were taken to a nearby field while Mazaudois and his family members, Pierre Vidalie and Louis Delord, were lined up, faces against a wall. A passer-by along with a neighbour, André Pommarel, were added to the group.

All were then shot in the back, the firing squad ensuring that the bullets were aimed at the heart side of the body. Mazaudois, on stumbling onto his knees, received a second bullet that killed him. However, on this occasion, the Germans did not apply their customary *coup de grâce* to the back of the head to the others. Pommarel later spoke of seeing the bullet that passed through him hit the wall and he played dead, then passed out through loss of blood. Somehow, despite passing out several times more, he managed to find his way home, a quarter of a mile away, and survived.

Prior to their deaths, the other men had been made to watch their homes stripped of anything the Germans thought valuable. Cash, jewellery, bicycles, sewing machines, silver and sides of bacon were amongst the items removed, before the château, along with the Larue house and two unoccupied houses were set alight. It took a while for the fires to get going, but eventually the flames did their work.

Such was the nature of 'action Brehmer'. The burning of houses and other property not only hit livelihoods in a spectacular manner, which was visible to whole communities near and far, but they also helped to hide the many other crimes committed. The bodies of executed victims were added to the fire and burned, making their remains difficult to identity. Any mutilation caused by torture could also be hidden in this way and the need to bother with any legalities associated with burial could be avoided. In larger properties, soldiers guarded doorways while the flames took hold to protect against any attempts to stifle the fire before it had spread. The soldiers also ensured that properties were thoroughly pillaged prior to being set alight. It was reported that as inhabitants rushed around their homes attempting to save belongings, women were raped in their own homes.[33]

One of the most astonishing examples of Brehmer's preferred methodology took place in Rouffignac, some 20 miles south-west of Périgueux. By the time the Brehmer Division visited on 30 March 1944, the German authorities were extremely well informed on the Resistance activity within a community that was so central to the local Maquis that it had earned the name '*Petit Moscou*'. It was not the first time the commune had been troubled. Groupe Rolland had narrowly escaped from the small hamlet of Peylon the previous November, and in several other instances attempts to surprise the *maquisards* had drawn a blank. Houses were pillaged as a result, several people were deported and further Resistance activity ensured that local informants had plenty of material to pass onto the German authorities, with details sometimes exaggerated to inflate their own importance to the Germano-Vichy cause.

On 30 March, following an ambush carried out by members of the FTP Gardette group, two injured Germans were taken prisoner and pushed into the back of a car belonging to the *maquisards*. On the way to their camp, the misguided decision was taken to make a stop in Rouffignac where the *maquisards* drew admiring groups of young inhabitants outside the Café des Sports. On finally arriving back at camp, word reached the group that the Germans were en route, so the prisoners were put back into the car and driven away. However, the vehicle carrying the prisoners came face to face with a German column and, although the young *maquisards* escaped, the car and prisoners were abandoned. The result for the Maquis was a destroyed camp and little else. Rouffignac and its people, on the other hand, suffered a much worse fate.

The following morning at half past eight, the town was surrounded by a unit of the Brehmer Division. The mayor was told to gather all inhabitants onto the Champ de Foire. Warning shots were fired at those trying to escape and an officer strode into the village school, instructing the children and their teachers to evacuate. In the meantime, as all inhabitants were gathering what little they could, the mayor and his secretary were interrogated but refused to speak up about what they knew of the Maquis.

On the Champ de Foire, men were separated into a single group and then further divided into those of 50 years of age or less, and the rest. Individual interrogations were carried out on the Champ de Foire until, at three o'clock, General Brehmer himself arrived. The sixty-four younger men were loaded onto two coaches and taken to nearby Azerat. Rumours abounded that the men were to be shot.

The rest of the population, including the older men, were told to gather valuables and vacate their properties by five o'clock at the latest. The local curé was informed that the church would be spared but he was to take vital items such as the archives to a safe location. According to the mayor, Fernand Lablenie, some twenty trucks were loaded with linen, supplies, furniture and other goods before being driven away to nearby Thenon. There, a large proportion of what had been taken was packed up for immediate exportation to Germany with the label, 'Gift from Rouffignac for the victims of Berlin'.

The fire began at nine o'clock that evening, and the population watched as their entire village burned to the ground. By six o'clock the following morning, only the church remained undamaged, along with three houses sheltered by it. However, the surviving dwellings did not last long as they were returned to on 2 April and burned down.

The male prisoners who had earlier been taken to Azerat were herded into a school courtyard where a dozen armed soldiers awaited them. Terrified, most were innocent of any crime but were lined up in three rows facing machine guns that were trained on them. An officer asked whether any of the men were Jewish. Pierre Khantine, a 29-year-old who had been actively engaged in Resistance activity, came forward. Punches were rained down on him in front of the gathered crowd before he was dragged away from the sight of the group and shot. Interrogations took place as the terrified men awaited their execution.

Then, a motorcycle carrying two officers arrived and brief discussions took place. The remaining sixty-three disbelieving men were loaded back on to the coaches and taken to the Daumesnil Barracks in Périgueux where they were held under dreadful conditions, but alive, for several weeks under strict instructions not to talk with other detainees. Further men from the village were brought in throughout the days that followed, while a repatriated prisoner of war, Lieutenant Asch was arrested, taken to Condat-le-Lardin and shot.

One of those interned in the now infamous Périgueux camp, Robert Nicolas, an apprentice plasterer, described the conditions:

There were a hundred men and women mixed together … We slept on the ground, on sawdust and dung, without latrines, without water; those who were ill received no care whatsoever. Any prisoner who seemed to have gone mad would be put in a cell and sent to Germany. I saw the boches force women and men to pick up all the excrement with their hands and take it away.[34]

Four or five days later the men were sorted by age. Sixteen men, including four gendarmes, were deported to work in Germany without being allowed to tell their families. Those who were a little older were released individually over the coming fortnight. The men who had been taken to Azerat had expected to die, and no doubt the soldiers who were tasked with killing them were surprised when they were spared. Although he denied it in later years, the mayor may well have accepted the offer of a destroyed village in place of sixty-four dead men. Perhaps this was why Rouffignac was, following the war, awarded the Croix de Guerre and the title of Martyred Village by General de Gaulle.

Events such as those at Brantôme and Rouffignac were 'statements' to the population; demonstrations of what would happen should the symbiosis with the local Maquis continue. The day after the twenty-five prisoners had been shot at Brantôme, Sainte-Marie-de-Chignac was chosen for a very similar show of force, being the spot where Hambrecht had been injured during a Maquis ambush. Once again, twenty-five prisoners were selected from the prisons of Limoges and Périgueux. The majority were Jews, but a few had been arrested in neighbouring Saint-Pierre-de-Chignac, including Hymian Granat and his 20-year-old son, and Isaac, whose mother Deborah had already been deported to Auschwitz. Several other Jewish residents of the village were chosen, including 40-year-old Tania Tennebaum, who had been arrested at the beginning of the month. Members of the Resistance were also included, as well as those who were only suspected or had been denounced, such as Jean Galinat, a 34-year-old baker who had been accused of having delivered bread to the Maquis.

Brought by heavily guarded coach to a place known as 'Les Potences' in Sainte-Marie-de-Chignac, those allocated were accompanied by a number of SS and Gestapo men from Limoges and Périgueux, including Hambrecht and Joseph Meyer. In the late afternoon the hostages were lined up along an embankment next to the Longueville farm and were relieved of their jackets. They were searched, and identity cards and personal papers were removed from them, after which they were riddled with bullets. While the firing squad was made up of Germans and Georgians, any prisoners still showing signs of life were finished off by North African auxiliaries of the BNA. The tangled bodies were stripped of jewellery, and, after pillaging and setting fire to the farm, the soldiers and police departed leaving the strewn bodies where they lay. However, when the bodies were discovered, two were missing – Tania Tennenbaum and an Italian prisoner named Joseph Camosetti had managed to stay perfectly still despite serious wounds, and both escaped to nearby woods.

The well-informed hunt for members of the Maquis was carried out with venom. On 26 March, Château des Farges, a suspected Maquis meeting point, was attacked. The owner, Jean Salzer, was absent but the house and barn where several Maquis members were suspected to have hidden were engulfed in flames. Maurice Dumonteil, a *charcutier* from Ribérac who rented one of the barns and a paddock, was shot and his body was thrown into the flames. Close by, one young *maquisard*, Clovis Raspingeas, who was acting as liaison agent, had managed to get word of the danger to the nearby group. He was caught, beaten and executed with a bullet to the back of the head at the side of the road after trying his best to flee.

In Lempzours on 28 March around fifty soldiers from the division turned up at the La Salle home of Adrien Thomasson. Having been accused of terrorism, he was told to fetch the key to his cellar in order to show the soldiers what was hidden there. They killed him in his cellar and, his wife and daughter having been kept away, set fire to the buildings. Only when the charred remains of his body were found weeks later did they know of his death.

Such summary executions were widespread that week. In Auriac-du-Périgord on 30 March, Henri Bonhomme was visited and wongly accused of being a local Maquis chief. After being beaten in his kitchen in front of his wife, he was driven to edge of the town and shot. The town's mayor, Antoine Laroche was taken to nearby La Borie where a farmer, who was not involved with the Maquis, was arrested, along with his son. They were killed there and then with several other tenant farmers, and the buildings set alight.

In Azerat, near Thenon, retired Doctor Trassagnac was accused of having a son in the Maquis. When his wife assured the soldiers that they had no son, the accusation was changed to having provided medical assistance to Maquis members. His wife was taken to the town hall and he was taken to a nearby field and executed, his body riddled with bullet holes and dumped behind a bush, covered with branches. The exhausted soldiers spent the night at the doctor's home, then pillaged and burned the house down.[35]

On the same day, they found the home of Monsieur Longueville and searched it from top to bottom. Living with his son of 15, Longueville kept an old revolver in a drawer, a souvenir of the Great War. Along with his son, he was taken to the town hall where both were beaten under interrogation with a leather belt. They were then taken to the edge of the village and shot while soldiers returned to their house and enjoyed a huge meal before burning the building down.

Earlier in the day, the Mayor of Azerat, his deputy and secretary had been interrogated and accused of helping the Resistance and supplying food tickets. Mayor Coulon, his deputy, Monsieur Lacoste, and his secretary, Madame Bonnefond, were to be taken to a spot a mile outside the town near Saint-Rabier. Louis Bonnefond, a postal worker, volunteered to take the place of his wife since she would be better able to take care of their 12-year-old child. This was accepted and all three men were murdered and buried.[36]

One of the most horrific of all the murders carried out during the week took place at the home of Justin Roby in Saint-Crepin-de-Richemont, north-west of Brantôme, on the edge of the Double Forest. Monsieur Roby lived on a small farm with his wife Joana, her 75-year-old father, Jean Bélard, and their four children. One of their sons, Camille, was a *réfractaire* from the STO and had been absent for some time. For reasons unknown, however, he was home when the troops from the Brehmer Division arrived on 27 March. His body was amongst the remains destroyed by fire and found later at the house. Camille's parents and 19-year-old brother had also been executed and thrown into the flames, along with his grandfather, Jean. The family's other two children survived because they were in school at the time of the massacre.

★★★

Brehmer's other targets were the Jews. With the arrival of the new division, Hambrecht could now engage his hitherto undermanned Gestapo agents alongside the auxiliaries such as Lafont and Villaplane's BNA and Brehmer's expert killers. The '*chasse de juifs*' (hunt of the Jews) could begin in earnest. In Hambrecht's own words written after the war, 'We proceeded with the arrest of all the Jews that we discovered, even if they had committed no act of Resistance.' Jew or Israélite, French or otherwise, little mercy would be extended to Jews. Women and children were to be arrested and sent to Drancy for deportation east. Furthermore, the rest of the population had to learn a lesson – protecting and sheltering Jews was not acceptable

– and with so many Jews having travelled south at the outbreak of war, the Dordogne was felt to have a significant Jewish 'problem'.

Marcel Ebstein had come to the Dordogne as a refugee from the Bas-Rhin, the north-eastern department containing Strasbourg and bordering Germany. Initially accommodated in Sarlat, he moved to Château-l'Evêque, just 10km north of Périgueux, when returning home ceased to be an option, Jews having been forbidden to return to their homes in Alsace-Lorraine.

It was in this small village on 28 March 1944 that Ebstein, 59, met a friend from the Centre d'accueil des Réfugiés for lunch and a drink. The village was surprisingly peaceful, despite the presence of an element of the Brehmer Division. The previous day, approximately 300 troops had stationed themselves in the village school and were, it seemed, taking the opportunity to rest, clean up and frequent local cafés. It was in one of these that several soldiers overheard Ebstein's conversation. He was followed home and soldiers forced their way in, ordering him to show his identification papers. These revealed his Jewish heritage and so, after beating him up, they told him to follow them. Ebstein was allowed to take a small suitcase with him, this sliver of hope perhaps the ultimate cruelty. He was taken beyond the limits of village, just 150m from the village school near to the route de Brantôme. He was told to lie face down on the floor and two bullets were fired into the base of his neck. The execution was carried out at half past seven in the evening and few people were around, so there was no one to witness it. Ebstein's corpse was only discovered the following morning by passers-by.

That evening, the mayor's secretary, Monsieur Ardillier, was forced to provide a list of all Jews and Israélites living in the commune. This information, though certainly incomplete, had been gathered officially from June 1941 when a census of Jews living in the unoccupied zone was taken on the date of the second *Statut de Juifs* (Jewish Law). Further censuses had been carried out in January 1942 for those Jews considered to be 'foreign', and then a further law, imposed by Vichy on 11 December 1942 after the demarcation line had been crossed, required all Jews in the southern zone now known as '*zone sud*' to carry the word '*juif*' or '*juive*' on their personal documentation including their *carte d'alimentation* (ration card) and *carte d'identité* (identity card).

Ardillier did what he could to delay handing the information held at the town hall over to the Germans. He also managed to warn a number of Jewish families overnight of the danger, and the word was successfully passed on. However, the following morning the Brehmer troops managed to arrest four men: 73-year-old Louis Einstein, Moïse Gardberg (61), Joseph Linz (49) and Jacques Kronenberger, who was 68. They were driven to nearby woodland above the main road to Brantôme and shot.

There is little doubt that Ardillier's quick thinking saved lives, including a whole family who lived nearby. On seeing the approach of the Germans, a further couple, the Oppenheimers, who lived on the edge of the Mesplier Woods where the executions were carried out, managed to escape via a window and hide in the woods.

On 29 March 1944, the women and children were spared deportation. However, a telegram was sent from the Prefect of the Dordogne to the Mayor of Château-l'Évêque: 'By order of the highest authority, only the family must attend the funeral of each of those killed. Any demonstration will bring with it the most severe of consequences.'[37]

Similar executions took place throughout the week. Mayors were called upon to provide lists that the Brehmer attachments supplemented with information they had received in advance and gleaned from elsewhere, such as from the likes of Paul Lapuyarde or the Service de Renseignements Généraux. But, Jewish families living in the area *were* protected to a large extent by individuals and families throughout the Dordogne. This was due to a number of factors. Firstly, the people of the towns and villages of the Dordogne had little experience of Jewish communities. Even in larger towns such as Bergerac, Jewish communities did not exist as they did in larger cities. The Jews represented in right-wing newspapers were almost cartoon figures, and the rural population simply did not identify those ordinary families who had come to their department as dangerous or subversive. The humanism of the French countryside shone through and a natural protective instinct, particularly amongst women who worked in the farmhouses while their men toiled in the fields, was evident.

Brehmer had his orders, however, and he showed little sympathy, nor did his officers, the Gestapo, the French auxiliaries or the soldiers who served under Brehmer. For them it was a question of numbers. In Corgnac sur-l'Isle, three French Jews were executed beside the river, one of whom had spent the whole day under duress showing the soldiers the location of several Maquis meeting places. In Sarliac, a list of Jews was demanded, leading to the arrest of a married couple by the name of Schvob, whose children were out at the time. Arthur Schvob was shot in nearby woodland, and the family home burned down.

A list was demanded in Preyssac-d'Excideuil and when the list showed no Jews in the commune, two non-Jewish prisoners, including the Président de la délégation spéciale (a position akin to mayor), were shot instead. In Nantheuil, north-west of the department close to Thiviers, four Jewish men who had been arrested several days earlier in nearby Ligueux were shot. Contemporary reports testify that the bodies, while not mutilated, were riddled with bullets. Three more were shot in Jayac the following day, and farms burned down.

La Bachellerie, a village 6 miles from Terrasson on the eastern edge of the Dordogne, just off the N89 road that stretched from Bordeaux to Lyon passing through Périgueux, was home to around 300 people in 1944. That population had been increased in 1939 when a number of refugees from Alsace-Lorraine had come to the area, and several Jewish families stayed on in 1940. Marguerite Lagorce ran the village bakery with her husband, Jean. They were a young couple, and their son Guy was born in 1937. When her husband was called up to the military in 1939 Marguerite took over the running of the business herself while her mother-in-law helped look after Guy. The need to keep going was heightened when she learned of the internment of her husband in a prisoner-of-war camp in Germany in 1940. Shortly afterwards, she received a visit from a Jewish family who had been exiled from Strasbourg and were in desperate need of help as they were unable to return home. The family were not asking for charity, Charles Netter, in his mid 40s, asked to be taken on as an apprentice *boulanger* (baker).

Marguerite took the family in while they looked for somewhere to live, and Charles Netter, despite having no experience or qualifications in the French art of breadmaking, thrived. Several weeks before the Germans came to La Bachellerie, however, he was paid a visit by two *miliciens* who told him to follow them out into the street, which he duly did. Clearly he was now in the line of sight of Denoix and his agents. Marguerite Lagorce bravely ran into the street and begged for Netter to return, saying that the bread was ready to be baked and if Charles was not returned immediately the whole batch would be lost. Surprisingly, he was allowed to return with the warning that he was to stay in the job and not flee, for if he did Marguerite and her family would suffer reprisals.

Marguerite was not averse to putting herself in danger, having already housed Gaston Hyllaire, known as 'Léonie', for a short time. He replaced Edmond Michelet as head of a number of Resistance networks when Michelet was arrested and sent to Buchenwald. However, bakers were easy targets for the Milice and the Germans because supplying the Maquis by any means was a charge that could easily be levied against them. During the Brehmer operation, for example, just 20 miles away in Chavagnac, a baker called Firmin Coulier, father of five children, was gunned down and put into his own baker's oven. Charles Netter did not run, probably because of the risk posed to his employer, but he and his family were in mortal danger.

La Bachellerie was the home village of Adolphe Denoix, from where his wife had been kidnapped just two weeks earlier. Her murder by *maquisards* had meant that it would inevitably become a focal point. On the morning of 21 March, *miliciens* from Limoges arrived in the village, arrested a dozen or so people, and took them back to Limoges for questioning. All were released in a matter of days but with a very severe warning – the Germans would be returning very soon.

On 30 March (and several subsequent days), the village had horror visited upon it. As a motorised column of tanks and trucks roared into the village that morning, shutters and doors were closed and the quiet streets emptied as terrified locals moved inside. Already the commune had been encircled, a tactic often employed by Brehmer, with machine guns placed on every exit and soldiers on each crossroads, behind hedges and hidden in ditches. Within the village, the soldiers began spreading out and rapping on doors, crashing their way into any houses that seemed empty.

The operation was led by the Gestapo of Périgueux and they drew on a list to which Denoix had no doubt paid special attention. A gendarmerie report collated by Adjudant Estrade, Commander of the Brigade of La Bachellerie later in the year, outlines in some detail the progression of events throughout the days to come. It also intimates that, in his opinion, the Germans were armed with lists which seemed to include information on those known to be communists, or suspected of so being, known Israélites, those of English nationality, and people suspected of having helped the Resistance in some way or another. Two German speakers were found to assist in the searches. One, René Laugénie, was a former prisoner of war, and the other, Maurice Gerst, was a refugee who was also Jewish.

Houses were ransacked and some set alight. One of the first people on the list was Henri Faucher, with the detail 'communist chief, founder of the cell'. When his home was found to be empty, it was searched and documents purporting to prove his guilt were brought out. Estrade reports a comment from a German officer who, on watching the house engulfed in flames, said, '*C'est la maison de Staline qui brûle* [It is the home of Stalin burning]'.

At the same time as the searches were taking place in the village, a further detachment headed to the nearby Château de Rastignac, built in 1811 and remarkable for its similarity in design to the White House in Washington DC. The owner, Jacques Lauwick and his staff were told to wait in the courtyard having been accused of harbouring two 'terrorists' and hiding armaments. This operation, led by Obersturmführer Thalman was, however, more than it seemed. Not mentioned on the gendarmerie report – because it was not widely known – was that Jacques Lauwick, through his sister-in-law and co-owner of the château, Madame Fairweather, had agreed to hold a collection of art in safekeeping for a friend of the family who happened to be a wealthy Parisian Jew. This man, Jean Bernheim, had moved to nearby Terrasson as a refugee and knew that his collection was under threat as the Germans were seizing Jewish possessions. This was not a normal collection. It contained paintings by the likes of Cézanne, Renoir, Van Gogh, Matisse and Manet so was of inestimable value. This visit by the Brehmer Division was no coincidence and had been ordered as part of the Einsatztab Reichsletter Rosemberg (ERR) in an attempt to gain control of goods of high value that had been seized from Jewish families.

At the beginning of 1944, the Gestapo found out about the collection through a contact only known as 'Suzanne' and the task of retrieving the collection was given to Brehmer by the Bureau de Sécurité in Paris. Thalman arrived at half past nine, along with an officer, two soldiers and a driver in a Peugeot 402. Once in the courtyard, where Lauwick was denied a chair for his 77-year-old mother-in-law to sit on, the family and staff were made to wait under watch for two hours. A guard was put on the main entrance steps and the sounds that escaped the château were those of all manner of items being smashed. At around midday, some of the staff, along with Lauwick and his family were taken to Azerat in the Peugeot while the others were told to disperse. Lauwick's wife was denied permission to return to the building to collect either clothes or identity papers.

The herdsman of the estate, Henri Belanger, was made to clear any barns and garages of any motorised or horse-driven vehicles, then to accompany two soldiers to a nearby farm. On his return, he saw further vehicles, including a truck, and soldiers carrying bundle after bundle of goods to them. Notwithstanding the hidden art collection, the château was home to a large number of rich pickings. Textiles, tapestries, silver, jewellery, art and furniture were taken. When Belanger was dismissed in the early afternoon he looked back from half a kilometre away to see the first flames climb. The fire was tended for days and no part of the building, nor that of the outbuildings, was allowed to survive. Nobody can account for the priceless works of art and whether they were ever retrieved because they haven't been seen since.

Arrests were made in La Bachellerie and those placed under watch were taken to a covered courtyard shared by a school and the town hall. The Germans were furious at the discovery of the empty homes of certain listed Jewish families. One of these, the Schupack family, were hidden in a waiting room by the deputy manager of the local railway station and another couple hid for thirty-six hours in a hearse after initially being protected by the owner of a guesthouse who took a huge risk in allowing them to stay a short while. Others were not so lucky and were arrested trying to flee. One family, the Schenkel family, had sensed the danger and got out of their house by a rear window, using a rope that tore into their father's hand. His name was Nathan and he had built up a small bric-a-brac business in the village since arriving from Strasbourg. Born in Poland in 1896, as had been his wife Esther two years later, he had naturalised as French in Strasbourg and the couple had five children. That morning, they made the heartbreaking decision to flee with only three of their children, Isaac, who was 12, Jacques (11) and Maurice, who was 9. Their other children, Cécile (14) and Alfred (7), had been chosen to represent the family at a gathering for Jewish Passover in Périgueux. They would be returning by the evening train, alone.

The Germans targeted the Lafarge garage and its owner, René, and son, Jean. They were arrested for having apparently repaired Maquis vehicles. The local maker of clogs, Monsieur Moïse Laroche, was also taken into custody, despite his protestations that he did not understand why he was being arrested. The protestations of René Laugénie, who informed the Germans that although Laroche had a Jewish first name he was neither

Jewish nor communist, were met with a rebuke from an officer that the information was not being requested. Charles Netter, the *boulanger*, was also arrested despite the pleas of his employer, Marguerite Lagorce.

The terrified Schenklers went to the home of the Faugeron family that morning. Their 14-year-old daughter Mady was friends with Cécile, one of the two Schenkel children in Périgueux for the day. They stayed for a while and were given breakfast and lunch before Nathan decided that his family would be safer elsewhere, and their presence also putting his hosts in danger. He took his family into woodland, leaving Mady Faugeron wondering where and how they would spend the night.

Those who had been arrested were sorted. Jewish women and children were taken to a nearby field, while ten men were led through town and slowly up to the top of a hill. Those with houses facing to the west could see the sad procession. Once at the summit of the climb the men were lined up. No time was wasted, the same two German Gestapo agents who had led the men to the top were tasked with killing them. The execution began on the left-hand side of the line, with bullets fired into the heart side of each man's back. There was a panicked shift away to the right, where the other executioner continued the operation. The clog maker, Laroche, was amongst the dead alongside his father, as were the garage owner and his son. There were no survivors, and a nearby landowner, Monsieur Meeckel, later spoke of what he saw, 'I'll never forget the horrible vision of those men falling forward, without a cry, like a game of boules and all my life I will see that tragic spectacle in my nightmares'.[38]

However, the killing was not finished. Maurice Gerst, 25, had acted as interpreter that day but could not escape the fate reserved for those of his Jewish heritage. He was shot nearby. Although René Laugénie had been unable to save lives, he did manage to dissuade the Germans from burning down certain buildings, in particular those in which the absent Jewish families had been living. The majority of these were rented from French landlords, having been requisitioned during the exodus of 1940. In fact, one of the houses belonged to a family member of Denoix and so was saved. This was the one from which the Schenkel family had escaped that very morning. The pillaging was extremely thorough. Anything of value, including leather shoes, tools, sewing machines, drapes, radio sets and accordions, was loaded onto vehicles and taken away. Houses that were not burned were turned upside down and trashed.

In the schoolyard, the Jewish women and children had waited for most of the day while the Brehmer Division did its work. In all, there were sixteen women or young girls and twelve children, as well as six men, who included two sergeants from the gendarmerie of La Bachellerie who had been accused of being too soft and lacking 'energy' in their pursuit of the Maquis. Marcel Michel, Mayor of la Bachellerie and former senator until he had been removed by the Vichy regime, was there too. At three o'clock in the afternoon, the Jewish women and children were taken to a nearby field, soon to be joined by Marcel Michel whose home had been searched but spared for the time being (it was burned two days later). The two gendarmes were free to go but were warned to be much more severe in their treatment of 'terrorists'.

That evening, Marcel Michel and the Jewish women and children were led from the field and boarded onto trucks, finding Monsieur Lauwick and his family from the château de Rastignac already on board. All were taken to the Daumesnil Barracks in Périgueux. Days filled with beatings and interrogations followed. The Lauwick family were released after three days and Marcel Michel returned to La Bachellerie a month later. All of those who had been arrested as Jewish had disappeared without trace.

Meanwhile, 18-year-old Yvette Lafon, who worked in Périgueux, was on the evening train home, dreaming of her coming wedding. Sitting in the same carriage on the short journey were two children whose family she knew well.[39] Fourteen-year-old Cécile Schenkel sat close to her 7-year-old brother, Alfred. As the train approached La Bachellerie, Yvette saw the flames rising from the Château de Rastignac and wondered what was going on. She got off the train, accompanied by the Schenkel children, at La Bachellerie. There were German soldiers everywhere and Monsieur Pasquet whispered to the young girl, 'Hurry up Yvette, get home quickly'. Yvette walked the short distance to the village with Cécile and Alfred sticking close to her. They were trembling and holding onto her skirt, as if for protection. She worked in Périgueux each day so was used to the presence of German soldiers, most of whom were polite to the general population. However, she could sense something different that night in La Bachellerie. There were soldiers with machine guns in ditches at the side of the road, some of whom were asleep. As they entered the village and drew level to the *Monument aux morts* (Great War memorial), they were stopped by an officer who asked them where they were going. The children squeezed in very tight to her and she saw the Faucher house, still in flames. Yvette told the officer that they were going home, and he allowed them on their way.

Yvette and the rest of the village did not fully understand the danger that such families were in. When both her front door and the home of the children were in sight she told them to run straight home and took herself inside. When the children got to their home they found nobody, their parents having fled that morning with their three brothers. Deciding against going to the owner of the house, their landlady Madame Raymondis, they were found moments later by 22-year-old Pierre Laugènie who, as a *cheminot* (railway worker), was also returning from work in Périgueux. He decided to take them to his home, where his mother and father, Marie and Louis, could decide what to do. On the way to La Fontaine Bachelière he was stopped and questioned by a soldier, but on showing his professional *laissez-passer* (permit) was allowed to go on his way. Pierre's mother fed the two children and set them up with somewhere to sleep in the room of her youngest daughter, Gisèle, who was 9. There they spent the night, but Gisèle was kept awake by the sobbing of the Schenkel children who wanted to know what had happened to their parents.

The following morning, Marie Laugènie answered the door. It was Madame Raymondis, the owner of the Schenkel home, who told the Laugènie couple that she needed to take the Schenkel children. Madame Laugènie refused but Madame Raymondis, a close relation of Adolphe Denoix, insisted. She threatened reprisals, saying that she knew Pierre's older brother René was in the Resistance. She threatened dire consequences for the whole family, including young Gisèle. The couple were left with no option but to hand the children over and they were led away by Madame Raymondis.[40]

The previous day, when Nathan and Esther Schenkel had fled the home of the Faugeron family, they had not got far before being picked up by the Germans. Nathan was arrested while Esther and the three other children were taken to the field from where they were driven to the Daumesnil Barracks in Périgueux. The Jewish families were locked away from the rest of the prisoners. The Schenkel family were not the only family to be intercepted when trying to escape; the same fate awaited the Grün family. Father Napthalie was arrested and taken away while his wife and 14-year-old son were taken to Périgueux with the other Jewish families.

Julien Borenstein, a Polish Jew who had been in Terrasson when the Germans had arrived on 30 March, arrived back in La Bachellerie the following day to find that most of the Jewish community had disappeared. His wife and two young daughters were missing, and his home had been turned upside down and torn apart. Mad with grief, he packed a small suitcase and, despite the protestations of neighbours, turned himself into the Germans. He was immediately taken to a spot near the railway station and executed.

The following day, on Saturday, 1 April, Napthalie Grün and Nathan Schenkel, both of whom had done all they could to get their families to safety, were taken to Azerat. They were added to a group of three other Jewish men who had been captured nearby and 15-year-old Anne-Marie Devaux watched through the gaps in the wooden slats of her barn as the group of men was 'pushed like animals going to the abattoir' against the wall of the cemetery.[41] She saw them 'collapse onto ground red with their blood', witnessing bullets smashing into the wall having passed through their bodies. But the worst was to come. One of the soldiers, she attested, on noticing something about the face of one of the victims, approached and smashed his heel down onto the jaw of the dead man. He then pulled out a dental frame that contained gold crowns. One of the three men executed alongside Grün and Schenkel was called Monsieur Cohen. He was a *Chevalier de La Légion d'Honneur* (Knight of the Legion of Honour) with a full pension awarded due to his exploits in the First World War. He also was an amputee, missing his leg and arm on the right side of his body.[42]

Around La Bachellerie, the operation continued for several days to come. Local administrators were arrested and taken to Périgueux. In Saint-Rabier, Jules Duteil, a 39-year-old factory worker and father of five was arrested, accused of being a communist. He, along with 44-year-old Marcel Moumaneix, the secretary in the town hall, father to six children and accused of supplying false identity cards, was executed. The wife of Marcel Moumaneix, who had given birth just three days previously, was forced to get out of her home and flee in order to escape the flames. A female Jewish Polish refugee named Léa Elefant, aged 39 and mother of a 6-year-old girl named Betty, was arrested for using a French identity card. Léa's husband had been in a prisoner-of-war camp since 1940. The young mother did her best to flee but was shot in the attempt; her body was thrown into the flames of her burning home.

Some friends who lived in the same block as Léa – a couple with the surname Scher – had decided during the morning, on seeing Germans in Saint-Rabier, that they had to flee. Their 8-year-old daughter Solange, who was like a sister to Betty, was left behind because, like Betty, she was at school and they felt that if she was safe anywhere then it would be under the protection of the teachers. At the end of the school day the two young girls emerged, searching for their mothers. They were taken by well-meaning boys to the town hall. From here they were seized by the Germans and taken to the Daumesnil Barracks in Périgueux. The two lost and terrified children had no parents to cling to and were looked after by two young assistants attached to the Jewish welfare organisation, Aide sociale israélite de Périgueux. They were Florette Feissel and Fanny Wolf, both of whom were also being deported. The young women mothered the children on board the long convoy No. 71 to Auschwitz-Birkenau, where, on arrival, they chose to hold the girls' hands as they were led straight into the gas chambers.[43]

La Bachellerie and its immediate surroundings had seen a total of twenty-four victims of executions, including fifteen Jews. On board the trains that made up convoy No. 71, which left Drancy on 13 April 1944 for the Polish death camp, were thirty-three people from that one commune. The list included sixteen boys and girls aged between 2 and 16 years. Of those thirty-three prisoners, only five returned, but none of the children made it back.

Charles Netter's wife, Adrienne, 12-year-old son, Yves and 8-year-old daughter, Monique, who had grown up alongside little Guy Lagorce in the family bakery, did not return. Some time later Guy asked his mother, 'Maman, are they going to kill us too?'[44] Esther Schenkel travelled to Auschwitz-Birkenau with all five of her children. Cécile was 14, Isaac was 12, Jacques, 11, Maurice was 9, while the youngest, Alfred, was 7. All were killed. Their father, Nathan, already murdered in Azerat, never had to learn the fate of the rest of his young loving family.[45]

During the week when the Brehmer Division carried out its operations in the Dordogne, 116 Jews were shot; 270 others, mainly Jewish women and children, were sent to Auschwitz following the horrendous journey that began in Périgueux.

The remaining Jews of the southern zone rightly felt scared. Many had gone into hiding while those remaining were unsure if they could consider themselves safe anymore. For Raphael Finkler the reality was sinking in. It did not matter that he did not practise the Jewish faith. According to the definition issued by Vichy authorities, neither he nor his family were exempt. They did not have a lot by way of property or money, but their lives were in danger. By May 1944, life was so perilous that Raphael's parents, Benjamin and Ida Finkler, could no longer go out into the street; staying indoors, in hiding, was just about their only option.

Then came a warning from an associate who worked within the police. They were in grave danger, and further round-ups were planned. Maryse Nicolas and her young aunt, Monette Leclerq, who were in constant touch with the Finklers, told them that they needed to get out of their apartment, as the address was obviously earmarked for a future round-up. As clandestinely as they could, they took Benjamin and Ida Finkler to their small apartment on the rue de la Boétie and for a short time hid them. This was impossible to maintain for long, especially given the importance of Monette and Maryse to the Resistance cause as liaison agents whose home could easily have been under surveillance. They decided that if they wanted to keep Benjamin and Ida safe they would have to get them as far away from the concentrated persecution of the Dordogne as they could. This would mean taking them into the former occupied zone and to their own home town of Pisany, near Royan.

Using all of their contacts and ingenuity, the young women procured what was needed to pass the demarcation line which was still operating as a frontier despite the total occupation of France. False identity cards were created and the Finklers took on new identities. Ida became Isabelle Blanc, and Benjamin became Benjamin Nortmer. The journey was dangerous, and it was important that neither Ida nor Benjamin spoke during the journey as both still had accents recognisable as Romanian. They also needed to travel separately, so Monette set off first with Benjamin. Maryse followed a day later. Both journeys went well and the passage through the demarcation line was tense but uneventful. When the couple were installed in the relative safety of the home of Louis and Méliane Nicolas, Monette and Maryse turned on their heels and returned to Périgueux, eager to carry on the vital work with which they had been entrusted. One month later, the rest of Raphael's family, including an uncle, an aunt and two cousins, one of whom was 8 years old, were arrested and deported to Auschwitz.

A meeting held on 9 May 1944 in Périgueux under the chairmanship of Lieutenant Colonel Hachette, who was commander of the forces charged with the maintenance of law and order in the Dordogne, concluded that a 'clean-up' of the agglomeration of Périgueux had become necessary. The operation had to take place immediately as any leak of information would be damaging to the eventual outcome. The round-up was by no means restricted to the removal of known Jews, it was equally aimed at bringing in members of the Resistance, those suspected of helping the Resistance, suspected communists and *Francs-maçons* in preparation for deportation. Using lists supplied by Paul Lapuyarde before his departure from the Périgord in order to take up a position as regional inspector of the LVF, further lists were drawn up that night for the arrests to come. Starting the very next morning, the town was to be surrounded and shut down. Eleven sectors were devised, and a member of the Milice was allocated to each, each in charge of further *miliciens* and police. Those arrested were to be taken to a cinema called Le Palace on the rue Bodin in order to be questioned and sorted accordingly.

The '*grande rafle*' (Great Round-up) of 10 May was a shock to the city dwellers of Périgueux, for whom the round-ups were assumed to be restricted to the Maquis-ridden countryside. In total, 211 men and women were rounded up that day and taken to Le Palace. Amongst them were key members of the ORA whose base of operations centred on the area. Lieutenant Raoul Christophe ('Krikri') was there, as was the wife of a doctor who was responsible for the health service of the FFI. As well as *Francs-maçons*, prison officers, road workers and local administrators, a diverse variety of other occupations were included. Several teachers and accountants were arrested, as was the owner of a local publisher and printer, Pierre Fanlac. Of those arrested, around ninety were sent to the holding camp at Saint-Paul-d'Eyjeaux, a mudbath of a camp with dreadful hygiene facilities in the Haute-Vienne. Others were deported to German concentration camps or sent to the submarine base in Bordeaux to work as forced labour on the Todt programme which was tantamount to slave labour.

'Krikri' managed to escape on 5 June during his transfer to Germany. He made it back to the Périgord, and rejoined the headquarters of the newly formed Forces Françaises de l'Intérieur (French Forces of the Interior, FFI) stationed at Breuilh.

7

COUNTER-ATTACKS

The Brehmer Division's success in clearing the area of Maquis groups was minimal, given the size of the operation. Any engagement with the paramilitary fighters had been haphazard or stumbled upon. Only the Groupe Lucien Sampaix had been actively targeted, and no *maquisards* were killed or captured during that operation. Most of its men dispersed, hid for a while, then either returned to other Maquis groups or to civilian life. A weekly report compiled by the Commissaire of Renseignements Généraux de la Dordogne, destined for the prefect and copied to superiors in both Limoges and Vichy on 8 April 1944, just four days after the end of the Brehmer operations, gives a fascinating, if rather one-sided view, of the department in the wake of the repressive measures. This does tally with what is known of the Brehmer plan, which never included frontal assaults on the Maquis, which would have failed. Brehmer's target had always been the civilian population, particularly those with proven or suspected links to the Resistance. His superiors had made it clear that the division should punish and scare the population into withdrawing their support or supplying information that would lead to further arrests. The police report betrays a confusion on the part of local Vichy administrators regarding the aims of the operations:

> The fast-paced capitulation of the gangs who have, for several months terrorised the Haute-Savoie, has surprised the population. These people, so tested by the 'purifying' operations undertaken by the German troops, are beginning to doubt the patriotism of the '*maquisards*' who

they deem responsible for the tragic events that have just played out in the Dordogne.

Many people blame the people of the Maquis for attacks on the undefended population, whilst at the very moment they find themselves in the presence of their armed enemy they only seek their safety by fleeing. It is said that they are only good at stirring up a hornet's nest.

The people are asking with a degree of insistence to be rid of the Maquis, but they are asking that, as in the Haute-Savoie, these operations be carried out by French forces.[1]

The event to which the commissionaire was referring was the defeat of the Maquis des Glières. In January 1944, the Maquis was squeezed under a state of siege in Haute-Savoie and eventually eliminated despite stern resistance.

While the events of the Haute-Savoie served as a warning to Maquis leaders around France of what sustained German repressive measures could achieve, it also inspired the French Resistance with tales of courage, pride and patriotism in the face of overwhelming odds. The defeat was turned into a propaganda victory, giving a boost to the French Resistance during the spring of 1944. The Maquis of the Dordogne were operating in a milder climate, amongst shallow valleys and sloping forests that they knew well, and to which guerrilla tactics were well suited, unlike the snowy mountains of the Glières. In the Dordogne, the Maquis easily outnumbered the Germans and could disperse into obscurity quickly, minimising losses. The Dordogne was never going to be another Haute-Savoie.

The Jews, the report informed, 'following operations by the German police in the course of which a great number … have been shot, are living in terror'. Furthermore, 'the arrest of the leaders of the *l'Entr'aide israélite* of the Dordogne … has reinforced their fear'. The report of the following week adds:

The recent operations by the German police have severely tested the Jewish community. 70 of them were shot (this figure is not exact since numerous bodies have not been identified). We count only around 300 Jews who have been arrested of which most have been taken to Paris, then onto an unknown destination. The Jews feel tracked and are trying to leave the department for a calmer region.[2]

In fact, 116 Jews were summarily executed during that week and 270 others, mainly women and children, were deported to Auschwitz. In the same report, the public were said to be regaining control of their emotions following the week of intense German activity. 'The public remain confused by such a large number of bodies and ruins. Too many innocent victims were created by the ugly bullets, it is said, and there is surprise that the French government did nothing to put an end to these reprisals.'[3]

Drawn from hundreds of letters opened by agents and other sources such as hearsay quoted by agents, prefect reports have to be questioned. To what extent did the NAP gain control of the flow of correspondence within the postal system? How influenced were the writers of the reports by their own beliefs and personal experience? The following statement seems particularly personal: 'A *milicien* was killed by German soldiers under the pretext that he was armed. Is this not proof, think the public, of a brutal and blind repression?'[4]

This suggestion that the Brehmer operations had got under the skin of even Vichy officials is countered once again by the claim that the public 'wishes, to avoid new reprisals, that police operations are undertaken against the "Maquis" by French police forces'.[5] There may have been some truth in this reassertion, but where the veracity of the report has to be questioned is in its claim that the *paysans* who had been 'severely affected by recent German police operations' wanted to be 'rid of the "Maquis"', the cause of their troubles'. Only a small proportion of the letters examined by the authorities were likely to have been written by the people of the countryside, whose lives often revolved around their own holdings. They were 'the privileged class' at that moment, and largely unaffected by food shortages. The Maquis were more likely to have been disliked within towns and villages where their appearance and action could lead to subsequent trouble for the civilian population. Despite the Brehmer operations, the people of the countryside would have been the least likely to have wished to see the back of the Maquis – and the survival of the Maquis groups relied heavily upon them.

The FTP based in the Ligueux Forest had, by April 1944, carried out some notable successful ambushes and, after most of them, Valentine Bussière's farmhouse served as a rallying point. Valentine and her parents continued to support the *maquisards* in whatever way they could. In that month, around forty hungry and tired young men came back to the house to seek provisions and hide from the German soldiers who suddenly seemed to be everywhere. They did not stay long, but it was long enough for their comings and goings to be noticed, and for the authorities to be informed.

During the night of 10 April most of the *maquisards* left the house to set up camp some 3km away. Only a handful of them remained and, due to sickness and injury, they were confined to bed where Valentine cared for them. Early on the morning of 14 April, Valentine noticed a single German soldier at the edge of the farm. She went back to the farmhouse and told her family that the '*Boches*' had arrived. Her brother fled without detection and headed for the camp, where he informed the FTP detachment of the imminent danger. Valentine's mother ran upstairs and told the remaining *maquisards* that they had to leave, which they did, also without being seen.

Valentine and her sister made for the stables where plenty of incriminating material was stored. After collecting a bag from the house, they gathered together parachute ropes, false identity cards and meal tickets and took them out towards the fields, making out that they were guiding a flock of sheep. They were noticed by the German soldier, who had returned to his position, and the girls ignored his calls and wild gesticulations for them to return. They sped up pretending not to hear, determined to buy time for the escaping three injured *maquisards*. Fortunately, the soldier decided against opening fire on them but minutes later the Bussière family home was searched and plundered by around fifty German soldiers. A large cannon was turned on it, and it was fired on repeatedly, burning it to the ground.

Valentine rushed to Périgueux and arrived at the flat of her contact Gaston Naboulet to find that he had fled. The door was opened by members of the Brigade Nord-Africaine and she was immediately arrested. She was taken to the Daumesnil Barracks in Périgueux where she was roughed up and questioned by Alex Villaplane. She gave nothing away and no evidence of any wrongdoing was found on her, so she was finally released and told to return two days later. The authorities held onto her identity papers as a guarantee. She did not return, knowing that she could easily procure new papers. She dyed her hair blonde, though it came out auburn, and then carried on with her work.

A meeting of regional FTP leaders held in Limoges on 16 February 1944 had resulted in a new offensive guerrilla strategy to be closely observed by all FTP chiefs. Each group must, it was decided, possess its own ambush group. With the war on the Eastern Front thinning the numbers of quality German troops on the ground in France, combined with a general insecurity amongst the Wehrmacht resulting in a higher concentration of troops in towns, it was necessary to make FTP men war-ready. Plans were drawn up to prepare all members of the Resistance for national insurrection.

As the German occupiers felt the pressure, they would need to call for reinforcements. Also, they would need to break up into small units to extinguish the fires of uprising. Both of these scenarios were ideal for ambushes. This would, they realised, lead to violent repercussions in the form of reprisals against the population, so ambushes should take place away from heavily populated agglomerations. Any attacks or ambushes needed to be well prepared, short and would need to draw heavily on the element of surprise. Should it seem likely that the ambush had prompted the support of a larger German unit, communication should be made so that men and resources could be protected.

As well as the issues of security and training, clothing, food, arms and shelter also had to be found. Some FTP leaders sensibly took the new arrivals – often generally those who simply wanted to be on the 'right side' in the months to come – in name if nothing else, hiding them in safe houses or farms throughout the countryside, but others could not contain their delight at the possibilities such a 'French' insurrection offered. There were, however, nowhere near enough arms to go around. Large concentrations of men would not only lead to a less mobile and more easily locatable army, but the *maquisards* simply did not have the weaponry or skill to take on heavily armoured Panzer units. Maquis redoubts had failed elsewhere in France, and small mobile units that could carry out short, sharp, well-planned attacks on German columns at their weak spots and inflicting maximum damage suited the lightly armed specialist fighters better.

When the Brehmer Division descended on the Eastern Dordogne at the end of March 1944, the Maquis knew better than to take it on. Instead, they retreated, broke up and waited to reform once the unbeatable unit had moved on. Only very small mobile units were left behind, with only very limited operations intended to harry the Germans. Antagonising such a unit further would have disastrous effects on the local population and could decimate the Maquis, who adopted the 'drop of mercury' strategy, coming back together later.[6]

The problem of more and more volunteers wishing to join the Maquis was one that had to be dealt with sensitively by the likes of SOE agent Jacques Poirier ('*Capitaine Jack*'). The orders coming in from London insisted that younger men who had recently arrived should be sent home, or provided with lodgings in farms to disperse to if this was not possible, each case judged on the merit of the potential recruit and the specific needs of the group. London's preference was for small well-trained groups, most of which were not only already in existence but fully operational. This was underlined with the directive that the Maquis should by no means exist in large concentrations of men. After the D-Day landing, when numbers swelled to unmanageable levels, Poirier was again pressured to send volunteers home and encourage small sub-units of men. However, he understood the reality on the ground and did not insist on all new men being sent away, a position which he rightly realised was untenable. "'They're crazy," I told Casimir and Jean-Pierre. "Do they think I can go to the Maquis commanders and tell them to send their boys home?'"[7]

AS barracks-style camps were less mobile than those of the FTP. Brigade RAC in the north of the department, led by Rodolphe Cézard, was a little different in that it was already mobilised into large teams and functioned as a light division with full services. From April it operated with two groups of fifty armed men. More commonly, however, AS Maquis were large and lacking mobility. This had brought its own problems when camps were discovered, and men and materiel lost as a result. The AS formed six *corps-francs*, including the Groupe Franc Roland, formed by Roland Clée in January 1944. With ten or fewer men, these units carried out smaller sabotage missions and occasionally located and eliminated collaborators. They also located supplies, scouted potential camp locations and protected the camps once settled. However, their primary role was the protection of the main camps, particularly during periods of transit.

Roland, who was responsible for the AS of the Dordogne Centre as well as being part of the *état-majeur* of the new Forces Françaises de l'Intérieur (FFI), understood very early compared to other militarily trained AS leaders the vulnerability of large concentrations of men, particularly when arms were lacking, and men were insufficiently trained in techniques of fighting with only light weaponry. Not wanting to undermine his own troops, he sent away men who could be just as important placed elsewhere in the overall system, such as gendarmes who were directed back to their stations where they could be of more immediate use.

Personalities played a large part in how the influx of new blood was dealt with. Some leaders, of FTP groups particularly, had little or no military training. Unlike Spanish Republicans, they might also have little under-standing of the need for self-discipline and structure and subsequently dismissed the idea of not accepting all-comers. Some of them had fallen into a lifestyle in which they were leaders for the first time, and adored the adoration afforded them by their men.

On 16 June, General Koenig, leader of the FTP, ordered larger groups to split into smaller bodies of men, but this order was ignored by some who were keen to retain overall control of their units. One of these, Jean Constantin ('Jean Bart') had no wish to 'demolish' his company, especially since he was proud of his recruits, who included police agents and gen-darmes from Périgueux and Ribérac. On 22 June, German soldiers of the 11th Panzer Division and Gestapo agents, reinforced by members of the BNA, were on a mission in the Vergt area when they located and arrested several *maquisards*. One of those arrested knew of the location of a large group of Maquis and gave its location away. Later that day, they attacked the Château de La Feuillade near Vergt where 300 of Constantin's men were assembled. Many of the men managed to get away after a significant battle, but there were arrests and two men were executed. A large amount of material vital to the Maquis was recovered from the site.

The Forces Françaises de l'Intérieur (FFI) had been in existence for several months but it only really became effective when a properly staffed headquarters was set up on the day following the Normandy landings. Prior to that, all manner of variations in strategies and personalities co-existed, meaning that Maquis units in the Dordogne more often than not went their own way. This happened to be the preference of the FTP anyway. Its three-sided leadership triangle issued directives and its company or group leaders were afforded the autonomy to run their group as they saw fit depending on the means available to them and their knowledge of the locality. While the FTP complained of armaments being sent by prefer-ence to AS groups, this also depended on personality and circumstance.

Contrary to SOE orders, operative Jacques Poirier got on particularly well with the FTP and struck up a good understanding with groups whose leaders demonstrated efficiency, guile and bravery. An unexpectedly strong working relationship developed with René Cousteiller ('Soleil') a tough-talking and uncompromising leader of men who had arrived from the Camargue and was known for his aggressive personality.[8] Cousteiller benefited from Poirier's admiration in as much as the young French SOE agent used the group and built up an understanding. As a result, equipment often found its way in the direction of Cousteiller. The relationship soured a little in the end, but it had already progressed immeasurably since the men's first meeting when Cousteiller threatened to kill Poirier. Poirier could not, however, work miracles. He did his best to arm each group adequately, but he could not change the fact that, prior to D-Day, London had prioritised the supply of weapons to other areas more exposed to those battles that would immediately follow the invasion of Normandy.

From April 1944, *corps-francs* groups of the AS were engaging more and more in sabotage missions. By the end of the month, by order of the R5 region leadership, Brigade RAC in particular were sending armed *maquisards* to carry out operations aimed at sabotaging railway lines and roads. Additionally, telephone lines were targeted with the hope that German troops could be further isolated and pushed into Périgueux and Bergerac, as well as Saint-Astier, a small town west of Périgueux which was home to several important military-based industries.

On an almost daily basis, successful operations were taking place on the railway in complicity with *cheminots*. Michaël Hambrecht, Gestapo chief in the Dordogne, later wrote:

> Even the great Wehrmacht units were attacked everywhere, but never openly, the roads were barricaded and the bridges destroyed. Many individual soldiers, or small groups of them, were ambushed ... The Maquis were forming themselves into gangs of several hundreds of men, armed with all the necessary weapons that had been parachuted in by English airplanes.[9]

★★★

Important message for Nestor: 'The giraffe has a long neck.'

When this message was broadcast amongst the nightly BBC London personals on the evening of 4 June 1944, two young men leapt to their feet and hugged. They had been waiting for the words for months, each evening huddled in a dark radio room listening to the wireless, waiting to see if the day would ever come. Jacques Poirier, code name 'Nestor' and known locally as '*Capitaine Jack*', had been trained in England and sent to France by the SOE. Although assumed to be English by local Resistance leaders, he was in fact French but decided to keep up the pretence. His companion that evening was Ralph Beauclerk, an Englishman who had been parachuted in to work in Poirier's network as a radio operator. His code name was 'Casimir' and along with Peter Black ('Jean-Pierre'), who had been sent to train the Maquis in the use of weapons and explosives, the men made up an effective triumvirate.

The message, broadcast from London, relayed in French and including the key phrase, meant that within twenty-four hours operations would commence for the invasion of France by Allied forces. Several days earlier Beauclerk had excitedly handed Poirier a piece of paper with a message that had arrived, double coded:

> Important message for Nestor *stop* Major operation scheduled in the next few days *stop* You will be notified by the BBC twenty-four hours before the operations commence *stop* The relevant message will be 'The giraffe has a long neck' *stop* Your task will be to sabotage railway lines, destroy petrol dumps, and maximize disruption to the enemy's lines of communication *stop* Execute well-timed guerrilla operations but avoid large-scale action that could expose the civilian population to reprisals.[10]

When the message arrived, Poirier knew that all the work he had put into preparing the Maquis leaders for this moment would be tested. He was, however, also wary of overexciting those same leaders. Two weeks earlier, he had received word that he should prepare landing sites for a large-scale parachute drop of Allied soldiers. As it happened, the drop turned out to be for no more than a dozen or so agents to help him, which he politely declined, being very happy with the people he already had. Having needed help in finding the sites and therefore involving certain senior leaders with limited amounts of information, he was dismayed when word got back to him that the Dordogne was about to be invaded from above.

In the case of the latest coded message, Poirier knew he needed to alert and prepare the leaders again. He could not give out the actual coded message, which was kept between himself and Beauclerk. He only told those who needed to know, including one of his more trusted companions, André Malraux, better known in Resistance circles as 'Colonel Berger'.

One of the great thinkers and writers of the day, André Malraux had already accomplished much as a writer, having travelled extensively and published a number of novels. The only one that Poirier knew anything about was *La Condition Humaine* and he was such a pragmatist that, at the time, he showed no interest in Malraux's public persona, even during a lunch in Paris with Albert Camus. Poirier was concerned that Malraux's image was too public and, as such, he was likely to get caught.

The great adventurer Malraux arrived in the Dordogne in the spring of 1944 and proclaimed himself in charge, despite having spent much of the war in the South of France doing little by way of resistance. He had fought in the Spanish Civil War, though his exact involvement is not completely clear. Malraux came into the Resistance when his two brothers were arrested and his involvement in the Resistance has been examined in some depth by Resistance historians, but Poirier placed great faith in him. He warmed to the man because of his commitment to the cause at hand.

Poirier was both surprised and amused by Malraux when one day the two of them, while driving through the Dordogne, came across an armoured German division. Skidding to a stop and turning the car, Poirier hoped to get away unnoticed, while Malraux fired a tiny pistol wildly in their general direction. Poirier also appreciated the incredible way Malraux, a talented orator, had with the men, inspiring them through speeches from the tops of tables, which riled and enthralled the young country folk in equal measure. For several months Poirier and Malraux became almost inseparable in the build-up to D-Day.

The advent of the Allied invasion in Normandy was a watershed moment for the Resistance and the French public at large. For those still openly supportive of the Vichy regime, fear grew as news of the Allied successes spread. Fear of reprisals occupied the minds of many. Prefect Jean Popineau fled to Vichy then Paris when he was sent a message by the Maquis to quit his post on pain of death. Other, less high-profile members of the public either slipped into hiding or looked at ways of melting into the Resistance. For most, including those who had neither resisted nor collaborated, the news was one of hope.

The event had been a long time coming and it was easy to believe that the end of the war was approaching. But there was still much to do. Throughout May, Jacques Poirier had been having more and more trouble dealing with the impatience and enthusiasm of Maquis leaders who, having waited for such a day for so long, were told that it was close. Parachutes supplied enough weapons or the numbers already engaged, but little more than that. When D-Day arrived, leaders expected an armed uprising, but there was nowhere near enough materiel to go around. Poirier chipped away at the leaders telling them that, should there be a mass recruitment due to an Allied invasion, they should stick to the plan and try not to swell their ranks. New recruits should be dispersed or sent home.

Between receipt of the news of the forthcoming invasion and the event itself, Poirier and Peter Lake, who had been concentrating his efforts in the east of the area, did their best to ensure that orders via personal messages on the BBC were followed. The orders indicated the various stages of the military plan to be activated within France by the Forces Françaises de l'Intérieur (FFI) as directed from London. 'Plan Vert' meant that train lines were to be sabotaged, 'Plan Violet' triggered the cutting of telephone lines and 'Plan Rouge' was the go-ahead for ambushes of the occupiers.

On receipt of the messages vast operations were undertaken. *Maquisards* of the FFI, along with local *cheminots*, successfully sabotaged the main rail routes from Bordeaux to Brive through Périgueux, as well as the Agen–Périgueux–Limoges track. Further attacks were carried out on other main lines such as Thiviers to Angoulême and Périgueux to Agen. Groups directed by SOE agents Philippe de Gunzbourg and George Starr hit lines westward in the direction of Bordeaux, and Peter Lake busily did the same in the eastern Dordogne. In Tulle, Jean Marsat led *cheminots* in cutting lines around that part of neighbouring Corrèze. Along the railways lay concentrations of equipment ready for transport and these too were attacked. Rail traffic was severely hampered, if not paralysed.

The message '*La Sorbonne a le toit rouge*' ('The Sorbonne has a red roof') indicated that road barricades should be set up throughout the region. Trees were felled, rocks were transported and old vehicles parked on highways to prevent movement. Crossroads were blocked and chicanes were set up, lined with armed *résistants* wearing armbands adorned with a 'V' or a cross of Lorraine. To guard and man the barricades was a French tradition that they were only too pleased to repeat.

It was likely, leaders were told, that German troops would soon traverse the area from the south. Maurice Loupias ('Bergeret') later claimed that he actually had to dissuade some of the road-blockers and encourage them to stick to the areas he had planned in advance.

London was explicit in its orders to Poirier. Everything should be done to harry German divisions and slow them down, as their early arrival in Normandy would threaten the establishment of an Allied bridgehead, should the invasion be successful. An insurrection was to be avoided, because 'a general uprising might imperil the local inhabitants'.[11] Indeed, the day before the Allied invasion even took place, SS-Brigadeführer und Generalmajor der Waffen SS Heinz Lammerding had set out his ideas for clearing the area that had become infested with 'terrorists' through a campaign of propaganda. This, he said, should include, ten days hence, the rounding up of 5,000 male 'suspects' in the Cahors–Aurillac–Tulle area and deporting them to Germany.

On hearing reliable news of the Allied landings, euphoria overcame some Resistance leaders and led them to act far too impulsively, which was a shock to Poirier and Lake. For example, in Champ de l'Ilot near Carlux, Maurice Loupias had proclaimed the Fourth Republic and proclaimed himself Prefect of Bergerac. There, French flags were flying out of windows, as they were in Sarlat, where, on 7 June the Maquis marched into town. Loupias claimed control of *résistants* north of the Dordogne river, while further south Philippe De Gunzbourg of the SOE did the same.

Despite claiming to have ample weaponry, they were setting up large, open groups of *maquisards* who could not possibly resist the advance of a Panzer division. Lucien Dubois proclaimed himself Mayor of Sarlat, while other *résistants* took up positions relating to law and order. The brigades of gendarmes from the surrounding area came to the town and swore allegiance. That night noted collaborators and *miliciens* were rounded up and arrested and 'the following day, 8 June 1944, the liberation of the town was complete'.[12]

Similar scenes took place in Belvès, where bells rang out as the Resistance set up a 'Comité de Libération', while volunteers carried out patrols, day and night, in towns and villages throughout. In Montignac, a regional headquarters was set up for the FFI and from the balcony of the town hall a proclamation was made, that of the institution of a 'Comité Français de la Libération'.

Few FTP groups joined in with the 'insurrection'. However, exceptions included Cousteiller ('Soleil'), who took up a position in Mouleydier, while in the Corrèze some FTP groups began an ill-fated takeover of Tulle.

Poirier and Malraux rushed to see 'Martial' (André Gaucher), head of the AS in the Dordogne and implored him to bring the leaders into line. The proximity of the Germans to such scenes made the situation perilous, 'If they stepped in, as they might within hours, there was every chance that a bloodbath might result'.[13] Promptly, orders were sent out to quieten the celebrations down. What Poirier and the commanders could not control were the scores of men, young and middle aged, who were leaving their homes and taking to the roads in search of a Maquis to join. Security breaches had to be avoided and the Maquis leaders had to stick to the plan, otherwise the whole thing could become a disaster.

On 7 June, a group led by Léon Cérisier undertook a raid on the prison of Mauzac. Meeting hardly any resistance from the French guards, its interns were taken to meet Philippe de Gunzbourg, and he sent them to various posts around the area of Bergerac.

In Périgueux, the Mouvements Unis de la Résistance (MUR) set to work in its quest to let the public know that the time had come to do exactly what those in command in London had wished to avoid:

> Frenchmen!
> The hour of insurrection has come.
> Every able man between 20 and 46 inclusive must present themselves immediately (within twenty-four hours) to the town hall in order to be registered in view of their participation in the liberation of the territory. Every Frenchman who does not conform to this order will be considered a deserter.[14]

It was unsurprising, then, that the Resistance was suddenly flooded with new recruits.

★★★

During the night of 8 June, a plane approached in the skies over the Dordogne from the south. It had flown from the northern Algerian city of Blida, carrying four men who parachuted down to fields outside Sarlat.

This was one of eighty Operation Jedburgh teams sent into France during the period just before, during and after D-Day. Each small team was meant to consist of three to four men, including an American, a Brit and a Frenchman.

This particular operation, code named Ammonia, sought to ensure that the Allies retained control over the *maquisards* on the ground. They were well trained, highly able agents who arrived in uniform so as to avoid any suspicion of them being spies. They were tasked with finding groups of *maquisards*, arranging them into teams, arming them and initiating them in the art of classical warfare. They were leaders of men, chosen to inspire local *maquisards* into action.

Four men dropped into the Périgord that night, a French captain named Raymond Lecomte, with his deputy, an American radio sergeant named Jacob B. Berlin, and an American captain called Benton McDonald Austin. As well as organising the Maquis, these agents also had the mission to cut communications between Brive and Montauban, and Montauban and Bordeaux. Having made contact with George Starr ('Colonel Hilaire'), whose HQ was in the Garonne, they set up base in Veyrignac.

Through Jacques Poirier they were allocated two teams of twenty men, one team from the AS and one from the FTP – although when the latter pulled out, a second AS team was allocated instead. They went to their task, then moved on to missions further south. Their stay in the Dordogne was brief and they saw a Resistance movement that was already working remarkably well. Their skills were better employed elsewhere.

★★★

A new appointment was made by officials in Vichy on 9 June and it was the second in command at Bergerac, Jean Calard, who was selected to become the new Prefect of the Dordogne. He was given the difficult task of holding together an area of France now seemingly set for uprising and insurrection. Unfortunately for Calard, one of his first duties was to deal with the news that the SS were coming his way.

The 2nd SS Panzer Division Das Reich, based in the area around Moissac and Montauban, less than 100 miles south of Bergerac, would be following instructions to proceed northwards towards Normandy. The Das Reich Division, with 20,000 men, was an impressive machine of war boasting tanks and armoured vehicles as well as experience that was second to none. Formed in 1939, it had helped invade the Balkans in 1941 and then fought in the USSR, where in 1943 its troops had been engaged in the savage battles on the Dnieper and in Kiev. Its men were tough, well used to the savagery of war and taking reprisals on citizens, and were a mixture of volunteers and the *Malgré-nous* (literally, 'against our will'), men from the Alsace-Moselle region who had been forcibly conscripted at the beginning of the war. It also contained conscripts from other parts of the Reich, including the Soviet Union, Romania and Czechoslovakia. They had been sent to the area around Toulouse and Montauban to reform, recuperate and train in preparation for their next mission, which was expected to be on the Western Front. The soldiers were young, but not overly so, and in fine physical condition.

Having finally received orders to move north at half past eleven on the morning of 7 June, the day after the Allied landings, the Das Reich Division finally set off on the morning of 8 June. Setting off from a point near Montauban, they were noisy and camouflaged with branches. Soldiers trained machine guns on the sides of the roads as the column moved slowly forward in the heat of the day, initially over hilly terrain.

Led by Heinz Lammerding, Das Reich was one of four SS Panzer divisions operating in France on D-Day. Once beyond Cahors, the capital of Quercy, it split into three main columns travelling separately in order to divide the attention of the local Resistance. The Der Führer Regiment, a lighter division led by Sturmbannführer Dickmann, took a forward position as a reconnaissance battalion following a slightly different route north in order to protect the left flank of the rest of the unit that headed through Figeac towards Brive.

On approaching Groléjac, a small village with a bridge across the River Dordogne, the Der Führer Regiment met its first battle. Here, the Rémy Company, an AS group from the Corrèze backed up by the 'Victor' Detachment led by Lucien Dubois, attempted an ambush on the head of the column coming their way. The short battle was over in twenty minutes, leaving five *résistants* and five civilians dead, including a man shot dead while fixing his car and refusing to acknowledge what was going on around him. A hotel on the river into which civilians had retreated was hit by a missile and began to burn with civilians still stuck inside. As they fled from the back entrance of the establishment they were shot dead. The

Der Führer Regiment moved on across the river, hardly delayed by the short battle and leaving bodies where they lay.

Less than 2 miles north of the river, in Carsac-Aillac, a surprised Maquis unit travelling in a truck was overcome, with four shot dead while another managed to flee to safety. Then, mistakenly taking a wrong turn towards Sarlat, soldiers of the Der Führer Regiment fired at civilians, killing thirteen in less than half an hour. A farmer driving oxen in the fields was killed, as was an 80-year-old blacksmith and a doctor, who was a Jewish refugee. Several properties were set alight before the column was redirected east along the northern edge of the Dordogne, reaching the riverside hamlet of Rouffillac on a crossroads from which the regiment could proceed north.

On a bridge heading south across the Dordogne, a direction in which the Panzer regiment had no need to go, a barricade constructed from beams procured from a local depot had been built. The hamlet was the base of a local Maquis, also named Rémy, led by Doctor Bezalel Auerbach ('Bernard'). The regiment approached, and shots were fired by *maquisards*, killing an advance motorcyclist. A bazooka was also fired, damaging an armoured half-track but there are no reports of further casualties on the German side. With insufficient weapons and numbers, the *maquisards* were forced to quickly retreat as the Germans began responding with automatic weapons.

When the area was clear, some of the Germans approached a restaurant near the bridge and demanded crêpes be made for them. When the owner refused, thirteen people, including eight women and two young girls, were rounded up and pushed inside the restaurant which was barricaded and burned, killing all those inside. Sadly, local *maquisards*, who lacked training, were firing too much and wasting ammunition while not understanding the range of their weapons and not using cover well in liaison with their commanders. They were never going to make inroads into the might of an armoured division. Too often, they opened up civilians to reprisals while they fled in the midst of battles that could have been avoided. Roadblocks were easily removed by units such as the Das Reich Division because they they had not been set alight.

Similar tragedies occurred along the route of the main column of the Das Reich Division that day, notably in Gabaudet, in Lot, where a gathering of boys and young men preparing to join the Maquis were discovered by a patrol. Ten were killed on the spot, including one young girl. Eighty others were arrested for deportation and later, for some unknown reason, released near Tulle.

The progress of the Das Reich Division through Lot and Limousin has been documented in other publications and the division's reputation preceded it. As it crossed Lot, Corrèze and eastern Dordogne into Limousin, Resistance activity certainly slowed it down. In doing so, the Resistance met its limited objective, that of delaying the various elements of the division and depriving it of its focus. However, the cost throughout the area was significant. In Tulle, the attempted FTP occupation led to a battle with the local German garrison and subsequent heavy German losses. The local occupying force, filled with ageing soldiers of dubious quality, struggled against an organised Maquis occupation until a detachment of the Das Reich Division arrived and circled the town, killing *maquisards* until the survivors were forced to retreat. As a result, on 9 June the SS, annoyed at having to intervene, took revenge by hanging ninety-nine local men from lampposts throughout the town.

The following day, elements of the Der Führer Regiment led by Dickmann headed to Oradour-sur-Glane, having been told of Maquis activity, stores of arms and the kidnap of a German officer there. The Maquis were apparently holding him in the town in preparation for a public execution. In fact, there was little in the way of activity in the town, no sign of arms and certainly no hostages. However, it mattered not, as it is likely those reasons were given later as excuses for the excess zeal of the commanding officers that day who rounded up the inhabitants of the town and executed them.

In all, 642 people died in Oradour-sur-Glane after it had been surrounded. The men were shot in barns, with only a handful escaping. The women and children were locked in the town's church and, after being sprayed with bullets, the church was set alight. One woman managed to escape by climbing out of a window and was found later, barely alive. One small child also escaped, having been told to run at the sight of Germans. But that was all. Locals were unable to retrieve the burned and unidentifiable remains for several days, and amongst the complete devastation of the town, bodies were also found in a well, hedgerows and in the oven of the *boulangerie*. As a show of force, it had limited effectiveness and was entirely unnecessary.

General Lammerding was a young general at 38, and his promotion owed more to the favour afforded him by Himmler on account of his administrative abilities than to militaristic talent. He agreed with the beliefs of the generals in Berlin that the Resistance should be dealt with as the convoy headed north. However, attacks on a convoy of the military might of the Das Reich Division would never amount to much and it is estimated that the whole division lost only thirty-five or so men out of 15,000 during the journey north.[15] Therefore, the decision of the generals, including Lammerding, to engage in operations of *ratissage* (violent raids) against the Maquis was folly.

The departure off the main route by Dickmann's Der Führer Regiment was one such needless operation. Souillac, south of Brive, had been marked as a Maquis hotbed when, in fact, the scuffle that had taken place there just days earlier had been nothing more than a minor attack by a local Maquis on a German outpost, with losses only incurred by the Maquis in the shape of three injured. Had the detour into the eastern Dordogne not been taken in order to address the Maquis there, progress would have been quicker still.

Lammerding refused to look beyond the twin strategy imposed on him from above to clear the way of Maquis for other regiments to follow, and to destroy any large concentrations of Resistance that could pose a problem for later periods of occupation. Though a mistake in the global story of the war, Lammerding and his officers were unable to resist the goading of the Resistance as they pecked away at the column's metal shell.

The journey north was long and slow. A stretch of over 700km was already going to take three to four days at least in an armoured convoy. Normally the journey would have been made by train, but Resistance in the southern zone had done remarkable work in rendering the tracks impassable. With lines being fixable in hours, the sabotage of tracks was insufficient, so instead the Maquis had concentrated on blocking the lines with sabotaged rolling stock, collapsing bridges and dynamiting tunnels. The road was the only option, therefore, and progress was bound to be slow. It was not until 10 June, when Lammerding reviewed his position and reported to his superiors of the 58th Panzer Corps, that he was instructed to entrain the tanks of the division in Périgueux, where at least some could be loaded onto flat beds and taken through to Coutras along the one piece of track that was passable. An armoured train operated along that line as a protective measure for several large industries in the Saint-Astier area west of Périgueux. From Coutras, lines northward from the Bordeaux area were in better condition.

Lammerding's report outlined a crippling paralysis of the area by the Resistance and not only spoke volumes of the work done by all arms of the Resistance in the area, but it also prompted the German Command Headquarters in France to order as an emergency measure a battle group of the 11th Panzer Division to help the Das Reich Division progress from the area, by ensuring 'restoration of peace and order and its maintenance by the strongest measures in the departments of Corrèze and Dordogne'. That division, based in the Bordeaux area, began its move eastwards while the Das Reich Division, originally headed in the direction of Clermont-Ferrand, diverted elements eastwards towards Périgueux, where its tanks could finally be loaded onto trains. Many of the tanks had had to wait for parts to arrive and so the movement was delayed and slow.

In order to get to Périgueux, the diverted elements of the Das Reich Division had to pass through Terrasson, the first major town within the eastern edge of the Dordogne, just 12 miles from Brive. Once there, they could proceed through the same villages that the Brehmer Division had trampled on its way towards Périgueux. Terrasson, home to around 3,000 people, had suffered its share of troubles already and was earmarked as a hotbed of Resistance despite the attentions of Brehmer. Its mayor, Georges Labarthe, wrote regular letters to his mother in Paris, painting a picture of a town terrorised by a Maquis that stole and pillaged in much the same way as the Germans.

The special attention accorded to the area by Brehmer in early April attests to how well protected the Maquis were. Those large numbers were well supplied by the *paysans* of the area and while those who lived in town did not like having goods requisitioned, generally it was accepted as necessary. Mayor Labarthe's claims that the Maquis made trouble only to flee at the first sign of combat, thereby leaving the population to suffer, is wide of the mark. On learning of the approaching Germans, several Maquis groups entered the town while the Battle of Tulle was raging on 9 June and began constructing roadblocks to slow down the advance of the German divisions that soon would be heading that way from Tulle. Labarthe called Roger Ranoux ('Hercule') to see him, which he did with a small number of men. Labarthe explained his concerns, that reprisals against civilians were apparently taking place near roadblocks and in urban areas. Ranoux agreed to take down the roadblocks and move them further outside town, to several kilometres before the column would reach the first buildings.

On the morning of 10 June, the town was in the hands of the Maquis who declared the Fourth Republic. A further meeting was held between Labarthe and the Maquis, and responsibilities for the day to come were agreed. Shots were heard outside town and the inhabitants, including the mayor, moved indoors. When the Germans arrived, they ordered Labarthe to round up the town's inhabitants to gather on a square and tanks were moved in all around to avoid any escapes. Soon a car arrived on which a *maquisard* was being carried. His name was Fernand Limouzy★ and his family were in the crowd. They did not give him away when the Germans yelled at the crowd, asking who knew him. A local doctor asked if he could attend to the young man but was refused. Meanwhile, Labarthe noticed that the town hall, located over the river in the old town, was ablaze. The young Limouzy was calling for his mother when one soldier pulled him by his arms and another two by the legs, towards a building with a balcony overlooking the square. A further soldier had climbed up to the balcony and dropped a rope down. Young Fernand Limouzy was hanged in front of everyone present, and Labarthe was told not to take him down for two days. The women and children were sent away, as were, a little later, men over the age of 50. There remained around 100 men within the square with machine guns trained on them.

Several women informed Labarthe that much of the old town was in flames. He asked and was given permission by the German officer for the remaining men to attend to the fire. Then, Labarthe claimed, while this was happening the officer demanded to be fed. Labarthe invited him to his home and they dined well, drank wine and he agreed that the men could go home once the fires had been extinguished. Also, according to Labarthe, a French-speaking medic through whom Labarthe had been communicating all day told him that the officer had decided that, since it was his wedding anniversary, he was in a good mood and Terrasson would not burn.

The Germans left the following morning (even, according to Labarthe, taking an injured older woman to the hospital on the way). After the war, Labarthe was painted locally in a very favourable light while the Maquis were accused of once again bringing terror on Terrasson. Labarthe was, however, 'a Pétainist up to the last minute',[16] – maybe not pro-German,

---

★ This young *maquisard* was a friend of Lucien Cournil, who was not present in the square that day.

but certainly anti-Resistance. Whether his actions that day were entirely as reported is almost impossible to ascertain, but he was an example of a local politician who did just enough when faced with an incredibly dangerous position to defuse a situation that could have become far worse. He was lauded and applauded for what he did. However, local whisperings never forgot that he entertained, ate and drank wine with the Germans that night.[17]

Documents have since emerged in the Bordeaux archives that Terrasson was likely never to have been destroyed because of its importance as a vital passage across the river, linking Bordeaux to Brive. As for the Maquis, they had done as asked and moved the barricade away from the populated area, and the only loss of life on 10 June 1944 in Terrasson was one of their combatants. Once more delays had been caused, if only slight ones.

The case of Terrasson that day is an interesting example of compromise prevailing. In one quirk of fate, the home of Chief of Milice Adolphe Denoix, located on the side of the road near a barricade, had been adorned with a huge red flag by the *maquisards* and so it was set alight by the Germans and destroyed.

The following morning, the column made its way through Brardville near Le Lardin, the location of the Christmas 1943 homecoming feast afforded to Ranoux and his men. It roared into La Bachellerie, the village that had suffered so terribly under the terror of Brehmer, setting alight its gendarmerie and firing at passers-by. Then it passed through Azerat, and into Thenon.

On 6 June, Thenon had become occupied by the AS Roger Group, led by Roger Deschamps and Roger Richard. With the British radio carrying message after message about the oncoming armada, all armed groups in the area had been instructed to cut communication lines, put up barricades, bring out the Maquis who had been stowed away in farmhouses and encourage young volunteers throughout the area to come forward and help in the insurrection. Men came from the gendarmerie and volunteers flooded forward, until it became obvious that there were insufficient arms and some were sent home until more weapons arrived.

Most of the *maquisards* set up in the old hospital, while the town hall and *salle du conseil municipal* (council chamber) were turned into dormitories. Martial Faucon was put in charge of the telephone exchange in the post office. When information came through as to the sheer size of the German column, the Maquis left the town and dispersed, sensibly not wishing to waste young life.

Geneviève Delliac was the 17-year-old daughter of the town's mayor and, her mother having died some years previously, she lived with just her father. It was overcast and drizzly on 11 June and he had gone to Auriac as part of his duties. Despite the relative proximity of Thenon to Terrasson, Geneviève had heard nothing of the events of the previous day and she decided to go to see her friend, Lily Deschamps, who was several years older than her and the young wife of a local leader of the Resistance. When she got there, her amazed friend looked at her and asked, 'What are you doing here?' Geneviève had not seen the oncoming monstrous caravan of armoured vehicles but, on comprehending the severity of the situation, she bounded out of the back courtyard and rushed home through neighbours' gardens.

The commanding officer of the convoy could see what had happened in the town and was furious. As well the barricades and obvious evidence of a Maquis occupation in the town hall and around the town, a truck that had been carrying *maquisards* was also found, abandoned. Geneviève looked on helplessly as Lily was driven up the street on a vehicle with a fixed machine gun.

Lily spoke German and had been commandeered as a translator. When asked to take the Germans to the mayor's home she could only do as she was told. The soldiers banged on the door and demanded the mayor. Geneviève told them that he was absent and the house was searched, though not well enough to find several hidden weapons that would have spelt disaster. Geneviève had just enough time to hang a white sheet from an upstairs window, a signal to her father that it was not safe to return home.

Geneviève was loaded onto the truck with Lily and taken to a point overlooking a valley that opened onto forestry near to the place where many of the *maquisards* would have fled. The abandoned truck that had been carrying *maquisards* was in a ditch nearby, and a large cannon had been trained on the woodland, ready to fire shells into the trees. The girls were questioned on where the *maquisards* were. Both girls held firm, claiming they knew nothing and were unable to help.

Suddenly, Geneviève was grabbed by the arms and pushed against the cannon, her face pressed up against its gaping barrel. She saw a soldier load a shell and prepare to fire. Lily looked on helplessly, terrified as the cannon was fired. As the smoke cleared she saw Geneviève on the ground. Her legs had given way through fear just as the cannon was fired, so the shell missed her. Shocked and tearful, she was pushed alongside Lily, temporarily deafened but luckily alive. Soon afterwards, the soldiers left. Thinking they would be executed when they were no longer needed, the young women hugged in relief as the last of the vehicles departed Thenon. Acquaintances and friends sobbed when they made their way through the town, having assumed them dead. Geneviève could not believe that she had survived the cannon, nor that the soldiers had not noticed her blouse made of parachute silk.[18]

Throughout 11 June, tanks and half-tracks converged on Périgueux. Many were taken to the Daumesnil Barracks, but they also lined up on the Place Francheville, along the Cours Fenelon and many other spots in the city. The heavy tanks and many other pieces of armoured equipment were loaded, on 13 and 14 June, onto fifteen trains, each pulling ten to twenty wagons out of the Dordogne and on to Coutras, then Poitiers and on to Normandy.

No further disruption of any note was encountered along the way. The Resistance had done all it could in the R5 region. In fact, it had hardly slowed the column at all, the German High Command had done that by itself, ordering senseless *ratissage* operations against the Resistance. But the *maquisards*, the supporting networks of *légaux*, *cheminots*, civilians, and even the likes of Georges Labarthe, had done their duty. The Das Reich Division had hated every minute it spent in the region.

None of the Das Reich Division remained in the Périgord beyond 14 June, but between 11 June and the departure of the division some elements accompanied the Gestapo and auxiliary forces, such as the BNA, on expeditions of repression around the region. On 12 June, such an operation was carried out amongst a number of communes north of Périgueux. Having accounted for five lives in Trélissac, a suburb of the city, and then another two in Antonne, the column headed into the area around Cornille. There, they arrested two men, one of whom, Izmul Frydman, was a Jewish refugee. He was the father of Paul Frydman and a friend of Raphael Finkler and 'Phil' Lichtenberg, who had travelled with them to join the Maquis on New Year's Day, 1944.

Izmul Frydman was shot just 300m from his home and his friend, Édouard Lauseille, was driven towards Les Piles, just 1½ miles east. Having already engaged the FTP groups of the Sorges area that day, the German column was returning to Périgueux through Les Piles when it was set upon by a small FTP detachment that had sprung up there since 6 June, led by Gaston Naboulet and including Valentine Bussière who, since her arrest by the BNA six weeks earlier, had been living semi-clandestinely without papers. The exact details of what happened in Les Piles on that day are unclear, but Valentine ensured that several *maquisards* who were injured in an upstairs room were removed by members of the group. Meaning to follow the group, she set off to retrieve one other recovering *maquisard* on the other side of the village. The Germans surrounded the small village and made a host of arrests. Shells were fired, killing one man and injuring two others. A 43-year-old man was killed on the side of the road and a Hungarian Jewish refugee was found in his home with his throat cut.

The division had been in the village less than an hour but, as well as having shelled properties, word spread that arrests had been made and the sound of a firing squad had been heard. When the Germans left, Valentine Bussière's parents and sister were amongst the first into the village to survey the damage and to look for her. Debris was scattered and burning. They recognised her hair as they approached what looked like a pile of bodies in front of a barn onto which burning wood had been thrown. As they got closer it was clear that some of the bodies were themselves still on fire. Valentine's dress and body were partially destroyed by flames, but her face was recognisable, as was the FFI armband on her arm. She had been shot in the chest twelve times. Five other people, including a married couple, lay burning along with the victims of the firing squad.

Legend has it that the last person to see Valentine saw her striding down the street towards the oncoming German column carrying a machine gun. The Germans returned to Les Piles that night and set fire to a further six houses. Nobody knows why. On their way back to Périgueux, they stopped at the home of Ideza Frydman, who had managed to get the body of her husband, Izmul, home. Her two sons Marcel, 18, and Paul, 20, were with her as she mourned her husband. The Germans burst in and shot all three of them. They set fire to the house and the burned remains of Paul Frydman and his family were found the following day. Only one person survived – 7-year-old Lazare Frydman escaped the carnage by hiding in a barrel.

★★★

As expectations of a 'national insurrection' spread more widely, intense activity took place elsewhere in the department. In the area around Mussidan, west of Périgueux, along the Isle Valley on the main rail and road link to Bordeaux, the 4th Bataillon FTP groups that had retreated to Lot and Lot-et Garonne during the Brehmer period were ordered to move into the area and take up position in Saint-Georges-Blancaneix where some locals had set up a small support network.

Having set off from Marminiac on 6 June and arriving at their destination two days later, they immediately received a request from the AS group 'Loiseau' for back-up in the area around Le Fleix, slightly further south-west in the Dordogne Valley (just minutes away from Saint-Antoine-de-Breuilh where Louis de la Bardonnie had first sent messages to London four years earlier). Word had come through via messages from London that the area was to be secured in preparation for a major operation arriving from London by air. This, in fact, was a ruse meant to throw the Germans off the scent of the real Allied plans, and instead the combined FTP and AS forces fought the 11th Panzer Division, which was trying to make its way to Bergerac where it had been told to support the struggling local garrison. The fighting lasted two days, throughout 8 and 9 June, and the column was prevented from crossing the Dordogne, having to turn around and take an alternative route after losing two armoured vehicles.

Mussidan was of strategic importance being a gateway along the valley of the Isle into Périgueux and onward to Brive and Limoges, therefore, the regional command of the FTP ordered Henri Borzeix, commander of the 4th Bataillon FTP, to occupy the town on 11 June. The men were given orders in Saint-Georges-Blancaneix on the afternoon of 10 June, and on the morning of 11 June detachments from the Groups Francs Roland (Roland Crouzille) and Kléber, as well as some back-up from Prosper, headed into the town. As just under 200 men rolled into town led by Borzeix and Crouzille, men who knew the town well were confident that the small number of Germans present there could be overcome. The men were well-armed, though extremely inexperienced and young, most had never been involved in combat or even realistic combat training. One *maquisard*, Jacques Chapet, was given a bazooka to use, 'Someone put a bazooka in my hands. I had never seen one before … I was simply told, "You put it on your shoulder, you will have a loader with you".' Another, Guy Léger, had never touched an automatic weapon before, 'When I was given a Sten sub-machine gun I had not even fired a hunting rifle before. My baptism of fire was Mussidan.'[19]

The *maquisards* took up key positions around the town, including the gendarmerie, town hall and railway station. An armoured train was expected, which passed through at intervals in order to protect a German garrison in nearby Saint-Astier where an underground factory constructed aircraft parts and transferred both parts and people to Bordeaux on a regular basis. The train itself carried a number of wagons in which German soldiers, young Luftwaffe men in the main, travelled protected by banks of sandbags. If the railway could be rendered unusable then the tanks that were being loaded at the station in Périgueux to join their detachments for the journey north would be severely delayed.

During the day, a second group of *maquisards* were instructed to approach the town from the other side of the river and destroy the river bridge. While some civilians aided *maquisards* in felling trees and setting up roadblocks, two detachments of Groupe Kléber (Claude and Jeannot), and parts of Groupe Franc Roland and Prosper positioned themselves at the station, in readiness for action should the train arrive and need to be neutralised. The train duly arrived at a quarter past ten, almost as soon as the men were in position. Jean Regazzoni (Groupe Kléber) recalled the battle:

> In front of the locomotive ... were harnessed two flatbed wagons serving as protection in case of explosion of mines on the track. Behind, linked to it, was the tender with its reserves of coal and water. Then two further flatbed wagons with slatted sides reinforced by steel plates and bags of sand. Two other mining wagons, which were shorter and deeper and in which men could stand, came next.[20]

At the rear of the convoy was the guard's carriage in which stood the train's French guard alongside further German soldiers. According to Regazzoni, in order to respond to the firing from the Maquis, the Germans were forced to go out into the open. Their grenades were all thrown too short and, stopped by the hedge, exploded in the branches or at the feet of the hedges.

Several Germans got out of the wagons. Jumping onto the ballast, they tried to get to the hedge but were mown down by a *maquisard*'s machine gun before the gunner was hit and killed: 'I asked my comrades to save their ammunition and only fire when they had a certain shot. I heard shouts from the other side of the train, towards the station, followed by a sustained exchange of gunfire. Then more cries, and silence.'

Regazzoni had served in the 35th Artillery Regiment, then became a *réfractaire* in February 1943. He joined the Maquis and there found his old friend from the army, Jean Mignon, or 'Zézé', who had been fighting in the Kléber Division of the FTP in the Double Forest for several months. Jean Mignon was killed in battle along with eight others at Mussidan that morning. Twelve more were injured during a battle that lasted over an hour. Luck, however, had deserted the Maquis. The railway station was just several hundred yards from the RN89, the main Bordeaux to Périgueux road, and by an awful coincidence a combat group from the 111th Grenadier Regiment of the 11th Panzer Division (which became known as the 'Ghost' Division), led by Colonel Wilde, was on its way to Limousin in order to relieve the Das Reich Division. Hearing and seeing the battle, Wilde's reinforcements were enough and, surprised and attacked from the rear, defeat for the *maquisards* was inevitable. With just enough time to gather their dead and injured onto a lorry, they escaped. To make matters worse, the plastic explosives expert had not shown up at the bridge so that could not be destroyed either. Surviving Germans apparently told Wilde that their men had been taken prisoner, then murdered and their bodies mutilated, but there is no evidence of this having occurred. It is more likely that it was a detail concocted to justify the events that followed.

Over the course of the afternoon, Wilde ordered his men to round up 300 local men from Mussidan and its immediate surrounding hamlets along the length of the RN89. Those arrested were aged between 16 and 60 years of age, though a number were younger still. This round-up was carried out under the pretext of a check of papers, and many of those rounded up knew nothing of the afternoon's events. A triage was conducted, with three streams of men sorted from each other – those who were to be executed as suspected terrorists, those who were to be deported and those who were to be released.

In some cases, the state of clothes or the length of stubble on chins were considered reasons enough to be suspected of being Maquis. At seven o'clock that evening, the war wounded and over 60s were released. All others waited nervously in the courtyard of the town hall. While the round-up was in progress, Gestapo boss Hambrecht was summoned, and at eight o'clock he arrived from Périgueux together with thirty or so men from the BNA led by Raymond Molange.* SS Colonel Charles Schmitt 'Willy' Sahm made the journey too, as did Gestapo agents including Joseph Kitz and Dr Willy Gersbach who, along with a visibly drunk Michaël Hambrecht, chose forty-eight men to be executed. Hambrecht had been given the go-ahead from his superiors in Limoges to kill fifty; all the other men were to be released the following morning.

The forty-eight chosen men were led, by around twenty members of the BNA and Hambrecht, along the main road and into a pathway near the town hall called the Chemin de Gorry, which opened out onto fields. The men were led silently in two rows with machine guns aimed at them and their hands above their heads. Hambrecht ordered the men in bad French, '*Fusillez-moi tout ça. Feu!* [Shoot all that for me. Fire!]. At quarter to nine they were shot in the back by machine guns at a range of just 2–3m. The North African mercenaries were told to look for anyone still breathing and finish them off with a bullet to the back of the head.

The evening was one of destruction and pillage in Mussidan. Shops and homes were looted and a further six people were killed in the street, while several rapes were reported. The mayor, Raoul Grassin, and his deputy, Camille Christman, were both separately tortured and when unable to supply any information as to the whereabouts of Maquis groups, were also murdered. Several locals watched from behind curtains.

The following morning, members of the local population who were worried for their men went to the Chemin de Gorry where they found the horrific sight of nearly fifty abandoned cadavers. Several of the bodies were mutilated beyond recognition. Four men had survived the shooting, one of whom was Marcel Charpentier, a waiter in a local café, who had climbed into a hedge. He was cared for and taken to hospital in Périgueux. Another, Antoine Villechanoux, survived horrific injuries by playing dead, pressing his face into the dirt and holding his breath. Two others died in hospital.

That day in Mussidan, fifty-two people were murdered in reprisal for the action of the Maquis, the tenth worst civilian atrocity in France during the war. After the war, German justifications given by the likes of Hambrecht and

---

* Raymond Molange replaced Alex Villaplane at the head of the BNA in the Dordogne. He is reported as being more sadistic and murderous than Villaplane, who had been recalled to Paris.

Clement Berghaus, an officer of the 11th Panzer Division who was also present that day, were built around the disproven story of the mutilated bodies of eleven German soldiers who died that day. However, the action was not untypical of what German panzer divisions were doing in the area following *L'ordonnance Sperrle* of March that year, by then a template for reprisals.

Further instructions had been issued by the Commander-in-Chief of the West on 8 June in relation to the need to subdue the Maquis by producing a climate of terror for a population considered complicit in the production and supply of everything the Maquis needed, including volunteers and encouragement. The German columns feared being attacked from the rear, just as they feared a communist uprising in south-western France. The order applied to Lot, Corrèze and Dordogne:

> The home of lasting rebellion in this region must be destroyed definitively. The result of this operation is of a capital importance for the future evolution of the west. Half successes in such operations are useless. Resistance forces are to be surrounded quickly and liquidated completely. In order to re-establish order and security, the most draconian measures must be taken to turn by the means of terror the inhabitants of these continually infested regions in order that they finally lose the wish to both host these resistance groups and be governed by them …[21]

In the south-west of the region around Bergerac, bloody battles were waged as the AS, under the command of Maurice Loupias, and Philippe de Gunzbourg further south, tried to wrest control of Bergerac. It was becoming more and more difficult as the local garrison were reinforced. With both de Gunzbourg and his immediate superior, Colonel George Starr ('Hilaire'), both being SOE agents, the areas around Bergerac and Sarlat had received a large number of parachuted weapons and materials since August 1943. So much so that Loupias claimed that Dordogne-sud could arm almost 5,000 men.[22]

One of the main aims of this southern force, as directed by messages from London, was that two large areas be protected for Allied parachute drops in the coming days. The indication arrived on 31 May, with the message '*la fée a un joli sourire*' ('The fairy has a pretty smile'). One of the sites was at Bourniquel, around 18 miles west of Bergerac and under the orders of de Gunzbourg, while another was at Saint-Sauveur, a small town on the northern bank of the Dordogne into which was ploughed a great number of resources. This came under the command of Bergeret and he set up command centre 11 miles to the north-east on the other side of Pressignac.

The parachute landings never came, with the *résistants* who had been used to protect the terrains, including Starr and de Gunzbourg, only learning that this was the case after liberation. However, nearby Mouleydier was defended manfully on a number of occasions, none more so than 11 June when René Cousteiller's Soleil Group had come to the area to help Loupias. Having received orders to set off the following morning to support a nearby barrage, the town came under attack before the FTP group could set off. Soleil's men helped beat the Germans back, but the town suffered several fires.

A similar battle took place a week later, but it was on 21 June when the Germans, attacking from both the south and the west, broke through Mouleydier. The population was rounded up and the men, of which there were around 120, were marched to Bergerac while the women and children were released. The town was set alight and 170 out of 200 buildings destroyed. The Germans headed north-west in the direction of Loupias' headquarters and Grand-Castang and, on reaching Pressignac, found large groups of Maquis still preparing to flee, the message not having got through from Mouleydier. By the time the Germans reached the empty headquarters a little further on, around sixty men had lost their lives, including nineteen prisoners who were finished off at Mouleydier, twenty-eight who were surprised at Pressignac and three more at Grand-Castang. The time had come for the Maquis to withdraw from the region.

The Battle of Mouleydier presented the Germans with a propaganda opportunity that they did not intend to give up. During the months of June and July 1944, a formidable propaganda unit was working behind the scenes of the 11th Panzer Division. The Kurt Eggers unit, named after a pro-Nazi poet and author who had been killed on the Eastern Front in 1943, specialised in creating, printing and distributing propaganda in the form of posters and leaflets that were intended to sap the morale of the Resistance and enemy troops. This dark propaganda often carried messages that appeared benevolent and friendly, while built on false information, rendering it highly cynical.

During that summer it launched SS Operation Skorpion West, with a view to dramatising and skewing the extreme events that the population had suffered, in particular where women and children had been victimised.[23] In a series of posters and leaflets based on the destruction of Mouleydier, photo montages of suffering (one including Denise Lareine carrying her young daughter) set against images of burning buildings were set on red backgrounds. Responsibility was shifted onto the Maquis, with the words 'Theft, Rape, Murder and Terror' under the title 'Villages in flames'. The subheading read '*Voilà le communisme*' ('This is communism'). Apart from the fact that only a small number of FTP fighters were ever involved in Mouleydier (Soleil Group on 11 June), the poster also put the fire down to large stocks of dangerous arms and ammunition that had accidentally, or otherwise, been set alight by the Maquis. They made no mention of the battles that had taken place there and claimed that the German Army intervened only to protect civilians from the dangerous communist terrorists, rather than repress them. Another poster showed a malignant terrorist against a backdrop of a burning town and murdered civilians. The title was '*Le chaos ou l'ordre?*' ('Chaos or order?')

Another leaflet, calling for the population to 'help the forces of order', was entitled 'They were preparing the Katyn★ of the Dordogne'. The photo showed a picture of a ceremony in front of the church in Bergerac attended by dignitaries in which prisoners of the Resistance were being returned to freedom by the Germans. The text read:

> In Bergerac, in front of the Church, in the presence of Monsieur the assistant prefect and of the Mayor, 180 inhabitants of Bergerac and its surrounding villages are returned to the French authorities. Made prisoner by the Maquis, they were in the middle of digging their own graves when the Wehrmacht delivered them at the last minute.

The prisoners referred to were mostly suspected collaborators, who had been arrested since 6 June and had been enthusiastically rounded up and taken to the prison at Mauzac. They were left behind when the Maquis had to retreat. Undoubtedly, they would have been badly treated – the months of the '*épuration*' ('purification') from society of those who had wronged the nation's interests would be proof of that, but the *maquisards* of that area were primarily AS and would not likely have executed them without some

---

★ A well-known slaughter of Polish opponents by Polish communists.

kind of trial. The propaganda tried to whip up fear in the population so that those who were a little more afraid of the Resistance might get behind the German cause.

★★★

The surge of civilians into the ranks of the Maquis created huge supply problems. The call in many towns and cities for 'national insurrection' was not compatible with the plans of Allied commanders, including de Gaulle and General Marie-Pierre Koenig, now commanding the FFI (only confirmed by General Eisenhower on 23 June). On 10 June, Koenig made a call from London for Resistance activities to be suspended as the Allies could no longer provide materiel support, but the message was hardly heard, even less followed. Having suffered four years of occupation, the French population at large sensed an opportunity to fight to the finish, so the message that Allied priorities now lay in the battle for Normandy did not get through.

Allied commanders knew that if the Germans could be defeated on the Western Front, they would cut their losses and begin to retreat from France anyway. The future of France, however, depended on the country liberating *itself*; for the Resistance to work alongside de Gaulle and the provisional government set up in North Africa to retain its full sovereignty. Roosevelt had ideas for a liberated France placed under an American occupation until full democratic normality could be installed. He dreaded what a communist France might look like as, for him, US borders post-war would need to stretch to the Rhine. His overall preference was for General Giraud, who was a five-star general, ranking higher than de Gaulle, who only was a recent two-star general.[24]

This was not the view of the people, however, and British intelligence reported this back to Churchill. Giraud was too entwined with Vichy and had never denounced Pétain nor his regime, only the German occupation. De Gaulle leading the French to liberation was the most stable bulwark against a communist France, and Churchill, despite not really liking the man, persuaded Roosevelt that the support of de Gaulle, or at least an acceptance of him leading the way in a French liberation, supported by the Allies, was the best representation for future stability in France and Europe.

In the Dordogne, the Maquis had long benefited from Allied parachuting of arms and equipment (though, as we have seen, this was patchy and unequal), but what the regional headquarters of the FFI really needed next was money. Some parachute drops over the previous two years had included currency and agents had smuggled in bundles of cash, but this was no longer sufficient for the needs of what had become a huge number of men. The local *paysans* could only supply so much food, and continual requisitions were beginning to harm the population's own needs, already stretched over a long period that had seen vast trainloads of produce sent to Germany. More requisitions from the population could result in both a drop in support for the cause and German reprisals on those who had been forced into co-operating.

André Gaucher ('Martial'), head of the general staff of the FFI for Dordogne, decided to approach Jean Calard, the former Assistant Prefect of Bergerac, who had in May been appointed to take over as departmental prefect when Jean Popineau had fled the area. Despite having been appointed by officials and having hands not completely clean of Maquis blood himself, Calard had shown signs of openness to the Resistance cause.

Gaucher sought a meeting with the prefect in order to try and negotiate access to some funds and, to his amazement, Calard proposed a method by which the Maquis might be able to take matters into their own hands. Two years previously, the Germans had told the Banque de France that due to the probability of Bordeaux, the capital of the Aquitaine and a town with a huge port and submarine base, being bombed, funds should be kept inland. Périgueux was chosen, and a sum of between 8 and 10 billion francs were stored in the bank's facilities there.[25] Security was such that the Maquis would not be able to locate the money while on site but, on the demand of the German naval authorities, funds were secretly transferred by armed guards on trains from Périgueux at regular intervals. As per the terms of Pétain's armistice, such 'administration' was run and funded by Vichy authorities. Calard suggested that he could pass on information as to when such a transfer was to take place, and the Maquis could hold up the train. Gaucher agreed to what sounded like an ideal plan and soon received word that a train would be running on 26 July.

Gaucher set about planning what would be one of the greatest train heists in history. The train, said Calard, would be carrying 2.28 billion francs, the equivalent in today's terms of around 370 million euros. The currency would be in the form of 5,000, 1,000, 500, 100 and 50-franc notes in 150 sacks weighing a total of 6 tonnes. The train would apparently be well guarded and armed, though it would likely be a wagon attached to a normal passenger train. Plans were formed. Raoul Christophe ('Krikri'), of the ORA, played a role in planning the heist and he would also be there on the day. Local AS Maquis drawn from the AS and ORA would carry out the heist, led by Groupe Franc Roland.

All *maquisards* now fought under the banner of the FFI, and armbands were worn by the men. A suitable place had to be found where the train would be slowing down, and so it was decided that it would be best to attack the train just outside a rural station. Being away from a town centre, not in sight of the main road that ran parallel to the track and with plenty of minor roads on which to make a quick getaway, Neuvic-sur-l'Isle was chosen, 20 miles west of Périgueux, beyond Saint-Astier and 7 miles before Mussidan. There was a good view from the single platform along the line, plenty of verges and greenery, a locomotive shed alongside the station and sabotages along the track meant that only a single track was in commission, meaning that no other train could pull up alongside. With a campaign of sabotages having been carried out against German fuel depots in Bordeaux, the slightly beleaguered Germans were spending more and more time within the town and barracks, with only main roads such as the N89 being patrolled regularly. Country roads were being patrolled less and less due to the fuel shortage and the ever-increasing grip that the Maquis were holding on the countryside.

The train, travelling in the direction of Bordeaux, would leave Périgueux at 6.25 p.m. Four Vichy inspectors would accompany the controller of the bank and his two deputies, and these men would be travelling in the unmarked carriage. Of the 100 or so *maquisards* involved in the daylight heist, some were directed to clear the surrounds of the station and hold the public back at a safe distance. Groupe Franc Roland would control the station itself as well as relieving the train of its prize and loading the sacks onto two trucks, one of which was driven by Gilbert Boissière, now working with Roland Clée. One of the trucks was petrol-driven while the other was a converted *gazogène* engine.★

While Groupe Franc Roland had been planning the attack for a week or so, the majority of the other *maquisards* had known of the mission for

---

★ The gasifier distilled wood or charcoal in a kind of boiler and provided a fuel gas to run the engine. It was ineffective and inefficient but widely used after the Germans started requisitioning fuel.

only an hour or two and did not know the details of what they were doing. At around half past six the *maquisards*, many in beige uniforms, entered Neuvic-sur-l'Isle and carried out their arrangements without any difficulty. They occupied the post office so that telephonic communication could be controlled and the *cheminots* were told what would be expected of them. The population were excited, and a Croix de Lorraine flag hung on the war memorial.

Anyone who would normally be in touch with other stations was to play on the idea of the train being delayed due to a series of problems with wagon couplings and the loading of goods for Germany. Several mines were set and a mortar and light machine gun were placed along the platform. The men hid along the sidings and waited for the arrival of the train. The Germans were based in Saint-Astier, 6 miles back along the track in the direction of Périgueux, and while the prospect of a patrol was unlikely, if word got to their barracks the Germans could get there before the operation was carried out. Furthermore, there was always the danger of patrols by *miliciens*.

At a quarter to eight, already half an hour late, the train came into view. Steam driven and looking perfectly normal, it pulled into the station and stopped. Roland Clée jumped up into the passenger wagon and told the passengers to keep quiet and keep all windows closed. One of Groupe Roland's men jumped onto the train driver's platform and the driver was more than happy to tell them that what they were looking for was in the first carriage.

On opening the wagon, the four inspectors and three representatives of the Banque de France who were present made no move to repel the 'bandits', following the orders that their respective employers had given them should something like this occur. The driver and mechanic, with the guns of Roland's men trained on them, were made to uncouple the wagon and manoeuvre it onto a side track in front of the shed. While the heavy sacks of money were unloaded and shared equally between the two trucks, Clée carried out an identity check amongst the passengers. The guards' pistols were discharged so that some element of resistance could be claimed.

As the trucks loaded with money sacks pulled away, two fell out onto the courtyard of the station. An employee shouted to alert the van driver and they were reclaimed. The train pulled away 2.28 billion francs lighter. Just before leaving the train, Raoul Christophe signed a requisition form for the sum total and handed it to the representative of the Banque de France. The haul arrived at its destination in Cendrieux at two o'clock in the morning. The *gazogène* truck had broken down and all 6 tonnes were loaded onto Gilbert Boissière's van just as the heavens opened, soaking the men and making the muddy tracks almost impassable. The weight of the money put incredible strain on the tyres of the truck and Gilbert Boissière was relieved to get the haul back to camp. On their return, those involved with the heist were congratulated and given a meal of sardines, some bread and a glass of red wine.[26]

On arrival at camp that night, one sack out of 150 was missing. There was no suggestion that anything untoward had happened, just that it must have fallen off the back of the overloaded lorry. It was too dangerous to go back for it. Someone that week must have come across a windfall of 15 million francs …

The money was looked after by members of the Comité Départmental de la Libération, including Maxime Roux, Treasurer of the Resistance of the Dordogne, who in the months to come would become the Prefect of the Maquis and eventually Prefect of the Dordogne at the time of liberation. It was kept in a number of locations and used to feed the Resistance in the final months of the war. It was also used to pay for hospitals in regions R5 and R6 and to help families of *résistants* who had lost everything. Some of it was paid back to the Banque de France after the war, but the majority of it had been written off by that institution. Some of it may have gone missing, but records are scarce and those in charge claimed after the war that every penny was accounted for. However, some was no doubt used as payment to free André Malraux when he got himself arrested by the Germans.

8

ENDINGS

The end was in sight, but the Germans would not be overcome by the Resistance. Only when the Allies gained the upper hand in Normandy and landed in Provence on 16 August did the Germans finally cut their losses and retreat. Before that, the French Resistance was forced to feel the bite of reality, losing much of the ground that it had gained before it could claim to have successfully hit the remaining German armies with a mortal blow.

Organisationally, the Resistance of the Dordogne and most of R5 was something of a jumble. When the Allies landed in Normandy on 6 June 1944 an *état-major* (general staff) was established for the FFI in the region. The FFI had been in existence for several months but most *résistants* still spoke of belonging to their own groups, associating with their leaders rather than their particular Maquis. The *état-major* of the FFI in the Dordogne in its initial form did not reflect the numbers of men on the ground. Its staff, headed by André Gaucher consisted of eight ORA representatives, four from the AS and only two FTP, of which neither was given a position of any authority. On the other hand, the FTP had around 3,600 fighting men, the AS around 17,800, while the ORA numbers were negligible by comparison.[1]

Regardless of the numerical discrepancies, this actually made sense in the context of the moment. The ORA consisted almost exclusively of professional soldiers, while the AS was, in the main, led by professional soldiers. The FTP was generally neither of these. Despite having led the way in guerrilla warfare, the organisation contained many foreigners and the FFI, as envisaged by Gaullists, needed to be led by the French. There was also the question of ideology. The FTP was, of course, based on communism and some of its leaders were all too eager to preach its doctrine. Maurice Loupias claimed that far too many men were joining the FTP unaware that they were joining a communist group, only to leave as they were repulsed by the doctrine forced upon them.

Both the AS and the ORA claimed to be apolitical. There were, however, still major differences between them. The ORA supported General Giraud while the AS were Gaullist. They both rejected Germany, but the removal of Vichy was, to both, a side feature of the process of the banishment of the Nazis, however welcome. The AS, whose leaders had built on a propaganda strategy set in place by its legal arms, had spent two years in overdrive regarding recruitment and training. The ORA had been based primarily on existing military personnel and, the AS felt, had not necessarily pulled its weight in terms of the training of recruits. The FTP had also put in huge efforts to recruit and, despite views propagated by the Germans and Vichy, had for the most part outgrown any early ambitions it had of returning France to a Front Populaire style left-wing government in which communism could grow to any sizeable proportion. French communism differed greatly to Bolshevism anyway, and the FTP, on the whole, had embraced Gaullism.

While certain members of the MUR accused the FTP of early 1944 of a lack of discipline, an eagerness to engage in independent actions that endangered themselves and civilians, a complete lack of military knowledge and even stealing parachutes and equipment (which no doubt they did), there were plenty of instances when AS leaders were guilty of similar mistakes. Over-concentration of large numbers of men in immobile camps, for example, had cost plenty of lives, and a lack of security in their processes had contributed to this. In the Dordogne, the AS claimed to have done their best to take the FTP in hand, guide and even support them financially, but the FTP refused all manner of such benevolence. This, to the likes of Ranoux, Cousteiller and Brouillet, appeared to be little more than an effort to subjugate.

The FTP benefited from the vision of SOE agents like Jaques Poirier in seeing through the 'badges' and looking at the quality of the men in question. This had, of course, been instrumental in the choice of men to lead the FFI, but the emergence of men like Cousteiller ('Soleil') helped to forge links between the SOE and the FTP that might not otherwise have so easily existed. 'Soleil' was a controversial figure during and after the war, for many reasons, relating to his personality and self-absorbed nature, but Poirier recognised in him a leader of men and a person of courage. While the leaders in London were less than eager to provide the FTP with arms and encouragement, Poirier, a Frenchman, along with the French intelligence service, the BCRA, recognised the potential of the FTP to carry out the kind of warfare that would be vital in the terrain of R5 if the Maquis was to carry out the plans that London had for it. Not a mass insurrection, but a means to 'make a mess'[2] for the Germans.

That the men and women of the FTP were successful in what they tried to do without anywhere near the arms they needed was a credit to their leaders. French or otherwise, the men were true to their leaders, and the pursuit of a common goal, that of the destruction of fascism, inspired and united them. The likes of Poirier, Peter Lake and Ralph Beauclerk were important in helping to guide Maquis tactics and provide training, just as were the agents of the Jedberg teams.

As the Das Reich Division was leaving the area, an *état*-major interallié (Allied general staff) was set up, firstly in the Château de la Vitrolle in Limeuil and then, when the Germans found Limeuil, it was moved to the Château de la Poujade in Urval. Each evening Beauclerk set up radio communications with England. Poirier surrounded himself with French men and women he could trust, including his own father (though this detail was never revealed during the war) and Robert Brouillet, his friend, Charles 'Le Bolshevik'. Poirier preferred people of talent and ingenuity over political preferences. He used three female liaison agents on whom he relied greatly, 'Georgette' Lachaud, 'Madeleine' Bleygeot and 'Nandou', otherwise known as Fernande Vidalie.

Poirier used the French expertise around him to protect his committee and for their knowledge of the terrain in which they were working, while André Malroux, 'Colonel Berger', proved to be very good at breaking down differences between leaders. They had more of an influence in the east of the department, into Corrèze and Lot, than they did in the west. In the north-west the units were more independent of each other, while in the south Philippe de Gunzbourg worked well with Maurice Loupias. Poirier had no idea who De Gunzbourg was, and when he learned that there was another SOE agent on his territory he had him kidnapped and questioned. Lines were established, but De Gunzbourg moved out of the area soon afterwards to prove that not even the likes of 'Captain Jack' were above the petty squabbles of Resistance.

Not until the region was liberated would the Resistance begin a process that would eventually lead to, at least in part, a united FFI. Just as Raymond Boucharel, mirroring the premature moves of AS men throughout the western Dordogne, was declaring himself Mayor of Nontron, Maxime Roux declared himself *prefect clandestin*. This meant that as well as the slightly less severe Jean Calard in place of Jean Popineau, who had fled fearing for his life, the Dordogne had a second unofficial prefect. Roux's full title was '*Maxime Roux, ancien inspecteur d'académie, préfet de la République en Dordogne*' ('Maxime Roux, former inspector of the academy, prefect of the Republic in the Dordogne'). This appointment was wildly early, given that he had been elected by no democratic process whatsoever in a country still fully occupied, but it gave the population a figurehead to look to, if only notionally,[3] much as de Gaulle had done on a wider scale. When Calard was forced to put up a notice in towns that further repressive measures equal to those in the northern zone could be expected if attacks were not stopped, Roux put his own version up encouraging the continuation of Resistance.

The German beast was wounded but it was not finished. During the two months that followed, the Resistance was hounded in the countryside by various elements of the Wehrmacht. The 11th Panzer 'Ghost' Division continued its operations *of ratissage*, a violent clean-up of Maquis groups. Kampfgruppe Wilde moved into the Corrèze and Lot-et-Garonne but was followed into the Dordogne by Kampfgruppe Bode, just as brutal and capable of suppressing *maquisards*.

In Razac-sur-l'Isle, the Germans threatened to execute thirty civilians if there was any repeat of the continual rail sabotage incidents that had plagued the SNCF Railway between Périgueux and Coutras. In response, Groupe Franc Roland decided to desist. At eleven o'clock on the evening of 13 June, five recently arrested *résistants* were dragged onto the Place Montaigne in the centre of Périgueux by Hambrecht, 'Willy' Gersbach, Charles Schmidt and four men of the BNA, and shot. Their bodies were abandoned to be dealt with by the public and the following morning a spontaneous cenotaph of flowers appeared.

The Germans' preference for remaining in control of urban areas and ceding control of the countryside to the Maquis suited them well. Once the Maquis showed itself in an urban area it could be attacked, but taking it on in the countryside, on its own terms and with its numerical strength, was useless. On 14 June, a support column was sent from the Daumesnil Barracks in Périgueux towards Bergerac to try and shore up security in the town. The journey resulted in violent clashes between Maquis and troops that achieved very little. Loupias had reminded men in the area of the need to prevent or badger large concentrations of German troops by engaging in guerrilla-style combat and demobilising the large numbers of men who had joined since the Allied landings and were no longer needed. But Maquis leaders who had drunk in the successes were not so eager to let their men go when they saw that the German presence was confined primarily to towns and main roads.

The threat from the Germans was still very real, however, and the Wehrmacht was showing no signs of retreat. As the cold, hard realisation that the occupiers were going nowhere set in, it seemed that the many barricades were, for the most part, making the lives of ordinary people difficult. Many were removed, often by civilians and sometimes by those who were arrested by German forces expressly for that purpose. In La Cavaille on the outskirts of Bergerac, two young men were made to dismantle a barricade that had been mined by the FFI, with the result that the explosion killed both men and injured the Germans.

The removal of barricades tied in with new orders issued by the regional FFI commanders on 30 June. Gaucher was furious about the successes that Kampfgruppen Wilde and Bode were having in the countryside, where they were employing smaller groups along country roads. Their very purpose for being in the area was now clean-up operations and these were damaging the morale of the population. In Sarlat, twelve civilians were shot following a series of ambushes just outside the town. Similar smaller events were taking place constantly, such as in Saint Cyprien where five inhabitants were shot.

Gaucher made it clear that German confidence was on the up and that the Resistance was suffering loss after loss because of group commanders' refusal, in many cases, to follow orders. He went as far as to say that many of the deaths and defeats could have been avoided had these orders, issued by the FFI command, been followed. As a result, each group would be inspected regularly by officers attached to the general staff and actions would need approval. The non-use of barricades was underlined so as to concentrate on the element of surprise, as was the importance of smaller numbers of men in any given place. Large groups were to be divided up, more *corps-francs* of six to twelve men were to be employed and groups should work together, in concentrations of no more than thirty or so at a time. The objective remained that all occupying forces should at no point feel secure, and where stocks of explosives allowed, rail sabotage could and should continue. The liberation seemed, to the disgruntled Maquis leaders, as far away as ever, and battles raged throughout the countryside with no particular gains made anywhere.

★★★

The time was coming for 'extreme collaborators' to flee if they were to survive. Alsatian François Collin had spent a year working for the Gestapo, and whether for financial or ideological purposes, the time had come to leave the Périgord if he wanted to survive. Eyewitness statements placed him at the pillaging of numerous houses, arrests, beatings and, on several occasions, firing at people in the street, albeit under the influence of alcohol. He had cosied up with Gestapo boss, Michaël Hambrecht, and other French Gestapo agents such as Paul Pradier. He had materially benefited from the deportation of Jews and had engaged in the arrest of a great many *résistants*. He was also placed at the Brantôme massacre of twenty-six hostages on 26 March, when he had aided the Brehmer operations and at Mussidan on 11 June, the day that fifty-two civilians were executed. He was also seen during the murder on the place de Montaigne in Périgueux of the five young *résistants* arrested on 13 June. He may not have pulled the trigger on any of these particular occasions, but he had been there and shared the guilt.

François Collin and Georgette Peynaud fled Périgueux just hours before the Maquis arrived. They fled to Germany where the girl disappeared from view. In their absence, she was acquitted of all but the most minor of crimes. Collin was sentenced to death, and when a traveller from the Périgord spotted him on the terrace of a café in the Vosges, he was arrested and returned to face justice in the Dordogne. On the day of his execution a friend who had known him since his arrival in Périgueux in 1940 wanted to be present. On passing by him, Collin gave him a brown jacket. 'Have this, it's my gift. I am paying because I lost.'[4]

Two years previously, on 9 March 1943, Paul Lapuyarde, then departmental delegate for the Légion des Volontaires Français (LVF) had made his way to the place du Marché au Bois in Périgueux. With the Relève having been transformed into the STO, sixty or so young men had gathered, waiting to go into the Office de Placement Allemande and sign their contracts. The LVF was not recruiting well, and Lapuyarde was using all the means he could to propagandise it, a 'French' legion that recruited volunteers to fight the war under German command. Lapuyarde was, not unusually, under the influence of alcohol and began to irritate the young men gathered there, so he was asked to leave by the director of the bureau. Enraged, he began calling out threats of arrest to several well-known notables who were also gathered nearby, including the mayor, Félix Gadaud. He claimed that he would get them arrested for belonging to the *Francs-maçons*, stating, 'I am from the Gestapo'. Lapuyarde was taken to the offices of the French police where he showed lists of around fifty well-known notables of the town whom, he said, he had been engaged to watch and inform on. Amongst the names was the Commissaire de Police Urbaine Jean Ruffel who, said Lapuyarde, would be arrested any day, although he had the power to prevent it. He listed names of officials who had already been deported and claimed that the preceding evening he had hosted a number of Gestapo agents. He added that his contacts had told him that 1,500 people from Périgueux were about to be arrested, and many would be shot. 'They all have to be swept away,' he said.[5] Realising the danger they ran by holding onto Lapuyarde, the police released him.

In a report written in August 1942 by Prefect René Rivière to the office of Pierre Laval, Lapuyarde was described as 'a widow, remarried in 1926 and separated in 1939, he has lived with a young girl of 22 years of age. He is the father of four children whom he never looks after.' Rivière revealed that he had been arrested and imprisoned in 1941 for having abused an administrative position in order to access personal and state files. He also described how Lapuyarde had been employed by the Service de Renseignement Militaire during the war period of 1939–40 and used the position to set up falsified files on local people, 'thumbing his nose to the most elementary level of discretion'. He refused to work with Lapuyarde whom he considered 'a violent man, devoid of scruples, who is not in possession of all of his mental faculties'.

Lapuyarde fulfilled the criteria that defined many 'extreme collaborators'. Seemingly unable to hold down relationships, driven by quick financial gain, dependant on alcohol, roundly mistrusted and disliked, psychologically unstable, something of a mythomaniac and profoundly violent, such men allowed themselves to stoop lower and lower into the depths of threat and criminality once they had become irredeemable in the eyes of the laws of the old republic. Lapuyarde was a man of Périgord whose vehement anti-Semitism and fascist purpose may have been driven by his own belief system or perhaps by a simple lack of intelligence with an ingrained need to follow the only code that would allow him to gain superiority over others. A full psychological profile of such people would be interesting in the modern age but, in reality, such people exist in society and always will. Fear of them may well be the key to understanding why so many of the normal public – anti-German certainly, anti-Vichy probably – stood by while others resisted.

People like François Collin and Paul Lapuyarde would not thrive in most circumstances, other than in a fascist society. For a man with visions of grandeur, Lapuyarde was small minded. On the night of 20–21 June 1943, in an effort to propagate further anti-Semitic feeling, he paid children between the ages of 10 and 12 years of age to attach stickers of yellow Jewish stars to the windows of businesses that were run by Jews. This was of little benefit as the processes of economic Aryanisation were already well under way, but it was a spiteful attack on the people themselves. His lack of success with the LVF (only forty-seven young men from the area were engaged with the service) riled him and he fell out with the Légion Française des Combattants. At the same time as threatening to have the French police arrested, he claimed that he had been targeted and reported on by the Légion for being anti-German and Gaullist. Paranoid, and perhaps even deranged, though usually in control of his actions, he wrote propaganda for the official press claiming that the only way to defeat communism was to support Doriot's PPF and the only way to be a true Frenchman was to fight with the Germans on the Eastern Front as a member of the LVF.

The lists he had with him, however, as early as his run-in with the police during his drunken outbursts in March 1943, were real and they were a result of the power that he was gaining. He did this by frequenting the right people, and in the Dordogne of 1943 and 1944 they were the

Gestapo. There is no doubt that he was a source of information to the Germans, and an extremely valuable one at that. Ample evidence suggests that lists provided by him led to the round-up by the FTP-MOI (in which nobody was hurt) of many 'anti-French', following the bomb of 9 November 1943, leading to their deportation. Lapuyarde provided lists for the 10 May 1944 round-up in which 210 Périgourdins were taken to the Palace Cinema, and it was his information that got Roger Laporte, an officer in the ORA, arrested on that day. Throughout 1943 he regularly met with Joseph Meyer of the Gestapo to supply information and on 10 November 1943, along with eight German soldiers, he was present at the arrest of communist Gaston Faure, whose wife Eugenie saw him. 'I saw him with my own eyes, sniggering when they put my husband in the car.'[6] Faure was deported.

The Resistance recognised that Lapuyarde was dangerous and tried to eliminate him at least twice. On the second of these occasions he was slightly hurt but needed to be hospitalised. He insisted on being guarded by German soldiers rather than French soldiers, who he did not trust. By the spring of 1944 he was spending time with Alexandre Villaplane whose BNA gave him a means to directly make arrests. He was responsible for the arrest of L'Abbé Jean Sigala, one of the founding members of Combat in the Dordogne as well as the commissioner of the urban police, René Gilles.

But there was one man that Lapuyarde suspected above all others – Charles Mangold, who appeared to be a peaceful Alsatian citizen and continued to live in Périgueux. Mangold was a neighbour of Hélène Dupuy, '*Maman de la Résistance*' and protector of Jewish families. Lapuyarde, however, suspected Mangold and sent François Collin, at that time one of his 'agents', to follow Mangold around the Saint-Astier area where, he suspected, Mangold had an abode.

The importance of Charles Mangold was such that a price of 100,000 francs had been put on his head. Since the arrival of the Germans in November 1942, Mangold had used his cover as a local government officer to carry on living in Périgueux and running the AS from there. Initially in charge of the AS in Périgueux, he took control of central Dordogne following the arrest of André Boissière in the first half of 1943. Everybody who met Charles Mangold, known as 'Commandant Vernois', knew that he had to lead the AS. Kind, patient, extremely well organised, courageous and seemingly invincible, he cycled the length and breadth of the central Dordogne attending meetings and ensuring that Maquis needs were taken care of. He worked with Jacques Poirier, Peter Lake and Ralph Beauclerk to ensure that the AS were first in line for armaments parachuted from London. He oversaw strategic matters and was universally loved by the men under his command, leaving the operational and militaristic decisions to the men under him such as Roland Clée.

Initially he set up home in an apartment right in the centre of the city, where he lived with his wife, Yvonne Seret, and son, Jean-Paul, himself involved with the ORA. It was only when Jean-Paul attended a meeting with an AS representative who turned out to be his father that Jean-Paul decided to work alongside him, initially as his liaison agent. However, when 'Marc' Goldman was arrested on 30 October 1943, having just dined with both Charles and his son in the Périgueux flat, and in full sight of both Jean-Paul and his father, the family abandoned the property. It is very possible that the trap had been set by Jean Gréber ('Aline'), a civil servant at the Prefecture de la Dordogne whose Resistance work was so well recognised by his contacts that he was given the job as head of the Noyautage des Administrations Publiques (NAP) in the heart of the regional command of the Mouvements Unis de la Résistance (MUR). He would have processed a lot of information and photographs of *résistants* while procuring false identity documents and would have known a lot about a lot of members. Subsequent suspicion arose that he supplied the photo of Marc Goldman ('Mireille') to the Germans as it was apparently taken by *maquisards* at the Durestal camp.[7]

Little is known about the circumstances surrounding Gréber's arrest in the final days of 1943, but he disappeared, only to emerge several months later under the protection of the Gestapo and was reported as having been seen in the Limoges offices of the Gestapo, moving freely. Whether he was a double agent from the beginning (which might explain the simplicity of the trap in which Goldman had been caught and his withdrawal from lunch at the Mangold flat a little earlier than everyone else) is unclear. It is quite possible that he was turned on his arrest. Several local historians such as Jacques Lagrange and Jacques Blanchard have claimed that Gréber was offered 10,000 per 'head' of those he turned in. I have been unable to find proof of this. However, Gréber's body was discovered sewn into a bag thrown into the Vienne, near Limoges. A police report from the Archives départementales de la Dordogne (1592 W) says:

Arrested in unknown circumstance by the Gestapo, he showed up in Limoges where, it is said, he turned over numerous *résistants* who he had known in the Dordogne and Haute Vienne. Was executed in Limoges (he was, according to some, thrown into the Vienne), before the Liberation, by members of the Resistance.

With the apartment abandoned, Charles found a safe house for his wife, while he and Jean-Paul took to the Maquis for several months, during which time he based himself with the Groupe Roger near Vergt. Charles Mangold visited his wife and son in Saint-Astier on the morning of 7 August then set off by bike with Jean-Paul. On reaching a crossroads known as '*Les Quatre routes*' on the southern limits of the small town,[8] the two men said their goodbyes. Jean-Paul had been sent to work away from his father, as the risk of the two men being caught together was too great. That morning Jean-Paul, now known as 'Popaul', headed south towards Vergt while Charles took the road to Bordeaux. At Razac-sur-l'Isle Charles Mangold was caught at a roadblock and arrested.

Before Jean-Paul Seret-Mangold had reached Vergt that morning, the postmistress intercepted information that the Germans were in nearby Église-Neuve-de-Vergt. On hearing this, the *maquisards* decided that the leaders of the AS, based in a farm at a place known as Les Jabauds near Vergt needed to be updated. Freddy Hauswirth volunteered to take a motorcycle belonging to his friend Jean-Paul and sped off in the direction of Vergt. Before getting to his destination Freddy swerved to avoid an automobile and crashed the bike. Hearing of what had happened, the local doctor, André Gaussen, examined Freddy who had suffered a serious head injury as well as multiple fractures. Managing to get hold of sulphamides, he was unsure of the prognosis for the young *maquisard*. Having received word of the crash, Claudette Négrier ('Coco'), who knew Freddy through her friend Jean-Paul, attended the doctor's examination and with her mother transferred Freddy to a nearby farm. Little by little he recovered as she became his full-time nurse, tending to him with devotion and care.

Charles Mangold was taken to the Daumesnil Barracks in Périgueux and questioned, enduring beatings and torture. For five nights he held up and gave nothing away. During that period, Jean Del Chiappo of the BNA was approached and offered a bribe in exchange for helping to free Mangold. He wanted to help, only for the money of course, but no longer had access to the prison. On the morning of 12 August, Charles Mangold decided to take away any further risk of succumbing to brutality. At peace with himself and having done his duty as a patriot he took the remains of a can of food and used the sharp edge to open the veins of his wrists. He lay down and awaited death, allowing the lifeblood to drain out of his body.

Towards the end of the afternoon, his jailers found what he had done. He was not yet dead and, determined that he would not be allowed to make the sacrifice, they dragged him to the infirmary, dressed his wounds tightly and injected him in order to make him conscious. He was seized under the arms and taken to a small courtyard outside the barracks, where a red-bricked wall was used for firing squads. He was shot, along with twenty-two other *résistants*, and all were thrown into a communal grave at the back of the courtyard that, up to that point, had been used only for the carcasses of animals. The liberation of the town was one week away.

The final month of Resistance in the Dordogne was as bloody as any that had gone before. However, a top-secret report written by William J. Donovan of the Office of Strategic Services (OSS)[9] for the attention of President Roosevelt as early as 6 July 1944 revealed that 'the achievements of French resistance since D-Day have far exceeded expectation'. In a detailed analysis, he explained that both the US and British secret services, using intelligence on the ground and gleaned from the skies 'credited the French resistance for much of the delay in the build-up of German forces in Normandy'. Railway disruption been most effective, as had the disruption of telecommunications. In the central, south and west of France:

> Guerrilla activities flared out openly, resulting in bitter fighting between German and Patriot forces, tying down substantial German forces and giving the Resistance control of large areas. The departments of Dordogne, Corrèze, Vienne, Ardeche, Indre, Ain, Jura and parts of Gers, Drome, Savoie, Haute-Savoie and Saone et Loire are in a state of general insurrection. Throughout these areas there are recurring engagements between resistance forces and German regiments and divisions.[10]

While ambushes and sabotages continued, there were some notable military victories too. On 24 July, a column of Germans headed towards Nontron, a town that had been 'liberated' by the Maquis some weeks earlier. On arriving at Javerlhac, a furious battle ensued led initially by the Groupe Manu of the 2nd Rac Division, whose leader Manuel Acébès was killed in the battle. Later they were reinforced by Jacques Nancy's Section Spéciale de Sabotage (SSS). The SSS group had been with Rodolphe ('Rac') Cézard's Rac Division since mid-June when the Nontron area had been liberated by the Resistance. With the help of the SSS that day, the Germans suffered heavy losses at the hands of Groupe Manu and other elements of the Rac Division – around fifty dead and twenty injured. The column turned and did not reach Nontron.

On 12 August a new general staff of the FFI was created, which recognised the FTP on an equal footing with the Corps-Francs de Liberation (CFL) made up primarily of the AS. In each section of the new command structure, AS and FTP captains and commanders were balanced. Yves Péron, known as 'Lieutenant Colonel Caillou', who had recently benefited from Allied air raids in Bergerac to escape from prison, was a professional soldier and took up an important leadership role on behalf of the FTP. Roger Ranoux ('Commandant Hercule') became joint commander, working alongside René Boillet ('Commandant Gisèle') of the CFL. André Gaucher ('Commandant Martial') continued to head up the état-major FFI. The changes were probably political in reasoning but brought some battle experience into the decision-making progress, none more so than Ranoux.

★★★

In the middle of a three-day battle in Saint-Foy-la-Grande, on the western tip of the Dordogne in which a determined local Maquis was gaining the upper hand over a retreating German Army, news came through of the Allied landings in Provence. As a consequence, on 16 August Hitler sent out an order that the south of France was to be abandoned and troops withdrawn to the west along a line stretching from Orléans to Montpellier, passing by Clermont-Ferrand. Over the coming days, the Germans began to withdraw from the Dordogne and, as they did, the *maquisards* moved into the towns. It was not a peaceful affair and battles raged as Périgueux and Bergerac were approached, but there was little willingness by the Germans to remain. *Miliciens* and their families left in their droves under the protection of the Germans, eager to be anywhere but where they were known. Throughout 18 and 19 August, Maquis groups moved towards Périgueux and the Germans left by train and road, either towards Bordeaux or towards Clermont-Ferrand. Though the Germans were allowed to leave the towns in relative safety, they continued to be attacked sporadically while outside of the cities.

Périgueux was officially liberated on 19 August 1944 and Bergerac on 21 August. Along the N89 towards Bordeaux, trees were felled and the Germans were harassed. At Roumanières, outside Bergerac, the German barracks were destroyed by the Germans themselves, and at Saint-Astier troops who were trying to destroy the production lines that had worked so efficiently in the past were fired upon and eight of the soldiers were killed. When the Germans found that they could no longer sustain Saint-Astier, an officer and seventy-seven prisoners capitulated and were made prisoner. Just a few hours after the surrender, a different column arrived there, not knowing of the German retreat from the town. They entered the town setting buildings ablaze and pillaging properties. The town's population fled to nearby safe spots, including woodland, and when they returned to town discovered the twenty-one bodies of executed civilians. They were lying, tangled, where they dropped, at the intersection with the road between Bordeaux and Périgueux, a place known as '*Les quatres routes*'. A place where, two weeks earlier, Charles Mangold had said goodbye to his son Jean-Paul for the very last time.

★★★

It was a sunny July afternoon when Norbert Hericord made his way from the station at Versannes to the top of a hill where he was due to visit some friends of the Maquis who were based there. Versannes is a tiny village midway between Périgueux and Mussidan, south of the main road in the direction of La Douze. When 17-year-old Norbert arrived at the farm he noticed a young woman of around 20 pacing in circles around the small yard. Following each step behind her was a *maquisard*, rifle aimed at her back. Norbert asked one of the *maquisards* what was going on and he was told that she had been picked up at the station, and was suspected of being a traitor. He watched as she was taken into a barn where a four-man improvised tribunal were going to judge her.

Ten minutes later they emerged; she was in tears. Gripped by her arms, she was led to an area behind the shed and Norbert heard two shots. Her grave had been dug before the hearing had even taken place. Seventy-two years later, he talked to a television reporter about what he had seen that day. The woman had got off the train and was unlucky enough to come across several *maquisards* at the platform. When they spoke to her, possibly joking with her or perhaps carrying out checks, she made the mistake, said Norbert Hericord, of responding. Her accent was not of the Périgord – she was from Alsace-Lorraine. This raised alarm bells, so the Maquis arrested her. She told them that she was there to visit her baby, being looked after with a family 3km away in Saint-Geyrac. Her reasons were not sufficient to save her life.

The killing was carried out by men whom Norbert Hericord called thugs – people who, had they not killed her, would probably still have killed others. Two of the names given by Norbert seventy-two years later have emerged in many contexts as belonging to men who committed crimes, particularly in the period of *épuration*, which was just beginning in July 1944. Sitting on the tribunal that day was also one man who was well-respected in that Maquis group and became a respected leader beyond the confines of his own unit.[11] The Maquis group was battle hardened, experienced and not known for wrongdoings. If events did occur as Norbert Hericord described, then it was a murder. Such were the times.

★★★

Crimes committed by Frenchmen under the command of the Germans, or under the command of Vichy authorities and dealt with directly by the Resistance were carried out over a period of months, broadly speaking, over the summer of 1944. In the Dordogne, where hated Gestapo auxiliaries had to be tracked down, the BNA led by Alex Villaplane had become symbolic of German brutality inflicted by the French on the French. The BNA was formed expressly in an effort to stem the growing success of the Resistance and turn an irresistible tide of Allied success. It stayed in the Dordogne for six months then returned to Paris. When the capital was liberated, and order resumed, many of its constituent members were located and brought to trial.

Before that, its leaders, Henri Lafont, Pierre Bonny and Alex Villaplane, were located and dealt with. Villaplane himself had been more a petty criminal than a mass killer, and his style was cynical rather than murderous. Circumstances had led to far more serious crimes and it is not clear how many, if any, people Villaplane killed by his own hand. He was, however, involved in beatings, sometimes wearing a smile, and he behaved in an extraordinarily cruel way. On sensing that the tide was turning against Germany, he began to play the role of a patriotic Frenchman trying his best to save the lives of his countrymen, but even this was usually done for some financial gain. In his trial in 1944 his prosecutor deemed him a schemer and a conman who committed 'the black-mail of hope'. For this alone, his execution on 26 December 1944 alongside Lafont and Bonny, condemned as one of the most despicable traitors in his country's history, was inevitable.

During the course of '*l'épuration sauvage*', the purge of traitors, collaborators and, sometimes, personal or political enemies, some 780 executions following a legal process, and at least 10,000 summarily, took place south of the demarcation line.[12] That period, during the insurrectional phase of the liberation from June to September 1944 (after which legal order resumed), scarred those who lived through it. A witness told me that the divisions caused by occupation were forgotten quickly, and another dismissed the events as 'stupidity that was tragic but quickly sorted out'. Both had engaged in the Resistance in some measure or another. However, the scars of the *épuration* added to the guilt of collaboration, particularly in the question of France's role in the Final Solution, contributed to the application of brakes on a proper analysis of the occupation in France for a number of decades. The uncomfortable questions that France had to face up to were eventually triggered by Marcel Ophuls' film *The Sorrow and the Pity* in the early seventies. After this, debates slowly emerged and are still ongoing as to France's acceptance of guilt in the events of the occupation. This book is not about the *épuration*, but it cannot be ignored.

Punishment of collaborators, on the other hand, began early and was one of the first roles of the AS of the combat network in particular. The 19 October edition of *L'Echo de Nancy* announced, 'A PPF militant is murdered by terrorists'. An official paper of the occupied zone reported:

Once again terrorists on the payroll of London and Moscow have mortally struck. Our friend René Bertinot … was, with his partner, one of those who are fighting courageously against the communists … After the armistice Bertinot left to set up in Tamnies in the Dordogne where he ran a farming business. It was here that our friend was murdered by terrorists.

When the likes of Doctor Victor Nessmann, Édouard Kauffmann, André Boissière, and many others, were arrested it was rare that the Germans were responsible for finding them unassisted. Denunciations were rife and networks were constantly decapitated. In the FTP, the 'lifespan' of a leader within the regional staff was so short (several months) that in 1944 they had to be incorporated into the Maquis camps. Bertinot, his wife Marguerite and another man, Pierre Brunschwig-Véry, were suspected of such denunciations and both men were killed. The woman fled, never to return to the area. Roger Verdier, another PPF member and *milicien*, was injured in Port-Sainte-Foy, then murdered in his hospital bed.

Marcel Ivert, a friend of the Gestapo and one of Paul Lapuyarde's men, who spent much of his time peddling goods in the black market while using the cover of a German Police card, was well known in Périgueux as the man in the green hat. He always wore a green Tyrolean with a feather in it. He was followed into a small bar on the rue Saint-Front in the heart of Périgueux and, while he sat and laughed with two girls at the bar, Jean Lestang and Jean Deix of the AS shot him twice, once in the head and once in the heart. Having carried out the killing, the two young men fled to the home of Hélène Dupuy, metres away from the Mangold's apartment, where they were kept safe while the commotion died down.[13]

Paul Lapuyarde escaped attempts on his life partly through luck, partly because of the added protection afforded to him by the German authorities. He fled Périgueux, but was recognised by a former *résistant* the next spring in Poitiers, where he had sought refuge. He was brought to Périgueux and, too late to be condemned by the Maquis who had given him forty death sentences *in absentia* in November 1944, was instead sentenced to death by the justice courts in Bordeaux. He was executed on 24 September 1945.

Renée Guimberteau lived in Mussidan and wrote an account in her diary of events as they unfolded. On 24 August 1944, she wrote:

> Today the party is in full swing. A big parade took place to the cemetery where sprays of flowers were laid on the graves of those that were shot on 11 June★ … The march of the *collaboratrices* [female collaborators] did not take place because the crowd would have torn them apart.[14]
>
> … [The] event did take place however on 2 September 1944 …

★ That day, fifty-two people were shot following FTP action in the town, which included an attack on a German train.

> This morning we had a real laugh. The FFI shaved the heads of all the *collaboratrices* ... There was a mad crowd. They marched them around all the streets then led them to prison.

The conduct of those involved with the early months of the *épuration*, following the liberation of the department in the final third of August 1944, can at least partially be understood with reference to the contemporary press. *Les Voies Nouvelles* expressed the popular view of those on the ground who had waited for an opportunity for vengeance:

> Périgourdins were very well amused the other evening by the passage of a most singular procession. A strange being, bizarrely human, led the dance. If you strained your eyes you could recognise feminine forms, and under an ivory bowl cranium painted with markings of infamy, menacing eyes and a slimy mouth: the hideousness of a piece of garbage. 'That's the *bicot*'s girl!' Explained the kids, incidentally. There was not a single expression of pity towards them.★

The shaving of heads was not exclusively reserved for women. In Bergerac, the owner of a bar called 'La Civette' had her head shaved along with her son. Both of them had a swastika tattooed on their foreheads and a single tuft of hair left growing at the top of their heads. Reporting the incident, *France Libre* of 8 September 1944 commented, 'On their blemished faces, there was no longer a look of triumphal vice but the ignominy of punishment ... When the crime is public, the reparation must also be public.'

Paul Lapuyarde's sister, an employee in a pharmacy, was saved from the clutches of the justice seekers of the *épuration* on the insistence of her employers that she had done nothing wrong. His most recent mistress, however, a 19-year-old named Yvonne, was abandoned by him to suffer the humiliations of the crowds who gathered to deal with '*les collaboratrices horizontales*'.

It is too simplistic to claim that most of *l'épuration sauvage* was carried out by members of the FTP, but the attitude of some of its leaders should be considered. Yves Péron ('Caillou'), who had been a prisoner of war until late in the war but ended up leading the region's FTP in libera-

---

★ '*Bicot*' was one pejorative term by which most locals referred to members of the Brigade Nord-Africaine.

tion, demanded that 'justice be done against traitors, [and] torturers of our imprisoned patriots'. He added, 'All the accomplices of the *Boches* must be punished and the punishment is death.' By 19 September, *Les Voies Nouvelles* recognised that 'yes, there could have been errors, but they have already been identified … Let us not forget that the possible excesses were the spontaneous reaction at a moment of daylight of a people too long oppressed, starved, betrayed.'

The Gaullist press reflected the approach that de Gaulle wanted to take, which was not altogether popular with the French people. Once again, there was an element of *attentisme* (wait and see) and of establishing that things be done properly. On 17 September 1944, under the title '*Justice et humanité*', the daily *Combat Républicain* reminded the public that 'the least doubt must be favourable to the accused … Would it not be better to absolve one guilty person than to execute an innocent?'

The *épuration* of activists against communism was carried out with venom by former members of the *Brigade Internationale* before they returned to Spain or Italy. FTP leader Andrej Urbanovitch, otherwise known as 'Doublemètre' was a Serbian of Jewish origin who became known for the arrest of many, and the elimination of a large number of political opponents and former collaborators. No doubt many of these were deemed just – 'sometimes preventative, often repressive and unjust'[15] – but they must be placed in the moment; one of great upset and political and social upheaval. Considered the chief '*épurateur*' of the Périgord, he had been present in Mussidan on 11 June 1944, and nearby the following day when fifty-two civilians had been killed. In the autumn of 1944, as head of the Service d'ordre patriotique, he was responsible for at least 700 arrests. He probably undertook something approaching fifty executions himself,[16] and some may well have been based on vengeance rather than justice. But he was not the only FTP name linked with such ventures. René Cousteiller ('Soleil') was amongst those investigated for killings and Urbanovitch was seen as the right-hand man of Yves Péron. During his time at the head of his court martial, death sentences were carried out on mere presumptions or denunciations and carried out almost immediately, leaving no possible recourse. He was tried several times between 1948 and 1956 and incarcerated in the prison of Cherche-Midi for a short time before an intervention by André Malraux, who he had known for a short time in 1944, led eventually to his freedom.

One of Urbanovitch's more famous investigations around the time of the liberation was the arrest of Maurice Chevalier, the film star and singer, who had entertained prisoners in camps during the occupation. He came to the Dordogne as a refugee with his mistress Rita Raya and his 'crime' of co-operation with the German forces very nearly led to his execution at the hands of Urbanovitch. A newspaper intervened and Urbanovitch granted Chevalier a pardon. The report revealed that Rita Raya was Jewish, and that Chevalier had saved a number of Jews in Paris during the war. Before that news was known publicly, he returned to Paris to large crowds of 'patriots' protesting against his presence in the capital and it took a filmed explanation, which was distributed and shown around cinemas in France to slowly exonerate him. However, former friend Josephine Baker remained very sceptical of his role, feeling that he had helped the Germans too much.

On 23 March 1945 the trial took place of the remaining members of the Brigade Nord-Africaine (the men in real power, Bonny, Lafont and Villaplane, having already been executed), while in April the return of many innocent French who had been deported sparked protest through a series of bombings starting in Beynac on 7 April in which *collaborateurs* or *collaboratrices* were targeted. Then, on 28 August 1944, Admiral Charles Platon who had been part of the Vichy government was executed by former *maquisards*.

The *épuration* is a subject to be fully explored elsewhere.

EPILOGUE

On 26 June 1944, as Kampfgruppe Wilde of the 11th Panzer Division continued their 'clean-up' operations in the area around Sarlat in the south-east of the Dordogne, a light detachment came to a bridge over the Dordogne at Castelnaud-la-Chapelle. It had been blown up and was still smoking. There was no sign of the perpetrators. If they wanted to cross the river they would have to take a railway bridge, some 200m further along the road. As the detachment restarted their engines, they found themselves under fire, bullets hitting their armoured vehicles and injuring several men, who dropped to the ground. The men on the hill nearby got ready for the fight, knowing that their trap had disturbed a hornets' nest. But the Nazis turned around and disappeared down the road from which they had come. The detachment's officers knew they weren't suited for the fight with a Maquis that knew every incline, every ditch and every group of trees around them. They would change their plans.

The group that had fired on the Germans was an FTP-MOI division led by Raphael 'Ralph' Finkler and his best friend Léon 'Phil' Lichtenberg. They had no idea why the Germans had turned around, and in battles all around Sarlat the Wilde group, and many other German divisions in the area, continued to win most battles in which they became embroiled. But some were being lost, avoided or deemed too difficult or too dangerous to pursue. The Maquis of the Dordogne had achieved what they set out to do.

That the Germans chose to withdraw from the area and regather their forces in the west of France should not take away from the success of the Maquis. When the columns of *maquisards* took to the streets of Périgueux and Bergerac, many celebrated, despite having no experience of these men.

These were men of the countryside, and the battle for the Périgord had been won on the slopes, forest roads and villages of the region. The people of the countryside – the *paysans* – had given their support and made sacrifices. They had sacrificed food, their own security and, too often, their livelihoods. Roger Ranoux – 'Colonel Hercule' of the FFI – recognised that without those *paysans* the Maquis would have failed.

But the people of the towns had done their bit, too. Living under the constant threat of arrest, with German and French agents based in urban areas, *résistance* could not be discussed in the streets or shops as might be the case in small communities like Siorac or Vergt. The Légion, the PPF, the Brigade Nord-Africaine, the Gestapo and Pétainists – all of whom were simply convinced that, in betraying Vichy, one was betraying France – were everywhere. Still, in towns networks grew under the noses of the enemy – in town halls, post offices, railway stations and workshops, in schools, churches, police stations, museums and within bars and cafés. The wheels of resistance gathered speed and absorbed the obstacles of repression and denunciations that weakened but never broke them.

In May 1945, former liaison agent Roger Meyer was in Algeria. Once Périgueux had been liberated, he joined up with the newly re-formed 26th Infantry Regiment and fought to liberate La Rochelle before being stationed in North Africa. On 10 May 1945, he received a telegram, sent from Nancy. It was from his sister, Jeannine, whom Roger had assumed had been lost in the camps of the east:

My dear Roger

Yes! It is me and I am writing to you after you have gone so long without news of us. We are in the North of Germany, delivered by our English friends. We will not be coming home together as Denise and Fanny are still resting, but I think we will have left by the 15th and we will be repatriated.

I send you warm kisses. Your sister
Jeannine[1]

When Roger got back to France he learned that Jeannine had been protecting him: both parents and one sister were already dead, the victims of the extermination camps. Jeannine had used the word 'we', knowing that, in fact, she was talking about her and her little sister, not, as Roger believed, the whole family.

Jeannine was in relatively good health but their youngest sister was unwell. Jeannine took Roger to see their sister. She was pale and skeletal, lying in a cot tended by sisters with her legs bent at the knees underneath her blankets. Her dark hair was thin. As the Allies advanced she had been made to march for three days in freezing temperatures. She had survived that death march and, despite her feet having been frozen, she had been brought back to Paris. She could barely speak but managed to string a single sentence together for her brother, 'You look handsome dressed as a soldier'. She could say nothing more. Several days later she died.

Roger Meyer knew little about Judaism as a religion at the beginning of the war but, like Raphael Finkler, he knew that he was Jewish. By travelling to the Dordogne, he survived, but his family did not. The Dordogne had known nothing about Jews at the beginning of the war. When Alsace Lorraine was annexed by the Nazis in June 1940 a policy of Germanisation that excluded non-French speakers and non-Alsatian natives as well as Jews was imposed. By the time Aryan evacuees returned home to Strasbourg after their sojourn in Périgueux and Limoges, the south-westerners who continued to host and settle in their Jewish guests had largely emerged from an innocent ignorance of what Jews were. The villages and small towns that had welcomed them and looked after them continued to do so as well as they could. Fear subsided, and human nature kicked in. Statistics around deportation and the implementation of the Final Solution in the Périgord clearly demonstrate that, despite heavy-handed and extreme repression together with forceful propaganda, the people of the Dordogne protected their human brothers and sisters. French historian Pascal Plas quite clearly marks out the Dordogne for special mention in this sphere. He calls the people who hid Jews, who were primarily women, the 'hidden heroes of the Resistance'. That the French authorities ever engaged in the implementation of Hitler's Final Solution is a black stain on France's past. Those sent to die in Germany from Vichy-controlled France were the only Jews deported from a European territory not occupied by the Germans. The nature of France's complicity in those deaths is a question to be explored elsewhere, but the depth of anti-Semitic feeling amongst the ruling classes, forced upon a wider public through war blame and horrific propaganda, is shocking. That these events occurred only two generations ago should continue to be an important aspect of the education of the young French today. There were many former *résistants* who visited schools to talk about their experiences, but they have become few and far between. We should all learn from them.

The Dordogne was singled out for repressive measures against its recently inherited Jewish population and, once it was clear that the Maquis were taking control of the countryside and the Wehrmacht and local authorities could not cope, the Germans decided to take special measures against the Resistance. They decided that pursuit of the Maquis – too numerous and on their own terrain – would be fruitless. Instead they targeted the population through twin tactics of severe repression and intense propaganda. Short, sharp operations were brutal but unsuccessful in the ultimate aim of turning the people against the Resistance. It is, of course, a question of percentages, as denunciations were rife. But as time went on these became targeted at individuals as security of networks increased and relations between the Maquis and *paysans* tightened. In some areas the Maquis took hold of country towns and villages and administered rules that were sometimes deemed tough. But, generally, they were fair and aimed at the benefit of the French, and were socialist in nature. Many *maquisards* overstepped the mark, and some acted criminally, but this was inevitable given the numbers involved and the relative power with which some personalities suddenly found themselves.

The liberation of the Dordogne was not the end of the war for the *maquisards* of the region. Most were redeployed towards the western coast, to fight around Royan, La Rochelle, the Médoc and on the Île d'Oléron. As the German army retreated west, divisions were left behind to man the Atlantic Wall. These battles between an isolated German army and Resistance battalions that felt abandoned but battled on manfully in trench warfare carried on into April 1945. A brigade for Alsace-Lorraine set off to fight in their homeland led, strangely enough, by André Malraux. The Bataillon Strasbourg included Jean-Paul Seret-Mangold and men from the Corrèze, Dordogne and Haute-Vienne. Freddy Hauswirth was still suffering follow-up problems from his motorcycle crash that included short, sharp and crushing headaches. To his regret he was unable to travel north to fight, but in 1946 he married Claudette – his 'Coco' – and she gave birth to the first of their three children the following year.[2]

The history of the Resistance in the Dordogne illustrates well the importance of women in the Resistance. From the many women liaison agents to those who worked in post officers or local administration, any form of Resistance as a *légal* was hugely dangerous. The Maquis is often celebrated and, of course, the fighting force was primarily male, but the the support of women like Maryse Nicolas and Monette Leclerq was essential to give and receive orders or carry documents and weaponry. It needed the likes of Valentine Bussière and her mother to provide care for the injured or to travel the countryside by bicycle, undetected. Women in towns, such as Hélène Dupuy, provided cover and safe houses for *maquisards* in need of safety, or for Jewish children who needed help to survive. It needed the likes of Alice Barrat at her restaurant in Saint-André-de-la-Double, providing help and guidance for young *réfractaires* trying to find their way to the Resistance and supplying vital links to local leaders so that outsiders could be rooted out. It required young women eager to provide a letterbox like Christiane Beau, whose father was killed in front of her, or to provide accommodation to *maquisards* in need of shelter like Alice Boubaud, who housed Jean-Paul Seret-Mangold in her *pharmacie* in Vergt. The role of the likes of Alice Garrigou cannot be overstated: Alice allowed meetings to take place at her establishment for orphans in Périgueux and provided a venue for Charles Mangold to direct operations, all the while putting herself under intense risk of discovery. The list goes on, but one further category should be mentioned.

The ordinary 'wives' such as Yvonne Seret, wife of Charles Mangold whose complicity in the AS was undeniable; Gaby Bloch, whose devotion to both her husband and the cause enabled the 'great escape' from Mauzac; and Denise de la Bardonnie, who guarded the door to her home, all the while protecting and enabling all that went on inside were invaluable. Rod Kedward talks of the 'woman at the doorway, prolonging police enquiries, misleading their search, feigning ignorance, covering tracks. As a vantage point of power, this otherwise marginalised position came into its own in the Resistance.'[3] This may have been a 'simple' role expected of their gender, but it carried enormous risks. One thinks of the delaying tactics of René Ségui's wife, finding time for her husband to bring his Resistance colleagues together and avoid arrest. The substantial contribution of women in the Resistance helped them progress in French society, while their witness accounts helped clarify gaps in memory or curb excessive accounts of events in later years.

Vincent García Riestra remembers the day that he was freed from Buchenwald, and recalls an American officer throwing up when coming into the camp faced with piles of dead bodies. Vincent had managed to stay alive by finding a job in the kitchens, but on liberation he weighed less than 5 stone and was suffering from tuberculosis. Franco had removed his Spanish nationality and there was no delegation to care for him. He stayed at the camp for a month before organising passage home with a French lorry driver, who took him part of the way back to his family in France. He was desperately ill for two years but survived and forged a career in construction. In 2017 the municipality named the lane on which his house is built after him, and he attended a ceremony with some of his grandchildren. He has dedicated his life to passing on his experiences to the young. He knows in which mass grave his father is buried and after years of searching was recently allowed by the Spanish authorities to put a plaque where it is thought his brother lies.[4]

Like so many of the leaders of the Resistance, Roger Ranoux entered politics, but unlike many he did not do so as part of the rehabilitation process of the Republic. Many of the men who, like him, excelled in leadership joined the new French army. He wanted nothing to do with the fight, and instead drove lorries for many years.[5] The man that once approached a Milice-manned control holding two unpinned grenades and told the guards that they must let his vehicle past or they and him would all die, lived a quiet life for a number of years. Only 24 years old at the time of liberation, he married Michelle, who was also a *résistante*. But he was an activist and, later in life, became a mayor and a politician, elected deputy for Sarlat in 1956 and later mayor of Montrem-Montanceix. His friend Lucien Cornil still lives in Le Lardin and visits schools regularly to talk of his experiences. During the passage of the Brehmer Division in the last week of March and first week of April 1944, Lucien's brother Jean's group, AS Maurice Dujarric, was the only Maquis to be actively pursued and he barely escaped with his life. Jean made the decision to go to Germany for the STO – a decision that hit Lucien hard. Eventually he came to accept the reasoning of his elder sibling. Lucien's youngest brother had died young, struck down by meningitis, and he himself was badly injured by a bullet. Jean went to Germany not for his own sake, but for his parents', so they should not be left with no sons at the war's end.

Raphael 'Ralph' Finkler and Léon 'Phil' Lichtenberg said goodbye to their many Spanish friends, who set off to Spain to try to liberate their homeland. They never saw the majority of them again. The men of the MOI set off for Angoulême – one of the hundreds of destinations to which *maquisards* were redeployed. 'Ralph' and 'Phil' were asked by Yves Péron, colonel to the General Staff of the FFI, to lead a Jewish company. Finkler was unsure, thinking the idea a political front, but agreed to lead a group of sixty men, attached to the Groupe Soleil, towards the battle of La Rochelle. Finkler and Lichtenberg named their company Groupe Paul Frydman after their friend who had set off with them into the Maquis. Paul Frydman had been murdered with his family at Les Piles by the 'Das Reich' on the same day as Valentine Bussière also met her fate less than a mile away. Finkler and Lichtenberg thought it a fitting tribute. Finkler returned from the Atlantic front to find his parents safe and well in the home of Louis Nicolas in Pisany. The father of Maryse and his wife had saved the lives of Finkler's parents, risking their own in the process, and they were later named *Justes parmi les nations* (Righteous among the nations). Both Finkler and Lichtenberg continued their work of educating the young on the dangers of nationalism and fascism throughout their adult lives.

It is impossible to be exact about the toll suffered by the population of the Dordogne during the occupation, but Périgourdin historian Guy Morquin presented some idea of the scale of it. In 148 towns or villages, 689 people were shot, of which 32 were women and 657 were men. A further 89 died in combat. 548 were deported and 136 arrested and incarcerated. There were 4,349 buildings set on fire in 80 different communes, and 2 villages were entirely destroyed in this way: Mouleydier, a town of 200 houses, and Rouffignac, with 105 houses. In the early 1990s the Dordogne branch of the Association Nationale des Anciens Combattants et Ami(e)s de la Résistance (ANACR) went slightly further and brought the number of deaths to 1,646, including victims from all backgrounds, regardless of their place of birth. It later went further still by adding 166 Jews deported in the autumn of 1942, bringing a figure of something in the region of 1,812 deaths. Guy Penaud mentions an approximate figure of 962 people deported for political reasons, or for being suspected *résistants*. This climbed from 31 in 1942 to 189 in 1943 and 649 in 1944. In a way, the numbers are inconsequential: each digit was life. To understand the times, you have to understand the people and the world in which they lived and died.

In his book about the Jews in the Dordogne during the period, Bernard Reviriego writes:

The story of persecution is the last link in the chain. The Dordogne as a whole suffered massively in its flesh and its property by the repression and reprisals of the occupying forces and its auxiliaries. Those men and women involved in the Resistance paid a very high price. Armed Resistance networks where French and foreigners worked hand in hand, resistance of the civilians who retained their legality, resistance of those that protected the Jews, but also resistance of thousands of others, humble, whose stories remain unknown. And while it is true that many Jews, thanks to the help of Périgourdins, were saved too many, alas, underwent deportation while others became victims of the systematic persecution and the mass executions of the spring and summer 1944.[6]

These stories are the tip of a monumental iceberg, not only in relation to what happened in the rest of the southern 'free' zone, not even in what happened elsewhere in France, but in what happened in the Périgourdin towns and cities, in single villages and around single dinner tables. Opposite the main municipal library in Périgueux stands the Cité scolaire Laure Gatet, named after the brave, young, intellectual daughter of a local headteacher who was arrested while working as a liaison agent for the Confrérire Notre Dame on 10 June 1942. Laure Gatet's name has become synonymous with education in Périgueux. I heard it often when I lived nearby, but it was just words – the name of a *lycée* – and nobody told me anything about the life of the young woman behind it. I didn't know who she was, and I never tried to find out. Arrested while compiling information on submarine movements near Bordeaux, she was a victim of denunciation and, during a period of torture and imprisonment, she refused to speak. Eventually, she reached Auschwitz on a convoy in late January 1943, where she died on 25 December 1943, numbered 31833.

GLOSSARY OF KEY TERMS

Armée Secrète (AS)	The armed fighting units of the Resistance after 1942 under the MUR.
Armistice army	A small army allowed for the defeated French following the fall to the Nazis in June 1940, mostly disbanded in November 1942.
Bureau Central de Renseignements et d'Action (BCRA)	The secret service of the Free French led from London by Colonel Passy (André Dewarin).
Chantiers de la Jeunesse	Vichy camps for the moral and physical betterment of young people.
Cheminot	Railway worker.
Combat	Initially a newspaper and eventually, through several name changes, one of the principal Resistance movements. Led by Henri Frenay.
Comité Départemental de la Libération (CDL)	Often set up as early as 1943, committees set up to aid liberation-era prefects through the post-war administrative challenges.
Comité Français de Libération Nationale (CFLN)	Formed in Algiers in 1943, first under de Gaulle and Giraud and later headed up by de Gaulle alone.
Commissariat Général aux Questions Juives (CGQJ)	Set up in 1941 to implement the Vichy government's anti-Semitic policies such as the confiscation of property.
Confédération Génerale de Travail (CGT)	The main trade union in France, formed in 1895.

Confrérie Notre Dame (CND)	A BCRA intelligence network setup by Colonel Rémy (Gilbert Rénault) and with strong ties to Louis de la Bardonnie in the Dordogne.
Conseil National de la Résistance (CNR)	Formed by de Gaulle's envoy to France, Jean Moulin, and a galvanising force between the various movements.
Croix de Lorraine	The Cross of Lorraine, adopted as the symbol of the Free French.
Délation	Informing, denounciation.
Demarcation Line	The line separating the northern occupied zone and the southern zone that initially remained notionally free of occupation.
Deuxième Bureau	French intelligence service.
Drancy	An internment camp in north-eastern Paris designed to hold Jews who would later be sent to extermination camps such as Auschwitz.
Épuration	The purge of collaborators that began as early as 1943.
État français	The name used by the French government under the German occupation.
Femmes tondues	Women whose heads were shaved for having had relations of various sorts with members of the occupying forces.
Forces Françaises de l'Intérieur (FFI)	The military forces of the Resistance within France, unified formally in June 1944.
Franc-maçonnerie	Freemasonry.
Franc-Tireur	A left-wing Resistance group that emerged from the Lyons area. Published a newspaper of the same name.
Francs-Tireurs et Partisans (Français) FTP(F)	The clandestine Communist Party's Resistance fighters.
Free French	Gaullist Resistance, initially led from outside of France.
Front National (FN)	Resistance organisation of 1941–44 organised by the clandestine Communist Party, though its membership was wider.

Front Populaire	An alliance of left-wing movements that included the French Communist Party and Radical Party that briefly held power between 1936 and 1938.
Gestapo (Geheime Staatspolizei)	Nazi secret police.
Gouvernement Provisoire de la République Française (GPRF)	An interim government of Free France between 1944 and 1946 following the liberation of continental France. Created a year earlier in Algiers.
Groupement de Travailleurs Étrangers (GTE)	Camps created where foreign workers deemed excess to the national economic need were obliged to work. Created in September 1940.
Groupes Francs (GP)	Resistance squads formed for short, sharp missions.
Groupes Mobiles de Réserve (GMR)	Vichy paramilitary police set up in regional brigades for whom the main purpose became the hunt for the Maquis.
Jour-J (D-Day)	The beginning of Operation Overlord, the landing of Allied forces in Normandy.
Légion des Volontaires Français Contre le Bolchevisme (LVF)	Volunteer unit that existed between 1941 and 1944. It recruited men eager to fight against Soviet Russia.
Légion Française des Combattants	French veterans legion whose members were often very supportive of Pétain.
Libération	Title of a newspaper published by Libération-sud.
Libération-sud	Resistance group set up in the southern zone by Emmanuel d'Astier de la Vigerie.
Main d'Oeuvre Immigrée (MOI)	Resistance group made up primarily of foreigner and Jewish members. Closely linked to the FTP.
Malgré-nous	Forced recruits to the German army from defeated or annexed territories .
Maquis	The clandestine Resistance fighters hidden in rural camps.
Marché noir	The black market.
Mers el-Kébir	An Algerian port where British ships destroyed French battleships with a huge loss of French life.

Milice	Squads of ultra-violent men organised to carry out the anti-Semitic and anti-Maquis work of the Vichy authorities.
Mont Valérian	An old fort in western Paris where many Resistance fighters were executed by the Nazis.
Mouvement Unis de la Résistance (MUR)	Formed by Jean Moulin in 1943 and comprising the three main movements of the southern zone: Combat, Libération-sud and Franc-Tireur.
Noyautage des Administration Publiques (NAP)	Resistance organisation of public service workers and officials led by the MUR.
Office of Strategic Services (OSS)	American intelligence services, the pre-cursor of the CIA.
Organisation de Résistance de l'Armée (ORA)	Resistance group that emerged from the Vichy army.
Parti Communiste Français (PCF)	The French Communist Party.
Postes, Télégraphes, Téléphones (PTT)	The national French communications company.
Préfecture	The seat of the préfet, the state administrator of a French département.
R5	One of the twelve military regions of the Resistance, R5 being the Limoges region.
Radio Paris	A Vichy France propagandist radio station.
Rafle	Round-up.
Relève, La	A volunatry programme created in June 1942 by Pierre Laval that aimed to return one French prisoner of war for every three workers that left for Germany.
Résistance-Fer	A Resistance group that emerged from the many railway workers' own groups.
Revolution Nationale	The official ideological programme of the Vichy state.
Schutzstaffeln (SS)	Originally Hitler's black-shirted guards, they made up several divisions that were sent to south-west France to recuperate from service on the Eastern Front. These included the SS 'Das Reich'.

Service d'Ordre Légionnaire (SOL)	Paramilitary section of the Légion Française des Combattants set up by Joseph Darnand in December 1941. The forerunner of the Milice.
Service de Travail Obligatoire (STO)	Vichy's forced labour service for men of military age. From February 1943 it obligated men to work in Germany.
Sicherheitsdienst (SD)	SS intelligence service.
Société Nationale de Chemins de fer Français (SNCF)	The nationalised French railway service that emerged from the takeover of private companies during the period of the Front Populaire.
Special Operations Executive (SOE)	Set up in 1940, a British intelligence and military organisation that helped the Resistance in a number of ways.
Statut des Juifs	Vichy anti-Semitism laws.
Tracts	Pamphlets or leaflets used for propaganda.
Vichy	A town near the much larger city of Clermont-Ferrand where the Pétain-led government was based.
Wehrmacht	The German army.

LIST OF PRINCIPAL CHARACTERS

Paul Armbruster	Early resistant who helped establish links that led to the CND.
Raoul Audrerie	Leader in the AS in the north-west of the Dordogne.
Ralph Beauclerk	'Casimir'; SOE agent sent to the Dordogne as Jacques Poirier's wireless operator.
Georges Bégué	SOE operative, born in Périgueux and sent back to the area.
Gaby Bloch	Wife of Pierre Bloch who helped him and other SOE agents escape from prison.
Pierre Bloch	Jewish politician who was an early *résistant* in the Dordogne.
René Bousquet	General secretary of the police in the Vichy regime.
Walther Brehmer	Commander of the Brehmer division, sent to the Dordogne in March–April 1944 to dismantle the Resistance through terror, and deal with the remaining Jews.
Robert Brouillet	'Charles le Bolshevik'; central point of contact between SOE and the Resistance.
Valentine Bussière	FTP liaison agent, prominent in the area north-west of Périgueux.
Roland Clée	AS leader based near Vergt.
François Collin	Alsatian in origin; a bar owner turned Gestapo agent.
Lucien Cournil	Teenage recruiter for Jeunesse Communiste from Le Lardin, near Terrasson.
René Cousteiller	'Soleil'; a communist who arrived in the Dordogne to lead an FTP battalion.
Louis de la Bardonnie	Gentleman farmer who housed an early Resistance group and one of the first links to London.

Charles de Gaulle	Low-ranking general in the defeated French army who, from London, launched the Free French movement.
Adolphe Victor Denoix	Head of the Milice for the Dordogne.
Hélène Dupuy	Central figure in the Périgueux Resistance; her flat provided a meeting point and was a home for Jewish children.
Raphael Finkler	A secondary school student in 1940; helped initiate an early clandestine network before becoming a *maquisard*.
Paul Frydman	Jewish friend of Raphael Finkler, who was an urban *résistant* before joining the Maquis.
Vincent García Riestra	Spanish teenage immigrant who became a liaison agent.
Laure Gatet	Daughter of a local headmaster and an academic ace herself; became liaison agent and information gatherer for the CND.
Michael Hambrecht	Head of the Sipo-SD (Gestapo) in the Dordogne.
Peter Lake	SOE agent sent to the R5 region as Jacques Poirier's right-hand man.
Paul Lapuyarde	Local man to Périgueux turned arch-collaborator.
Pierre Laval	Pétain's right-hand man; twice prime minister and head of the Vichy government.
Monette Leclerc	Aunt of Maryse Nicolas though only a little older; worked closely with her niece.
Léon Lichtenberg	Close friend of Raphael Finkler; first an urban *résistant* before joining the Maquis.
Maurice Loupias	'Bergeret'; leader of the AS in the area around Bergerac.
André Malraux	Well-known French writer who entered into the Resistance at a late stage, 'taking command' of elements of the Resistance in the Dordogne
Charles Mangold	Alsatian who became chief of the AS in the Dordogne.
Roger Meyer	Alsatian Jew, recruited into the Resistance while still at school to become a liaison agent.
Edmond Michelet	Brive-based and later a politician under de Gaulle; author of some of the earliest acts of Resistance.
Luce Million	Known locally as Soeur Marie-Philomène; nun who worked in a hospital in Périgueux and lived in Thiviers.

Jean Moulin	Former prefect in the occupied zone who fled to London; sent by de Gaulle to the southern zone to unify the Resistance movements.
Claudette Négrier	Young villager whose father ran a café that served as a central meeting point for the Resistance in Vergt.
Maryse Nicolas	Originally from the occupied zone, came to Périgueux and joined a Resistance group before becoming a liaison agent.
Jacques Poirier	French-born SOE agent sent to the Dordogne to prepare the Resistance for the Allied invasion.
Jean Popineau	Vichy-appointed prefect of the Dordogne.
Roger Ranoux	'Hercule' (because of his height); young communist *maquisard* who became an FFI leader just prior to liberation.
Albert Rigoulet	'Le Frisé'; Dordogne farmer who was an early active *résistant*.
Maxime Roux	Headteacher who became 'Prefect of the Maquis' before becoming prefect of the department of the Dordogne.
René Segui	'Violette' (first to use); former soldier and early AS leader before being forced into hiding.
René Tallet	'Violette'; decommissioned soldier who became an important figure in the AS.
Alexandre Villaplane	Former captain of the French football team who was employed by the Gestapo as part of the Brigade Nord-Africaine.

NOTES

1 Peace and War

1 Recorded interviews at the Archives Départmentales de la Dordogne 14 AV 67, 69.
2 Jourdan, J.-P., and Simon, P., 'L'Aquitaine, une terre de gauche?', *Parlement(s)*, *Revue d'histoire politique* (2005/3(HS 2)) (2005), pp.40–54.
3 Rolli, P., *La Dordogne dans la Seconde Guerre mondiale*, p.21.
4 Archives départementales de la Dordogne 3 X 29, quoted in Rolli, La Dordogne dans la Seconde Guerre Mondiale, p.21.
5 Archives departementales de la Dordogne, 14 AV 15.
6 Rolli, P., *La Dordogne dans la Seconde Guerre mondiale*, p.14.
7 Ibid., p.12.
8 Kedward, H.R., *La vie en bleu*, p.234.
9 Léon Lichtenberg, speaking in 2009.
10 Amicale des Anciens Résistants et Amis du Bataillon Violette, *La Résistance racontée aux jeunes … et à leurs parents*, p.20.
11 In the manifesto of Brazzaville, 27 October 1940.
12 Jackson, J., *The Fall of France: The Nazi Invasion of 1940*, p.144.
13 L. Cournil, interview with author, Le Lardin, December 2017.
14 Kedward, H.R., *Resistance in Vichy France*, p.250.
15 Charbonnel, Daniel, *Laure Gatet: Une intellectuelle en Résistance*, p.30.

2 National Renewal

1 Penaud, G., *Histoire de de la Resistance en Périgord*, p.46.
2 Alary, E., and Vergez-Chaignon, B., *Dictionnaire de la France sous l'Occupation*, p.343.
3 Ibid.
4 Paxton, R., *Vichy France: Old Guard and New Order*, p.172.
5 L. Cournil, interview with author, Le Lardin, December 2017.

6 Archives départementales de la Dordogne 7 AV 65.

7 Archives départementales de la Dordogne 7 AV 53 – under married name Sonya Subac.

8 Plas, P., and Kiener, M., *Enfances juives*, p.49.

9 Paxton, R., *Vichy France: Old Guard and New Order*, pp.169–71.

10 ADD, Cabinét du prefect 1W.

11 Rolli, P., *La Dordogne dans la Seconde Guerre mondiale*, p.62.

12 Ibid., p.64.

13 ANACR Dordogne., *La Résistance de 1939–1945 en Dordogne*, p.45.

14 Ibid., p.46.

3 Networks and Secret Armies

1 Buckmaster, M., *They Fought Alone: The True Story of SOE's Agents in Wartime France*, p.45.

2 Churchill, P., *Duel of Wits*, p.246.

3 ANF (72AJ/35-72AJ/89) Piece 7G Témoignage de Jean-Philippe Charles le Harivel, alias Georges 15.

4 Stafford, D., *Secret Agent: The True Story of the Special Operations Executive*, p 189.

5 ADD, Cabinét du préfet, Rapport de gendarmerie 1 W 1757.

6 Penaud, G., *Histoire de de la Resistance en Périgord*, p.68.

7 Kedward, H.R., *La vie en bleu*, p.282.

8 Kedward, H.R., *Resistance in Vichy France*, p.235.

9 From resistancefrancaise.blogspot.com/2013/01/noms-de-guerre-pseudonyms-de-la.html.

10 Charbonnel, J., *Edmond Michelet*, p.50.

11 Kedward, H.R., *La vie en bleu*, p.285.

12 ANACR Dordogne, *La Résistance de 1939–1945 en Dordogne*, p.94.

13 Beau, G., and Gaubusseau, L., *R5 Les SS en Limousin, Périgord et Quercy*, p.39.

14 *La Marseillaise du Centre: organe régional du Mouvement de libération nationale* (1944).

15 Beau, G., and Gaubusseau, L., *R5 Les SS en Limousin, Périgord et Quercy*, p.31.

16 Kauffmann's story is from reseaualliance.e-monsite.com/pages/biographie-des-membres/edouard-kauffmann-bis.html.

17 Penaud, G., *Histoire de de la Resistance en Périgord*, p.99.

18 ANF (72AJ/232) Dossier 9 *Notes et rapports sur des missions et des projets d'organisation conduits dans la région du Sud-Ouest, janvier 1942–mars 1942.*

19 Gildea, R., *Fighters in the Shadows: A New History of the French Resistance*, p.121.

20 ANACR Dordogne, *La Résistance de 1939–1945 en Dordogne*, p.23.

21 André Roulland, AS Groupe 'Alberte', quoted in ANACR Dordogne, *La Résistance de 1939–1945 en Dordogne*, p.69.

22 Marrus, M., and Paxton, R., *Vichy France and the Jews*, p.257.

23 Ibid., p.256.

24 Plas, P., and Kiener, M., *Enfances juives*, p.49.

25 Ibid., p.70.

26 Kedward, H.R., *In Search of the* Maquis: *Rural Resistance in Southern France 1942–1944*, p.7.

27 Colonel Passy (Andre Dewavrin), quoted in Moulin, L., *Jean Moulin*, p.345.

28 Ibid.

29 Ibid., p.344.

30 Ibid., p.345.

31 ANF (72AJ/35–72AJ/89) 72AJ/60 n.3 Piece 28 Témoignage de Raymond Boucharel.

32 ADD (7 AV 56).

33 Kent, S., and Nicolas, N., *Agent Michael Trotobas and SOE in Northern France*, p.55.

34 Ibid., p.56.

4 *The Rise of the* Maquis

1 Bellanger, R., *Dordogne en Armes*, pp.19–23.

2 Viaud, M.T., 'Problèmes stratégiques et Tactiques des Maquis de Dordogne', in *La Résistance et les Français: Lutte armée et Maquis* (1995), p.258.

3 Faucon, M., 'Regards sur FTP', in *ANACR Dordogne, La Résistance de 1939–1945 en Dordogne*, p.143.

4 Penaud, G., *Histoire de de la Resistance en Périgord*, p.117.

5 Kedward, H.R., *In Search of the Maquis*, p.20.

6 Ousby, I., *Occupation: The Ordeal of France 1940–1944*, p.265.

7 Penaud, G., *Histoire de de la Resistance en Périgord*, p.102.

8 L. Cournil, interview with author, Le Lardin, December 2017. On this point, M. Cournil was clear. It may not always have run so smoothly throughout the war but in this area there was always a good degree of understanding between the two.

9 Speech by Raymond Pivert, *La Chapelle*, 26 October 1986.

10 C. Hauswirth, interview with author, Boulazac, December 2017.

11 Caminel, N., 'En souvenir d'Alice', in *Sud Ouest* (2014).

12 ADD (14 J 12).

13 ADD (14 J 10) Les PTT en Dordogne durant la guerre de 1939–1945.

14 Broch, L., Ordinary Workers, Vichy and the Holocaust: French Railwaymen and the Second World War, p.121.

15 Ibid., p.25.

16 Chubilleau, B., 'Maryse & Moncttc: Fines fleurs de la Résistance', in Famosa (2015), pp.60–4.

17 R. Finkler, conversation with author, Périgueux, October 2016.

18 Archives départementales de la Dordogne 1W 1803.

5 *Turning Tides*

1 Marrus, M., and Paxton, R., *Vichy France and the Jews* (1981), p.306.

2 Ibid., p.307.

3 ADD (14 J 9) Pastoral letter *sur la personne humaine* by Mgr Jules-Géraud Saliège, archevêque de Toulouse. This letter was found by an agent of the *Renseignements généraux* in a letterbox in Périgueux, 23 August 1942.

4 Plas, P., 'Les populations juives dans la Région de Limoges: entre refuge et persécutions 1940–1944', in Plas, P., and Kiener, M. (eds), *Enfances juives* (2006), pp.30–55.

5 Ibid., pp.48–52.

6 ADD (7 AV 46 et 47).

7 Ibid.

8 ADD (14 J 7) Opération du Gestapo en Dordogne, Corrèze et Haute-Vienne en 1943.

9 Ibid.

10 ANACR Dordogne, *La Résistance de 1939–1945 en Dordogne*, p.103.

11 Charbonnel, J., *Edmond Michelet* (1987), p.51.

12 Ibid., p.53.

13 ADD (1 W 1838) Fonds du cabinet du préfet 'L'arrestation de Marc Goldman'.

14 Interview with Vincent García Riestra, Trélissac, December 2017.

15 Ibid. M. Garcia continues to be proud that his father wanted to ensure that everyone could eat, regardless of their political beliefs.

16 Interview with Vincent García Riestra, Trelissac, December 2017.

17 Quoted in Rolli, P., *La Dordogne dans la Seconde Guerre mondiale*, p.123.

18 ADD (1W 1838) Fonds du cabinet du Préfet.

19 Ibid.

20 Kedward, H.R., *In Search of the* Maquis: *Rural Resistance in Southern France 1942–1944*, p.97.

21 ADD (1W 1815-1) Rapport du Préfet, 27 September 1943.

22 Ibid., quoted in Rolli, P., *La Dordogne dans la Seconde Guerre mondiale*, p.121.

23 ADD (1W 1815-2) December note by prefect.

24 Ibid., Rapport du Préfet, 31 January 1944.

25 Ibid., December note by prefect.

26 Raphael Finkler, interview with author, Périgueux, December 2017.

27 Kedward, H.R., *In Search of the* Maquis: *Rural Resistance in Southern France 1942–1944*, p.132, note 33.

28 AD24 (Archives départementales de la Dordogne) 1W1815-2.

29 ADD (1W 1838) Fond du cabinet du préfet – Note du service des renseignements généraux sur l'activité de la Résistance en Dordogne au 16 octobre 1943.

30 This account of the story has been compiled drawing on a number of accounts, several details of which differ significantly. Michel Maureau's work, and the account contained within journalist Dominique Richard's book *Le Roman noir du Périgord*, seem to be the most reliable. A novel that attempts to piece together the story called *Les Démons de Soeur Philomène* by Jean-Luc Aubarbier is a good read. A 2011 Jean-Pierre Denis film called *Ici-Bas* (*Here Below*) also tells a much-changed version of the story. This film is notable, however, for its excellent depiction of the Périgord in 1943.

31 For example, Dutheillet de Lamothe, A., *Bataillon Violette* (Saint-Yrieix-la-Perche: Imprimerie Fabregue, 1975).

32 This quote is taken from Richard, D., and Siméon, A., *Le Roman Noir du Périgord* (Périgueux: Fanlac, 2001), p.32. The attributed source is an account written in 1975 by Alfred Dutheillet de Lamothe, Captain Fred of Tallet's Bataillon Violette. The quote itself is impossible to verify fully, but the presence of the priest throughout is confirmed by several eyewitness accounts.

33 Chassain, H., 'La fin de soeur Philomène', in *Sud Ouest* (2012).

34 Quoted in Richard, D., and Siméon, A., *Le Roman Noir du Périgord* (Périgueux : Fanlac, 2001).

35 L. Cournil, interview with author, Le Lardin, December 2017.

36 Ibid.

37 ADD (14 AV 68) Recorded interviews with Roger Ranoux, Montrem, 2009.

38 L. Cournil, interview with author, Le Lardin, December 2017.

39 An anecdote relayed by M. Cournil, as well as by Roger Ranoux in recorded interviews.

40 R. Finkler, interview with author, Périgueux, August 2017.

41 Ibid.

42 This story is told in the film *L'Armée du Crime* (*Army of Crime*) (Robert Guédiguian, 2010).

43 While M. Finkler cannot be certain that this was the case, it is the only explanation he has been able to offer for his, Léon Lichtenberg and Paul Frydman's designation to the FTP-MOI.

44 Gillot, J.-J., *Chroniques des années de guerre en Périgord*, p.136.

45 'La princesse Wolkonski n'est plus', in *Sud Ouest* (8 June 1967).

6 Collaboration and Repression

1 ADD (1W 1838).

2 Quoted in Rolli, P., *La Dordogne dans la Seconde Guerre mondiale*, p.130, note 217.

3 Ibid.

4 Emmanuel Chevet, 'Gendarmerie et maquis sous l'Occupation en France (1943–1944)', in *'Force est faiblesse', Guerres mondiales et conflits contemporains* (2011/2, 242) (2011), p.131.

5 ADD (14 J 7).

6 Ibid., Comité de histoire de la 2ème guerre mondiale – Forces allemandes de l'occupation et gestapo. Report by the *police judiciaire* on the trial of François Collin and Georgette Peynaud, 2 May 1945.

7 Ibid., Procès-Verbal, Direction de la police nationale – Affaire: COLLIN, François, PEYNAUD, Georgette Objet: Trahison, Meurtre recel.

8 Kedward, H.R., *In Search of the* Maquis: *Rural Resistance in Southern France 1942–1944*, pp.188–9.

9 From resistancefrancaise.blogspot.com/2011/06/le-pont-lasveyras-16-fevrier-1944.html.

10 R. Delon, quoted at resistancefrancaise.blogspot.co.uk/2011/06/le-pont-lasveyras-16-fevrier-1944.html.

11 P. Chartrain, quoted at resistancefrancaise.blogspot.co.uk/2012/05/paul-chartrain-dit-leclair-gendarme-et.html.

12 A. Cubertafon, quoted in Amicale des Anciens Résistants et Amis du Bataillon Violette, *La Résistance racontée aux jeunes … et à leurs parents* (2015).

13 ADD Fonds de la presse: PRE 32-54 (L'Argus du Périgord) and PRE 264-5 (Le Courrier du Centre).

14 Lagrange, J., *1944 en Dordogne.*

15 Thibaud, P., 'Une stèle en mémoire des victimes civiles', in *Sud Ouest* (2012).

16 This remarkable insider account was provided by Raphael Finkler, the only survivor from within Le Canadier (Périgueux, October 2016). Most elements of the story from the official point of view are clearly evidenced through police reports from the prefecture. ADD (1W 1838 and 1W 1793).

17 ADD (1 W 1793) Note sur l'assaut du maquis de Veyrines-de-Domme.

18 Ibid., Obsèques des *maquisards* de Veyrines-de-Domme.

19 ADD PRE 1-237 L'Avenir de la Dordogne, 27 March 1944.

20 Penaud, G., *Histoire de de la Resistance en Périgord*, p.193.

21 Letter from Roger Meyer's mother can be viewed at lesresistances.france3.fr/documentaire-limousin/lettre-de-la-mere-de-roger-meyer.

22 Letter from a neighbour of the Meyer family can be viewed at lesresistances.france3.fr/documentaire-limousin/lettre-du-voisin-des-meyer.

23 ADD (1W 1838) Cabinet du préfet.

24 Ibid., circulaire 2221.

25 Quoted in Penaud, G., *Histoire de de la Résistance en Périgord* (2013), p.193.

26 Penaud, G., *Les Crimes de la Division 'Brehmer'*, pp.8–9.

27 ADD (1W 1838) Fonds du cabinet du préfet.

28 Rolli, P., *La Dordogne dans la Seconde Guerre mondiale*, p.202.

29 Penaud, G., *Histoire de de la Resistance en Périgord*, pp.201–3.

30 Penaud, G., *Les Crimes de la Division 'Brehmer'*, p.9.

31 ADD (14 J 10).

32 *Le Figaro*, 3 October 1945, p.25.

33 ADD (E DEP 7331) Fonds des archives communales de Périgueux, Rapport sur les crimes de guerre en Dordogne.

34 Quoted at crdp.ac-bordeaux.fr/cddp24/cnr99/rouffig.htm.

35 ADD (E DEP 7331) Fonds des archives communales de Périgueux, Rapport sur les crimes de guerre en Dordogne.

36 ADD (14 J 10) Les PTT en Dordogne durant la guerre de 1939–1945.

37 The events of the Brehmer operations are drawn from a multitude of secondary sources in additional to archival material from police reports and contemporary research into war crimes carried out by the prefecture. Guy Penaud's books listed in the bibliography were vital, as well as *1944 en Dordogne* by Jacques Lagrange. Other authors, including Jean Marc Parisis, Patrice Rolli, Martial

Faucon and Bernard Reviriego, have done the hard work in recording the many accounts of this short and horrific period.

38 Faucon, M., *Scènes du temps de Guerre en Périgord*, p.324.

39 Ibid., pp.366–444.

40 Ibid.

41 The events of La Bachellerie detailed here are drawn from a number of secondary sources as well as police records from the Archives départementales de la Dordogne.

42 Faucon, M., *Scènes du temps de Guerre en Périgord*, pp.304–6.

43 Ibid., p.365.

44 Ibid., p.357.

45 An excellent book was written about this family's story: Parisis, J.-M., *Les Inoubliables* (Paris: Flammarion, *2014*).

7 Counter-attacks

1 ADD (1W 1815-2) Rapport du Commissariat des Renseignements généraux de la Dordogne, semaine du 1 au 8 avril 1944.

2 Ibid., semaine du 8 au 15 avril 1944.

3 Ibid.

4 Ibid.

5 Ibid.

6 Viaud, M., 'Problèmes stratégiques et Tactiques des Maquis de Dordogne', in *La Résistance et les Français: Lutte armée et Maquis* (1995), p.259.

7 Poirier, J.R.E., *The Giraffe has a Long Neck* (1995), p.135.

8 Hastings, M., *Das Reich: The March of the 2nd SS Panzer Division Through France June 1944* (1981), p.53.

9 Quoted from Hambrecht's diaries, written in 1947.

10 Poirier, J.R.E., *The Giraffe has a Long Neck* (1995), p.137.

11 Ibid., p.139.

12 P. Géradou, quoted in ANACR Dordogne, *La Résistance de 1939–1945 en Dordogne*, p.306.

13 Poirier, J.R.E., *The Giraffe has a Long Neck*, p.138.

14 Penaud, G., *Histoire de la Resistance en Périgord*, p.275.

15 Hastings, M., *Das Reich: The March of the 2nd SS Panzer Division Through France June 1944*, p.217.

16 L. Cournil, interview with author, Le Lardin, December 2017.

17 Labarthe's account is recounted fully in Hastings, M., *Das Reich: The March of the 2nd SS Panzer Division Through France June 1944* (1981).

18 G. Delliac, quoted in Faucon, M., *Scènes du temps de Guerre en Périgord*, pp.70–5.

19 Rolli, P., *La Dordogne dans la Seconde Guerre mondiale*, p.189.

20 ANACR Dordogne, *La Résistance de 1939–1945 en Dordogne*, pp.352–6.

21 Rolli, P., *La Dordogne dans la Seconde Guerre mondiale*, p.203.

22 ANACR Dordogne, *La Résistance de 1939–1945 en Dordogne*, p.344.

23 Thanks to Patrice Rolli for providing me with further information on this campaign during a meeting in Périgueux during August 2017.

24 FDR Presidential Library and Museum, The President's Secretary's File (PSF), 1933–45, Box 31, France – De Gaulle, Charles, 1944–45, New York.

25 Richard, D., and Siméon, A., *Le Roman Noir du Périgord* (2001).

26 Penaud, G., *Les Milliards du Train de Neuvic* (2003).

8 Endings

1 Penaud, G., *Histoire de de la Resistance en Périgord*, p.526.

2 Poirier, J.R.E., *The Giraffe has a Long Neck*, p.140.

3 Penaud, G., *Histoire de de la Resistance en Périgord*.

4 Lagrange, J., *1944 en Dordogne*, loc. 4835.

5 Gillot, J., *Chroniques des Années de Guerre en Périgord*, p.65.

6 ADD (14 J 9) Procès-verbal.

7 Gillot, J., *Chroniques des Années de Guerre en Périgord*, p.85.

8 Seiler, R., *Charles Mangold: Chef de l'Armée Sécrète en Périgord*, pp.161–2.

9 OSS was the precursor to the CIA. The President's Secretary's File (PSF), 1933–45, Box 3,1 France – De Gaulle, Charles, 1944–45, 6 July 1944, New York, Memorandum for the President, Performance and Potential of French Resistance.

10 Ibid.

11 *Dordogne: une jeune alsacienne aurait été tuée en juillet 1944 par des maquisards la prenant pour une espionne allemande*, France3-regions.francetvinfo.fr (2016).

12 Bourdrel, P., *L'épuration sauvage*, pp.495–8.

13 The details of these events are drawn from both Lagrange, J., *1944 en Dordogne*, and Gillot, J., *Chroniques des Années de Guerre en Périgord*.

14 Tronel, J., *Regard sur l'Épuration et les femmes tondues en Dordogne* (2010).

15 Gillot, J., *Chroniques des Années de Guerre en Périgord*, p.78.

16 Bourdrel, P., *L'épuration sauvage*, p.495.

Epilogue

1 *Télégramme de Jeannine Meyer* (2018), lesresistances.france3.fr/documentaire-limousin/telegramme-jeannine-meyer.

2 Claudette Hauswirth, interview with the author, Boulazac, December 2017.

3 Kedward, H., 'Resiting French Resistance', in *Transactions of the Royal Historical Society* (9) (1999), p.276.

4 Vincent García Riestra, interview with the author, Trelissac, December 2017.

5 Borrinet, R., and Feynant, N., *Hercule*, p.73.

6 Reviriego, B., *Les juifs en Dordogne, 1939–1944*, p.13.

BIBLIOGRAPHY

Archives

Archives Nationale de France

Archives du Comité d'histoire de la Deuxième Guerre mondiale (ADF)

    72AJ/35-72AJ/89 Résistance intérieure : mouvements, réseaux, partis politiques et syndicats

    72AJ/220-72AJ/248 France libre et résistance extérieure

Archives départementales de la Dordogne★ (ADD)

    14 J 1-47 Papiers des correspondants du Comité d'histoire de la 2ème guerre mondiale

    1 W Cabinet du préfet

    14 AV Recorded Interviews

    PRE fonds de la presse

FDR Presidential Library and Museum

    The President's Secretary's File (PSF), 1933–45, Box 31 France – De Gaulle, Charles, 1944–45, New York

Books

Alary, E., and Vergez-Chaignon, B., *Dictionnaire de la France sous l'Occupation* (Paris: Larousse, 2011)

Amicale des Anciens Résistants et Amis du Bataillon Violette, *La Résistance racontée aux jeunes ... et à leurs parents* (Neuvic sur l'Isle: Les Livres de l'Îlot, 2015)

ANACR Dordogne., *La Résistance de 1939–1945 en Dordogne: La Lutte Contre le Nazisme et le Régime de Vichy* (Périgueux: Imprimerie Moderne, 1996)

Aubrac, L., *La Résistance expliquée à mes petits-enfants* (Paris: Éditions de Seuil, 2000)

Baruch, M.O., *Le Régime de Vichy 1940–1944* (Paris: Éditions Tallandier, 2017)

Beau, G., and Gaubusseau, L., *R5 Les SS en Limousin, Périgord et Quercy* (Paris: Presses de la Cité, 1969)

Bellanger, R., *Dordogne en armes* (Périgueux: Éditions Fontas, 1945)

Berthon, S., *Allies at War* (New York: Carroll & Graf, 2001)

Borrinet, R., and Feynant, N., *Hercule* (Périgueux: La Lauze, 2003)

Bourdrel, Philippe., *L'épuration sauvage* (Paris: Éditions Perrin, 2002)

Broch, L., *Ordinary Workers, Vichy and the Holocaust: French Railwaymen and the Second World War* (Cambridge: Cambridge University Press, 2016)

Buckmaster, M., *They Fought Alone: The True Story of SOE's Agents in Wartime France* (Watford: Odhams, 1958)

Cadroas, P., *Blessent Nos Cœurs ... de femmes dans la guerre (1939–1945)* (Ribérac: Pierre Cadroas édition, 2006)

Charbonnel, D. (ed.), *Laure Gatet: Une intellectuelle en Résistance* (Périgueux: Cité scolaire Laure Gatet, 2013)

Charbonnel, J., *Edmond Michelet* (Paris: Beauchesne, 1987)

Churchill, P., *Duel of Wits* (London: Hodder and Stoughton, 1953)

Cobb, M., *The Resistance: The French Fight Against the Nazis* (London: Simon & Schuster, 2009)

Cobban, A., *History of Modern France: Volume 3 1871–1962* (London: Penguin, 1965)

Coustellier, R., *Le Groupe Soleil dans la Résistance* (Périgueux: Fanlac, 1998)

Diamond, H., *Fleeing Hitler: France 1940* (Oxford: Oxford University Press, 2007)

Dutheillet de Lamothe, A., *Bataillon Violette* (Saint-Yrieix-la-Perche: Imprimerie Fabregue, 1975)

Faucon, M., *Brehmer à Azerat* (Bordeaux: Memoria-Edition, 2010)

——, *Scènes du temps de Guerre en Périgord* (Saint-Sardos: Éditions de l'Oustal, 2016)

Foot, M., *SOE: The Special Operations Executive 1940–46* (London: BBC, 1984)

Gaulle, C. de, *Mémoires de guerre: L'appel 1940–1942* (Paris: Presses pocket, 1980)

Gildea, R., *Fighters in the Shadows: A New History of the French Resistance* (London: Faber & Faber, 2015)

Gillot, J., *Chroniques des Années de Guerre en Périgord* (Clermont-Ferrand: De Borée, 2013)

Hastings, M., *All Hell Let Loose: The World at War 1939–1945* (London: Harper Press, 2011)

——, *Das Reich: The March of the 2nd SS Panzer Division Through France June 1944* (London: Michael Joseph, 1981)

——, *The Secret War: Spies Codes and Guerrillas 1939–1945* (London: William Collins, 2015)

Jackson, J., *France: The Dark Years 1940–1944* (Oxford: Oxford University Press, 2003)

——, *The Fall of France: The Nazi Invasion of 1940* (Oxford: Oxford University Press, 2003)

Kedward, H.R., *In Search of the* Maquis: *Rural Resistance in Southern France 1942–1944* (Oxford: Clarendon Press, 1993)

——, *La Vie en Bleu: France and the French Since 1900* (London: Penguin, 2006)

——, *Occupied France: Collaboration and Resistance 1940–1944* (Oxford: Blackwell, 1985)

——, *Resistance in Vichy France* (Oxford: Oxford University Press, 1978)

Kent, S., and Nicolas, N., *Agent Michael Trotobas and SOE in Northern France* (Barnsley: Pen and Sword, 2015)

Kersaudy, F., *De Gaulle et Roosevelt* (Paris: Perrin, 2006)

Laborie, P., *Le Chagrin et le venin: Occupation. Résistance. Idées reçues* (Paris: Éditions Bayard, 2011)

Lagrange, J., *1944 en Dordogne* (Périgueux: Éditions Pilote 24, 1993)

——, *Dictionnaire de la Résistance en Dordogne* (Périgueux: Éditions Pilote 24, 2007)

Lormier, D., *La Résistance* (Paris: Éditions Gründ, 2012)

Marcot, F. (ed.), *Dictionnaire Historique de la Résistance* (Paris: Robert Laffont, 2006)

Marrus, M., 'French Protestant Churches and the Persecution of the Jews in France', in C. Rittner, D. Smith and I. Steinfeldt (eds), *The Holocaust and the Christian World* (Yad-Vashem, 2000), pp.88–91.

——, and Paxton, R., *Vichy France and the Jews* (New York: Basic Books, 1981)

Martin, J., *Portraits de Résistants* (Paris: Édition J'ai Lu, 2016)

Maureau, M., *Pont Lasveyras, nouveaux témoignages* (Périgueux: Fanlac, 2005)

——, *Pont Lasveyras: Un drame de la Résistance en Dordogne-Nord* (Périgueux: Fanlac, 2004)

Moulin, L., *Jean Moulin* (Paris: Presses de la Cité, 1969)

Neville, P., *France 1914–69: The Three Republics* (London: Hodder & Stoughton, 1995)

Ophuls, M., *The Sorrow and the Pity: A Film by Marcel Orphuls* (New York: Outerbridge & Lazard, 1972)

Ousby, I., *Occupation: The Ordeal of France 1940–1944* (London: John Murray, 1997)

Parisis, J.-M., *Les Inoubliables* (Paris: Flammarion, 2014)

Paxton, R., *Vichy France: Old Guard and New Order* (New York: Columbia University Press, 1982)

Penaud, G., *Histoire de la Résistance en Périgord* (Bordeaux: Éditions Sud Ouest, 2013)

——, *Histoire secrète de la Résistance dans le Sud-Ouest* (Bordeaux: Éditions Sud Ouest, 2011)

——, *La 'Das Reich' 2e SS Panzer Division* (Périgueux: La Lauze, 2005)

——, *Les Crimes de la Division 'Brehmer'* (Périgueux: La Lauze, 2004)

——, *Les Milliards du Train de Neuvic* (Périgueux: Fanlac, 2003)

Plas, P. and Kiener, M., *Enfances juives* (Saint-Paul: Souny, 2006)

Poirier, J.R.E., *The Giraffe has a Long Neck* (London: Leo Cooper, 1995)

Quétel, C., *La Seconde Guerre Mondiale* (Paris: Perrin, 2015)

Reviriego, B., *Les juifs en Dordogne, 1939–1944* (Périgueux: Fanlac, 2003)

Richard, D., and Siméon, A., *Le Roman Noir du Périgord* (Périgueux: Fanlac, 2001)

Robertson, C.L., *When Roosevelt Planned to Govern France* (Boston: University of Massachusetts Press, 2011)

Rolli, P., *L'Occupation Allemande en Périgord* (Mussidan: Éditions l'Histoire en partage, 2013)

——, *La Dordogne dans la Seconde Guerre mondiale* (Mussidan: Éditions l'Histoire en partage, 2014)

——, *La Phalange nord-africaine en Dordogne* (Mussidan: Éditions l'Histoire en partage, 2014)

Rousso, H., *Les Années Noires: vivre sous l'occupation* (Paris: Gallimard, 1992)

Seiler, R., *Charles Mangold: Chef de l'Armée Secrète en Périgord* (Paris: L'Harmattan, 2014)

Shennan, A., *De Gaulle* (London: Longman, 1993)

Stafford, D., *Secret Agent: The True Story of the Special Operations Executive* (London: BBC, 2000)

Sweets, J.F., *Choices in Vichy France: The French under Nazi Occupation* (New York: Oxford University Press Inc., 1986)

Touchard, J., *Le Gaullisme 1940–1969* (Paris: Éditions de Seuil, 1978)

Vinen, R., *The Unfree French: Life Under the Occupation* (London: Allen Lane, 2006)

Webster, P., *Pétain's Crime: The Full Story of French Collaboration in the Holocaust* (London: Macmillan, 1990)

Articles

Albert, R., and Hervé, R., 'Connus ou inconnus, mais Justes' (Conseil représentatif des Institutions Juives de France, 2007)

Archives départementales de la Dordogne, 'Les femmes dans la Résistance', in *Mémoire de Ia Dordogne Revue semestrielle des services du patrimoine departmental* (10) (1991)

Bachelier, C., 'La SNCF sous l'Occupation allemande, 1940–1944' (Paris: Rails et histoire, 1996), chapter 6. Available at: www.ahicf.com

Caminel, N., 'En souvenir d'Alice', in *Sud Ouest* (2014)

Chadwick, K., 'Our Enemy's Enemy', in *Media History* (21:4) (2015), pp.426–42

Chassain, H., 'La fin de soeur Philomène', in *Sud Ouest* (2012).

Chevet, E., 'Gendarmerie et maquis sous l'Occupation en France (1943–1944). Force est faiblesse', in *Guerres mondiales et conflits contemporains* (242) (2011), pp.121–39

Chubilleau, B., 'Maryse & Monette: Fines fleurs de la Résistance', in *Famosa* (15) (2015), pp.60–4

'Dordogne: une jeune alsacienne aurait été tuée en juillet 1944 par des *maquisards* la prenant pour une espionne allemande' (2016). Available at: France3-regions. francetvinfo.fr

Gildea, R. 'Lettres de correspondants français à la BBC (1940–1943). Une pénombre de la Résistance', in *Vingtième Siècle. Revue d'histoire* (2015/1 (125)) (2015), pp.61–76

Gosset, J., '"Ralph" et "Phil", le destin croisé de deux volontaires', in *Aperçus d'histoire sociale* (107–9) (2013), pp.74–80

Jourdan, J., and Simon, P., 'L'Aquitaine, une terre de gauche?', in *Parlement(s), Revue d'histoire politique* (2005/3(HS 2)) (2005), pp.40–54

Kedward, H.R., 'Resiting French Resistance', in *Transactions of the Royal Historical Society* (9) (1999), pp.271–82

Millington, C., 'Vichy France, Collaboration and Resistance' (2012). Available at: frenchhistory.wordpress.com

Poznanski, R., 'Rescue of the Jews and the Resistance in France: From History to Historiography', in *French Politics, Culture & Society* (30(2)) (2012), pp.8–32

Préfet de la Dordogne, *1944–2014 Calendrier des manifestations* (Périgueux: Préfet de la Dordogne, 2014)

Richard, D., 'Un été 44: Les milliards du train de Neuvic', in *Sud Ouest* (2014)

Rittner, C., Smith, S.D., and Steinfeldt, I., *The Holocaust and the Christian World* (Yad-Vashem, 2000), pp.88–91

Rolli, P., 'Quand le Périgord était occupé', in *Sud Ouest* (2015)

Salvat, A., 'Et Hercule libera Périgueux', in *Sud Ouest* (2014)

See, Kwang-Yew, 'The Downfall of General Giraud: A Study in American Wartime Politics', in *Penn History Review* (18) (2011), pp.36–48

Thibaud, P., 'Une stèle en mémoire des victimes civiles', in *Sud Ouest* (2012)

Tronel, J., 'Intoxication et propagande noire en Dordogne: opération SS Skorpion West', in *Histoire pénitentiaire et Justice militaire* (2015)

——, 'Problèmes stratégiques et Tactiques des Maquis de Dordogne', in *La Résistance et les Français: Lutte armée et Maquis* (Besançon: Annales littéraires de l'Université de Franche-Comté, 1995), pp.257–67

——, 'Regard sur l'Épuration et les femmes tondues en Dordogne', in *Histoire pénitentiaire et Justice militaire* (2010)

Viaud, M., 'L'épuration en Dordogne', in *Annales du Midi: revue archéologique, historique et philologique de la France méridionale* (104) (1992), pp.417–28

Novels Based on Real Events

Aubarbier, J.-L., *Les Démons de soeur Philomène: Roman* (Paris: Éditions Jean-Claude Lattès, 2003)

Brunaux, H., *De l'Or et des Sardines: Le roman vrai du plus grand casse de tous les temps* (Arlès: Éditions du Rouergue, 2013)

Websites

judaisme.sdv.fr/histoire/shh/dordogne/index.htm
lemussidanaisdanslasecondeguerremondiale.over-blog.com
lesresistances.france3.fr
memoires-resistances.dordogne.fr
resistancefrancaise.blogspot.co.uk
www.ajpn.org/archive dordogne
www.cheminsdememoire.gouv.fr/
www.cnd-castille.org

ACKNOWLEDGEMENTS

Thank you to the many people who helped me write this book. In particular I was lucky to have the support of a number of eminent historians who guided me through the process of piecing the jigsaw together. Rod Kedward is an invaluable source of advice and inspiration, and without him I would have fallen at the first hurdle. Thank you also to those who read and critiqued the manuscript in its many versions. Hanna Diamond, Matthew Cobb, Caroline Moorhead and Robert Gildea all gave their time freely to do so and I am eternally grateful.

In France the wonderful local historian Patrice Rolli met me, put me right on a number of issues and gave me access to his amazing collection of photographs, while Guy Penaud also allowed me to use his documentation. Thank you to Nicolas Cournil and the rest of the staff at the Archives Départmentales de la Dordogne for their patience and for helping me locate so much vital material. Jean-Paul Bedoin put me in touch with interviewees Vincent García, Claudette Hauswirth and Lucien Cournil, while 'Ralph' Finkler inspired me on the occasions I visited him in his Périgueux home. He may not remember our first meeting in 1997 but I certainly do!

Thanks too to Chrissy McMorris at The History Press for showing interest in my idea and guiding me through the writing process. Finally, my wife Kate and my boys Joseph and Elliot have given me support and eternal patience during the research and writing of this book, and to them most of all I owe a huge debt of gratitude.

INDEX

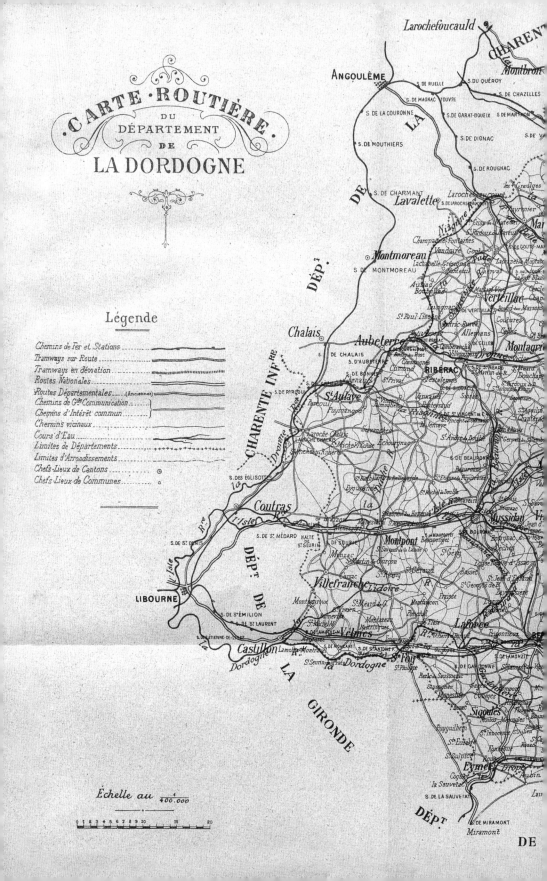

CARTE ROUTIÈRE

DU

DÉPARTEMENT

DE

LA DORDOGNE

Légende

Chemins de Fer et Stations ....
Tramways sur Route ....
Tramways en déviation ....
Routes Nationales ....
Routes Départementales ..... (Anciennes)
Chemins de Gde Communication ....
Chemins d'Intérêt commun ....
Chemins vicinaux ....
Cours d'Eau ....
Limites de Départements ....
Limites d'Arrondissements ....
Chefs-Lieux de Cantons .... ⊙
Chefs-Lieux de Communes .... ○

Échelle au 1/400.000

0 1 2 3 4 5 6 7 8 9 10   15   20